P9-CDU-753

ORGANIZATION THEORY AND PUBLIC ORGANIZATIONS

ORGANIZATION THEORY AND PUBLIC ORGANIZATIONS

The Political Connection

FLORENCE HEFFRON
Department of Political Science
University of Idaho

PRENTICE HALL
Upper Saddle River, New Jersey 07458

Library of Congress Cataloging-in-Publication Data

Heffron, Florence A.
  Organization theory and public organizations.

  Includes index.
  I. Public administration. 2. Organizational
change. 3. Organizational behavior.
4. Organization. I. Title.
JF1525.073H44 1989   350   88–19714
ISBN 0–13–642208–X

List on page 26 from *Democracy and the Public Service,*
Second Edition, by Frederick C. Mosher.
Copyright © 1968, 1982 by Oxford University Press, Inc.
Reprinted by permission.

Editorial/production supervision and
   interior design: Scott Huler
Cover design: Lundgren Graphics, Ltd.
Manufacturing buyer: Peter Havens

© 1989 by Prentice-Hall, Inc.
A Pearson Education Company
Upper Saddle River, NJ 07458

All rights reserved. No part of this book may be
reproduced, in any form or by any means,
without permission in writing from the publisher.

Printed in the United States of America

10 9 8 7 6

ISBN 0-13-642208-X

Prentice-Hall International (UK) Limited, London
Prentice-Hall of Australia Pty. Limited, Sydney
Prentice-Hall Canada Inc., Toronto
Prentice-Hall Hispanoamericana, S.A., Mexico
Prentice-Hall of India Private Limited, New Delhi
Prentice-Hall of Japan, Inc., Tokyo
Pearson Education Asia Pte. Ltd., Singapore
Editoria Prentice-Hall do Brasil, Ltda., Rio De Janeiro

CONTENTS

PREFACE

Organizations are the primary means by which public policy is implemented. Understanding organizations and the ways they affect and are affected by the behavior of their members is essential for public managers, public employees, policy makers, and everyone concerned with public administration. The primary concerns of organization theory are understanding and explaining organizations: their structures, the variables that affect their behavior, their internal processes, and the ways they affect and are affected by the behavior of their members. Until recently, research in these fields has been concentrated on private sector, for-profit organizations, and the resulting theoretical principles have been incorporated into public administration.

However, public organizations are clearly different from business organizations, and to understand public organizations managers must recognize these differences and how they affect organizational behavior. Nevertheless, public organizations are still organizations, and as such they are affected by the same general variables as their private sector counterparts. Consequently, organization theory can teach us a great deal about the behavior and management of public organizations as long as it recognizes the basic differences between the two sectors. The purpose of this book is to apply the major approaches of organization theory to public organizations.

The book covers both macro organization theory and organizational behavior, discussing the structure of organizations and the major contingencies that affect structure and organizational behavior: environment, goals, technology, strategy, and size. The distinctive nature of those contingencies in the public sector—the political connection—is highlighted and exemplified. Attention then shifts to internal organizational processes: change, conflict, and internal organizational politics and culture. All of these concepts and approaches teach us a great deal about organizations; applying them specifically to a variety of public organizations, as the book does through both cases and examples, expands our understanding of the differences between public and private sector management and of their similarities as well.

The final chapters of the book shift focus to the management and behavior of individuals in organizations and impacts, positive and negative, of organizations on individuals. Again the focus is exclusively on public organizations and public employees. The book concludes with an attempt to assess by what criteria public organizations should be evaluated.

Although writing this book frequently appeared to be one of the most solitary endeavors I have undertaken, in reality many people assisted in various ways. I would particularly like to thank Mark A. Emmert, Mark L. Weinberg, and Nicholas P. Lovrich, who reviewed the manuscript and made many helpful suggestions. In addition, Gina Reid and Barbara Tornow, who willingly typed, proofread, and suffered through seemingly endless revisions, have earned my enduring gratitude. Similarly, Linda Britton, a graduate assistant, did a superb job in helping prepare this manuscript for publication. Finally, to my public administration students, past and present, graduate and undergraduate, who provided the inspiration to write a book on public organizations, a special thank you.

Florence Heffron
University of Idaho

INTRODUCTION: ORGANIZATIONS

"Whatever is good for man can only be achieved through modern organization."[1]

Organizations are the central actors in contemporary society, the primary instruments that we use to accomplish our social, political, economic, and, in many instances, personal goals. In the private sector organizations produce, process, and market the endless variety of consumer goods and services that make our lives more enjoyable. In the public sector, organizations defend us from foreign attack; protect us from criminals, unsafe consumer products, and unhealthy air and water; build and maintain our highways and airports; educate our children; and provide myriad services that enhance the overall quality of life in our society. Individual personal goals—meaningful work, income security, professional advancement, recognition, and growth—also usually require organizational settings for their achievement.

Despite its omnipresence and beneficence, modern organization also has its darker side, for it is equally true that "much of what is bad for man can also only be achieved through modern organization." Illegal and dangerous drugs, widespread oppression and denial of human rights, and toxic chemical wastes are also organizational outputs. For individuals, success in large-scale organizations requires conformity, obedience, and a willingness to subordinate their own goals to those of the organization. From the time of Karl Marx to the present, many writers have charged that the depersonalization and specialization characteristic of modern organizations have carried a high cost to the worker in stress and, ultimately, alienation. In the political system, the necessary reliance on large-scale bureaucratic organizations to implement public policy has raised questions about the responsiveness, representativeness, and accountability of government at all levels. Politicians, the media, and interest groups have frequently alleged that these same organizations are also a major source of waste and inefficiency in the public sector.

However one evaluates the overall contribution organizations have made to contemporary society, understanding them and how they operate may be one of the most important determinants of individual and societal survival, success, and happiness. The role of organizations is equally important in public administration and public policy: administration is primarily the management of organizations and people in them, and almost all public policies are implemented by organizations. In contemporary public administration, the continuing scarcity of financial resources makes understanding and improving public organizations essential to the maintenance and improvement of the quality of public service delivery.

ORGANIZATIONS ARE ALL THE SAME

Organization is a comprehensive term encompassing entities as large and diversified as the Department of Defense and General Motors and as small and simple as the single-owner restaurant employing four people or the Police Department of Wallace, Idaho, which has only three employees. An examination of these contrasting organizations reveals that they share certain common features:

1. They involve two or more people, working to accomplish
2. A common goal or goals through
3. Coordination of activities, which involves
4. Some type of structure.

Scott and Mitchell combine these factors to define an organization as "a system of coordinated activities of a group of people working cooperatively toward a common goal under authority and leadership."[2] Any entity possessing these characteristics is an organization, and organizations vary in size, type and number of goals, structural characteristics, and types of coordinative processes utilized. A public organization is any organization created by government. Although public organizations differ from business or private organizations on the specific nature of each or all of these four dimensions, at the most basic level they share these four common dimensions with private sector organizations.

ORGANIZATION THEORY

"A theory is an abstraction of real life . . . a set of interrelated concepts, definitions and propositions about relationships between the concepts," the purpose of which is to explain and predict the behavior of the unit of analysis.[3] Specifically, organization theory is concerned with the anatomy— the *structure*—and the physiology—the *interrelationships* and *functions*—of key components of organizations, primarily the individuals and groups that compose them. There is some disagreement as to whether the physiology of organizations, more commonly referred to as organization behavior, is a separate area of inquiry or a subfield of organization theory. Those who oppose its inclusion in organization theory argue that the proper focus for organization theory is the organization: its structure, goals, technology, and environment. They feel that organization structure is the dependent variable, and the primary concern of organization theory is to identify and analyze the key independent variables associated with different types of organization structure.[4] Organization behavior then emerges as a separate area of inquiry whose goal is "to understand the behavior of people in organizations. . . . Individuals, small groups, total organizations and the interaction of the organization with the external environment comprise the units of observation for organization behavior."[5] But if organization theory has as its goals understanding why organizations function as they do and determining how they should be designed and managed to achieve maximum effectiveness, then it should focus on both structure and behavior.

Theory may also be either descriptive or prescriptive. That is, it may be focused on explaining the concept under examination or it may be concerned with identifying relationships and conditions that *should* exist. Because public organizations play a crucial role in the political system, public organization theory has traditionally been deeply concerned with the "ought" as well as the "is" of organization.

As a general field of study, organization theory is relatively young. Until organizations assumed an increasingly important role in society, there was little interest in or need for organization theory. As organizations developed and their sphere grew more encompassing, organization theory emerged as an academic and practical field of inquiry reflecting the basic concerns of organization management—attempting to determine the best way to structure and run organizations. The primary value sought was to maximize organizational rationality, which was—and by some theorists still is—narrowly defined as efficiency: the ratio of outputs to inputs.[6] The earliest approaches emphasized structure, arguing that structure controlled individual worker behavior and that the perfect structure, if it could be determined, developed, and utilized, would perfectly control individual behavior, essentially eliminating the need for concern with individuals.

These early approaches became collectively known as Classical

Organization Theory; its most well known theorists and practitioners were Frederick W. Taylor, Lyndall F. Urwick, Luther Gulick, James Mooney, Alan Reilly, and Henri Fayol. What united these theorists was their belief that organization management was a science and that uniformly applicable laws and principles could be identified and would result in the best, the most efficient, organization. Taylor, in *The Principles of Scientific Management*,[7] emphasized the analysis of work processes, relying heavily on time and motion studies to determine the "one best way" to perform all tasks within the organization. Once this was determined, the next crucial step for management was the scientific selection and training of employees in the one best way to perform their tasks. Taylor has been extensively and perhaps justifiably criticized for his somewhat heavy-handed treatment of workers and his ignorance of the complexities and subtleties of worker motivation.[8] In Taylor's defense, he believed that workers and management did and should share a "mutuality of interests," which focused on money—desire for higher wages for the worker and higher profits for management. Nevertheless, Taylor's approach to workers was condescending and basically dehumanizing.

The other classicists focused on principles of organizational structure, and their concepts of organization have become staples in the lexicon of organization theory: "span of control," "unity of command," "the scalar chain," "division of work," organization by purpose, process, place, or clientele.[9] They were as convinced that there was one best way to structure organizations as Taylor was that there was one best way to perform a task, and they subsequently have been criticized for their simplistic and unrealistic approach. One of the most devastating of these criticisms came from Herbert Simon, who convincingly demonstrated that their scientific principles were more like proverbs: "For almost every principle one can find an equally plausible and acceptable contradictory principle."[10] Despite criticism, however, the principles continue to play an important role in contemporary organization theory, particularly in the public sector. Their argument for a strong single executive whose power is enhanced by a hierarchical command structure and a limited span of control remains central to the recurring attempts to reorganize both state and federal governments, both because those principles have been so frequently violated to the frustration of elected chief executives and because they appear to enhance the possibility of democratic accountability by centering responsibility on a single elected official.

The organizational structure that emerges from adherence to the principles is the classic bureaucracy defined and described in the writings of Max Weber. Weber's analysis of the "ideal type" bureaucracy became the foundation for all subsequent organization theory. First published in 1921, Weber's essay on bureaucracy was not translated into English until the late 1920s. For Weber, bureaucracy based on legal-rational authority was the most efficient form of organization, a form that was destined to dominate all other forms because of "its purely technical superiority over any other form of organization."[11] The identifying characteristics of bureaucracy were:

1. Fixed and official jurisdictional areas, controlled and ordered by written rules and regulations;
2. Clear division of labor, with authority and responsibility equally clearly designated, maximizing specialization and expertise;
3. The arrangement of all positions into a hierarchy of authority;
4. All officials appointed on the basis of qualifications—expertise;
5. Work viewed as a vocation, a full-time occupation;
6. Uniformity and impersonality in treatment, "without regard for persons."[12]

As Weber predicted, bureaucracy did become the dominant form of organizational structure in the industrialized world. And as its dominance expanded, organization theorists and practitioners came to realize that from its greatest advantages as an organization form also sprung its greatest dysfunctions. The rules, the impersonality, the fixed and inviolable chain of command, the specialization so characteristic of and invaluable to a bureaucracy could and frequently did become red tape, dehumanization, rigidity and inflexibility, and boring, monotonous, and unsatisfying work. When a bureaucracy degenerated to this level, its rationality and efficiency were diminished, and the task for organization theory thus became discovering methods for remedying the seemingly inherent dysfunctions of bureaucracy.

One of the first of these attempts was the Human Relations approach of Elton Mayo and Fritz Roethlisberger and William Dickson.[13] The concept of organization central to Weber and the classical theorists was machine bureaucracy, and the human beings who worked in that machine tended to be regarded as important but nevertheless interchangeable parts. The Human Relationists came to regard organizations as social systems composed of individuals whose attitudes, values, beliefs, and behaviors were shaped by forces and factors external to the organization and by the informal associations and groups internal to the organization. The focus of organization theory shifted to the informal organization—understanding it and developing methods to utilize it to facilitate the accomplishment of the formal organization's goals. Mayo, in particular, emerged as the foremost pluralist of organization theory. Like pluralists in political theory, Mayo believed (based on his experiments) that groups, not individuals or structure, were the most important organizational factors and the key to understanding and controlling individual behavior. Primary groups were the instruments of society through which the individual acquired attitudes, goals, and opinions. Within the organization, work groups were a key source of norms, behavioral cues, and motivation. For the individual, work groups satisfied social needs and provided opportunities for status, self-expression, and security. No matter how well designed the formal structure, if the informal organization—the work and social groups—was working counter to its purposes, the organization would deteriorate in overall performance.

By the 1940s the Human Relations approach had merged into the Humanist school of administration. The Humanists narrowed the focus of organization theory to the individual worker, and their ultimate goal was the creation and development of human-centered organizations—organizations designed to fulfill the needs and wants of human personality. Some of the most well known of the humanists are Robert Golembiewski, Chris Argyris, Rensis Likert, Warren Bennis, Douglas MacGregor, and Robert Presthus. They shared a disenchantment with bureaucracy and a disavowal of its superiority as an organization form:

> The bureaucratic form of organization is becoming less and less effective, . . . it is hopelessly out of joint with contemporary realities. . . . (1) Bureaucracy does not adequately allow for personal growth and the development of mature personalities. (2) It develops conformity and "group-think." (3) It does not take into account the "informal organization" and the emergent and unanticipated problems. (4) Its systems of control and authority are hopelessly outdated. (5) It has no adequate juridical process. (6) It does not possess adequate means for resolving differences and conflicts between ranks, and most particularly, between functional groups. (7) Communication (and innovative ideas) are thwarted or distorted due to hierarchical divisions. (8) The full human resources of bureaucracy are not being utilized due to mistrust, fear of reprisals, etc. (9) It cannot assimilate the influx of new technology or scientists entering the organization. (10) It modifies personality structure so that people become and reflect the dull, gray, conditioned "organization man."[14]

The Humanists sought an organization that satisfied the needs of individuals and maximized flexibility and adaptability. The concepts that they emphasized were job satisfaction, job enrichment, democratic management, and sometimes self-actualization, concepts diametrically opposed to those of classical theory. Whatever their true intention, the Humanists directed attention away from formal organization structure to the behavior of individuals within organizations. Although ascertaining how to develop and maintain the maximally productive organization remained an important goal in organization theory, creating organizations that satisfied workers' human needs and goals also emerged as an equal and sometimes conflicting goal.

The emphasis of the Humanists on individuals led some critics to disparage Humanism as the "people without organizations" approach, much as the Humanists had criticized classical theory as "the organization without people" approach. Many Humanists responded to this criticism by expanding their scope to organization development (OD), a contemporary multimethod approach that seeks to create organizations that emphasize equally their concerns for productivity and people. OD practitioners and theorists, such as Robert Blake and Jane Mouton, Golembiewski, and Likert, emphasize the use of applied behavioral science methodology to diagnose and develop organizations. Among the tactics used in OD are team building, intergroup problem solving, confrontation meeting, goal setting and planning, and third-party facilitation.[15] The fully developed organization is characterized by an open problem-solving climate, authority based on knowledge, decentralized decision making, collaboration, and a reward system that recognizes both the achievement of the organization's mission and the growth of people within the organization.

A new example of an old approach to organization theory paralleled the development of organization development: the rise of the New Management Science, the foremost theorist of which is Herbert Simon.[16] The New Management Science reemphasizes organizational rationality as the primary goal of organization theory. Recognizing the basic nonrationality of individual human beings, the approach once again shifts the focus to creating an organizational structure and climate that can control and manipulate the individuals within the organization to achieve organizational rationality. The unit of analysis becomes the *decision*, and ensuring that administrative man reaches rational decisions is to be facilitated through a carefully designed and computerized management information system. To the Humanists, this brings organization theory full circle, back to the rigid authoritarianism of the classical theorists:

> Organization based on rational man administrative theory is similar in important respects to the organization of traditional administrative theory. . . .
> In Simon's organization, it is management that defines the objectives and tasks, management that gives the orders downwards; it trains—indeed indoctrinates—the employees; it is management that rewards and penalizes.[17]

In the seventies and eighties two new theoretical approaches have provided additional insights into the actual operations of organizations. The first of these, the cultural school, views organizations as minisocieties, each with its own distinct cultural values, norms, folkways, and socialization processes. For the cultural theorists, the formal, rational aspects of organizations are less significant than the deeply rooted, almost subconscious, aspects of their culture.

The second of the new approaches, the power and politics school, views organizations as political systems permeated with conflict and power struggles to determine who gets what, when, and how. In the ceaseless struggle for power, everybody plays, and who wins depends on the resources and skills of the participants; formal authority does not guarantee success in organizational politics. The rational, mechanical aspects of organization are considered clearly less important in determining organizational behavior than the informal aspects—in this instance the political games and strategies in which participants engage.

Organization theory has indeed come full circle, and the enduring conflicts that characterize the field remain unresolved: formal versus informal structure as the proper focus of analysis, rationality versus humanism as the proper approach, equity versus efficiency as the goal of organizations, and the responsibility or lack thereof of the organization for the development and satisfaction of its employees—ultimately, conflicting theories of human nature and personality. What becomes apparent is that organizations are far more complex and complicated than was initially believed; as important as it is to understand them, we are a long way from that understanding.

BUT ORGANIZATIONS ARE ALL DIFFERENT: OPEN SYSTEMS AND CONTINGENCY THEORY

Two major contemporary organization theories were not covered in the preceding section: open systems theory and contingency theory. The two theories differ significantly from those previously discussed, primarily because both deny that there is one best way to structure and run organizations or that there is a limited number of immutable principles that are uniformly applicable to all organizations in all situations. Both theories emphasize situational analysis: the identification and analysis of multiple variables that affect and determine organizational behavior and effectiveness.

Open Systems Theory

A system is "a set of units with relationships among them," and the totality of the system is greater than the sum of its parts.[18] Traditional organization theory viewed organizations as "closed systems"; it regarded "the enterprise as sufficiently independent to allow most of its problems to be analyzed with reference to its internal structure and without reference to its external environment."[19] Open systems theory, in contrast, views all organizations as open systems, entities that exist in a dynamic and interdependent relationship with their environment, receiving resources from that environment, transforming those resources into outputs, and transmitting them to the environment (see Figure 1). Environmental reaction to those outputs is fed back to the system as an input, and the cyclical dependency of the relationship is maintained. To survive—and survival is the primary goal of an open system—organizations must acquire and develop negative entropy. Closed systems experience entropy, "the tendency to chaos, disorder, disintegration . . . their parts wear out and cannot be

FIGURE 1. **Organization as Open System**

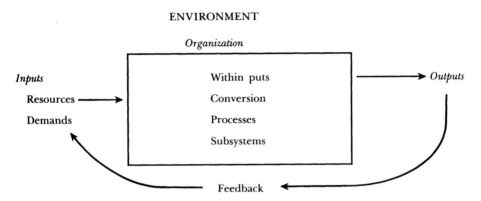

replaced."[20] Open systems, by importing more energy resources from their environment than they expend, can acquire negative entropy. Successful open systems achieve steady state equilibrium through dynamic homeostasis:

> In adapting to their environment, systems will attempt to cope with external forces by ingesting them or acquiring control over them. . . . Social systems will move towards incorporating within their boundaries the external resources essential to survival. . . . [T]he steady state becomes one of preserving the character of the system through growth and expansion.[21]

Open systems are also characterized by increasing differentiation and elaboration of roles through specialization and by equifinality, the principle that systems "may achieve their purposes using diverse sets of inputs and different configurations of system components . . . [and] outputs may be attained by transforming inputs in different ways."[22] In other words, for open systems there is no one best way but rather a variety of ways of achieving a goal.

In open systems, environment emerges as the crucial variable for organizational survival. To understand an organization, one must understand its environment. Managing an organization successfully requires constant monitoring of the environment and constant responsiveness to changes in that environment. A structure well adapted to one type of environment may become archaic and obsolete if it does not respond to change in the environment. Similarly, management practices that may have worked well for years may become unsuccessful if personnel, recruited from a changed environment, are no longer responsive to them, and a product or service once highly demanded may thus be rendered obsolete or irrelevant.

Open systems theory provides a framework for analyzing and understanding all organizations. It does not completely negate the validity of any earlier or contemporary organization theories. Open systems theory merely encourages us to recognize that organizations are all the same but that they are all different. To the extent that all organizations are viewed as open systems, they all share certain similarities whether they be private (business), public (governmental), quasi-governmental, or nonprofit organizations. At the same time, however, all organizations are different: they exist in different environments; require and utilize different types of inputs; have different goals, structures, and conversion processes; vary tremendously in size; and produce different kinds of outputs.

Contingency Theory

Contingency theory emphasizes the differences among organizations and seeks to identify those variables—contingencies—that affect organizational structure, performance, and effectiveness. One contingency that has received extensive research attention is the impact of different types of environments on organizational behavior. James Thompson, for example, identified two major environmental dimensions—stability and homogeneity—as "crucial contingencies" for organizational structure.[23] Thompson argued that an organization will adapt to an unstable, heterogeneous environment by decentralization, an increase in monitoring units, and a complex divisional structure. Similarly, Laurence and Lorsch linked environmental stability to the degree of differentiation, formalization, and centralization of organizational structure.[24] The impact of organizational technology—the basic work flow, process, and methods used by the organization—has also received considerable attention from contingency theorists. The variability of tasks and the nature of the intellectual search necessary to deal with variations were identified by Charles Perrow as having a direct impact on organization structure.[25] Burns and Stalker linked technological and market stability with two types of management style: mechanistic, a formal bureaucratic style of management, was identified as most successful with stable technology, whereas technological and market instability required a more flexible, organic style of management.[26]

Other contingency theories have emphasized internal variables that affect organization performance and effectiveness. Fred Fiedler focused on leadership style and developed a contingency model of leadership effectiveness, arguing that situational forces—those in the leader, the subordinates, and the situation—determined what constituted a successful leadership style; and that style could vary from extreme laissez-faire leadership to extreme authoritarianism.[27] Victor Vroom applied similar logic to worker motivation and job performance and concluded that management of a subordinate should respond to the characteristics of the subordinate.[28]

Contingency theory substituted "it all depends" for the "one best way" and directed organization theory towards identifying the major variables in an organization's internal and external environments, analyzing how they interact and the results produced by that interaction. Like open systems theory, contingency theory does not totally negate any of the previous approaches to organization theory; rather it cautions against the universal application of any one organizational structure or management style. Admittedly, this makes the task of organization design and management more complex. Instead of mastering a set of principles, managers must first master the skills of situational analysis, then understand a wide variety of theories and principles, and finally learn to select from those principles the ones applicable to an immediate situation. The complexity, untidiness, and almost "untheoretical" nature of contingency theory are its greatest weaknesses. But from the perspective of this book, one of its most important contributions is that it provides a critical link enabling the organization theories developed for private sector organizations to apply to public sector organizations. .

Organization theory is generic; no separate public organization theory has yet emerged. A reasonable suspicion has long existed that public organizations may be so different from private organizations that understanding, structuring, and managing them requires an entirely different set of theoretical premises. One of the more troublesome and persistent questions in public organization theory has been to what extent, given the differences between public and private organizations, is business organization theory applicable and relevant to public organizations? Contingency theory provides a vague and tentative answer: it all depends.

PUBLIC VERSUS PRIVATE: SOME ORGANIZATIONS ARE MORE DIFFERENT THAN OTHERS

Initially, neither public administration nor organization theory recognized any essential differences between public and private administration: what was good (from an organization theory perspective) for General Motors was equally good for the federal government. Woodrow Wilson was one of the earliest and most articulate proponents of the universal applicability of administrative principles and the basic similarity of business and public administration: "The field of administration is a field of business. . . . [A]dministration lies outside the sphere of politics. Administrative questions are not political questions."[29] The obvious distinguishing characteristic of public organizations, their political connection, was thus rendered irrelevant, and the basis was established for a science of administration. To Wilson, politics and the nature of the political system were so separable from administration that even the basic form of government, democratic or authoritarian, had no impact on organizational structure or administration. There could be "but one rule of administration for all governments alike. So far as administrative functions are concerned, all governments have a strong structural likeness; more than that, if they are to be uniformly useful and efficient, they *must* have a strong structural likeness."[30]

The dichotomy between politics and administration, which dominated public administration theory in the first four decades of the twentieth century, provided the theoretical basis for the application of the principles of scientific management to the public sector. The failure of this approach in public administration might be interpreted as proof of the difference between government and business until one realizes the approach was not especially successful in business either and was gradually displaced by newer approaches to organization and management. In academic public administration, the response was to emphasize the "political" and to deemphasize the "administration." The differences between business and public administration appeared so substantial that the possibility of successfully applying theory developed for one sector to the other seemed minimal.[31] But no new discrete theory of public organization developed, and public managers learned and applied techniques developed in the private sector. Matrix organization structures, organization development, management by objectives, and a variety of other approaches developed in the private sector were transplanted into the public sector—with the same mixed results they had in the private sector.

Identifying the special characteristics of public organizations has proven difficult. Rainey, Backoff, and Levine analyzed the major approaches that had attempted to differentiate between public and private organizations and noted, "None of these approaches can succeed in drawing a clean line between sectors; there are always intermediate types and overlaps on various dimensions."[32] Nevertheless, they concluded, "It seems clear that one could identify large groups of organizations which represent a hard core of public and private organizations, in that they are distinct on a number of basic characteristics (and magnitudes). . . . It seems reasonable to speak of 'typical' government and business organizations."[33] Among the most important differences between public and private organizations that they identified were the following:

1. Environmental factors: Public organizations are subject to less market exposure than their private counterparts and have less incentive for efficiency. Revenue for public organizations depends on appropriations from political branches, not on market performance. At the same time, public organizations are subject to more formal legal constraints and to political influences from diverse sources and groups.
2. Organizations—Environmental transactions: Environmental transactions of public organizations have been identified as more coercive, broader in impact, and more subject to public scrutiny and to expectations that they are responsive, accountable, and fair.

3. Internal structures and processes: Public organizations have vague, multiple goals that are difficult to measure and are frequently conflicting. Equity is as important as efficiency, and authority is likely to be fragmented and weak. Public organizational performance is likely to be characterized by caution and less innovativeness.

4. Personnel: Public employees may have higher dominance and flexibility needs and lower work satisfaction and organizational commitment.[34] Top executives have shorter tenure and more limited time perspectives. The nature of goals makes measuring employee performance more difficult.[35]

This list of differences appears impressive, and at a minimum it indicates that great caution should be exercised in applying business organization theory to the public sector. However, determining whether the identified differences are actually characteristic of "typical" public or "typical" private organizations is complex. The public sector is vast, encompassing organizations that vary tremendously in size, goals, management flexibility, innovativeness, and funding sources. Some public organizations do have specific, measurable goals—fire departments and the Internal Revenue Service, for example. Others have vague, multiple, conflicting goals, but so do many private organizations. A for-profit nursing home, for example, may have as goals both making a profit and providing quality nursing and custodial care to patients, and the latter is not only potentially in conflict with the former but also very difficult to quantify and measure. Some public organizations are innovative, such as NASA; some are rigid and inflexible—the department of corrections of most states are prime examples of rigidity. In the private sector, such high-tech firms as Techtronic, Apple, and Hewlett-Packard are clearly innovative and allow considerable management flexibility; the American steel industry, however, has displayed rigidity and stagnation that puts the most hidebound government bureaucracy to shame, raising the question whether dependence on market transactions does result in greater organizational efficiency. While most public organizations derive their funding from appropriations, not all do: the U.S. Postal Service, the Tennessee Valley Authority, Conrail, and many local sanitation departments charge fees for services. At the state and local level, as tax sources have become less reliable or available, more and more services are being financed by user fees. The distinctions become even more blurred when government contractors are considered.

Even the existence of legal and formal constraints is not quite as distinguishing a characteristic as it once seemed. The legal constraints on private business may not be as exacting as those on public organizations, but regulations regarding labor relations, working conditions, worker safety, fair treatment of consumers and competitors, environmental protection, and tax codes characterize the specific environments of many private organizations.

Organizational environments differ tremendously, but the differences do not depend solely on the "privateness" or "publicness" of the organizations. Some public organizations have stable, peaceful, supportive environments and are subject to minimal public scrutiny or interest; this is typical in those policy arenas, characterized as subgovernments (such as agricultural subsidies and veterans' benefits), where a limited number of participants, congressional subcommittee members and staff, bureaucrats and representatives of affected interest groups controls policymaking and implementation.[36] Other public and private organizations have chaotic, rapidly changing, hostile, complex environments—the Environmental Protection Agency and Hewlett-Packard, for example. Simplicity or complexity of the technology used has little to do with whether an organization is public or private. Time horizons of organizational management range from long-range, planning, careerist orientation (the U.S. Forestry Service, IBM) to crisis orientation and rapid personnel turnover (the new high-tech firms, and inner-city schools). Similarly, organizations appear to go through a life cycle, at varying speeds, regardless of their publicness or privateness.

Was Woodrow Wilson right? Both open systems and contingency theories suggest that he was partially right and partially wrong. Administration and organization management are different from politics, but in the public sector they are never completely divorced. The goal of organization theory is to understand organizations; the goal of public organization theory is to understand public organizations. To do that we must understand the environment, of which politics is an unavoidable component, in which those organizations exist; we must identify and understand the crucial contingencies that affect organizational structure and performance; and we must understand how individuals affect and are affected by organizations. By taking an exclusively public perspective and analyzing only public organizations, we may be able to determine why they behave as they do and to evaluate their performances. This will allow us to determine under what circumstances each of the private organization theories are applicable to public organizations. Organization theory is not exclusively a field of business any more than organization is, and questions of organization are intensely political because they explicitly involve questions of distribution of power.

SCOPE AND COVERAGE OF THE BOOK

The primary objective of this book is to help readers develop an understanding of public organizations. Organization theory that was developed primarily to explain the behavior of business organizations will provide the basic framework, but it will be specifically modified and expanded to enhance its applicability to public sector organizations.

The book is divided into two major sections. The first section is concerned with organizational structure, environment, goals, technology, culture, strategy, size, and age, as well as basic organizational processes: conflict, politics, and change. A variety of public organizations will be used to examine organizations and their environments, goals, and technologies and the interactions among these variables. This section also considers two major issues of particular contemporary concern in organization theory generally and public administration specifically: organizational decline and cutback and management of organizational conflict. The section concludes with a consideration of organizations as individual cultures and the impact of values, norms, and socialization processes on organization and member behavior.

The second section of the book, starting with Chapter 8, shifts the focus of attention to organization behavior. Psychological theories that have played a major role in contemporary humanist organization theory are examined, and the role of work in the lives of individuals and how that role affects work behavior is analyzed. Theories of motivation and the particular problems of motivation in the public sector are covered in Chapter 9. Stress and burnout, a severe form of alienation characteristic of human services professions (which tend to be concentrated in the public sector) are covered in Chapter 10. The final chapter examines the difficult and challenging task of measuring and evaluating organizational effectiveness. Even in the private sector, where it is frequently assumed that effectiveness is much simpler to define and measure, no agreement exists on the appropriate definition of organizational effectiveness. In the public sector, the definition and measurement of organizational effectiveness are complicated by the ambiguous and conflicting goals of public organizations and by the necessity of considering conformity with political and social values in any valid measure of public organization effectiveness.

NOTES

1. David K. Hart and William Scott, "The Organizational Imperative," *Administration and Society* 7, no. 3 (November 1975): p. 259.
2. William G. Scott and Terence R. Mitchell, *Organization Theory: A Structural and Behavioral Analysis* (Homewood, Ill.: Richard D. Irwin, 1976), p. 29.
3. Stephen Carroll and Henry Tosi, *Organization Behavior* (Chicago: St. Clair Press, 1977), p. 39.
4. L. L. Cummings, "Toward Organizational Behavior," *Academy of Management Review* (1978): p. 4.
5. Andrew J. Dubrin, *Casebook of Organizational Behavior* (New York: Pergamon Press, 1977), p. 4.
6. Hart and Scott, "The Organizational Imperative," p. 152.
7. Frederick W. Taylor, *The Principles of Scientific Management* (New York: Norton, 1967), originally published in 1911 (New York: Harper & Bros., 1911).

8. See, for example, David Schuman, *Bureaucracies, Organization and Administration* (New York: MacMillan, 1976), pp. 70–79.
9. See L. H. Gulick and L. E. Urwick, *Papers on the Science of Administration* (New York: Institute of Public Administration, Columbia University, 1937).
10. Herbert Simon, *Administrative Behavior*, 2nd ed. (New York: Free Press, 1966), p. 20.
11. From *Max Weber: Essays in Sociology*, ed. and trans. H. H. Gerth and C. W. Mills (New York: Oxford University Press, 1946), p. 214.
12. Ibid., pp. 196–204.
13. See Elton Mayo, *The Human Problems of an Industrial Civilization* (Cambridge: Harvard University Press, 1933); F. J. Roethlisberger and William Dickson, *Management and the Worker* (Cambridge: Harvard University Press, 1939).
14. Warren G. Bennis, "Beyond Bureaucracy," in Bennis, *American Bureaucracy* (New York: Aldine, 1970), pp. 3–6.
15. John J. Sherwood, "An Introduction to Organization Development," in Robert T. Golembiewski and William B. Eddy, eds., *Organization Development and the Public Sector, Part I* (New York: Marcel Dekker, 1978), pp. 208–209.
16. See Simon, *Administration Behavior; The New Science of Management Decision* (New York: Harper and Row, 1960). See also Richard M. Cyert and James G. March, *A Behavioral Theory of the Firm* (Englewood Cliffs: Prentice-Hall, 1963).
17. Chris Argyris, "Some Limits of Rational Man Organization Theory," *Public Administration Review* (May/June, 1973): p. 255.
18. Ludwig Bertalanffy, "General Systems Theory," *Yearbook of the Society for General Systems Research* 7 (1956): pp. 1–10.
19. F. E. Emery and E. L. Trist, "Sociotechnical Systems," in *Management Sciences Models and Techniques*, vol. 2 (London: Pergamon Press, 1960), p. 84.
20. Daniel Katz and Robert L. Kahn, *The Social Psychology of Organizations* (New York: John Wiley & Sons, 1966), p. 34.
21. Ibid., p. 25.
22. Donald D. White and H. William Vroman, *Action in Organizations*, 2nd ed. (Boston: Allyn & Bacon, 1982), p. 11.
23. James D. Thompson, *Organization in Action* (New York: McGraw-Hill, 1967), p. 39.
24. Paul Laurence and Jay Lorsch, *Organization and Environment, Managing Differentiation and Integration* (Homewood, Ill: Richard D. Irwin, 1969).
25. Charles Perrow, *Organizational Analysis: A Sociological View* (Belmont, Calif.: Wadsworth, 1970).
26. T. Burns and G. M. Stalker, *The Management of Innovation* (London: Tavistock, 1961).
27. Fred Fiedler, *A Theory of Leadership Effectiveness* (New York: McGraw-Hill, 1967).
28. Victor Vroom, *Work and Motivation* (New York: John Wiley, 1967).
29. Woodrow Wilson, "The Study of Administration," *Political Science Quarterly* (June 1887): pp. 209–210.
30. Ibid., p. 216.
31. See Nicholas Henry, "Paradigms of Public Administration," *Public Administration Review* (July/August 1975): pp. 378–386.
32. Hal Rainey, R. Backoff, and Charles Levine, "Comparing Public and Private Organization," *Public Administration Review* (March/April 1976): p. 234.
33. Ibid., p. 235.
34. Ibid., p. 236–237.

35. Graham Allison, "Public and Private Management: Are They Fundamentally Alike in all the Unimportant Particulars?" in Barry Bozeman and Jeffrey Strausman, eds., *New Directions in Public Administration* (Monterey, Calif.: Brooks/Cole, 1984), pp. 36–37.
36. Randall Ripley and Grace Franklin, *Congress, the Bureaucracy and Public Policy,* 4th ed. (Chicago; The Dorsey Press, 1987), pp. 8–9.

1

ORGANIZATION STRUCTURE

The formal structure of an organization consists of its internal division of labor and the coordinating mechanisms used to maintain control and secure the cooperation of individuals and units. The most visible manifestations of formal structure are the organization chart and the written rules, regulations, and procedures of the organization. For the classical organization theorists, structure was not only the essential aspect of organizations but also the focus of organization theory: "The theory of organization, therefore, has to do with the structure of coordination imposed upon the work division units of an enterprise."[1]

Although later theorists reduced structural concerns in importance, formal structure still constitutes one of the primary concerns of practical organizational management. For the organization, structure is the basic means of achieving goals, defining status relationships, channeling communications, and influencing relationships with the external environment.[2] For the individual within an organization, structure is equally important. Through work division it determines the specific nature, scope, and authority of the individual's position. The coordinating mechanisms define work groups and thus structure the immediate interpersonal relationships of the worker, and the hierarchy limits and specifies the opportunities for career advancement. Finally, the basic nature of the structure, whether it is tall (many steps in the hierarchy) or flat (few steps) appears to have a direct impact on job satisfaction.[3]

In the public sector, the structure of federal and state executive branches has been a frequent source of frustration and a focal point of attention for presidents, politicians, and scholars. From Franklin Roosevelt through Ronald Reagan, presidents have periodically focused on the structure of the executive branch, created study commissions, and attempted to reorganize "the one best way." The Brownlow Commission (1937), the first and second Hoover Commissions, the Ash Council, and the Grace Commission were all presidential study commissions whose concerns centered on the structure of the federal executive branch. The fixation with organizational structure has been duplicated at the state level, typified by then-governor Jimmy Carter's major overhaul of Georgia state government in 1972. Government agencies are organized, criticized, and reorganized continually.

Although structure is certainly not the sum total of an organization, it is an important part of it. The right structure may not guarantee an effective organization, but structural inadequacies can cause a variety of problems for workers, for managers, for clientele, and—in the public sector—for those who seek ultimate control of the organization: elected executives, legislators, interest groups, or the courts.

THE DIMENSIONS OF STRUCTURE

The structure of an organization reflects the way the organization has handled two basic processes: work division and coordination. Work division involves identifying the major activities the organization performs, breaking those activities even further down into tasks and subtasks, and assembling those subtasks into positions. What has been rendered asunder must, however, be put back together again through coordinating mechanisms such as a hierarchy, mutual adjustment, and standardization of work processes, outputs, or skills.[4]

The resulting structure can be characterized on the basis of three different dimensions: formalization, centralization, and complexity.[5] Formalization refers to the extent to which jobs, activities, and behavior are standardized and to the means by which this standardization is accomplished.[6] Centralization is the degree to which decision-making power and control are concentrated,[7] and complexity measures the number of different types of occupational specializations employed by the organization, the number of levels in the hierarchy, and the extent of geographic dispersion.[8]

Formalization

Job Standardization. "Specialization belongs to the natural order. . . . Division of work permits reduction in the number of objects to which attention and effort must be directed and has been recognized as the best means of making use of individuals and of groups of people."[9]

The first step in formalization is designing individual positions and clearly identifying the tasks, skills, knowledge, and ability required for each position. The classical theorists made clear that positions should be designed to maximize specialization; the number of tasks to be performed by any individual should be limited so that through constant repetition skill would be enhanced and efficiency increased. Frederick Winslow Taylor went beyond this to insist that for every identifiable task, there could be determined "the one best way" to perform that task, and then workers could be trained, persuaded, and coerced to perform it that way. Just as standardization of parts in machines allowed for interchangeable parts, standardization of jobs made workers equally interchangeable. Predictability, stability, and order—prime organizational values—result from specialized, standardized jobs.

Standardization and specialization also satisfy other organizational values. They are likely to reduce labor costs, promote automatic coordination, minimize discretion, and enhance the dispensability of individuals. If tasks can be so clearly specified and routinized that only minimal skill and training is required, then unskilled labor can be hired at relatively low cost, and training costs can be reduced. And the more standardized the task, the less important the specific individual who performs it, because that individual can easily be replaced with minimal disruption to the organization. If it can be determined exactly what, when, and how each task needs to be done to contribute to the organization's function, fewer methods of control and coordination will be needed throughout the organizational process.

William Scott and David Hart contend that dispensability is a basic value of contemporary organizations:

> The organizational imperative requires that nothing and no one be indispensable and that, indeed, dispensability be a prized attribute. Modern American society is built upon the dispensability of things, and our economy is founded upon the necessity of the dispensability of products through the consumption cycle. . . .
>   What is less well understood is how individuals in a society that exalts dispensability might come to view themselves. . . . The organizational imperative requires that all people believe they are dispensable and, further, that this is a good thing. Modern organizations cannot tolerate necessary individuals. If they did, organizations would become dependent upon those individuals, and such a situation is anathema to managerial thought and practice. . . .
>   At all levels and in all capacities, personnel must be immediately replaceable by others of similar abilities with a minimal loss of efficiency during the transition.[10]

The more standardized the job, the more dispensable is any particular individual who might hold it.

In the public sector, job standardization offers two additional advantages: the minimization of discretion and the development of a civil service system based on equal pay for equal work. Discretion, the ability of the individual employee—especially street-level bureaucrats such as policemen, welfare workers, teachers, and inspectors—to determine when, how, and on whom to enforce the law, has long bedeviled public managers and analysts. Although long recognized as an essential part of the work life of street-level bureaucrats, the power vested in them to make, in many cases, the final determination of what the law says and what public policy actually is, poses a challenge to the democratic notion that laws or policy must be made by elected representatives. To a very limited extent, job standardization can limit discretion by trying to ensure that what these employees do is determined by organizational managers who are presumably more in touch with legislative or chief executive intent. This in turn helps maintain the fictional dichotomy between politics and administration that has never been completely abandoned in public administration theory. Such standardization may also ensure that all employees occupying similar positions behave similarly and treat clientele similarly, thus enhancing the possibility of equal justice under the law.

Finally, job standardization allows for the classification of positions that have similar duties and require similar skills, knowledge, and ability into pay grades under a civil service system. To a certain extent, the spirit of Frederick Taylor lives on in today's public personnel practices.

> Job classification is the process of categorizing positions according to the type of work performed, the type of skill required or any other job-related factor. Classification simplifies job analysis, for it means that a standardized job description and qualifications standard can be written for an entire group of positions.[11]

Standard Operating Procedures

> Bureaucratic formalization is one method for reducing uncertainty in formal organizations. Official procedures provide precise "performance programs" which prescribe the appropriate reactions to recurrent situations and furnish established guides for decision-making.[12]

The position description defines the tasks the worker is to perform; standard operating procedures, embodied in the policy manual or handbook (under whatever title the organization uses), direct the worker *how* to perform those tasks. Standard operating procedures represent the organization's repository of wisdom on the most appropriate response to specific situations.

In 1960, Herbert Kaufman's *The Forest Ranger* detailed the elaborate formal and informal mechanisms used by the United States Forest Service to maintain control over its widely dispersed regional and district forests.[13] At the center of these mechanisms was the *Forest Service Manual*, which described in detail the appropriate response to practically any problem or situation that Forest Service personnel might confront. Twenty-eight years later, the Forest Service has undoubtedly changed in many respects, but the *Forest Service Manual* survives and thrives, all twenty-plus looseleaf volumes of it. The manual is the composite of the directives that have been issued by the Forest Service:

> The Forest Service Directive System is the basis for the management of internal program and administrative direction.
> a) [it] sets forth legal authorities, objectives, policies, responsibilities, delegations, standards, procedures, and other instructions that apply to more than one subunit of the issuing unit.[14]

The manual spells out the organization, the general procedures to be used in planning, budgeting, range management, and external relations with Congress, other agencies and interest groups and other levels of government. The reach of the *Forest Service Manual* is comprehensive; it does not limit its attention solely to broad management concerns but deals with the trivia of forest management as well; for example, it discusses where to develop swimming sites—"only where it is possible to mitigate hazardous conditions"—and then defines what constitute hazardous conditions.[15]

The detailed written specification of standard operating procedures is certainly not unique to the Forest Service. Rare is the government agency, whether federal, state, or local, that does not have a policy manual to guide and control employee behavior. The Internal Revenue Service publishes its internal guidelines in the multivolume *Internal Revenue Manual*. The audit section of that manual is published separately as the *Audit Examination Handbook For Agents*, and it exceeds in specificity the strictures of the *Forest Service Manual*. For example, specific instructions are provided to auditors on how to conduct the initial interview in income tax audits:

> (1) The initial interview is the most important part of the examination process. The first few minutes should be spent making the taxpayer comfortable and explaining the examination process and appeal rights. This would also be a good time to ask the taxpayer if he/she has any questions. . . .
> (4) Remember, the taxpayer is being examined and not just the return. Therefore, develop all information to the fullest extent possible. If the appearance of the return and response to initial questions lead the examiner to believe that indirect methods to determine income may be necessary, the factors in Chapter 500 should also be covered at this time.[16]

Like other aspects of formalization, standard operating procedures are intended to ensure uniformity, predictability, stability, and control within the organization. They also limit discretion and reduce uncertainty for employees and clients. Thus, they should enhance the efficiency and effectiveness of the organization. That they limit innovation, stifle creativity, depersonalize clients, and diminish the significance of their individual problems may be viewed as either an advantage or disadvantage. To the organization, that is the purpose of standard operating procedures; to the individual, that is the essence of their dehumanizing nature.

Formal Rules and Regulations. Organizations require obedience from their members, and conformity to organizational rules is an essential part of that obedience. Many organizations attempt to control the behavior, appearance, and beliefs of their members through elaborate systems of formal rules and regulations. When to report to work; when to take a coffee break; when to go to lunch; and how to address superiors, inferiors, peers, and clients are all subjects addressed by organizational rules. The military is the prototypical organization seeking to regulate nearly every aspect of the lives of its members. Air Force Regulation (AFR) 35–10 establishes the dress code for uniformed personnel and includes the official organizational justification for such a code:

> (1) The American public and its elected representatives draw certain conclusions on military effectiveness based on what they see; that is, the image the Air Force presents. The image must instill public confidence and leave no doubt that the service member lives by a common standard and responds to military order and discipline.[17]

Among other standards of dress, the regulation specifies that "headgear will not be worn . . . while indoors except by armed security police in the performance of their duties." The United States Supreme Court may not normally be thought of as being a collective of organization theorists, but when it was required to rule on the constitutionality of that regulation when applied to prohibit the wearing of a Yarmulke and thus violating religious freedom, the court majority displayed an impressive understanding of the logic of formalized organizations.

> To accomplish its mission the military must foster instinctive obedience, unity, commitment, and esprit de corps . . . the essence of military service is the subordination of the desires and interests of the individual to the needs of the service.
>
> The considered professional judgment of the Air Force is that the traditional outfitting of personnel in standardized uniforms encourages the subordination of personal preferences and identities in favor of the overall group mission. Uniforms encourage a sense of hierarchical unity by tending to eliminate outward individual distinctions except for those of rank. The Air Force considers them as vital during peacetime as during war because its personnel must be ready to provide an effective defense on a moment's notice; the necessary habits of discipline and unity must be developed in

advance of trouble. We have acknowledged that "[t]he inescapable demands of military discipline and obedience to orders cannot be taught on battlefields; the habit of immediate compliance with military procedures and orders must be virtually reflex with no time for debate or reflection."[18]

Although it may be an extreme example, the military is not the only public organization that seeks through its formal system of rules to regulate the appearance of its members through required dress codes. Fire departments, prisons, and police departments likewise require personnel to wear uniforms and maintain the proper appearance. In 1971, the Suffolk County Police Department promulgated Order 71–1, which established hair grooming standards applicable to male members of the police force.

> 2/75.1 HAIR: Hair shall be neat, clean, trimmed, and present a groomed appearance. Hair will not touch the ears or the collar except the closely cut hair on the back of the neck. Hair in front will be groomed so that it does not fall below the band of properly worn headgear. In no case will the bulk or length of the hair interfere with the proper wear of any authorized headgear. The acceptability of a member's hair style will be based upon the criteria in this paragraph and not upon the style in which he chooses to wear his hair.[19]

Also included in the order were specifications for sideburns (neatly trimmed and tapered), mustaches (not to extend over the top of the upper lip), beards (prohibited), and wigs (to be worn only to cover "natural baldness" or physical disfiguration). The Supreme Court as organization theorist found these regulations as justified for the police as for the military:

> The overwhelming majority of state and local police of the present day are uniformed. This fact itself testifies to the recognition by those who direct those operations, and by the people of the States and localities who directly or indirectly choose such persons, that similarity in appearance of police officers is desirable. This choice may be based on a desire to make police officers readily recognizable to the members of the public, or a desire for the esprit de corps which such similarity is felt to inculcate within the police force itself. Either one is a sufficiently rational justification for regulations so as to defeat respondent's claim based on the liberty guarantee of the Fourteenth Amendment.[20]

Rules and regulations may also extend to the off-work behavior of public employees. Teachers may be prohibited from frequenting taverns and bars; FBI agents were, until fairly recently, prohibited from cohabiting with members of the opposite sex unless they were related by blood or marriage, and homosexuality is grounds for dismissal by many public agencies.

In all organizations the written rules and regulations are supplemented by a set of unwritten, informal rules and regulations. These unwritten rules emanate from top management, from peers, from subordinates, from clients, and from the community and society in which the organization exists. Organizations that do not have written dress codes usually have unwritten dress codes. Few public universities today have written dress codes for faculty and administrators, but expectations do exist: faculty members should not look like janitors or students. For them to do so makes life too complicated and unpredictable for others in the organization, for students, and for the public. Inappropriate dress may elicit a variety of negative reactions, from disrespect to criticism and sarcastic comments. Nonconformity may be tolerated, but the nonconformist had best have a thick skin.[21]

In the most highly formalized organization, typified by the military and prisons, few aspects of organizational behavior will escape regulation, either formally or informally. The reasons for this have been well explained by the Supreme Court, but many of the dysfunctions it causes are apparent: the destruction of individuality, the invasion of privacy, the stifling conformity that crushes creativity and innovation come quickly to mind. One of the more ironic consequences of excessive reliance on rules was identified by Michael Crozier in *The Bureaucratic Phenomenon*—it destroys the dependence of subordinates on superiors:

> Every member of the organization, therefore, is protected both from his superiors and his subordinates. He is, on the one hand, totally deprived of initiative and completely controlled by rules imposed on him from the outside. On the other hand, he is completely free from personal interference by any other individual.[22]

Professionalism. The aspects of formalization discussed to this point have all concerned methods imposed internally by organizations. Behavior standardization of employees may, however, be primarily caused by forces external to the organization. Professionalization is the dominant method for standardizing behavior, attitudes, and values of employees from outside the organization. A profession shares most or all of the following characteristics:

1. "Professional decisions and actions are governed by universalistic standards . . . derived from a body of specialized knowledge . . . [the mastery of which] requires a period of specialized training."[23]
2. Professional expertise is specific and limited to a rather narrowly defined area.
3. The "professional's relations with clients are characterized by affective neutrality. . . . Professional codes of ethics condemn emotional involvement with the client."[24]
4. Professional control is exerted through two methods: the extensive training, socialization, and educational requirements imposed on the members of the profession, embodied in the profession's code of ethics; and continuing control exerted on the professional by professional organizations and peers.[25]

5. The community provides sanctions and supports for what members of the profession do.

Frederick Mosher was one of the first political scientists to become concerned with increasing professionalization in the public service. He identified the following agencies as having become professionally dominated:

Federal

Agency	*Agents*
All military agencies	Military officers
Department of State	Foreign service officers
Public Health Service	Public health doctors
Forest Service	Foresters
Bureau of Reclamation	Civil engineers
Geological Survey	Geologists
Department of Justice	Lawyers
Department of Education	Educators
Bureau of Standards	Natural scientists

State and Local

Agency	*Agents*
Highways and other public works agencies	Civil engineers
Welfare agencies	Social workers
Mental hygiene agencies	Psychiatrists
Public health agencies	Public health doctors
Elementary and secondary education offices and schools	Educators
Higher education institutions	Professors
Attorneys general, district attorneys, legal counsel	Lawyers[26]

Occupations increasingly seek professional status because the prestige, the income, and the autonomy associated with professionalization are appealing to most workers.[27] To Mosher's list of public professions should be added at least two occupations aspiring to achieve professional status: the police and public administrators, though it should be noted that both occupational categories are far from achieving full professional status. For some, the professionalization of the police offers a solution to the vexing problem of police discretion: "the key is providing individual officers with an internalized commitment to serve social interests"[28]

Others see it as a method for enhancing the formalization of police organizations:

> On the purely administrative level the goal of those in favor of professionalization is to carry the bureaucratization of the police to its highest degree. . . . They want those advantages in scientific administration that Max Weber has described as the fruit of the fully developed bureaucratic mecha-

nism: "Precision, speed, unambiguity, knowledge of the files, continuity, unity, strict subordination, reduction of friction, and of material and personal costs."[29]

For still others, police professionalization is a way to increase the status, prestige, and—not incidentally—the pay of the police. Such professionalization would require basic agreement on the skills, knowledge, and values that all police officers should possess. Educational programs would then be established, ensuring that all police officers receive similar training, and then a professional association with the power to establish professional norms and enforce educational requirements and the norms could be established.

Since the early 1970s, the National Association of Schools of Public Affairs and Administration (NASPAA) has attempted to develop and enforce standards for public administration education and training, with the ultimate goal of establishing public administration as a profession.[30] NASPAA has emphasized organizational autonomy for public administration programs, deemphasis of liberal arts training, establishment of required core courses for M.P.A.s, and enforcement of their standards through peer review and ultimately accreditation. The end result of this professionalization, at least from NASPAA's view, would be a professional core of public administrators at all levels of government and in all public agencies. Similar to the police, public administrators have a long way to go before they can make a valid claim to professional status.

Reliance on professionalization as a formalization technique has both advantages and disadvantages from the organizational perspective. On the positive side, professionalization is cheaper for the organization because society or the individual pays the cost of the majority of vocational training. Fewer organizational resources need to be committed to indoctrination and socialization, as these too have at least been partially accomplished through professional training. To have successfully completed their professional education, individuals must have learned considerable self-discipline and demonstrated an ability to conform to the demands and expectations of authority. Problems occur, however, when there is a conflict between the organization's goals, values, or activities and those of the profession to which the individual belongs. "Professionals have commitments and loyalties to a reference group composed of other professionals and to a definite set of normative standards governing their work, besides their commitment to the organization."[31] Generally, professionals manifest less organizational loyalty and deeper job commitment than nonprofessionals, and they are more likely to have an outer reference group orientation.[32] These problems are mitigated or eliminated when the employing organization has effective control over the educational process, as is true with the military and, to a somewhat lesser extent, with the Forest Service.

In the public sector, professionalization poses serious problems not just for public organizations but for the political system and society as well. Professionalization of public education has obviously not solved the problem of providing quality education for a mass society. It has, however, increased the autonomy of teachers, isolated the schools from direct community control, and legitimated the refusal of the professional to submit to performance evaluation by the taxpayers or by elected branches of government.[33] These characteristics of professionalism were demonstrated in the initial reactions of teachers' organizations to the concern expressed by both the public and politicians about the perceived deterioration of public education. The teachers' unions and professional associations vigorously resisted attempts to link pay and performance or to evaluate the competence of teachers and their basic skill levels, arguing that teachers' performance cannot be evaluated and that the more meaningful measures are "objective indicators" such as per-pupil expenditures or teacher-student ratios. Ironically, in some states, the teachers have achieved, from an organizational perspective, a bizarre victory. Conceding that the quality of education is poor (and teachers do have considerable control over that), the teachers have argued successfully that they should be paid more, which will somehow result in improved education.

The social work profession, which is predominantly a public sector profession, has also come in for its share of criticism. Street has charged that the professionalization of social work has resulted in the perpetuation of inequality and poverty—that instead of attempting to move the poor out of poverty, the professionals have been more concerned with maintaining control of social programs directed at the poor.[34] Further, defining the problems of poverty, criminality, and illness as individual pathologies and focusing efforts on changing (and blaming) individuals, the professionals have effectively prevented broader economic or social approaches from emerging as possible solutions to these problems.[35] The result has been the emergence of an "I'm OK, You're Not OK" ethic in dealing with clients.

Mosher identified a further problem with professions and the public service:

> There is a built-in animosity between the professions and politics. . . . Most of the professions . . . won their professional spurs over many arduous years of contending against the infiltration, the domination and the influence of politicians (who to many professionals are amateurs at best and criminals at worst). . . . Professionalism rests upon specialized knowledge, science, and rationality. There are *correct* ways of solving problems and doing things.[36]

Politics, in contrast, rests upon bargaining, compromise, and imperfect responses to intractable problems.

The attempt to professionalize the police and public administration raise further doubts about the compatibility of professionalism and politics. Clearly, police discretion and police behavior have been and continue to be serious problems. The prospect of professionalization is a tempting solution: if the police were all well educated and trained, if they had internalized the proper set of professional values, if they were to enforce these standards on themselves, we would not have to worry about how they treated suspects or the public. Or would we? Who determines what values they should internalize? What will those values be? How do we control the police, if their first line of responsibility is to their professional association? In other words, "Who guards the guardians?"

Similar problems exist with the professionalism of public administration and particularly with the emerging standards of NASPAA. Although knowledge of political and social process is still included in the requisite skills for public administrators, increasing emphasis is placed on quantitative techniques and methods and rationality as dominant values. The potential for conflict with politics, political superiors, and political values is limitless.

Automation. The ultimate in formalization is best achieved by replacing human beings with machines. "The operating core transcends a state of bureaucracy—in a sense it becomes totally bureaucratic, totally standardized, but without the people—and the administration shifts its orientation completely. The rules, the regulations, and the standards are now built into machines, not workers."[37] Machines do not have interpersonal relations, so management is freed from having to deal with problems that arise from human situations. Machines—automatic bank tellers, for example—treat everyone equally, thus eliminating unequal treatment or abuse of discretion.

In addition to all of the preceding advantages, computers clearly have other advantages over human beings. They can retain far more information than a single human being can; they can recall stored information more quickly, solve complex problems more rapidly, and solve them repeatedly without error. They can model complex situations, simulate, project, and make rational decisions. For Herbert Simon, their capabilities and potential have changed the basic concerns of organization design and structure: "The major problems of governmental organization today are not problems of departmentalization and coordination. . . . Instead they are problems of organizing information storage and information processing—not problems of division of labor, but problems of the factorization of decisionmaking."[38] Simon believes that the ultimate result of information processing technology will be to make public decision making more rational.

Like every other method of extreme formalization, automation—particularly computerization—entails costs, some of which will be borne by the organization, some by the workers, some by clients and the public, and some by the political system. Machines are expensive, and the rate of change in the technology is such that most systems are obsolete nearly as soon as they are installed, which means that the organization must either use obsolete machinery or spend more money. Further, though machines are predictable and produce more uniform outputs than humans, they do break down—computer programs develop glitches, and word processors lose manuscripts. A human clerk may make an error that on a human scale does cost money; but when a computer system goes haywire, it is capable of making billion-dollar errors.

For workers, automation is intimidating; it means acquiring new skills, which may not be within their capabilities, and ultimately threatens the loss of jobs. If automation is to save money (and in addition to increasing formalization, that is one of its major advantages), the savings are likely to be realized through decreased personnel costs. For clients and the public, the increased depersonalization involved in public sector automation is a cost. Machines are uncaring, unfeeling, and unresponsive, qualities that are antithetical to what clients and the public want and need from their public servants. In a society where public attitudes towards government are apathetic and frequently antagonistic, automation carries the risk of increasing the extent and intensity of both attitudes. Finally, the conflict between rationality and politics seems especially pronounced in the movement towards computerized decision making. To believe in rationality is to believe that there is one right answer to complex problems, that there is indeed a "one best way," and that essentially eliminates the need for politics.

The Quest for Uniformity. Formalization is a key dimension of an organization's structure, and organizations vary tremendously in the amount of formalization that they need, desire, and have achieved. As we have seen, organizations use a variety of techniques to achieve formalization, and each technique has advantages and disadvantages for the organization, for its employees, for its clients, and for the political system.

Centralization

Centralization measures the degree of concentration of decision-making power in the organization. Maximum concentration is achieved when all decision-making power is concentrated in one individual. This definition, though basically simple, regrettably spawns a need for further definitions, particularly of the terms power, authority, decisions, and decision making. Unfortunately, not all organization theorists agree on how these terms should be defined.

Weber defined power as "the probability that one actor within a social relationship will be in a position to carry out his own will despite resistance."[39] Authority is "the probability that certain specific commands (or all commands) from a given source will be obeyed by a given group of persons."[40] Authority is tied to legitimacy: individuals obey authority because they believe that the person in authority has the right to issue commands. Authority "in the official hierarchical sense is the *right* to command"; and power is "the capacity to secure the dominance of one's values or goals."[41] From the organizational perspective, determining who has authority is a complex problem. On one hand, the hierarchical system implies that individual authority within the organization is vested in positions by the organization. In Max Weber's bureaucracy, authority is vested in the position and not the person, and so identifying authorities and the dispersion of authority within the organization involves examining the organizational chart and the position description. The classical theorists agreed with Weber and added to the lexicon of organization theory terms such as "chain of command" and "scalar chain": "the chain of superiors ranging from the ultimate authority to the lowest ranks."[42]

Chester Barnard, however, viewed authority as based on the willingness of subordinates to cooperate and obey. According to Barnard, for a person to accept a command as authoritative, several conditions must be met:

> (1) he can and does understand the communication; (2) at the time of his decision, he believes that it is not inconsistent with the purpose of the organization; (3) at the time of his decision he believes it to be compatible with his personal interest as a whole; and (4) he is able mentally and physically to comply with it.[43]

Taken to its logical extreme, Barnard's concept of authority leads to the conclusion that all organizations are basically decentralized, because each worker actually determines whether each decision will be followed, and hence each has decision power. However, Barnard qualifies his almost anarchic view of organizational authority by pointing out that in reality most orders within an organization are automatically obeyed because they fall within subordinates' "zones of indifference." That is, individuals will accept many orders automatically and are "relatively indifferent as to what the order is so far as the question of authority is concerned."[44] Stanley Milgram's experiments on obedience demonstrated that within our society at least, most people have very wide zones of indifference. They will obey orders that violate their own moral principles and inflict pain on other individuals as long as the orders are given by a person in a position of authority.[45]

Different types of authority further complicate the measurement of concentration of authority in an organization. In addition to position, at least two other bases of organizational authority exist: authority can be based on competence and on personality. Particularly in highly specialized, professionalized organizations, professionals may not occupy positions of authority, but in many situations their knowledge and expertise determines what is actually done. The power struggle between specialists and hierarchical position holders is endemic to contemporary organizations. Weber distinguished between authority based on position (bureaucratic authority) and authority based on the personal attributes of the individual exercising it (charismatic authority). We have come to realize that even within bureaucratic organizations, charismatic authority continues to exist. Fayol and Barnard recognized the distinction between "official authority" and "personal" authority.[46]

Measuring organizational centralization also requires an understanding of the decision-making process. A decision is a choice; it includes, however, not just a verbalization of what choice has been made but also the actual behavior subsequent to that. If, for example, a prison warden feels that guards are treating prisoners too harshly and issues a directive requiring guards to be respectful and courteous in their relationships with prisoners, yet the guards continue to treat the prisoners harshly, the organizational decision is not what the warden ordered but what the guards actually did. Little agreement exists as to how organizations do or should make decisions.

Basically, any decision-making process resembles the steps commonly identified for the policy-making process in government:

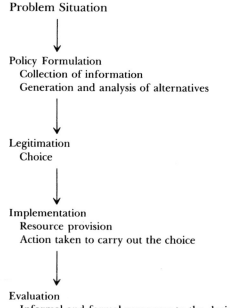

Problem Situation

Policy Formulation
    Collection of information
    Generation and analysis of alternatives

Legitimation
    Choice

Implementation
    Resource provision
    Action taken to carry out the choice

Evaluation
    Informal and formal responses to the decision[42]

The length of time and the scope and breadth of activity that occurs at each step vary with individuals, problems, and organizations. Centralization describes the extent to which the entire decision-making process is controlled by a single unit or actor.

When the complexity of the decision-making process is added to the difficulties of identifying and defining power and authority, the measurement of centralization becomes exceedingly difficult. It requires determination of how much involvement top management has in gathering and interpreting the information that is used in making decisions, and the control it has over executing decisions once made. Similarly, the discretion vested in first-line supervisors over budgets, hiring, firing, performance evaluation systems and rewards, purchasing, and establishing new projects also needs to be measured.[48] By these measures, most public agencies appear to be moderately to highly centralized, because control over routine administrative functions, such as budgeting, purchasing, and personnel, is usually not left to the discretion of lower-level management.

Measurements of centralization should also be related to formalization. Although an organization may decentralize decision making to lower levels, if all lower-level managers have been indoctrinated to the point that they will make the same choices as top management, not much meaningful decentralization has occurred.

The advantages and disadvantages of centralization are subject to debate. Centralization is both a virtue and a vice in the hierarchy of American political values. Decentralization, "grass roots control," is a basic American political value, based on the belief that decentralized government is more responsive to the needs of the people and less dangerous than centralized government.

> Decentralization is often recommended as a way of rendering government more susceptible to change. By encouraging diversity, decentralization may also encourage innovation through experiment . . . by multiplying centers of decision, and access for sources of suggestion . . . by reducing the uses and scale of bureaucracy, decentralization may diminish resistance to change.[49]

The structure and powers of the national executive branch directly reflect our entrancement with the notion of decentralization: multiheaded agencies and fragmentation of programmatic responsibilities among various agencies and levels of governments are a result of the attempt to prevent concentration of power. Decentralization is also praised for encouraging flexibility and adaptability and for permitting faster and better decisions (because they will be made by those with the best and most immediate knowledge of problems). Decentralization is supposed to improve the quality of personnel, increase morale and motivation, and ease burdens on communication channels, increasing organizational effectiveness and efficiency. Finally, decentralization is said to facilitate rapport with clientele.

Centralization, however, also has its supporters, frequently the same presidents whose campaign speeches tout the virtues of decentralization. The underlying theme of most proposals for reorganization of the executive branch have been based on the need to centralize power in the president:

> [Their] guiding principle is integrated organization—one that links related tasks at successive levels all the way to the top. Such a structure facilitates leadership, direction, supervision, and evaluation from a responsible chief executive. Although hierarchical by design, the organization is viewed as an instrument of democratic government, since top management is responsible to an elected official and accountable to laws democratically made.[50]

Centralization maximizes control; control minimizes discretion.

Centralization is offered as a corrective to the disadvantages of decentralization. One of the major problems associated with decentralization in public organizations is the likelihood of decentralized organizations becoming captives of their local constituencies. Philip Selznick's *TVA and the Grass Roots*[51] provides clear documentation of the perils of creating a decentralized agency that becomes so responsive to dominant local interests, in this case conservative farm groups and land grant colleges, that it resists such policy changes as civil rights enforcement mandated by the central government. Semiautonomous units of decentralized organizations are responsive, but they are likely to be responsive to the most powerful established interests of the locality at the expense of the less powerful and less organized interests.[52] The substantive result of decentralized government organizations is likely to be nonuniform policy that perpetuates inequality and obscures responsibility and accountability. Further, political control is essential in public organizations. This makes decentralization doubly problematic; by definition, decentralized organizations are not subject to central control, but at the same time, it may not be politically or legally possible for public organizations to decentralize responsibility along with authority.

Decentralization may be expensive for the organization: either the advantages of specialization must be forgone or specialists must be duplicated throughout the organization. One specialist increases efficiency; duplicating specialists increases expenses. Particularly in times of resource scarcity, decentralization is contraindicated. Unnecessary expenses must be curtailed, and duplication limited. In addition, when expenditure cuts must be made, they can usually be made only through centralization: no independent unit is likely to agree that it can make cuts, and all units will feel that other units could be cut.

Complexity

Organizations are based on specialization and division of labor. In turn, specialization and division of labor require coordination, the assembly of positions vertically and horizontally to ensure that the system operates as a unified whole. The complexity of an organization's structure comprises three aspects: horizontal differentiation, vertical differentiation, and spatial dispersion. Horizontal differentiation describes the extent and type of job specialization within the organization; this includes departmentation, the grouping of specializations to achieve coordination. Vertical differentiation describes the nature and depth of the hierarchical structure created to coordinate the groupings achieved through departmentation. Spatial dispersion is simply the extent to which the organization is physically divided into geographically separated units.[53]

Complexity begins with the diversity of job specializations that the organization employs. An organization that primarily employs lawyers and the support staff they need (for example, a state attorney general's office) faces fewer coordination problems than an organization that employs doctors, lawyers, pharmacists, chemists, biochemists, and nutritionists (such as the Food and Drug Administration). Conflicting professional norms, orientations, and status struggles can wreak havoc in an occupationally diverse organization unless an effective basis of departmentation is chosen. Unfortunately, selecting an effective basis is extremely difficult, and organization theory provides at best ambiguous or conflicting guidance.

Classical organization theorists, particularly Gulick and Urwick, identified four major bases of departmentation: purpose, process, clientele, and material and place.[54] Although those bases were debunked by Herbert Simon,[55] they continue to resurface in business textbooks on organization design[56] and in political reorganization studies. Their survival and dominance may have less to do with their theoretical precision than with the reality that no one, including Herbert Simon, has come up with a better, more practical set of terms or concepts for designing organizations.

Purpose. Purpose-based organization brings together "all of those who are at work endeavoring to render a particular service" or perform a particular function.[57] The plea for purpose-based organization is standard in contemporary studies of organization of the federal government:

> There is a need to reduce the number of departments, to use major purpose as the criterion for grouping functions . . . to bring about meaningful coordination of related programs on behalf of the president.[58]

> Within the integrated structure, the basic guide for organization is to combine functions according to purposes served.[59]

> The organizing principle of a department should be a national purpose or objective; and the broader the better.[60]

Gulick and the proponents of purpose-based organization see its major advantages as providing for more-integrated programs with a better relation of activities aimed at accomplishing specified goals. Political reorganizers perceive purpose-based organizations as facilitating executive control over the organization. The basic problem with using purpose as a basis in government is the difficulty in ascertaining the purposes of a particular program, policy or law: "Federal programs are likely to have multiple purposes. Disagreements as to priorities among diverse and sometimes conflicting objectives are a major source of current controversies."[61]

Is the purpose of the variety of federal programs directed at the poor to alleviate the misery of poverty, or cure it? To control the poor, or to provide subsidies to those who provide services to the poor? Is the purpose of a public university to provide an educational opportunity for all citizens of the state, to provide vocational training, to conduct funded research, or to serve the needs and interests of the state? If purposes cannot be identified, then purpose-based organizations are impossible to construct.

Process. Process-based organization "brings together in a single department all of those who are at work making use of a given skill or are members of a given profession."[62] The purported advantages of process-based organization are that it guarantees maximum utilization of up-to-date technical skills, enhances morale (because specialists communicate and feel most comfortable working with persons of a similar specialization), and encourages the development of career systems. Process-based organization carries the inherent risk that coordination, communication, and identification with the organization's purposes are more difficult to achieve and maintain. Professionals tend to identify primarily with their profession and place loyalty to profession above loyalty to the organization. Certain professions, notably the legal profession, tend to be more concerned with procedure—how things are done—than with substantial accomplisment. Further, professions have their own jargon, and constant association and continuous interaction with other members of the profession can turn jargon into a language difficult for nonprofessionals to comprehend. Anyone who has struggled to understand "legalese" or "computerese" understands the communication problems that this can breed throughout the organization. Professionalism may lead to arrogance—contempt for anyone not a member of the profession and an insistence on accepting the professional's point of view: "If you knew what I know, then you would know that this is the correct decision." Mechanisms to coordinate disparate professional groups are also complicated. In assembling the hierarchy, which specialization should prevail? If, for example, an engineer is selected to supervise or coordinate the activities of lawyers, doctors, and social scientists, all of the identified problems are magnified. Even if a generalist is chosen for the coordinating role, the problems will remain.

Clientele or Material.   Clientele- or material-based organization is organization based on either the persons or things with which the organization deals. The Veterans Administration (VA), the Department of Labor, and the Bureau of Indian Affairs are examples of federal organizations that are clientele based; the Nuclear Regulatory Commission is an example of a material-based organization. Clientele-based organizations are viewed with considerable disfavor by government organization theorists because they are particularly susceptible to dominance by and identification with the clientele. They come to view things from the perspective of the client special interest groups and elevate their desires over that of the more general public interest. The irony is that this is usually precisely why the organization was created: the VA is supposed to serve and represent veterans; the Department of Labor was created at the insistence of organized labor to provide it at least symbolic representation at the national level.[63] In addition, clientele-based organization simplifies the problems of dealing with government for the client group, since at least theoretically all services and programs directed at one group are contained in a single agency, eliminating the bureaucratic runaround that can be frustrating to individuals seeking advice or assistance.

Organization by place, at least to an extent, is inevitable in geographically dispersed government organizations. It brings together all of those who work in a given geographic region, regardless of the activities they perform. As a basis for government organization, place-based organization has advantages and disadvantages similar to clientele-based organization. It facilitates access for citizens and is likely to result in more responsiveness to local needs, but it may encourage organization members to identify with local interests. Beyond that, place-based organization has many of the same advantages and disadvantages that have been identified with decentralization.

Simon was particularly critical of these four "proverbs" of classical theory. As he pointed out, selecting any one basis meant that "at any given point of division the advantages of three must be sacrificed to secure the advantages of the fourth."[64] Further, the terms are ambiguous and the "principles of administration give no guide as to which of these competing bases of specialization is applicable to any given situation."[65] This criticism is unfair—the principles do provide guidance: the creators or managers of the organization must decide which of the advantages they wish to maximize. Once that decision is made, then the appropriate basis of organization can be selected. The choice is essentially a value judgment, but in politics, value judgments are inescapable. At least the principles provide some guidance as to how to maximize achievement of particular goals in public organization structure. Despite their problems, the classical bases continue to be used in both the private and public sector. In practical terms, they provide more guidance than Simon, who, after stating that a structural description of an organization should "designate for each person in the organization what decisions that person makes, and the influences to which he is subject in making each of these decisions,"[66] stopped at "the first step in the reconstruction of administrative theory—the construction of an adequate vocabulary and analytic scheme."[67]

Once positions have been assembled into units, supervisory positions must be created and units grouped into a coordinating structure. One of the key determinations at this point is the appropriate span of control for supervisors. Span of control refers to the number of subordinates reporting to one supervisor. The classicists insisted that the span of control be kept narrow, that one individual could not effectively supervise more than six or seven subordinates.[68] This was based on theoretical work of V. A. Graicunas, who demonstrated that as the number of people in a group increased, the number of possible social relationships increased geometrically according to the formula $n(n-1)/2$. Thus, in a group of seven people, twenty-one different relationships were possible, and this was considered the maximum number that any person could monitor.[69] Such limited span of control generates two organizational problems: it increases the number of hierarchical levels, which increases communication problems,[70] and it may increase worker dissatisfaction and decrease willingness to accept responsibility and exercise initiative.[71]

Too wide a span of control is a chronic complaint of elected chief executives in the American political system. Jimmy Carter frequently pointed out in his 1976 presidential campaign that when he was first elected governor of Georgia, more than two hundred separate agencies reported directly to the governor.[72] Although this seems excessive, most governors and mayors find that they too have spans of control that exceed thirty. The president of the United States has long been confronted with a similar problem. In 1937, the Brownlow committee found that one hundred separate agencies reported directly to the president.[73] Despite persistent reorganization efforts, in 1985, twelve cabinet departments, fifty-eight independent agencies, and fifty-eight government corporations, enterprises, and private corporations organized to provide contractual services were in the president's span of control.[74] That the heads of many of these agencies were not directly removable by the president only added to the complexity of his management situation.

Subsequent research has indicated that in the private sector, at least, there is no magic number for establishing an effective span of control. Spans of control of seventy operate successfully,[75] and the Bank of America functioned with a span of control of six hundred.[76] Effective span of control must be based on the level of intensity of required supervision which in turn depends on levels of professionalism, interdependence of group members, and amount of guidance required.[77] For the public sector, achievement of desired political values must be added to these considerations.

Geographical dispersion is the final element of complexity. By any measure, the Department of Defense (DOD) is a complex organization, but few organizations, private or public, surpass it in geographical dispersion, with its bases and facilities scattered throughout the United States and the world and at sea as well as on land. The Forest Service, although not as dispersed as DOD, also has had to confront the problem of maintaining control over a geographically decentralized organization. Both organizations rely on extensive formalization—a formal chain of command and such techniques as extensive reporting requirements, field inspections, and rotation of personnel to maintain compliance with organization policies and procedures.

Formalization, centralization, and complexity are the major dimensions of an organization's formal structure. Although formal structure has been somewhat deemphasized as the focus of contemporary theory and may not be as interesting as organizational behavior, it is a critical aspect of an organization's function and adaptive capacity and is a source of many of the problems for workers that are the subject of countless behavioral inquiries and normative studies. Excessive formalization and centralization can result in restrictive, repetitive, confining jobs that undermine and destroy satisfaction. In the public sector, structure has consistently been of concern because of its relevance to establishing and maintaining responsive, responsible, and effective government agencies. Formalization, centralization, and complexity vary in degree from organization to organization. The varying configurations of the three dimensions form the basis for the classification of organization structures that is the subject of the following section.

A TYPOLOGY OF ORGANIZATION STRUCTURES

Machine Bureaucracies

Machine bureaucracies closely resemble Weber's ideal bureaucracy. They rank high on all measures of formalization: jobs are standardized, written procedures and rules and regulations proliferate, control and authority are centralized, span of control is limited, and hierarchy is pronounced and multilayered. Horizontal and geographical complexity vary; some machine bureaucracies are horizontally and geographically complex, others are not.

The punitive-custodial prison is an extreme example of a machine bureaucracy. Such prisons are characterized by elaborate hierarchical rankings with military titles. Rules govern every aspect of the guard's job, behavior, and appearance.

> In order to maintain the conditions of deprivation and restriction believed necessary for "taming" prisoners, employees as well as criminals . . . must be

denied extensive opportunities to make decisions. Communications are formal in nature, restricted as far as possible to rules and commands. . . .

Employees are given explicit orders, ordinarily in the form of rules, for manning their posts and performing their duties. . . . The ideal employee is a kind of robot who carefully observes the conduct of offenders in his charge and reports rule violations to his superiors for disciplinary action.[78]

Despite the professionalization of its officer corps, the military, at least the uniformed services portion, also fits the basic requisites of machine bureaucracy: highly formalized, centralized, and vertically complex. Utilizing an intense indoctrination program that begins with basic training and continues throughout the member's service, the military organizations seek a dedication and unquestioning loyalty from members. Few aspects of the individuals' lives are exempt from attempted control by the organization. Control is exercised through an elaborately structured hierarchy with clearly defined ranks and status symbols, with orders flowing down the chain of command. Standard operating procedures exist for nearly every activity performed within the organization.

Obedience to commands is accepted and required:

Responsibility for the execution of orders rests ultimately on the tactical commander (and the ordinary soldier) on whom the various orders and directives tend to converge. He has no recourse but to obey; discipline is his primary virtue. His judgments concern only how to overcome the external difficulties he encounters in the execution of orders.[79]

Police and fire departments also fit the machine bureaucracy model:

Modern police forces are quasi-military bureaucratic organizations. Many believe that police systems need to be organized along the lines of the military so that they will be prepared and trained to respond at a moment's notice to unpredictable criminal events and public disturbances. That departments are organized bureaucratically insures that there are clear lines of responsibility between the different organizational divisions, personnel and offices. . . .

Although the mass media frequently portray police work in a glamorous and adventurous light, the realities of police work and its bureaucratic requirements are often routine. . . . Rather than chasing criminals every waking moment, patrol officers spend a large portion of their time doing the paperwork necessary in their job. They must follow procedures and rules that may make little sense to them and that may seem to have little bearing upon their job performance. But failure to comply may lead to disciplinary action.[80]

The work of firefighters is also frequently portrayed as glamorous, but it too is carried out within the confines of a paramilitary bureaucracy with rules and specified procedures governing every aspect of the work situation.

Machine bureaucracies are surely the worst-case examples that Warren Bennis and other critics had in mind when they launched their attacks on bureaucracy in general. Machine bureaucracies have been attacked as being rigid, inflexible, unwilling or unable to adapt to change, inefficient, inhuman, undemocratic, generally destructive of the spirit and soul of their employees, and a constant source of frustration to members of the public who must deal with them. They are in many respects what Douglas McGregor called Theory X Organizations, based on a pessimistic view of human nature that requires that workers must be constantly directed, controlled, pushed, punished, and persuaded in order to work.[81] To a certain extent, machine bureaucracies are all that their critics allege, but for all that, they continue to survive, to perform their assigned functions, to attract members and employees for life careers, members who are not really all that dissatisfied with their organizations.

To its members, a well-run machine bureaucracy offers order, stability, predictability, and clear expectations of duties, authority, responsibility, and behavior. Ambiguities about status and prestige are nonexistent. Esprit de corps, a sense of belonging, an opportunity to identify with something beyond the individual are intrinsic to many machine bureaucracies. Perhaps people should not want these things, but many people do and thus find working in these bureaucracies a comforting and satisfying experience.

Machine bureaucracies do emphasize specialization, and their standard operating procedures are a distillation of the organization's experience at handling the problem situations it has repeatedly confronted. For many situations, this does maximize efficiency and effectiveness. There probably is "one best way" to fight fires, and if it has been discovered, then it makes sense to follow it. As much as any organizational form can, machine bureaucracies stress uniformity, competence, and fairness.

From a societal perspective, the control aspect of machine bureaucracies, particularly for the police and the military, is desirable and necessary. Both are organizations whose members are authorized to use coercion, including deadly force. To ensure that deadly force is used only in necessary and proper circumstances is a constant concern in all societies, and so the organizations and all of their members to whom we have entrusted that power must be subject to control by the political system. At least in theory, machine bureaucracy provides maximal control over all organization members. For other public organizations the need for control may not be so urgent, but it is still important to ensure their accountability and responsibility.

Controlling discretion remains an unsolved problem in the public sector. Whatever the virtues of allowing employees to be creative and self-expressive in their work, it is not desirable that this result in a lack of uniformity in treatment of the public and clients (unequal justice) or that public servants invent the law as they apply it. Although machine bureaucracy is intended to control discretion, it has not succeeded, particularly with the police. Its failure to do so has led to a search for alternatives. The two most frequently suggested alternatives have been increased formalization or another form of organization. The most commonly identified alternative is professional bureaucracy. Advocates of that alternative should examine how well it has functioned in other public agencies.

Professional Bureaucracies

Professional bureaucracies differ from machine bureaucracies in two key dimensions: centralization and formalization. The essence of professional bureaucracy is that its operative functions are performed by professionals, specialists who have received their training and indoctrination outside the organization. Their skills, attitudes, values, and norms have been imparted to them before they enter the organization, and theoretically the tasks they perform are so complex and complicated that they require a high degree of expertise. Consequently, hierarchical control is diminished: no one can tell the experts how to perform assigned tasks— they alone possess the knowledge and skill necessary to perform them. Authority is based on expertise, not hierarchical position, in this type of organization. Formalization, at least formalization emanating from within the organization, also decreases. Schools, hospitals, the Environmental Protection Agency, and the Food and Drug Administration are examples of public sector professional bureaucracies.

As indicated earlier, elementary and secondary teaching has been granted the status of a profession. Teachers must be certified by the state, and to obtain that certification most are required to have a certain educational background that includes academic coursework in substantive subjects plus a large component of education courses. Presumably, this imparts expertise in both the substance and process of teaching. Consequently, once in the classroom, the teacher is close to being sovereign. Administrators have little control over the instructional work of teachers or the methods they use.[82] Authority is decentralized; job standardization is minimized. Schools illustrate an interesting aspect of formalization in professional bureaucracies that deal with dependent clientele. While the formalization of the behavior of professional employees may be left to external sources, rules and regulations, written and unwritten, proliferate for the clientele. Public school students find that their behavior is closely regulated to the point that their rights to even the most basic aspects of privacy are sometimes abrogated. The Supreme Court again affirmed this organizational need for order at the expense of the constitutional rights of clientele in 1985:

> Against the child's interest in privacy must be set the substantial interest of teachers and administrators in maintaining discipline in the classroom and on school grounds. Maintaining order in the classroom has never been easy, but in recent years, school disorder has often taken particularly ugly forms: drug use and violent crime in the schools have become major social problems. . . . Even in schools that have been spared the most severe disciplinary problems, the preservation of order and a proper educational environment requires close supervision of schoolchildren, as well as the enforcement of rules against conduct that would be perfectly permissible if undertaken by an adult.[83]

Hospitals are professional bureaucracies that are considerably more complex than elementary and secondary schools. At the operative level they are clearly dominated by professional staff, but the professional staff is composed of multiple and frequently competing professional groups: doctors, nurses, and medical technicians. Each professional group has its own status hierarchy: within the medical profession, surgeons, primary care physicians, anesthesiologists, radiologists, and obstetricians compete for status and authority. The nursing hierarchy is stratified on the basis of specialty and education: R.N.s, L.P.N.s, and nurse's aides. Concurrent with the professional hierarchies, an administrative hierarchy also operates, and hospital administration is emerging as a separate profession.[84] The consequences of these dual hierarchies are increased conflict and continuing power struggles within the organization as each professional group attempts to protect its own autonomy and status. From a management perspective, these problems of coordination and control are considerably more difficult to resolve than those in a machine bureaucracy.

Social work agencies illustrate the limitations of professionalization as a control of discretion. Social workers have long struggled to establish their occupation as a profession, and while they may not have succeeded to the degree that doctors or lawyers have, they have achieved many of the goals of professionalization. In many states, social workers are licensed by the state; licensing requires completion of a specified educational curriculum and success on a state administered examination. In turn, many state and local public welfare agencies will hire only licensed social workers. Nonetheless, the promised benefits of equal treatment and successful control of discretion have not materialized.

> A number of studies have shown the insidious effects of staff discretion, given agency autonomy and client overload. . . . [S]taff were able to reward clients who had knowledge of the bureaucratic ropes and caused fewer problems than ignorant clients.[85]

Case workers in a state public welfare system were found to have developed a classification of "good" clients and "bad" clients, the former to whom they offered all the options for payments allowable under regulations and the latter to whom they gave payment options only when asked specifically.[86]

Professionalization may exacerbate the problem of control of discretion because professionals are likely to insist on autonomy and the need— and the right—to treat individuals unequally, based on their individual situations as determined by the professional.

The Environmental Protection Agency's (EPA) recent history illustrates the problem of maintaining political control over professional bureaucracies. The EPA employs a variety of professionals essential for the accomplishment of its mission to maintain or improve the quality of our natural environment. Predictably, "many employees' strongest loyalties [are] to the air, water, pesticides, solid waste and radiation programs in which they worked, and to their professional discipline, such as engineering, chemistry, biology, and the law."[87] As long as the programmatic and professional commitments of these employees were compatible with the direction pursued by the political leadership of the agency, the organization functioned relatively harmoniously. When a change in political leadership resulted in an attempted weakening of policy enforcement, the reaction from the professionals within the organization was predictable. Accompanied by budget cuts and reductions in force, the change in policy direction resulted in sagging morale and an increase in "voluntary" resignations. "Nowhere has low morale and the brain drain at EPA been more severe than among competent scientists and scientist managers."[88] Resistance to and resentment of the new leadership by the professionals resulted in an internal organizational environment characterized by conflict, disillusionment, and near paralysis. EPA was truly a "battered organization."[89]

Professional bureaucracy is a common organization form in the public sector, and because it is a "fashionable" structure, it is perceived by some occupations and organizational theorists as preferable to machine bureaucracy.[90] Although it appears to be more democratic than machine bureaucracy because it decentralizes authority within organizations, this appearance is deceptive. Professional organizations that control the indoctrination and evaluation of their members are not themselves democratically run; the standardization of behavior that they impose results in a type of conformity and control similar to that imposed internally by machine bureaucracies. Further, as has been illustrated, professional bureaucracies do not usually extend whatever semblance of democracy they internalize to clientele. Finally, in the public sector, this form of organization creates problems for maintaining political control and responsiveness.

Adhocracy and Matrix Organizations

Bureaucracy has been characterized as a "mechanistic" form of organization most suitable for stable conditions and generally incapable of innovative, adaptive behavior. To its critics, it is the dinosaur of organizational forms because rapidly accelerating change in technology, the society, and the economy are characteristic of both the present and the future. Since bureaucracy cannot adapt, it is doomed to extinction. In its place, a new organizational form was predicted to become dominant: the "adhocracy" of *Future Shock*.[91] Adhocracies, as Warren Bennis described them, would "be adaptive, rapidly changing *temporary systems*, organized around problems-to-be-solved by groups of relative strangers with diverse professional skills."[92] Such organizations would be low on formalization, extremely decentralized, and ephemeral.

Whatever the extent of adhocratization of the private sector, adhocracies have been extremely rare in the public sector. The basic reason for their rarity is the definitional assumption that they are organized around problems-to-be-solved. The problems that public sector organizations are created to handle are frequently problems that have no final or known solutions: crime, poverty, environmental pollution, ignorance, illness, and international conflict are not temporary problems, and their solutions remain unknown. Even the one government organization that is most commonly identified as having been an adhocracy, the National Aeronautics and Space Administration (NASA), created in 1958 and still in existence in 1989, is obviously not temporary.

If temporariness is an essential characteristic of adhocracy, and it would seem to be, then its most common usage in the public sector has been in the various study commissions created to examine specified problems and recommend solutions, which may or may not be followed. The Grace Commission, the National Commission on Social Security Reform, and the Commission on Pornography created by the Justice Department exemplify this type of organizational form. All were assigned a specific problem to investigate, and when they completed their investigations, they were disbanded. Presidential campaign organizations might also be classified as adhocracies. The candidates must construct, finance, and manage a nationwide organization with one goal—to secure the nomination and election of the candidate. The organizations are by necessity decentralized, frequently lacking any type of formalization, and decidedly temporary, particularly if the candidate loses. Task forces are also a form of adhocracy commonly used in the public sector. Frequently, task forces are formed to deal with a problem that overlaps the boundaries of several organizations or even governmental jurisdictions. The Seattle-Tacoma, King County, Washington, area was the scene of over thirty murders of prostitutes occurring from 1984 to 1986, which were known as the Green River Murders. To solve the crimes, a Green River Task Force, composed of city, county, and state law enforcement officers, was created. As of 1989, however, the crimes had not been solved. For the most part, however, adhocracies remain rarities.

Which is not to say that other forms of organic organization are not used in the public sector. Organic systems are characterized by fluid, nonhierarchic structures, with authority based on knowledge, competence, and expertise rather than hierarchical position. They have a "network structure of control, authority and communication," and the content of communication consists of information and advice rather than instructions and decisions.[93]

Matrix organizations are organic systems. Instead of a hierarchical structure with a single, clearly defined chain of command and communication system, matrix organizations feature a dual chain of command and a complex, networking communication system. Matrix organizations are of two basic types: temporary and permanent. Temporary matrices rely heavily on project management. "A project is a specific time-constrained task, the performance of which cuts across the traditional lines of structure and authority within a given organization."[94] A task is identified, and a project manager is designated and given authority to assemble a project team composed of people drawn from units throughout the organization. When the project is completed, the team is disbanded and members are returned to their base units. In the interim, they are subject to the authority of both the project manager and their usual supervisors. Permanent matrix organizations have identified an enduring duality of major functions for which they maintain dual chains of command. Many universities use a permanent matrix structure for the dual functions of graduate and undergraduate education. A graduate college with a separate dean exists parallel and equal to undergraduate colleges of letters and science, business, engineering, and so forth. Faculty members are assigned to individual departments and have the dual functions of both graduate and undergraduate education.

NASA has long been the prime example of a project-management-oriented matrix organization in the public sector. NASA was created in 1958, taking over the functions, responsibilities, and organizational style of the National Advisory Committee on Aeronautics, which for forty-three years had had the primary responsibility for basic and applied aeronautical research. NASA was given additional direct operational responsibility for manned space exploration: the Mercury, Gemini, and Apollo programs, the Skylab program, and the Space Shuttle Orbiter. In the early years, NASA struggled to find the appropriate organizational structure, organizing and reorganizing constantly.[95] What eventually resulted was an extremely complex, decentralized matrix organization that relied heavily on the use of outside contractors to perform essential organizational functions. Compounding the complexity was the geographical decentralization of NASA's research centers, laboratories, and space centers.

Just as bureaucracy is subject to "bureaupathologies,"[96] matrix organizations are subject to their own pathologies: power struggles, anarchy (no one identified as clearly in command or responsible), groupitis (pressure for all decisions to be group decisions), excessive overhead, and decision strangulation (decision making is slowed by the inability of team members to make decisions without clearing them with supervisors) and the consequent escalation of conflict to higher levels.[97] NASA had long been subject to all of these problems plus the human problems of matrix organization: stress and anxiety resulting from ambiguity of responsibility and authority, brevity of work relationships, role conflict, and anxiety over job reassignments when projects ended. "Project personnel . . . tend to be more frustrated by what they perceive to be make-work assignments than do members of functional organizations, and . . . they worry more about being set back in their careers."[98]

NASA was touted as a model government agency as its successes accumulated: the space walk, the man on the moon, the space shuttle flights. Then on January 28, 1986, the Space Shuttle Challenger exploded and seven astronauts died. As the investigation to determine what went wrong proceeded, NASA's prestige plummeted and it became a badly discredited agency. General Accounting Office reports revealed repeated instances of waste, contract mismanagement, and spending abuses "in virtually every aspect of NASA operations."[99] Some, but by no means all, of the blame can be attributed to the inherent flaws of a matrix organization:

> Organizational components that were supposed to work closely together—the Marshall, Kennedy, and Johnson Space Centers—have behaved like quasi-independent baronies, uncommunicative with one another and the top. . . .
> The result: an organization in which the flow of vital information up and down was as flawed as the now notorious O-rings. . . .
> It was a failure of NASA's command system. . . . Managers from the Marshall Center, in trying to explain to the presidential commission why they had not relayed to the top vehement objections of Thiokol's engineers, presented their judgment as a matter of routine decisionmaking at the appropriate level of the organization. . . .
> Keeping abreast of what is happening down in the ranks has always been tough for NASA's leaders because the agency's component organizations have fiercely defended their own turf. . . .
> On NASA's organizational charts, Marshall has an ambiguous chain of command. Normally, it reports to the Johnson Space Center in Houston, . . . though Marshall is not under the Johnson Center's management control. It also reports to the Office of Space Flight at NASA headquarters.[100]

The advantages of the matrix structure are as pronounced as its disadvantages. It has a built-in flexibility and ability to respond to problems as they develop. It allows for optional use of specialists. It minimizes monotony and boredom for employees, providing them with work that is diverse and challenging though always temporary.

Committee Structures and Plural Executives

The forms of organization examined thus far, even the most decentralized, have been based on single individuals as designated sources of leadership, whether of position or expertise. In bureaucracy, of course, single individuals are designated as supervisors at all levels up to and including the top of the organization. Even matrix organizations designate single individuals as project managers and chief executives. An alternative form of organization is to have plural executives either at the top of the organization or throughout the organization: administration by committee.

Multiheaded agencies are common in government. Legislatures in particular are fond of creating agencies headed by commissions whose members share equally in controlling and directing the agency. The Federal Communications Commission, the Consumer Product Safety Commission, and the Federal Trade Commission are examples of federal agencies with plural executives. Politically, multiheaded agencies provide a way to prevent concentration of power in a single person, allow for representation of diverse interests in decision making, and make the agency more responsive to legislative control. From administrative perspective, a plural executive allows diverse input into decision making, encourages debate and deliberation, and permits the dispersion of the work load.

The disadvantages of a plural executive were well summarized by Alexander Hamilton in the *Federalist Papers*, number seventy.

> [It] enervates the whole system of administration. . . . [T]he mere diversity of views and opinions would alone be sufficient to tincture the exercise of the executive authority with a spirit of habitual feebleness and dilatoriness. . . . [It] tends to conceal faults and destroy responsibility. . . .
> The plurality of the executive tends to deprive the people of the two greatest securities they can have for the faithful exercise of any delegated power, first the restraints of public opinion which lose their efficacy, . . . second, the opportunity of discovering with facility and clearness the misconduct of persons they trust.[101]

The Congress of the United States is an organization that is controlled and operates primarily through committees. An organization chart of either the House or the Senate would show a flat structure with decision making decentralized in the multimember standing committees. The operations and outputs of Congress clearly illustrate the advantages and disadvantages of a committee structure. On the positive side, such a structure maximizes opportunity for member participation in decision making. The committees encourage specialization so that decision making is not only participatory but also reflective of both expertise and the diverse points of view represented within the organization. Conversely, the committee structure does not just decentralize power, it fragments it—with the result that the decision process always operates slowly and sometimes cannot operate at all. Indecisiveness, hesitation, and slowness become the most notable characteristics of the organization. The participatory, decentralized nature of the decision process determines the way decisions are most commonly made: through bargaining, negotiating, and compromises. The decisions thus reached may not be most appropriate for the problems or issues at stake but instead are an inconsistent conglomeration of ideas put together to obtain majority support.

Conglomerate Structures

A conglomerate structure combines several independent units with no important interdependencies.[102] One of the best examples of a governmental conglomerate organization is found in the state government of Idaho. The Department of Self-Governing Agencies (Table 1–1) consists of twenty-three separate boards and commissions, which operate as autonomous units except for some minor administrative housekeeping chores. The logic behind the creation of such a department is specific to the public

TABLE 1–1.   Idaho Department of Self-Governing Agencies

Promoting Idaho Commodities

    Idaho Apple Commission—advertising and promoting Idaho apples
    Idaho Bean Commission—marketing and development of Idaho beans
    Idaho Cherry Commission—advertising and promoting Idaho cherries
    Idaho Dairy Products—promotion of Idaho dairy products
    Idaho Potato Commission—advertising and promoting Idaho potatoes
    Idaho Wheat Commission—marketing and development of Idaho wheat
    Idaho Prune Commission

Professional Licensing and Regulation

    Athletic Director—supervising boxing and wrestling in Idaho
    Board of Pharmacy—protecting public health, monitors controlled substance abuse
    Board of Accountancy—licensing and enforcement
    Board of Dentistry—enforcement of the Dental Practices Act
    Board of Engineering Examiners—licensing and enforcement
    Board of Medicine—licensing, enforcement, and education
    Board of Nursing—licensing, enforcement, and education
    Public Works Contractors State License Board—licensing and enforcement
    Real Estate Commission—administration
    Real Estate Commission—education
    Board of Registration for Professional Geologists—board of professional geologists
    Board of Optometry—administration
    Idaho Outfitters and Guides Board
    Certified Shorthand Reporters Board

sector. In 1974, the legislature, at the urging of the governor, decided to reorganize the state executive branch. One of the major goals of the reorganization was to reduce the Governor's span of control, so a decision was made to limit the number of cabinet departments to twenty-one. One departmental slot was to be kept vacant to accommodate any new priorities or problems that might occur in the future. The other nineteen department slots were rather quickly allotted. This left a rather large and motley group of agencies as organizational orphans. Since the agencies were not without political strength, a solution acceptable to them had to be discovered. The result was the cabinet-level Department of Self-Governing Agencies.

The old federal Department of Health, Education and Welfare (HEW, reorganized as the Department of Education and the Department of Health and Human Services in 1979) resembled a conglomerate structure. Although health, education and welfare could be considered to be part of a broader human resource function, in reality they are very separate functions, controlled by separate, independent, and established professions. At the time of HEW's creation they were already represented in established bureaus, which were combined into one department. The result was a conglomerate department, with minimal interdependency between its three major units, whose secretary was relegated to housekeeping and coordination.[103]

Despite the difficulties inherent in coordination and control of conglomerates, they do have some organizational advantages. Sheer size frequently translates into power and survivability in the political arena. And political commitment to individual programs tends to wax and wane; a program that loses favor may be protected by the parent organization from some of the adverse consequences of political neglect or hostility. The diversity and size of a conglomerate may also assist it in attracting new resources and new programs because it may be able to demonstrate that it already has the expertise and experience necessary to implement it. Thus, HEW succeeded in obtaining authority to implement the College Work Study and Adult Basic Education programs in the Johnson administration's War on Poverty.[104] Conversely, if budget cuts must be made, they may be spread throughout a diverse structure without seriously damaging the overall organization, thus possibly saving member organizations from extinction.

Simple Structure

The simple structure organization ranks low on all measures of complexity, low on formalization, and high on centralization. It is usually a two-tiered organization: the boss or head and the subordinates. The head of the organization is the source of decisions, authority, and control. Simple structures are usually associated with small organizations: small towns, small school districts, small businesses.

Simplicity is appealing in an era of complex, massive, impersonal organizations. Because authority is centralized, decisions can be made and implemented quickly. The form allows maximum flexibility and clear accountability with minimum goal displacement. All of these advantages depend completely on the ability and personality of the leader; if the leader lacks ability or for some reason is removed from office, the organization is likely to flounder and collapse. Further, the lack of formalization can easily result in abuse of power and arbitrary behavior. In the public sector particularly, the personalized nature of small organizations is problematic, maximizing discretion and resulting in unequal treatment of citizens and employees and offering little, if any, opportunity for career growth and advancement. Representation of diverse interests is minimal. Smallness also tends to result in organizational vulnerability; the simple structure may prevent the organization from diversifying support and surviving adverse environmental conditions.

CONCLUSION

This chapter examined the major dimensions of organization structure—formalization, complexity, and centralization—and the major types of organization structures that result from varying combinations of these dimensions. Each of the major forms of organization exists in the public sector. Each structural form has advantages and disadvantages for organizational function, for employees, for clients, for the public, and for the political system. No "one best way" of organization emerges.

Starting with the next chapter, attention is focused on the contingency factors, the situational variables, that are associated with the development, survival, and effectiveness of the major organizational types. Contingency theorists have associated six major situational variables with organization structure: the organization's environment, goals, technology, strategy, size, and age. The relationship among these variables is complex, as the variables are interrelated, particularly for public organizations. The environment is often the source of organizational goals, but large public organizations are capable of manipulating both their environments and goals. Goals and environment determine the nature of the technology the organizations will use, which in turn affects the organization's structure. The structure of the organization, professional bureaucracy for example, may control the technology and thus control or change the goals of the organization. Some variables may push the organization towards one type of structure; other variables may pressure it towards a different structure.

Ultimately, for the organization the crucial problem becomes determining the most effective structure given a particular configuration of situational variables. This in turn leads to determining what constitutes an effective organization.

NOTES

1. Luther Gulick, "Notes on the Theory of Organization," in L. Gulick and L. Urwick, *Papers on the Science of Administration* (New York: Institute for Public Administration, 1937), p. 7.
2. Lee Sproull, Stephen Weiner, and David Wolff, *Organizing an Anarchy* (Chicago: University of Chicago Press, 1978), p. 141.
3. John Ivancevich and James Donnelly, "Relation of Organization Structure to Job Satisfaction, Anxiety-Stress, and Performance," *Administrative Science Quarterly* (June 1975): p. 279.
4. Henry Mintzberg, *The Structuring of Organizations* (Englewood Cliffs, N. J.: Prentice-Hall, 1979), pp. 5–6.
5. Stephen R. Robbins, *Organization Theory* (Englewood Cliffs: Prentice-Hall, 1983), p. 45.
6. Ibid., p. 61.
7. Ibid., p. 76.
8. Ibid., p. 47.
9. Henri Fayol, *General and Industrial Management*, trans. Constance Storrs (London: Pitman Publishing Ltd., 1949), p. 20.
10. William G. Scott and David Hart, *Organizational America* (Boston: Houghton-Mifflin, 1979), pp. 66–67.
11. Donald E. Klingner and John Nalbandian, *Public Personnel Management: Contexts and Strategies* (Englewood Cliffs, N.J.: Prentice-Hall, 1985), p. 160.
12. Peter Blau and Richard Scott, *Formal Organizations* (San Francisco: Chandler Publishing Co., 1962), p. 240.
13. Herbert Kaufman, *The Forest Ranger* (Baltimore: Johns Hopkins Press, 1960).
14. *U.S. Forest Service Manual*, sec. 1103–1.
15. Ibid., sec. 2300.
16. *Tax Audit Guidelines For Internal Revenue Service Examiners*, Internal Revenue Manual, p. 4231–12.
17. Air Force Regulation 35–10, pp. 1–12a (1) and (2) (1978).
18. *Goldman v. Weinberger*, 106 S. Ct. 1310 (1968).
19. From *Kelley v. Johnson*, 425US238, 240 (1976).
20. Ibid., 248.
21. Informal rules will be discussed more extensively in Chapter 7.
22. Michael Crozier, *The Bureaucratic Phenomenon* (Chicago: University of Chicago Press, 1964), p. 189.
23. Blau and Scott, *Formal Organizations*, p. 60.
24. Ibid., p. 61.
25. Ibid., p. 63.
26. Frederick C. Mosher, *Democracy and the Public Service* (New York: Oxford University Press, 1982), p. 115.
27. See Harold Wilensky, "The Professionalization of Everyone," *The American Journal of Sociology* (September 1964): pp. 137–58.

28. Lee W. Potts, *Responsible Police Administration* (University of Alabama: University of Alabama Press, 1983), p. 139.
29. Arthur Niederhoffer, "From Bureaucracy to Profession," in W. Clinton Terry III, *Policing Society* (New York: John Wiley, 1985), p. 166.
30. See Daniel M. Poore, "The Impact of NASPAA's Standards on Defining the Field of Public Administration," in Joseph A. Uveges, ed., *Public Administration: History and Theory in Contemporary Perspective* (New York: Marcel Dekker, 1982), pp. 85–104, and Richard L. Scott, "Public Administration as a Profession: Problems and Prospects," *Public Administration Review* (May/June 1976): pp. 253–259.
31. Oscar Grusky and George A. Miller, *The Sociology of Organizations* (New York: Free Press, 1970), p. 475.
32. Leonard Reissman, "A Study of Role Conceptions in Bureaucracy," *Social Forces* (1949): pp. 305–10.
33. John W. Meyer and Brian Rowen, "The Structure of Educational Organizations," in John W. Meyer and W. Richard Scott, *Organizational Environments* (Beverly Hills, Calif.: Sage Publications Inc., 1983), pp. 71–96.
34. David Street, "Bureaucratization, Professionalization and the Poor," in K. Gronbjerg, D. Street and G. Scittles, eds., *Poverty and Social Change* (Chicago: University of Chicago Press, 1979).
35. Rosemary C. Sarri and Yeheskel Hasenfeld, eds., *The Management of Human Services* (New York: Columbia University Press, 1978), p. 9.
36. Mosher, *Democracy and the Public Service*, p. 118.
37. Mintzberg, *The Structuring of Organizations*, p. 258.
38. Herbert Simon, *Administrative Behavior*, 3rd ed. (New York: Free Press, 1976), p. 307.
39. Max Weber, *The Theory of Social and Economic Organization*, trans. A. M. Henderson and Talcott Parsons, Talcott Parsons, ed., (Glencoe, Ill.: Free Press, 1947), p. 152.
40. Ibid., p. 324.
41. John M. Pfiffner and Frank P. Sherwood, *Administrative Organization* (Englewood Cliffs: Prentice-Hall, 1960), p. 77.
42. Henri Fayol, *General and Industrial Management* (London: Putman Publishing Ltd., 1949), p. 38.
43. Chester Barnard, *The Functions of the Executive* (Cambridge: Harvard University Press, 1968), p. 165.
44. Ibid., pp. 167–69.
45. Stanley Milgram, "Some Conditions of Obedience and Disobedience to Authority," *Human Relations* (1965): pp. 57–76.
46. Fayol, *General and Industrial Management*, pp. 19–21; Barnard, *The Functions of the Executive*, p. 173.
47. Charles O. Jones, *Introduction to the Study of Public Policy*, 3rd ed. (Monterey, Calif.: Brooks/Cole Publishing Co., 1984), p. 29.
48. Robbins, *Organization Theory*, p. 88.
49. Charles E. Gilbert, ed., "Implementing Governmental Change," *Annals of the American Academy of Political and Social Sciences* (March 1983): pp. 9–10.
50. Emmette Redford and Marian Blissett, *Organizing the Executive Branch* (Chicago: University of Chicago Press, 1981), p. 4.
51. Philip Selznick, *TVA and the Grass Roots* (Berkeley: University of California Press, 1949).
52. Charles Gilbert, "Implementing Governmental Change," p. 10.

53. Robbins, *Organization Theory*, pp. 45–57.
54. See Gulick, "Notes on the Theory of Organization," pp. 21ff.
55. Simon, *Administrative Behavior*, pp. 30–35.
56. See, for example, Mintzberg, *The Structuring of Organizations*, pp. 108–113; Daniel Robey, *Designing Organizations* (Homewood, Ill.: Richard D. Irwin, 1982), pp. 312–335; Robbins, *Organization Theory*, pp. 49–50.
57. Gulick, "Notes on the Theory of Organization," p. 21.
58. Alan L. Dean, "The Management of The Executive Branch," *Annals of the Academy of Political and Social Science* (March 1983): p. 81.
59. Redford and Blissett, *Organizing the Executive Branch*, p. 20.
60. Peter Szanton, "So You Want to Reorganize the Government?" in Peter Szanton, *Federal Reorganization* (Chatham, N.J.: Chatham House Publishers, Inc., 1981), p. 21.
61. Harold Seidman and Robert Gilmour, *Politics, Position and Power* (New York: Oxford, 1986), p. 20.
62. Gulick, "Notes on the Theory of Organization," p. 23.
63. Dean, "The Management of the Executive Branch," p. 81.
64. Simon, *Administrative Behavior*, p. 28.
65. Ibid., p. 33.
66. Ibid., p. 37.
67. Ibid., p. 44.
68. L. Urwick, *The Elements of Administration* (New York: Harper & Bros., 1945), pp. 52–54.
69. V. A. Graicunas, "Relationship in Organization," in Gulick and Urwick, *Papers on the Science of Administration*, pp. 183–87.
70. Simon, *Administrative Behavior*, pp. 26–28.
71. James Worthy, *Big Business and Free Men* (New York: Harper & Row, 1959), pp. 110–111.
72. Jimmy Carter, *Keeping Faith* (New York: Bantam Books, 1982), p. 69.
73. President's Committee on Administrative Management, *Report With Special Studies* (Washington, D.C.: Government Printing Office, 1937), p. 32.
74. Seidman and Gilmour, *Politics, Position and Power*, p. 253.
75. Joan Woodward, *Industrial Organization: Theory and Practice* (London: Oxford University Press, 1965), p. 62.
76. Pfiffner and Sherwood, *Administrative Organization*, p. 161.
77. Robey, *Designing Organizations*, pp. 338–340.
78. Donald R. Cressey, "Prison Organizations," in James G. March, *Handbook of Organizations* (Chicago: Rand-McNally, 1965), p. 1045.
79. Kurt Lang, "Military Organizations," in March, *Handbook of Organizations*, p. 852.
80. W. Clinton Terry III, *Policing Society*, p. xiii.
81. Douglas McGregor, *The Human Side of Enterprise* (New York: McGraw-Hill, 1968).
82. John W. Meyer and Brian Rowan, "The Structure of Educational Organizations," in Meyer and Scott, *Organizational Environments*, pp. 74–75.
83. *New Jersey v. T.L.O.*, 83 L. Ed. 2d 720, 733 (1985).
84. See Charles Perrow, "Hospitals, Technology, Structure, and Goals," in March, *Handbook of Organizations*, pp. 947–952.
85. Howard Aldrich, "Centralization versus Decentralization in the Design of Human Service Delivery Systems," in Sarri and Hasenfeld, *The Management of Human Services*, p. 58.
86. Peter H. Rossi, "Some Issues In the Evaluation of Human Services Delivery," in Sarri and Hasenfeld, p. 244.

87. Howard Messner, "The Environment Inside EPA," *The Bureaucrat* (Spring 1986): p. 56.
88. Russell Peterson, Audubon Society President, quoted in *Congressional Quarterly* (July 31, 1982): p. 1829.
89. Messner, "The Environment Inside EPA," p. 55.
90. Mintzberg, *The Structuring of Organizations*, p. 37.
91. Alvin Toffler, *Future Shock* (New York: Bantam Books, 1970).
92. Warren Bennis, "Post-Bureaucratic Leadership," in Warren Bennis, ed., *American Bureaucracy* (New York: Aldine, 1970), pp. 166.
93. Tom Burns and G. M. Stalker, *The Management of Innovation* (London: Tavistock Publications, 1961), p. 120.
94. Richard L. Chapman, *Project Management in NASA*, (Washington, D.C.: Government Printing Office, 1973), p. 3.
95. W. Litzinger, A. Mayrinac, and J. Wagle, "The Manned Spacecraft Center in Houston: The Practice of Matrix Management," *International Review of Administrative Sciences* (1970): pp. 1–8.
96. James Thompson, *Modern Organizations* (New York: Knopf, 1961), p. 154.
97. S. M. Davis and P. R. Laurence, *Matrix* (Reading, Mass.: Addison-Wesley, 1976), cited in Mary Ellen Simon, "Matrix Management at the U.S. Consumer Product Safety Commission," *Public Administration Review* (July/August 1983): p. 361.
98. Chapman, *Project Management in NASA*, p. 105.
99. "NASA Wasted Billions, Federal Audits Disclose," *New York Times*, April 23, 1986, p. 10.
100. Michael Brady, "NASA's Challenge: Ending Isolation at the Top," *Fortune* (May 12, 1986): pp. 20–29.
101. Alexander Hamilton, "Federalist no. 70," in *The Federalist Papers* (New York: New American Library, 1961), pp. 427–429.
102. Robbins, *Organization Theory*, p. 239.
103. Seidman and Gilmour, *Position, Politics and Power*, pp. 182–183.
104. Redford and Blissett, *Organizing the Executive Branch*, p. 87.

2

ORGANIZATIONS AND THEIR ENVIRONMENTS

Organizations are creatures, captives, and controllers of the environments within which they operate. The relationship between an organization and its environment is dynamic and multifaceted. Public organizations are created in response to demands from groups, organizations, or powerful individuals in the general environment, and their goals and purposes, at least initially, are determined by environmental forces. They depend on the environment for the financial and human resources necessary to carry out their activities. Once created and operational, they must develop and maintain environmental support and acceptance of their activities—"if they do not, they do not last long."[1]

Organizational structure is also partially determined by organizational attempts to adapt to their environments. The population ecology school of organization theorists argues that resource constraints and competition for resources in the environment results in a type of organizational Darwinism, selecting for survival the organizations, and organizational forms, best adapted for the environment: "Selection of new or changed organizational forms occurs as a result of environmental constraints. Organizations fitting environmental criteria are positively selected and survive, while others either fail or change to match environmental requirements."[2] In the struggle for survival, organizations will vary their activities and structures, selecting and retaining the most successful adaptations.

One of the major criticisms of population ecology theory is that it overlooks the extent to which powerful organizations create or manipulate their environments.[3] While small, powerless organizations may exist at the mercy of their environments, large, powerful organizations, such as the Department of Defense, use a variety of strategies and tactics to modify and control their environments. The organizational-environmental relationship is in reality reciprocal and dynamic.

Organizational environments have two basic components: the general environment common to all organizations within a particular society and a specific environment unique to the individual organization. The general environment consists of societal and cultural values, political and legal norms and values, and economic, demographic, and technological conditions in society. The specific environment of individual organizations consists of those organizations, groups, and individuals with which the organization directly interacts. Both the general and specific environments affect organizational structure, goals, and behavior and are in turn affected by them.

THE GENERAL ENVIRONMENT OF AMERICAN PUBLIC ORGANIZATIONS

The general environment shapes the attitudes and values of the public toward governmental activities and organization as well as the attitudes and values of the employees that organizations recruit. It is the source of the problems that public organizations are assigned to solve and the determiner of the technology available to deal with those problems. The general economic environment determines the availability or scarcity of resources for the public sector. The basic political and legal values determine the ultimate goals of and the basic constraints on public organization behavior. Although the general environment may appear remote and tangential to the routine functioning of an organization, it shapes the specific environment; any significant changes in the general environment are likely to be transmitted to specific organizational environments.

Social and Cultural Values

The United States is a socially and culturally diverse nation, and its dominant social values superficially reflect that diversity. Individualism, materialism, equality, conformity, pragmatism, rationality, the Protestant work ethic, belief in progress, and obedience to authority are characteristic values of contemporary American social culture. Initially, many of these values appear to inherently conflict. In reality and practice, the values are compatible and combine to create a contextual environment supportive of bureaucratic organization.

The belief in rugged individualism is deeply rooted in American culture. The central tenet of individualism is the belief that the individual is the source and determiner of all values. Each person has the right and responsibility to decide what is in his or her best interest and to pursue that interest without interference from others. From that central tenet comes the belief that the individual is solely responsible for success or failure in his or her life. While it might seem that individualism is incompatible with conformity and organizational life, individualism actually establishes the groundwork for both. In the pursuit of individual identity and the attempt to establish one's worth, individuals judge themselves through comparison with the status and position of others. Success and failure are socially determined; in the quest for success, then, being like others becomes very important. Ironically, to be different is to be a failure. Thus conformity in looks, behavior, and material acquisition is a requisite for individual success.

Beyond the pressure to conform, individualism also results in a frightening and unnatural isolation. Individualism is a doctrine of aloneness, setting each individual apart from and in competition with others. Humans are social animals, as the human relations school of management demonstrated and as most social psychologists would agree, but individualism denies that and forces them to face the world alone and on their own. According to individualism, even family and community are to be sacrificed in the pursuit of individual ego gratification. In practice, however, the human need to belong does not disappear. Denied other outlets, it finds expression in structured organizational life, with its requirements for conformity and obedience and its offer of something larger with which to identify. As large organizations become the dominant actors in social, economic, and political life, individualism reinforces their power. To succeed in the conventionally defined sense means to succeed in organizations: to achieve the status, power, prestige, and income indicative of success, most people must work in the dominant organizations in society. Success within the organization requires people to play the game by the organization's rules and conform to its norms, values, and expectations.

Economic materialism, the belief that material possessions and money are the best measure of a person's worth, is a natural outgrowth of individualism. Individual success has to be measured by some standard, and in this society the standard is visible, external possessions. Again, organizations play a central role. They produce the material objects that we prize, and they are the predominant means by which people may earn the money necessary to purchase these objects.

Equality is a natural concomitant of individualism. In the American value system, equality is defined as a requirement for equality of opportunity. Guaranteed the equal right to compete, the individual bears the burden of actual success or failure. The lack of even basic equality of opportunity for certain groups in society has long troubled the American social and political conscience, but attempts to eliminate basic discrimination have always been limited by the insistence that no encroachment on individualism accompany them.

The Protestant work ethic combines individualism, equality, conformity, and material accumulation and elevates them to the status of a divinely inspired doctrine. In the quest to prove one's worth to God, one must work, strive, and succeed. Beginning with the Calvinist doctrine of predestination, the individual was simultaneously stripped of control over his or her own destiny and compelled to bear alone "the destiny which had been decreed for him from eternity." The result was "a feeling of unprecedented inner loneliness of the single individual."[4] Although seemingly nothing the individual did mattered—and consequently his or her behavior on earth might seem irrelevant—the Protestant work ethic did not let the individual off that easily. "Thus, however useless good works might be as a means of attaining salvation, . . . they are indispensable as a sign of election."[5] Thus, man must work, and "waste of time is thus the first and, in principle, the deadliest of sins."[6] This in turn leads to extreme pressures toward uniformity of life and ultimately the accumulation of wealth, which according to Max Weber fueled the development of capitalism. Although as religious doctrine, the Protestant work ethic eschewed material consumption, in this country it became a secular doctrine, and in its secular guise the sign of being one of the elect was not just hard work but all the material trappings that can be purchased as a result of success. The cumulative effect of these deeply ingrained social values was to encourage conformity and obedience to authority.

In *The Organizational Society*, Robert Presthus summarizes basic American cultural values as

> a distrust of theory, considerable respect for size and quantitative standards, respect for power, an unchallenged belief in a high degree of social mobility (based upon the ideal of equal opportunity), great disparity in consumption levels (validated by *personal* success or failure), and a pragmatic ethic that often makes success the test of truth.[7]

Pragmatism as a philosophical belief emphasizes flexibility, practicality, experience as the test of reality, and workability as the test of truth. "There is no final truth. . . . Truth . . . is that which proves useful in an ever-changing, ever-surprising human situation."[8] Without absolutes, everything is relative. If it works, it is good; nothing succeeds like success. For individuals as for organizations, pragmatism supports survival of the fittest as the operative value system.

The belief in rationality as the ideal lends support to both pragmatism and organizational life. Rationality is based on positive science, which stipulates that truth can be obtained only through use of the scientific method. Knowledge must be based on experience and direct observation. Intuition and subjective forms of knowledge are "irrational." In rational decision making, problems are clearly defined, goals are clear and attainable, alternative ways to achieve those goals are developed, their consequences are predicted, their costs and benefits are weighed, and the best alternative is selected and implemented. From an economic and organizational perspective, the ultimate goal of rationality is to always select the course of action that most efficiently attains goals. That no human being is capable of complete rationality diminishes the importance of humans and elevates the importance of organizations: "The rational individual is, and must be, an organized and institutionalized individual."[9] Of course, the totally irrational individual will probably also be institutionalized, but that is the purpose of organizations: to constrain and overcome our irrationality. The quest for rationality not only requires that individuals become organized but also justifies the use of control and any techniques necessary to achieve rationality and its greatest benefit, efficiency. Bureaucracy triumphed, as an organization form, because of its ability to maximize rationality.

The composite result of these socio-cultural values has been the creation of an institutional environment that legitimates rationalized bureaucracy as the preeminent organizational form. "Institutional environments are broadly defined as including the rules and belief systems as well as the relational networks that arise in the broader societal context. In modern societies, an important category of the rules and belief systems that arise are sets of 'rational myths.' . . . They identify specific social purposes and then specify in a rule-like manner what activities are to be carried out . . . to achieve them."[10] Large, powerful, bureaucratic organizations emerge as the dominant and most successful type of organization. They pressure other organizations to adopt a similar structure, and those organizations that "create unique structures, lack acceptable legitimated accounts of their activities. Such organizations are more vulnerable to claims that they are negligent, irrational or unnecessary."[11]

Scott and Hart contend in *Organizational America* that the "organizational imperative" has changed basic American social values.[12] The argument presented here is somewhat the opposite: basic American social values have always been compatible with the organizational imperative, and they nurture and promote it. Once dominant, however, the organizational ethic has resulted in a modification of those values. For the good of the organization (what is good for organizations is good for society), individuals can be compelled to surrender basic individual rights and forced to submit to lie detector tests, urine analyses, tests, and similar intrusions into their privacy. For the good of the organization (what is good for the organization is good for the individual), individuals can be compelled to participate in "wellness" programs, behavior modification, sensitivity training, and psychological counselling. As long as large organizations are successful at satisfying individual and societal needs, the socio-cultural environment will remain supportive of their existence and power. Beyond that, large organizations, public and private, have achieved such power that they are capable of manipulating their general environment to ensure support even if they cease to satisfy the needs and desires of society.

The Political and Legal Environment

The general political environment in the United States has determined and continues to determine the structure and behavior of public organizations. One of the basic political beliefs that has permeated American political culture from the founding of this country has been a fear and mistrust of governmental power. The writers of the Constitution designed a political system that they believed would prevent government from ever becoming too powerful. At the national level this was accomplished by separation of powers, or rather separate institutions sharing powers, so that the three major branches of government—legislative, executive, and judicial—would constantly check the exercise of power by each other. Governmental power was further limited through creation of a federal system that divided power between the national and state levels of government.

Separation of powers has resulted in continual conflict between the president and Congress over control of executive agencies. The president, as chief executive, has long contended that he should have ultimate authority over their finances, personnel, powers, and structure. Congress has been equally insistent that as the legislative branch it has final authority because it appropriates, passes the laws, creates agencies, and checks on how they have exercised their powers. This conflict has had a lasting impact on the structure and powers of the executive agencies. Congress has demonstrated a propensity toward proliferating independent agencies, partially to thwart easy presidential domination by expanding the president's span of control, partially to placate interest groups, and partially to facilitate congressional committee oversight. Congress has also preferred multi-headed agencies (commissions) for similar reasons and has preferred to fragment responsibility for specific policy areas by overlapping and duplicating functions among various agencies. Although Congress has granted the president limited reorganization authority in the past, it has seldom approved reorganizations that would have strengthened presidential control at the expense of congressional power.

Federalism has had an equally important impact on the structure of the executive branch. Created and maintained in fear of excessive centralization, federalism has evolved into a fragmented, uncoordinated system of government. In domestic policy, federal agencies often have responsibility for programs that will in reality be implemented by state or local government agencies. The federal agency makes the rules and disburses the funds, but the local agencies actually implement the policy. The result is decentralization and, frequently, lack of uniformity in policy impact, which provokes federal agencies to increase formalization: more rules and regulations aimed at achieving uniformity. Another result has been congressional attempts to control the structure of state governments. To facilitate national policy implementation, Congress has frequently required state governments to create a "single state agency" to administer federal funds. The Federal Highway Act, the National Health Planning and Resources Development Act of 1974, and the School Lunch Program, as well as community health, urban planning, and countless other federal programs have mandated the structure of the state agency charged with their enforcement.[13]

Red tape, excessive formalization, has been one of the more chronic criticisms of government agencies. The underlying cause of red tape, however, is the constitutional legal system, particularly the requirement that agencies must provide due process of law in any action that infringes life, liberty, or property. Due process in turn has come to require that all rules, policies, and procedures be written and available for public inspection. It requires that people be treated equally and fairly and that quasi-judicial procedures be followed in a variety of circumstances. Failure to provide due process may result in a court challenge and nullification of an attempted action. Nothing is more offensive to due process than the arbitrary and capricious exercise of discretion, so attempts to control discretion have resulted not only in increased formalization but also increased centralization.

Equally important in the legal and political environment are the values intrinsic to democratic political theory that require government to be responsive, representative, and responsible. For Congress and the president, responsiveness, representation, and responsibility are presumably achieved through the electoral process. For the bureaucratic agencies at all levels of government, the requirements are not so easily met. Failure to satisfy these requirements, however, diminishes the legitimacy of the agencies and of government as a whole. One of the basic theoretical and practical problems associated with the expansion of power of executive agencies has been determining to whom they should be responsive and responsible and who they should represent.

One of the primary methods of ensuring responsiveness and responsibility has been "overhead democracy," based on the belief that responsiveness and responsibility should be to the elected branches of government. Overhead democracy stresses the importance of control mechanisms of the chief executive, the legislature, and the courts over agency action. This results in a strong preference for bureaucratic organization and its hierarchy of positions, where authority and responsibility are synonymous and centralized at the top, and written rules and regulations guide and control employee behavior and permit review and oversight by the courts, the executive, and the legislature. The unresolved dilemma of this concept of responsiveness and responsibility is to whom responsiveness and responsibility is owed when the three branches conflict. Separation of powers guarantees that this will frequently occur, and even the ideal type bureaucracy will be unable to resolve the conflict. If the conflict is between the president and Congress, top-level political executives will probably offer at least public responsiveness to the president, whereas the career service will either be silent or respond to Congress. When the courts are involved in the conflict, agencies will take their cue to appropriate response from the political branches.

Another method of promoting bureaucratic responsiveness is the inner check. The inner check stresses the importance of the values, attitudes, and ethics of the employees to ensuring their continuing responsiveness and responsibility to the public and political superiors. Similar to professionalism, the inner check relies less on organizational control of behavior than on inculcated individual values to ensure conformity and uniformity of behavior. The problems with this approach lie in the absence of a clear, consistent, widely agreed upon set of values and a method for instilling those values. And as with overhead democracy, no agreement exists on to whom responsiveness and responsibility are owed or how conflicts may be resolved. The problems may be particularly severe at the level of the individual public employee:

> The tax auditor reviewing a tax return is faced with supporting efficiency (reviewing the most returns possible), fairness (taking time to inform me of what he is doing), accountability (responding to his appointed superior who says take it easy on middle income returns), and the rule of law (doing precisely what the regulations stipulate). The caseworker faces the rule of law (which specifies eligibility), responsiveness (listening to all applicants), honesty (reporting the exact income figures), expertise (judging whether an applicant is truly in need), and efficiency (processing the most cases possible). . . . What does one do?[14]

The New Public Administration of the 1970s attempted to answer that question. For its adherents, the inner check was the primary answer to the responsiveness, responsibility, and representation problems. The dominant value that public administrators were to internalize and relentlessly pursue was social equity. The three major branches of government were viewed as lacking commitment to social equity and were thus given an insignificant role in controlling public agencies: "The procedures of representative democracy presently operate in a way that either fails or only very gradually attempts to reverse systematic discrimination against disadvantaged minorities. Social equity, then, includes activities designed to enhance the political power and economic well-being of these minorities."[15] The organizational structure advocated by the new public administration was "modified bureaucratic," emphasizing "decentralization, devolution, projects, contracts, sensitivity training, organization development, responsibility expansion, confrontation and client involvement."[16] Although many of the structural changes advocated have occurred to a certain extent throughout the public sector, the overriding value of social equity seems somewhat archaic in the political climate of the 1980s; and without that value commitment, the problems of responsiveness, responsibility, and representation of the public service are unsolved.

Representation in the public service has proved to be as difficult to define and implement as responsiveness and responsibility. In dealing with public organizations, three types of representative bureaucracy have been identified: demographic, attitudinal, and substantive.[17] Demographic representation requires that the demographic characteristics (race, sex, age, socioeconomic class) of the public service at all levels closely resemble that of the general population. Attitudinal representation requires that the values and beliefs of the public servants resemble and reflect those of the general public. Substantive representation is more complex and the definition more open to argument: it is defined as either acting in the best interests of the public (or clientele or constituents) or carrying out the expressed desires of the public. No clear link exists between the three types: an organization may be demographically representative but not substantively representative, or it may be attitudinally representative but neither demographically nor substantively representative.[18]

The quest for representation has had a decided impact on public organizations. Affirmative action programs have been aimed at increasing demographic representation by increasing the number of minorities and women at all levels of the public service. Organizations have responded reluctantly to this pressure from the legal environment: "When faced with demands for affirmative action, organizations will attempt to limit uncertainty by complying, but will try to minimize the effect of the change on the organization by placing women and minorities in subunits isolated from the core activities of the organization."[19]

The push for decentralization, devolving program responsibility and power to lower levels of government, is based in part on the desire to achieve attitudinal representation. The underlying presumption of decentralization is that units of government closest to the people will be most attuned to the people's needs and desires. The desire to improve substantive representation was an integral part of the New Public Administration, and the New Public Administration supported decentralization as a method to achieve this. The requirements for citizen participation in program administration reflect the desire to improve substantive representation. By 1980, 155 federal programs required some form of direct citizen participation in implementation.[20] Whether decentralization is the best way to increase representation of public administration is questionable, as was pointed out in Chapter 1. Critics of citizen participation have also questioned its efficacy as a representational technique because participants are not necessarily representative of the general public and are easy prey to cooptation by organization administrators.

Public Attitudes Towards Government and Public Service. The general fear and mistrust of government that is indigenous to our political culture has in recent years surfaced as an outspoken opposition to government in general and bureaucracy in particular. In political campaigns, the press, election results, academic writing, and public opinion polls, negative attitudes towards government have been constantly and vociferously expressed.[21] The result has been the creation of a generally hostile environment for the public service. One of the most visible effects of this hostility has been decreased financial resources for the public sector. Whether through property tax limitations at the state and local levels or budget cutbacks at the national level, public organization resources have diminished, frequently at the same time that demands for public services have increased. Public employee morale has suffered, and the ability of agencies to implement programs has been impaired.

Ironically, this generally negative attitude toward public agencies largely disappears when individuals are asked to evaluate their personal experiences with specific public bureaucracies. As Goodsell documents, surveys have repeatedly shown that sizeable majorities of those who have had direct contact with a wide variety of government agencies report that they believe they are treated fairly and considerately and are generally satisfied with the experience.[22] The likely consequences of this dissonance in attitudes was summarized by Robert Kahn and his associates in 1975:

> If people do not link their own experiences with governmental services to their ideals of public bureaucracies, they can be supportive at one level and destructive at another. . . . [P]eople respond realistically to their own experience, but they do not carry that realism to more general issues, with a resulting inconsistency of belief. Unless people get more involved with policy reform and bridge that inconsistency, we can expect that they will accept populist dogma far sooner than programs based on sweet reason.[23]

The Technological Environment

The technological environment refers to the "external technology potentially available to organization, . . . the knowledge about technical processes existing outside the organization."[24] One significant aspect of the technological environment of public agencies is the extent to which advances in machine-based technology have outstripped advances in human-based technologies. Computers and automation have been changing at breathtaking rates, and technological change puts pressure on all organizations to adapt to, adopt, and utilize the new technology. Failure to do so threatens an organization with obsolescence and extinction, but the incorporation of new technologies causes change throughout the organization: training and personnel needs change, structure must be adjusted to accommodate the new technology, and resources must be reallocated.

Unfortunately, the technology to deal with poverty, crime, illiteracy, mental illness, and a variety of other problems that the public sector is expected to solve has not advanced at the same rate as technology for producing material goods or processing information. We know little more today about how to control crime or rehabilitate criminals than we knew in 1900; the causes and cures of poverty remain elusive; and in education, although billions of dollars annually are expended, no "clearly understood and effective technical process for obtaining desired outcomes" has yet emerged.[25] One result of this has been increased impatience with governmental attempts (and failures) to solve complex social and economic problems, which leads to at times overly simplistic and optimistic approaches to these problems: "If we can put a man on the moon, why can't we cure poverty?"

Technological change in the general environment has had other effects on the public sector. The technological advances that made possible a mass production, mass consumption society also resulted in environmental degradation and depletion of natural resources, problems the private sector is unable or unwilling to solve, and which consequently have become the responsibility of the public sector. Once again, the technology to solve those problems has not advanced at the same rate as the technology to create them. The advances in information technology and their adoption by public organizations have had mixed results. The computerization of work processes in agencies such as the Internal Revenue Service and the Social Security Administration has expanded their administrative capabilities and enabled them to carry out functions which would otherwise be impossible. At the same time, opportunities for invasion of individual privacy have been equally magnified. Computerization has also increased the potential for depersonalization of public service delivery; no human bureaucrat ever totally depersonalized contacts with clientele the way computers have. Depersonalization may ultimately result in increased public alienation, which in turn may increase negative reactions to government in general.

The ability to collect, process, and analyze massive amounts of data has increased reliance on statistical indicators as an objective measure of social and human conditions. The unemployment rate, faithfully calculated and announced every month, has become for many the major measure of the economic health of the country. The reliance on what is, at best, a somewhat arbitrary measure of unemployment frequently obscures the depth of the problem because neither the underemployed, the part-time worker, or those terminated within the month surveyed are included in the most commonly reported rate. The Consumer Price Index suffers from similar inadequacies as a complete and accurate measure of the inflation rate's impact on individuals. Technological advances have made these measures possible; their simplicity has made them appealing, comprehensive measures of complex and multifaceted problems. For those attempting to solve these problems—usually public agencies—such oversimplification is misleading and rarely helpful.

Generally, the technological environment is characterized by rapid change, complexity, uncertainty, and "fundamental unknowability," introducing an element of turbulence into the specific environments of many organizations. Its complexity and increasing specialization have resulted in "an increasing escalation of key decisionmakers from the technological base." Technology is cumulative and over time "changes contribute to the evolution of a new system that no single person or group of people can know." Finally, technology has "developed such a momentum as to be essentially out of control and beyond manageability. The effects of massive technological change are, given existing circumstances, irreversible."[26]

The Human Environment

The major components of the human environment are the demographic characteristics of the population, the major changes that are occurring in those characteristics, and the educational, attitudinal, and behavioral characteristics of the most important resource organizations obtain from their environment—human beings. Some of the recent changes in the population most significant for public organizations have been the post–World War II baby boom, the declining birth rate, the "graying of America," and shifts in the geographic distribution of the population. The post–World War II baby boom, referred to by demographers as "the pig in the python," has had a continuing impact on the economy and society. The education system was the first institution to be overwhelmed by the baby boomers. From elementary schools through higher education, more resources had to be allocated to the educational system to provide more classrooms, more teachers, and more facilities to accommodate the huge increase in the school-age population. The criminal justice system was overloaded to the breaking point when the baby boomers entered their crime-prone years, ages sixteen through twenty-five. As the baby boomers entered the job market, the economy strained to accommodate the influx of new workers, but without a high economic growth rate, the unemployment rate inevitably increased.

At each phase of its passage through the python, the baby boom has left behind new problems of adaptation. From an overload of students, the educational system was confronted with steadily declining primary, secondary, and postsecondary enrollments, and this trend is expected to continue through the 1990s. Organizations that expanded and hired sizable numbers of employees at approximately the same time will be confronted with the age-lump phenomenon in the near future. As the group of employees of similar age moves up the hierarchy, it will block promotion and career advancement for those who entered later and may result in organizational stagnation. When the baby boomers reach retirement age, they will strain the capacities of social security and pension systems as well as change the demands for social services placed on the political system. Baby boomers have also demonstrated a tendency to postpone marriage and childbearing and to have smaller families than previous generations. This may result in a labor shortage in the early part of the twenty-first century and increased intergenerational conflict over public policies, services, and taxation.

Geographical shifts in population distribution from the Frostbelt to the Sunbelt, and in some cases back, and from cities to suburbs also add to the complexity and uncertainty of the environment of the public sector. Those areas losing population face declining tax bases, an aging and inadequate economic base, a population whose needs for public services remain high, and deterioration of essential public facilities. Those areas gaining population confront sharply increased demands for public services, a lack of basic public facilities (schools, highways, housing, and water and sewer systems), and political systems unprepared to cope with the problems. When the economies in those boom areas slump, as has occurred in Texas and other oil-producing regions with the decline of oil prices, governments are even less prepared to cope with the problems than their Frostbelt counterparts. Population and industrial shifts from city to suburbs continue and present severe problems of adjustment to both the cities and the suburbs.

The skills and attitudes of the human resources that the environment supplies are subject to change and not easily predictable. The educational level of the population is constantly increasing, but the quality of this education and its relevance to providing the requisite skills for work and organizational life are debatable.[27] Our educational system does not respond rapidly to changing employment prospects. "Educational institutions . . . crank out larger and larger numbers of graduates whether there are appropriate jobs waiting for those graduates or not. If there are not enough suitable jobs, students eventually get the word and change options."[28] The result is periodic surpluses and shortages in specific occupational categories: engineers, teachers, doctors, computer scientists. This results in an overly educated population that feels undervalued and unneeded. A college education, or even more so a graduate degree, may at the same time produce a questioning mind, an expectation and longing for better things and a better quality of life, a deficiency in specific skills needed by business and industry, and a dissatisfaction with the rather pedestrian jobs that are often the only ones available.[29]

Rapid technological change exacerbates the problem. Even if workers were provided the appropriate skills and knowledge during their educational process, those skills quickly become obsolete as technology changes. This increases both stress for individuals and problems of recruiting and training for organizations. Depending on the responses of organizations, this may also result in chronic high unemployment for society.

The Economic Environment

The structure, function, and health of the general economy constitute additional input to the public sector. The strength of the economy, whether measured by growth rate, unemployment rate, inflation rate, or interest rates, determines both the availability of financial resources and the scope and magnitude of the problems the public sector will be expected to solve. Like so many other aspects of the general environment, the economic environment is highly changeable and difficult to predict. Although governments are compelled to project economic changes for budgetary purposes and have done so for decades, the projections have been uniformly wrong and subject to challenge and disagreement within the community of economic forecasters.

One of the most frequently identified trends in the general economy is the decline of the manufacturing segment of the economy: production of steel, automobiles, and durable goods of all types is declining and by some predictions on its way to extinction. No consensus has emerged as to whether government should intervene to prevent this decline, and if so, what actions it should take. Given the impact of factory closings on labor, local economies, and ultimately the entire economic system, and the centrality of these industries to national defense capabilities, a wide variety of public organizations will be affected by this development whether or not government becomes directly involved.

Although some forecasters see the decline of the manufacturing sector as more than offset by increases in the "information economy" of high-tech industries,[30] others are less sanguine about the postindustrial society. The service sector is the most rapidly increasing segment of the economy, but many of the jobs being created are low-skill, low-paying positions. This raises the unpleasant possibility of increased downward mobility in a society that has always stressed the possibility of upward mobility as an intrinsic social belief.

One final aspect of the American economy that has a direct impact on the public sector is its domination by a relatively few extremely large and powerful corporations. By 1982, one hundred corporations controlled over two-thirds of the assets, profits, and sales in the manufacturing segment of the economy. The concentration of assets was even greater in transportation, insurance, retailing, utilities, and banking.[31] Particularly for the government agencies that are supposed to regulate the activities of these corporations, their size and power is a constant problem. No government regulatory agency at any level of government can match the resources of a General Motors, for example. Hostile environments threaten organizational effectiveness and ability to survive, and when powerful corporations constitute a major portion of an agency's environment, rare is the agency that will ceaselessly and fearlessly antagonize them. Though it is probably not politically wise to contend publicly at this point that "What's good for General Motors is good for the country," it is also true that the size and economic importance of the biggest of the corporations makes them central to the health of the American economy. Consequently, protecting and promoting these corporations is a predictable response from the public sector.

The Current Environment of Public Organizations

A turbulent environment is one composed of many interdependent factors that affect each other in a bewildering complexity of ways. It is characterized by an extreme rate of change, making prediction difficult or impossible.[32] From some perspectives, the general environment of public organizations appears to have become increasingly turbulent in recent years. Rapid, unpredictable change has been endemic in some sections of the general environment, most notably the technological sphere. Similarly, change has been marked in the economic and human sectors. These changes have posed continuing and serious challenges to the political system, which has frequently appeared to be unable or unwilling to cope with them. Negative public attitudes toward politics and bureaucracy have increased the overall hostility of the environment.

Bureaucracy remains the dominant organizational form in the public sector, despite the contentions of some theorists that it is hopelessly inadequate. "Our public organization structures are woefully obsolete . . . the importance of developing a new organizational design cannot be overstated."[33] As indicated, however, many aspects of the general environment pressure public organizations to maintain bureaucratic structures. Consequently, governmental responses to environmental change have taken forms other than structural modification. To a certain extent, the policies of the Reagan administration represent typical organizational responses to a turbulent or at least disturbed-reactive environment: domain modification, decentralization, and increased effort in public relations. Domain has been modified through cutbacks in services provided in order to remove some interest groups, institutions, and problems from the federal government's domain. Decentralization—in this case, pushing problems down to lower levels for solution—has also been attempted. Similarly, increased public relations activities have been undertaken by the president to convince the general public that everything is better than it might appear. To a certain extent these strategies have been successful for the federal government. Hostility and negativism toward government has decreased, and its environment appears less volatile than it did before 1981. Nonetheless, the ultimate success of these strategies is far from certain. Problems have not been solved; they either have been pushed down to state and local governments, complicating those environments, or are being ignored and are probably increasing in seriousness.

The conceptualization of the general environment as turbulent may be somewhat misleading. To begin with, not all spheres of the environment have been subject to rapid or unpredictable change. Even in the technological environment the rate of change has been uneven; technological advance in many areas of special concern to the public sector has been slow or nonexistent. Political values and institutions have remained remarkably stable, and relevant social values have not changed dramatically. If anything, political and social values have reacted to rapid changes in the technological and human environments by becoming more conservative. And although the economy has undergone considerable change, the changes have been predictable. The major problem has been our inability to either accept the predictions or suitably cope with the problems they portend.

The forces of change in the environment have, to a certain extent, been countervailed by the forces of stability, and this is precisely the reason bureaucracy remains dominant. It too is a force of stability, predictability, and order, and in the public sector those are powerful human and political values. Further, in the public sector, political values are of overriding importance, and they continue to support bureaucracy. The final reason for the continued dominance of bureaucracy may be the nature of alternative forms of ogranization that have been developed to replace it. As indicated in Chapter 1, the organic, adaptive organizations are extremely difficult to control, coordinate, and manage; they may even be so complicated that they exceed human managerial capacity.

As important as the general environment is for the normal, continuous functioning of an organization, it is less important than the specific environment. The specific environment of an organization may largely shelter it from both the turbulence and hostility of the general environment. Conversely, the specific environment may be considerably more turbulent or hostile than the general environment, requiring the organization to take adaptive measures not required of the overwhelming majority of other organizations.

SPECIFIC ENVIRONMENTS

Every organization operates in a specific environment composed of those organizations, groups, and individuals with which it directly interacts. Its specific environment is largely determined by its domain, its area of operation (based on the functions it performs or services it provides), and the clientele it serves.[34] For public organizations, specific environments include clientele groups, legislatures, chief executives, and other organizations that may be allies, competitors, or contractors. Depending on the organization, the specific environment may include other interest groups, such as professional groups or public interest groups, the media, members of the public, the courts, and other appointed political executives external to the immediate organization. The specific environment is the source of demands for organizational outputs, of resources, and of feedback—response to organizational activity. Thus it varies over time depending on changes in organizational activity, changes in the general environment, and changes in the demands placed on the organization.

Environmental Dimensions

One of the major concerns of open systems theorists has been identifying the most significant dimensions of organizational environments and developing classifications or typologies of environments. This difficult challenge has not yet been satisfactorily met. Classifications are important for developing generalizations on environmental impacts on organization structure and behavior; but to be valid, those classifications must include and be based on all the significant dimensions. The fewer dimensions identified, the fewer types of environment will be identified, and the greater the ease of classification and development of general principles—but the less accurate the characterization of the environment and its impact. As the number of relevant dimensions increases arithmetically, the number of environmental types increases geometrically, making generalization difficult. Unfortunately, there is no agreement on what the most relevant dimensions are.

Although theorists differ on what they consider the most important dimensions, five major environmental dimensions have been identified: stability-turbulence, homogeneity-heterogeneity, clusteredness-randomness, scarcity-munificence, and hostility-supportiveness.

Stability-Turbulence   The stability-turbulence dimension measures the rate and magnitude of change in the environment. Like all of the dimensions, it is a continuum; it ranges from static, unchanging environments to those characterized by constant, uncontrollable, and unpredictable change. Although no organization has a perfectly stable environment, many government organizations, such as professional licensing boards, the Veterans Administration, and many fire and police departments, have basically stable environments. For these organizations, the major actors in their environment are known and relatively unchanging. Professional licensing agencies—state medical boards, for example—are largely self-supporting, have the general support of relevant political actors, and have demonstrated considerable ability to keep new actors, consumers, for example, from becoming important environmental influences. Potential competitors—chiropractors, osteopaths, nurses—have long been identified, and their positions and tactics are known.

A stable environment is above all a predictable environment. The Veterans Administration has succeeded in maintaining a relatively closed and stable environment populated mainly by the Senate and House Veterans' Affairs Committee, the American Legion, the Veterans of Foreign Wars, and the Disabled American Veterans. Frequently categorized as an "iron triangle" in political science studies of policy making, this policy arena has remained remarkably stable and intact despite resource scarcity in the general environment and attempts by the president and other interest groups, most notably the Vietnam Veterans Association, to disrupt its stability.

It might seem that police and fire departments confront a turbulent environment because of the nature of their functions, but this is rarely the case. For police departments, the major environmental actors are well known, as are their attitudes toward and expectations for the department. The mayor, the city manager, the city council, the public, the press, and even the clientele are relatively unchanging. Even the crime rate, or increases in it, are predictable if uncontrollable. Fire departments are likely to have similarly stable environments.

At the opposite end of the spectrum, the Department of Defense (DOD) and the Environmental Protection Agency (EPA) face turbulent environments. The Department of Defense must contend with uncontrollable and frequently unpredictable changes from foreign governments, from a Congress that vacillates constantly on whether to increase, decrease, or stabilize defense spending, from rapid technological developments, from contractors, and from the public. Perhaps no other government organization devotes a greater proportion of resources to the attempts to establish stability and predictability in its environment than DOD. The scores of policy analysts, intelligence officers, public and congressional information officers, statisticians, computer experts, and decision analysts that the Pentagon employs are all involved in trying to smooth out and make more certain a highly turbulent environment.

The EPA has also faced a highly turbulent environment in recent years. Presidential attitudes and actions towards the agency have varied from extreme hostility to general support, sometimes changing on a day by day basis. Top administrators have been appointed, been removed, and resigned with great frequency. Congressional attention has waxed and waned, and Congress has varied from support to hostility. Interest group involvement has intensified, and the problems that the agency is assigned to handle have proliferated: acid rain, PCBs, and asbestos in the environment are not only complex problems but problems whose definitions are not clearly established and whose solutions are unknown. Interorganizational conflicts, with the Occupational Safety and Health Administration over asbestos, with the Department of Agriculture over pesticides, and with state and local governments over water pollution control have intensified. Resources have fluctuated. Little has remained unchanged in EPA's environment.

The stability of its environment has a tremendous impact on an organization. A stable environment permits and encourages formalization, the development of routines, rules, and standard operating procedures.[35] "In a highly stabilized environment, the whole organization takes on the form of a protected or undisturbed system, which can standardize its procedures from top to bottom."[36] Burns and Stalker, in a study of manufacturing firms, found that stable environments were associated with mechanistic structures; organizations that had more unstable environments were likely to have more organic structures.[37] These findings were supported by Lawrence and Lorsch, who in their investigation of firms in the plastics industry found that formality of structure had a negative correlation with uncertainty in the environment.[38] Bennis argued that environmental turbulence would be paralleled by turbulence within organizations. Thus, an extremely turbulent environment would lead to temporary organizations.[39]

Unfortunately, other theorists have come to different conclusions about the impact of environmental instability on organizations. Katz and Kahn pointed out, in response to Bennis, that "for every step taken in this new direction, organizations have taken two steps in more conservative directions to deal with environmental change."[40] Fred Emery argued that the most common organizational response to increased turbulence has been increased bureaucratization.[41] Some organizations, it seems, respond to turbulence by adopting decentralized, less formal structures and others respond by increasing centralization and formalization.

Resolving these contradictions is difficult, and it is always tempting to respond to the question of what determines the organization's response with, "It all depends." First, stability-turbulence is only one dimension of the organization's environment, and the other dimensions are equally important in determining organization behavior. A specific organization may have a turbulent environment that pushes toward an organic structure, and other dimensions that push toward a mechanistic structure. The DOD, as indicated, has a turbulent environment, but it is also a machine bureaucracy. This is due partly to imperatives from the general environment, partly to its response to other environmental pressures, and partly to its use of techniques and strategies other than structural change to respond to and control environmental uncertainty.

Organizations attempt to reduce uncertainty in their environment by several methods. First, they may *increase* internal control and regulation. This is "aimed at producing a disciplined, unified system that can move quickly to meet environmental threats or changes."[42] For the DOD, this is a primary strategy for dealing both with unpredictable foreign "enemies" and with equally unpredictable domestic organizations and actors. Other techniques include cooptation of the unpredictable actors, environmental manipulation through public relations and propaganda,[43] and the creation or expansion of boundary-spanning agents (special units or departments that deal with unpredictable elements and thus protect the operating core). Boundary-spanning agents include public information offices, legislative liaison offices, and contract management offices (to deal with contractors), all of which increase the capability of the organization to collect and process information about change in the environment.[44] The DOD has used, with varying degrees of success, all of these techniques to decrease environmental uncertainty.

If turbulence does not guarantee that an organization will have an organic structure, stability does seem to predict a mechanistic structure, at least with public organizations. The general political, legal, and social environment fosters a strong preference for bureaucratic structure in the public sector. Consequently, in the absence of compelling pressure from the specific environment, public organizations will have a bureaucratic structure. Stability supports bureaucracy; therefore, a stable environment will usually have a bureaucratic form of organization.

Homogeneity-Heterogeneity. The homogeneity-heterogeneity dimension of an organization's environment is based on the number and diversity of constituencies that influence the organization. The more numerous and diverse the relevant constituencies, the more complex and heterogeneous the environment. Complexity in the environment has several effects on an organization. For public organizations, this may lead to goal ambiguity as different constituencies define the goals of the organization differently and pressure the organization to accept their definitions of the goals.

The EPA is an example of an organization with a diverse and conflict-plagued environment. Environmental groups perceive its goal to be protection and improvement of the environment, regardless of the costs involved, but affected industries are likely to emphasize cost in environmental regulation. The pressure from the president and congressional committees tends to vacillate between the two positions. Countervailing pressures from these diverse sources decrease the capacity of the organization to formulate and pursue clear and consistent goals.

Since the increase in activism of public interest groups in the late

1960s, most regulatory agencies have had heterogeneous environments. The Occupational Safety and Health Administration, the Nuclear Regulatory Commission, the Federal Trade Commission, and the Food and Drug Administration operate in environments of high diversity and conflict. External conflict is frequently reflected by increased conflict within the organization, particularly between top-level political executives and permanent civil servants, since the two groups may have differing perceptions as to which constituencies are most powerful or legitimate. The ultimate result of prolonged and intense environmental conflict may be organizational paralysis, which will persist until the organization resolves its internal conflicts.

Environmental complexity is also associated with organizational complexity and decentralization. To adapt to a diverse environment, an organization will increase its internal differentiation.[45] The Federal Communications Commission's (FCC) response to increased heterogeneity in its environment during the late 1960s clearly illustrates how increased environmental complexity leads to increased organizational complexity and differentiation. As cable television organizations became increasingly powerful and were perceived as a threat by the FCC's traditional major constituency, network stations, the FCC was pressured to regulate cable. The structural response of the FCC was to create a new bureau for cable television. Similarly, the emergence of vocal groups arguing for regulation of children's television resulted in the creation of the Children's Television Bureau. The increased differentiation is likely to be accompanied by decentralization, as the organization attempts to "localize" conflict by turning it over to specialized units.[46]

Heterogeneity will also increase the organization's need for information and expertise. More specialists will be required to deal with different aspects of the environment, and thus organizational complexity will again be increased. Heterogeneity may also lead the organization to attempt to contract its domain in order to remove conflicting constituencies from its environment. When the FCC's attempt to defuse the conflict between network television broadcasters and cable by differentiation and decentralization proved unsuccessful, the FCC pursued a policy of deregulation of cable: it contracted its domain to simplify its environment.[47]

Simple, homogeneous environments, though less prone to conflict, may also pose problems for organizations. For example, the organization may become too dependent for its survival on a single constituency.[48] This appears to be one of the major causes of "regulatory capture," which has occurred in the past with regulatory agencies—for example, the Civil Aeronautics Board (CAB).

Organizational survival depends on the ability of the organization to draw resources and support from its environment. With only a single, major constituency, an organization will attempt to satisfy that constituency; antagonizing it will result in hostility and lack of support. As long as the environment remains simple, satisfying the major constituency is a successful strategy for organizational survival. If, however, the environment becomes more complex, and the original constituency is opposed by powerful new forces or the constituency becomes divided or weakened, the organization may be endangered. Thus, the CAB, which became over-reliant on the major airlines, could not survive in an environment that became increasingly heterogeneous. Similarly, the Veterans Administration, with its reliance on the older, established veterans groups, may ultimately endanger its own survival as those groups become weaker and newer groups more vocal.

Clusteredness-Randomness. The clustered-randomness dimension of an environment involves the degree of interconnection among components of the environment. In a random environment, constituents are highly dispersed, discrete entities with no significant interactions or connections. Few public organizations have environments that are highly random. A fire department's environment might be classified as moderately random, although obviously interconnections do exist among political institutions in its environment. Its clientele are normally dispersed and, in the absence of an arson ring, not interconnected. Randomness makes it less likely that any one environmental actor's behavior can have a significant impact on the organization, and the organization can deal with its constituents on a one-to-one basis.

Most public organization environments are highly interconnected. Network analysis is a contemporary approach to measuring interrelationships and interactions among organizations in a given policy area.[49] An interorganizational network is "a number of distinguishable organizations having a significant amount of interaction with each other."[50] Networks can be either tightly coupled, having "many points of interaction where information, advice, help and resources are shared and traded . . . [and allowing] people [to] move freely among the organizations," or they can be loosely coupled with minimal interaction.[51]

An example of a tightly coupled network is the current nuclear power policy arena. The Nuclear Regulatory Commission has primary responsibility for nuclear power development and regulation. Its environment is crowded and clustered and consists of the following major actors:

1. Other federal agencies, including the Department of Energy, the Department of Defense, the Department of the Interior, and the Department of Transportation.
2. The House Committee on Energy and Commerce, the Senate Committee on Energy and Natural Resources, and Congress as a whole.
3. Utility companies, insurance companies, financial institutions, and other industrial and commercial interests.

4. State and local governments.
5. The courts.
6. A wide variety of interest groups.[52]

The result is a complex network of organizations in constant interaction with each other. The environment is both heterogeneous and clustered, with the result that policy decisions are difficult to make and even more difficult to implement.

Clustered environments are far more intricate and complicated to operate in than random environments. They constrain the freedom of the organization to make and implement decisions and require it to devote more time, resources, and attention to management of the environment than random environments do. They also require more integration among units that interact with the environment.[53]

Scarcity-Munificence.   Environments are also classified according to the abundance of resources that they contain.[54] Organizations depend on the environment for human, natural, financial, and technological resources. The availability of these resources and any change in their availability directly affects the organization's ability to function. Any organization needs a constant supply of qualified and competent employees. In times of high employment and an expanding economy, public organizations generally experience some problems in recruitment due to their somewhat lower pay scale and negative attitudes toward public service. For the most part, this is balanced by the greater security of public jobs and the government's position of monopsony for certain occupations—particularly police and fire protection.

The United States Army is an example of an organization whose ability to recruit sufficient human resources underwent a drastic change. Before 1973, the Army was assured of adequate human resources because it had the power to draft those resources from the environment and did not have to depend on attracting candidates as almost all other organizations must. Congress repealed the draft in 1972; starting in 1973, the Army was forced to compete with other organizations, public and private, for human resources.

The response of the Army to this situation illustrates the problems and reactions of organizations confronted with scarcity of an essential environmental resource. First, more organizational resources had to be allocated to personnel. By 1978, the General Accounting Office estimated that the all-volunteer Army was costing about $3 billion a year in increased personnel costs.[55] Boundary-spanning units and public relations and recruitment efforts were expanded and became more visible and expensive. Scarcity required the organization to modify its standards. To a certain extent this meant lowering recruitment qualifications, but it also required the Army to diversify its recruitment efforts and open up to groups that it had previously been somewhat reluctant to recruit: women and minorities. This, in turn, forced changes in both formal and informal rules of the organization. In many instances diversification resulted in increased organizational conflict.

In 1975, Stau and Szwajkowski hypothesized that organizations under conditions of environmental scarcity would be much more likely to engage in illegal action than those in munificent environments.[56] Although they were concerned with financial resources and business firms, their basic hypothesis was confirmed by behavior of Army recruiters. Under pressure to meet demanding recruitment quotas, recruiters engaged in a variety of unethical and illegal behaviors: falsifying exam scores, supplying potential recruits with advance copies of exams, and making false promises of career opportunities to wavering or doubtful volunteers.

Chapter 5 will examine in detail public organizational responses to financial resource scarcity. Briefly, a reduction in the availability of financial resources, particularly if prolonged or permanent, affects nearly every aspect of organizational behavior, from structure to strategy, to goals, to personnel policies, to organizational effectiveness, and even to survival.

Hostility-Supportiveness.   An environment characterized by scarcity could also be classified as a hostile environment, but even munificent environments may be hostile. "Hostility is influenced by competition, by the organization's relationships with . . . other outside groups as well as by the availability of resources to it."[57] Aside from resource scarcity, some public organizations operate in environments that are essentially hostile and resistant to the organizations' activities. For private sector organizations, prolonged environmental hostility is likely to result in extinction, but many public sector organizations, because of their basic functions, must cope with a chronically hostile environment. Police departments continuously deal with a clientele that is resistant to their purposes and activities. Frequently suspects, criminals, victims, the general public, and even the courts are hostile to the police, individually and collectively. Police departments respond to hostility by high formalization, centralization, and organizational attempts to increase esprit de corps and identification with the organization.

The Occupational Safety and Health Administration (OSHA) also confronts a generally hostile environment, mainly as a result of its assigned responsibilities. Created to regulate—and regulatory agencies generally encounter hostility from those they regulate, at least initially—OSHA has always had to contend with hostility and resistance from the business organizations that constitute a major segment of its environment. The recent resistance of the president and the Office of Management and Budget to its activities has escalated environmental hostility for OSHA. For some regulatory agencies, the primary response to hostility is placation; changing organizational activities, usually by reducing them, in an attempt to appease those most hostile to their activities. In a homogeneous environment this may succeed, but in a heterogeneous environment like OSHA's, placating one set of actors usually antagonizes another. Increased complexity, creating more and more diverse organizational units to relate to hostile elements in the environment, is an alternative response to hostility.

"Extreme hostility in its environment drives any organization to centralize its structure temporarily."[58] Extreme hostility threatens the survival of the organization; if the organization is to survive, it must respond in a unified manner. Centralization of power decreases response and decision time and permits the organization to cope successfully with extreme hostility. Similarly, formalization will also increase if survival requires an immediate and integrated response.

The specific environments of organizations vary tremendously along the five major dimensions. Even limiting consideration to the extremes of each dimension, a total of 252 different environmental classifications is possible. When gradations within each dimension are recognized, the number of different possible environments becomes astronomical. Complicating the situation even more from the organization's perspective, environments change, sometimes gradually but other times rapidly. To survive, an organization must monitor its environment and adapt to the demands the environment places on it. Structural configuration is one method of organizational adaptation. Figure 2–1 summarizes the major structural relationships with each environmental dimension. Unfortunately for organizations and for theoretical simplicity, the dimensions are, to a large extent, independent. Consequently, one dimension of an organization's environment may promote low centralization while another promotes high centralization.

An organization confronted with disparities in the dimensions of its environment may respond by selective decentralization and structural differentiation or by selecting the structure indicated by the dimension that is most threatening to its survival. NASA's environment, subsequent to the explosion of the space shuttle, could be characterized as turbulent, heterogeneous, clustered, with scarce resources, and hostile. As Figure 2–1 indicates, no consistent structural configuration emerges. If hostility were the most threatening dimension of NASA's environment, then NASA would probably increase centralization, formalization, and complexity. As has been indicated, this is precisely the direction the agency appears to be moving. But when no single dimension dominates, structural differentiation is a more likely response to environmental disparities.[59]

Another approach to clarifying the relationship between structure and environment has been to develop typologies of environments and

FIGURE 2–1. Structural Relationships and Environmental Dimensions

	Stability-Turbulence	Homogeneity-Heterogeneity	Clusteredness-Randomness	Scarcity-Munificence	Hostility-Supportiveness
Complexity	Low High	Low High	High Low	Low High	High Low
Centralization	High Low	High Low	Low High	High Low	High Low
Formalization	High Low	High Low	Low High	High Low	High Low

match them with the indicated structure. Because five dimension results in an unwieldy number of environmental types, most typologies are based on two dimensions, usually the stability-turbulence dimension and a complexity dimension measuring either homogeneity or interconnectedness of environment.

Emery and Trist used the stability and diversity dimensions to develop four basic environmental types, each with a basic organization type most likely to emerge and be successful. A Type I environment is placid-random, with a low rate of change and dispersed actors with little or no interconnections. Organizations with this type of environment are likely to be small and to have simple structures. A Type II environment is placid-clustered, composed of environmental actors divided into recognizable and potentially powerful coalitions; its rate of change is slow. Organizations in Type II environments are likely to be larger with hierarchical, centralized structures. Type III environments are disturbed-reactive, highly interconnected, and unstable. Organizational structures move toward increasing complexity and decentralization. Type IV, turbulent environments, are marked by accelerating change, complexity, and unpredictability, requiring Type IV organizations to adapt a matrix structure.[60]

The general consensus among organization theorists is that bureaucracy is best suited to stable, simple, noninterconnected environments, and that complex, dynamic, interconnected environments require a more organic, flexible structure. The introduction of extreme hostility or resource scarcity into an organization's environment, however, takes precedence over the other dimensions and will push an organization toward increased centralization and formalization. Given the current situation of both scarce resources and general hostility toward government organizations, theory would predict that most public organizations would be bureaucratic, and if hostility or scarcity continues or increases, so will the degree of centralization and formalization in these organizations.

STRATEGIES AND TACTICS FOR MANAGING THE ENVIRONMENT

Structural modification is one type of organizational response to environmental pressure and change. Environmental turbulence, scarcity, and hostility pose the greatest challenges to organizational effectiveness and survival. To deal effectively with any or all of these conditions, organizations are likely to use the following techniques: forecasting, domain modification, rationing, stockpiling, contracting, coopting, and advertising and public relations campaigns. Forecasting, attempting to predict significant changes that will affect the organization, provides advanced warning of trouble spots and opportunities. Domain modification involves expanding or contracting the organization's domain by determining "what aspects of the environment are to be of concern, what phenomena should be noticed and what variables should be introduced into the criterion function for the organization's performance."[61]

Consider the following example. Predictions of declining birth rates and consequent decreases in the school-age population constitute a serious threat to public schools and universities. The threat is magnified by property tax limitations that will cause revenue shortages. Both sets of institutions have already begun to respond to the challenge. The main strategies that public elementary and secondary schools have used to combat that threat are third-party soliciting and increased public (community) relations campaigns.[62] Particularly in bond issue elections, schools have relied on third parties, the teachers unions and parents organizations, to win support for increased funding. Universities have used student and community groups to pressure legislatures to increase appropriations. They have also increased public relations efforts, and many have hired marketing experts to help them sell their services. Although domain contraction is a typical response to scarcity,[63] educational institutions have attempted to expand their domains. Many universities now offer Elderhostel programs, summer programs that combine educational and recreational opportunities to appeal to older people; most have expanded their continuing education programs and have expanded off-campus and video course offerings. Domain expansion, although an unusual strategy, allows the organization to protect its operating core and avoid personnel reductions.

For most organizations confronted with hostility or resource scarcity, domain contraction is a more likely response. The Federal Communications Commission, confronted with increasing hostility from diverse regulated groups and interest groups, cable television companies, television stations, radio stations, responded with deregulation, a form of domain contraction. Domain contraction alleviates hostility by eliminating an unpopular action and thus resistors to that action from the environment. Regulatory agencies whose actions provoke resentment or resistance commonly opt for domain contraction. Similarly, organizations suffering from severe resource scarcity may be forced to eliminate programs and services. Rationing—allocating services on a priority basis—may also be used in scarce environments. Some police departments faced with personnel and monetary shortages have established priorities for investigation. The Spokane, Washington, police department, responding to financial resource scarcity, announced that starting in 1987, it will investigate property crimes only where losses exceed $250. Hospitals that perform organ transplants have dealt with the constant shortage of organs by establishing a rationing system to determine who, among a surplus of patients, receives transplants.

Contracting out—privatization—has become increasingly common in recent years. At all levels of government, for a wide variety of services, contracting out has become a dominant strategy. Refuse collection, fire protection, hospital services, transportation, social welfare, and even prisons and police services have been contracted out by state and local governments, largely in response to environmental scarcity or hostility. In a way, contracting is a form of domain contraction, in that an expensive or troublesome organizational activity is shifted away from the organization, and the complaints, resentment, and demands associated with that service are also shifted to the new provider.[64]

At the federal level, the Department of Defense is the biggest contractor in dollar terms, contracting for everything from research to weapons and equipment and basic management functions; but countless other federal agencies contract for goods and services. "The trend reflects political expediency because third-party arrangements permit the president and Congress to take credit for acting without assuming responsibility for program design, administration and results."[65] Contracting may also be cheaper, though the evidence on this is definitely mixed.

Cooptation is "the process of absorbing new elements into the leadership or policy-determining structure of an organization as a means of averting threats to its stability or existence."[66] Selznick's classic study of the Tennessee Valley Authority (TVA) documented how TVA defused hostility towards its activities by coopting the groups and organizations that were its most vocal opponents. Martha Derthick detailed the Social Security Administration's use of advisory councils composed of labor and business representatives to build support for agency programs and policies.[67] Community Action Agencies used citizen advisory boards to coopt potential adversaries to their policies. Cooptation, in addition to reducing environmental hostility, also creates allies who may assist the organization in its struggle to increase the resources available to it.

SUMMARY

All public organizations in the United States share a similar general environment, and certain aspects of that general environment, particularly the constitutional-legal component, put pressure on public organizations to adopt bureaucratic structures. Social values also support bureaucracy. Given the importance of these factors, the dominance and persistence of bureaucracy throughout the public sector is not surprising..

At the same time, every public organization has a unique specific environment within which it operates. Organizational survival depends on successful adaptation to the characteristics of that environment. An organization's environment consists of five major dimensions, and each dimension pressures the organization to conform its structure to its specific demands. Increasingly, three specific dimensions of public organization environments appear dominant: turbulence, scarcity, and hostility. Although a turbulent environment requires an organic, flexible structure, considerable evidence indicates that when confronted with uncertainty, organizations seek predictability and order. Unable to find that externally, they may seek to find it internally, through bureaucracy. Both scarcity and hostility pressure organizations to increase centralization and control. Thus, the composite force of environmental pressures appears to support bureaucracy as the dominant form of public organization.

Structural adaptation is only one of several responses organizations can take to maintain or restore equilibrium in a changing environment. Organizations can manage their environments by creating or expanding boundary-spanning units, through cooptation, cooperation, and domain modification. Public organizations have less flexibility in altering their structures than do their private counterparts, so they tend to rely more heavily on environmental management techniques than structural change.

NOTES

1. James March and Johan Olson, "Organizing Political Life: What Administrative Reorganization Tells Us About Government," *American Political Science Review* (June 1983): p. 284.
2. Howard Aldrich, *Organizations and Their Environments* (Englewood Cliffs: Prentice-Hall, 1979), p. 29.
3. Charles Perrow, *Complex Organizations*, 3rd ed. (New York: Random House, 1986), p. 213.
4. Max Weber, *The Protestant Ethic and The Spirit of Capitalism*, trans. Talcott Parsons (New York: Charles Scribner's Sons, 1958), p. 104.
5. Ibid., p. 115.
6. Ibid., p. 157.
7. Robert Prethus, *The Organizational Society*, (New York: St. Martin's Press, 1978), p. 91.
8. David Minar, *Ideas and Politics: The American Experience* (Homewood, Ill.: Dorsey Press, 1964), p. 359.
9. Herbert Simon, *Administrative Behavior*, 3rd ed. (New York: Free Press, 1976), p. 102.
10. W. Richard Scott, "Introduction: From Technology to Environment," in John Meyer and W. Richard Scott, *Organizational Environments* (Beverly Hills: Sage Publications, 1983), p. 12.
11. John Meyer and Brian Rowan, "Institutionalized Organizations: Formal Structures as Myth and Ceremony," in Meyer and Scott, *Organizational Environments*, p. 31.
12. William G. Scott and David K. Hart, *Organizational America* (Boston: Houghton-Mifflin, 1979).
13. Harold Seidman and Robert Gilmour, *Politics, Position and Power*, 4th ed. (New York: Oxford University Press, 1986), pp. 201–202.
14. John Worthley, "Ethics and Public Management: Education and Training," *Public Personnel Management* (1981): pp. 43–44.
15. H.George Frederickson, "Toward a New Public Administration," in Frank

Marini, ed., *Toward a New Public Administration: The Minnow Brook Perspective* (Scranton: Chandler Publishing Co., 1971), p. 309.

16. Ibid., p. 312.
17. Frank Thompson, "Types of Representative Bureaucracy and Their Linkage: The Case of Ethnicity," in Robert T. Golembiewski, Frank Gibson, and Geoffrey Cornoy, *Public Administration*, 3rd ed. (Chicago: Rand McNally, 1976), p. 578.
18. Ibid., p. 589.
19. H. Barton Milward and Cheryl Swanson, "Organizational Response to Environmental Pressures: The Policy of Affirmative Action," *Administration and Society* (August 1978): p. 124.
20. Terry L. Cooper, "Citizen Participation," in Thomas D. Lynch, ed., *Organizational Theory and Management* (New York: Marcel Dekker, Inc., 1983), p. 13.
21. Charles Goodsell, *The Case For Bureaucracy*, 2nd ed. (Chatham, N.J.: Chatham House, 1985), pp. 1–13.
22. Ibid., pp. 19–32.
23. Robert L. Kahn, Barbara Gutek, Eugenia Barton, and Daniel Katz, "Americans Love Their Bureaucrats," in Francis E. Rourke, *Bureaucratic Power in National Policymaking*, 4th ed. (Boston: Little, Brown, 1986), pp. 291–292.
24. Daniel Katz and Robert Kahn, *The Social Psychology of Industry*, 2nd ed. (New York: John Wiley, 1978), p. 136.
25. John W. Meyer, W. Richard Scott, and Terrence Deal, "Institutional and Technical Sources of Organization Structure: Explaining the Structure of Educational Organizations," in Meyer and Scott, *Organizational Environments*, p. 61.
26. Kenyon DeGreene, *The Adaptive Organization* (New York: John Wiley, 1982), p. 240.
27. Ibid., p. 241.
28. Ibid., p. 241–242.
29. Ibid., p. 242.
30. John Naisbett, *Megatrends* (New York: Warner Books, 1982).
31. *Statistical Abstract of the United States, 1984* (Washington, D.C.: Government Printing Office, 1984), pp. 536–546.
32. Katz and Kahn, *The Social Psychology of Industry*, p. 125.
33. Louis C. Gawthrop, *Public Sector Management, Systems and Ethics* (Bloomington: Indiana University Press, 1984), pp. 3–4.
34. James Thompson, *Organizations in Action* (New York: McGraw-Hill, 1967), p. 27.
35. Aldrich, *Organizations and Their Environments*, p. 67.
36. Henry Mintzberg, *The Structuring of Organizations*, (Englewood Cliffs, N.J.: Prentice Hall, 1983), p. 271.
37. T. Burns and G. M. Stalker, *The Management of Innovation* (London: Tavistock, 1961).
38. P. R. Lawrence and J. W. Lorsch, *Organization and Environment* (Boston: Harvard Business School, 1967).
39. Warren Bennis and P. E. Slater, *The Temporary Society* (New York: Harper and Row, 1968).
40. Katz and Kahn, *The Social Psychology of Industry*, p. 133.
41. Fred Emery, *Futures We Are In* (Leiden, The Netherlands: Martinus Nijhoff, 1977).
42. Katz and Kahn, *The Social Psychology of Industry*, p. 131.
43. Ibid.
44. Thompson, *Organizations in Action*, pp. 20–24.

45. Stephen L. Fink, R. Stephen Jenks, and Robin Willits, *Designing and Managing Organizations* (Homewood, Ill.: Richard D. Irwin, 1983), p. 285.
46. Mintzberg, *The Structuring of Organizations*, p. 273.
47. Florence Heffron, "The Federal Communications Commission and Broadcast Deregulation," in John Havick, ed., *Communications, Policy and the Political Process* (Westport, Conn.: Greenwood Press, 1983), pp. 61–65.
48. Fink, et al., *Designing and Managing Organizations*, p. 279.
49. See Charles Perrow, *Complex Organizations*, pp. 192–208.
50. J. Kenneth Benson, "The Interorganizational Network as a Political Economy," *Administrative Science Quarterly* (June 1975): p. 230.
51. Perrow, *Complex Organizations*, p. 202.
52. Robert T. Nakamura and Frank Smallwood, *The Politics of Policy Implementation* (New York: St. Martin's Press, 1980), p. 117.
53. Fink et al., *Designing and Managing Organizations*, p. 285.
54. Katz and Kahn, *The Social Psychology of Organizations*, p. 127.
55. Pat Towell, "Resumption of Registration of 18-year-olds Considered," *Congressional Quarterly* (April 21, 1979): p. 4.
56. B. Straw and E. Szwajkowski, "The Scarcity-Munificence Component of Organizational Environments and the Commission of Illegal Acts," *Administrative Science Quarterly* (1975): pp. 345–354.
57. Mintzberg, *The Structuring of Organizations*, p. 269.
58. Ibid., p. 281.
59. Ibid., p. 282.
60. Fred Emery and E. L. Trist, "The Causal Texture of Organizational Environments," *Human Relations* (February 1965): pp. 21–32.
61. William McWhinney, "Organization Form, Decision Modalities and the Environment," *Human Relations* (1968): p. 272.
62. Stephen Robbins, *Organization Theory* (Englewood Cliffs, N.J.: Prentice-Hall, 1983), p. 363.
63. Barry Bozeman and E. Allen Slusher, "Scarcity and Environmental Stress in Public Organizations," *Administration and Society* (November 1979): p. 339.
64. An extensive literature on contracting out has developed. For the strongest case for contracting see E. S. Savas, *Privatizing the Public Sector* (Chatham, N.J.: Chatham House Publishers, 1982). AFSCME, one of the strongest arguments against contracting is found in *Passing the Bucks*, 1983.
65. Seidman and Gilmour, *Politics, Position and Power*, pp. 121–122.
66. Philip Selznick, *TVA and the Grass Roots* (Berkeley: University of California Press, 1949), p. 13.
67. Martha Derthick, *Policymaking For Social Security* (Washington, D.C.: Brookings Institution, 1979), pp. 89–109.

3

ORGANIZATION GOALS

In the Introduction, an organization was defined as "a system of coordinated activities of a group of people working cooperatively toward a common goal under authority and leadership."[1] Although almost all organization theorists agree that goals are an integral part of organizations, they do not agree on the precise definition of goals or how to identify or determine what constitutes organizational goals. Further complicating the definitional problem, organizations have different types of goals: substantive goals (those related to the organization's purpose), systems goals (concerned with the health and survival of the organization as a system), and the separate, frequently conflicting goals of individual members of the organization.

CATEGORIES OF ORGANIZATION GOALS

Substantive Goals

An organization's substantive goals can be defined as the purposes the organization is attempting to achieve. "Goals represent the reason for the organization's existence. . . . Without some purpose there is no need for the organization. Goals summarize and articulate that purpose."[2] Goals are future oriented: "A goal never exists; it is a state which we seek, not one we have."[3] Business theorists distinguish between an organization's mission and its goals. A mission is an organization's function in society—the products it produces and services it provides—whereas goals are "the intentions behind decisions or actions, the states of minds that drive individuals or collectivities of individuals . . . to do what they do."[4] Thus for an automobile manufacturer, producing cars is its mission, and making a profit is one of its goals.

For public organizations, the distinction between mission and goals is, or should be, less clear, and the terms tend to be used interchangeably. The Soil Conservation Service (SCS) defines its mission as "providing national leadership in the conservation and wise use of soil, water, and related resources."[5] Identifying a goal separate from this is almost impossible. The SCS was not formed to make a profit, and certainly making a profit is not its intention. Efficiency, though a criterion for evaluating organization performance, is not a goal. No one creates an organization to maximize efficiency. What shapes the decisions of the SCS and its management is its mission, for the mission is an end in itself. In public organizations, the mission is the general overall purpose of the organization; the substantive goals are the more specific activities or functions undertaken to achieve that mission.

Simon defines organizational goals (missions) as "the constraint sets and criteria of search that define roles at the upper levels of management."[6] The goals of the organization are internalized by individuals and applied during performance of their duties. In decision-making situations, goals emerge as constraints limiting the alternatives that will be considered and determining how those alternatives will be evaluated. For the SCS, the mission is an overriding constraint that decisions and actions must be weighed against.

Missions are extremely important to public organizations. They provide a sense of legitimacy, direction, and purpose, serve as criteria for performance evaluation for the overall organization and for individual employees, and reduce uncertainty within the organization.[7] They are also an important recruitment device, particularly in the public sector where potential employees are attracted to public service by the functions that the organizations perform. The mission provides a motivating force for individuals within the organization and serves as a continuing source of cohesiveness for the organization. Finally, the mission and the substantive goals derived from it provide a rationale for organization design and structure.

Perrow classified substantive organizational goals into three categories: official, operative, and operational. Official goals or missions are the general purposes of the organization as described in the charter or public statements by key officials. Official goals are primarily intended to show the purpose of the organization to key constituencies. Operative goals, inferred from the actual operating policies of the organization, indicate what the organization is really trying to do. Operational goals, which are more specific and are measurable, are used to guide behavior and evaluate the performance of employees.[8] Thus, the official goals of the Equal Employment Opportunity Commission are to "eliminate discrimination based on race, color, religion, sex, national origin, or age in hiring, promoting, firing, wages, testing, training, apprenticeship, and all other conditions of employment."[9] Its operative goals include maintaining presidential and congressional support, maintaining satisfactory relationships with key civil rights groups, and avoiding excessive antagonism with major businesses. Operational goals include investigating a certain number of cases, negotiating a specific number of settlements, and filing and winning a certain number of court cases.

Official goals are symbolic, frequently not attainable and not even meant to be attained. They are intended rather to provide symbolic reassurance to interest groups or the public at large.[10]

> An antipoverty program that falls short of the mark may nonetheless assure people that the government is concerned about poverty. Equal Employment Opportunity legislation assures people that government, officially at least, does not condone descrimination in hiring on the basis of race, sex and nationality. Apart from whatever effects such policies have on social conditions, they may contribute to social order, support for government and personal self-esteem.[11]

Although symbolic goals serve important political purposes, they may cause severe problems for the organizations to which they are assigned. Appealing symbolic goals may attract to the organization members who are committed to those goals. The discovery that those goals are not really what the organization is trying to accomplish may result in disillusionment, frustration, stress, low morale, and staff burnout. Clientele groups, too, may eventually grow weary of symbolic reassurance and demand positive action or withdraw their support from the organization. Similarly, Congress and the president may forget that the goals were meant to be symbolic only and become impatient and hostile as a result of the organization's failure to achieve the unintended. Finally, evaluators, whether in house or external, have a tendency to take symbolic goals seriously and use them as a basis for evaluating organizational effectiveness, which guarantees a negative evaluation.

Systems Goals

Once created, organizations develop a momentum of their own and, as open systems, attempt to ensure their own maintenance, growth, and survival. Their systems goals may even become so important that they override the substantive goals the organization was created to achieve. The organization acquires intrinsic meaning for its members and supporters, whose careers and livelihood depend on the organization's survival. For external supporters, the existence of the organization provides symbolic reassurance. Consequently the organization's survival, even if substantive goals are not being accomplished, emerges as "the ultimate constraint for every system."[12]

In a munificent and supportive environment, survival may require only minimal attention or resources and thus neither conflicts nor competes with substantive goals. But when environmental hostility, turbulence, or scarcity is encountered, the organization's survival may be threatened. When this occurs, survival becomes the preeminent goal and may displace substantive goals. Regulatory agencies are particularly likely to confront environmental hostility as a direct result of their substantive goals: their environments are populated primarily by regulated groups who are opposed to being regulated. Pursuing their mission vigorously would increase the level of hostility in their environment; without contervailing support, this hostility could cause the organization to lose resources and ultimately be abolished. From a systems perspective, the logical and mandatory organizational response is to pursue the course of action most likely to result in organizational survival. Frequently, that requires abandonment of substantive goals, "selling out" to regulated groups in order to decrease their hostility and gain their support.

This quest for survival partially explains the disappointing performance of such economic regulatory agencies as the Civil Aeronautics Board, the Interstate Commission, the Federal Communications Commission, and the Federal Power Commission and their counterparts at the state level, particularly before the development of consistently active and vigilant public interest groups. Vigorous and consistent pursuit of their substantive goals would have resulted in a hostile environment devoid of political support. Public agencies must have political support to survive, and if that requires modification or abandonment of substantive goals, systems logic dictates that the agencies do so.

Beyond merely placating hostile environmental actors, some organizations actually attempt to control and manipulate their environment. Usually an organization tries to control its environment to establish predictability, stability, and support so that it can pursue its substantive goals. In some cases, however, an "organization may become so obsessed with dominating the forces in its environment that the quest for autonomy comes to look more and more like the lust for power."[13]

The Federal Bureau of Investigation under J. Edgar Hoover was in some ways dominated by an insatiable desire to control its environment at the expense of its substantive goals. Environmental control in this case required manipulating, placating, coopting, or neutralizing three major groups: the public, Congress, and executive branch superiors. Public support was a key element, and this was gained through a consistent and elaborate public relations effort that spanned decades. The creation of the "Public Enemy Number One" designation that was awarded to such criminals as John Dillinger and Alvin Karpis set the stage for well-publicized and dramatic arrests by the FBI. Radio and television shows glorifying G-men created and maintained a mystique about the agency and particularly its director: "Hoover had transformed the FBI into an article of the national faith and its rigid hierarchy matched that of any religious order. Hoover's personal supremacy was as absolute as any pontiff's and he wielded his power with the imperious assurance of one ordained."[14]

Congress was similarly neutralized. As politicians, members of Congress were fully aware of the FBI's overwhelming public support and hesitated to interfere with it on that basis alone. However, Hoover left little to chance and

> systematically detoothed the watchdog committees of Congress with a statistical razzle-dazzle unmatched in legislative manipulation before or since. Each year, the Bureau appropriations request was supported by statistical tables captioned Convictions, Total Sentences, Fugitives Located, Automobiles Recovered, and Fines, Savings and Recoveries. The right side of the chart indicated Percent Increase or Decrease, . . . [and] decreases were virtually nonexistent. . . . Hoover's statistics always went up, and somehow they simultaneously documented the FBI's dramatic triumph over crime last year and the compelling need for more FBI agents and appropriations next year. . . . As a result, FBI budget requests routinely swept through Congress untouched.[15]

When Hoover's "official and confidential" files on members of Congress and the executive branch were added to these techniques, few if any members of Congress were inclined to criticize or interfere with the agency. High ranking executive branch officials, daunted by Hoover's public and congressional support and apprehensive over whether he might have assembled an official and confidential file on them, were equally unlikely to interfere with the agency.

Hoover's control of the agency's environment was so complete that the FBI approximated a closed system. The substantive goals of the agency were subordinated to systems goals. To maintain its public image, the agency had to concentrate on easily solved crimes or hand-picked "public enemies," neglecting more serious but less easily controlled crimes—particularly organized crime. Civil rights violations were given even lower priority, and the lack of minorities within the agency was pronounced. Relationships between the FBI and state and local law enforcement agencies ranged from manipulative to hostile, because by cooperating, the FBI might have diminished its own publicity. The agency was practically autonomous, and the autonomy was vested exclusively in the director. The organization itself was largely at his mercy and suffered the inevitable results when Hoover died. Much of the resentment and hostility that had been repressed under his regime was ultimately released; unaccustomed to having to operate as an open and accountable system, the FBI floundered.

Organizational growth is a systems goal related to both survival and control. Growth is an indication of a healthy organization. It permits the organization to provide better career opportunities to employees, and it lessens internal conflict over allocation of resources. A growing organization is likely to be regarded as successful and accorded increased prestige. Size is also equated with power; the larger the organization, the more control it exerts over its environment, and the more resistant it is to attacks against it.

Public organizations may be even more prone to pursue growth as a goal than private sector organizations. Plagued with vague and frequently unattainable goals—the Department of Defense will never finally and completely ensure the national security of the United States, and no Police Department will ever eliminate crime and ensure domestic security—public organizations are pushed toward growth from two directions. First, the inability to accomplish goals fuels the conviction that if only the organization were larger and had more resources it could come closer to goal accomplishment; because no one really knows how to accomplish these goals, arguments that more is not necessarily better rarely prevail. Second, failing to seek growth may be interpreted by politicians as a lack of commitment to organizational mission. A brief glance at congressional authorizing and appropriating committee hearings during the Reagan administration reveals that many committee members viewed administrative agency officials who did not seek growth as being opposed to the goals of their organizations.

Systems goals need not interfere with substantive goals. They are, in a sense, natural goals inherent to organizations. Nonetheless, under certain circumstances, systems goals can supercede substantive goals in importance for the organization, causing the organization to pursue systems goals at the expense of substantive goals. The associated circumstances of goal displacement will be examined later in this chapter.

Individual Member Goals

Just as organizations are goal oriented, they are also collectives of individuals, and those individuals have personal goals that they pursue in the organizational setting. One of the newest approaches to organization analysis, economic theory, starts with the premise that the individual, not the organization, should be the basic unit of analysis for organization theory. In its starkest form, economic theory claims that organizations are "purely political arenas, with no goals of their own . . . marketplaces whose structure and processes are the outcomes of complex accommodations made by actors exchanging a variety of incentives and pursuing a diversity of goals."[16] For these theorists, individuals embody the economists' concept of human nature: they are self-interested, motivated primarily by greed and the desire for self-aggrandizement, and willing to cheat to achieve their goals.

Agency theory, one of the major economic approaches, views social life and particularly organizational life as a series of contracts. From the organizational perspective, two of the most important principles of agency theory are adverse selection and moral hazard. The principle of adverse selection is concerned with the problems and perils of the recruitment and selection process from the organization's perspective. The employer is handicapped because of insufficient information about the true abilities and characteristics of potential employees. The potential employees however, are fully aware of their abilities. The result is that when the employer offers a job at a particular salary, the best among the potential employees, believing they are worth more, will not accept; the mediocre or worse, knowing their true worth, will accept. "The poor employer ends up with many of the less qualified and few of the highly qualified; he or she cannot discriminate among the applicants because they all say their type is appropriate to the salary, and the employer loses the best."[17]

Adverse selection, despite its academic sounding language, is in reality the Peter Principle applied to the hiring process, with the same result: the organization gets stuck with incompetents. Its accuracy is questionable for the private sector, and even more so for the public sector. By starting with the assumption that salary is the sole criterion used by the best employees in selecting jobs, agency theory ignores the vast literature of psychological theory that indicates that individuals have complex motivations and seek various goals in their jobs, including satisfying and meaningful work. Particularly in the public sector, the mission of the organization, its basic purpose, and the opportunity to work toward that purpose is for many potential employees more important than maximizing income. The ranks of police officers, firefighters, social workers, teachers, and college professors are replete with individuals who chose and remain in their careers and organizations because they believe in the importance of the task they perform even if the pay is lower than that offered elsewhere.

Moral hazard concerns the employees' behavior after being hired. Although the words are different and couched in economic jargon, the concept is old and was initially stated by Frederick Taylor: "Underworking, that is deliberately working slowly so as to avoid doing a full day's work, soldiering as it is called in this country, hanging it out, as it is called in England . . . is almost universal in industrial establishments . . . and the writer asserts without fear of contradiction that this constitutes the greatest evil with which the working people of both England and America are now afflicted."[18] Agency theorists call it "substituting leisure for work."[19] Evidently, once on the job, the individual's primary goal changes from maximizing income to maximizing leisure, and the employer is confronted with the continuing problem of controlling the workers' built-in propensity for minimizing effort on the job.

Agency theory presents an overly simplistic and misleading picture of both organizations and individuals. Nevertheless, it does highlight the importance of individual goals and their potential conflict with organization goals. Unquestionably, individuals have personal goals, which they seek to achieve within the organization. These goals are not limited to monetary gain or maximizing leisure but include the desire for status, power, satisfactory interpersonal relationships, meaningful and inherently satisfying work, and career development and advancement. Although personal goals differ from individual to individual, they are shared, common goals and as such constitute organizational goals as well.

ESTABLISHING ORGANIZATION GOALS

Organizations are not just goal-oriented entities; they are multiple-goal-oriented entities. They pursue substantive goals, systems goals, and individual member goals. Further complicating the situation, multiple goals are likely to exist within each goal category, and these goals frequently conflict. One of the most critical tasks the organization faces is the determination of its actual, operative goals. This frequently involves translating vague mission statements into specific, purposive directives and resolving conflicts among conflicting goals.

The missions of public organizations are usually determined externally, by legislatures and elected executives. The almost inevitable result of goal determination by the political process is vague, ambiguous goal statements. The passage of legislation requires the creation of coalitions within the legislature. To gain the support of diverse interest groups and individuals, statutory goals must usually be kept so vague that they can be interpreted to satisfy all of the various conflicting interests necessary for passage. Thus statutes abound with terms such as "maximum feasible participation," "equality of opportunity," "special needs of educationally deprived students," and "full employment." While these terms have tremendous political appeal, they are subject to various interpretations and provide no specific direction for the organizations that they are supposed to guide.

Publicly assigned missions are likely to be misleading or confusing in two ways besides vagueness. As previously indicated, many times these missions are intended for symbolic purposes only. The Housing Act of 1949, for example, stated the general goal of "providing a decent home and suitable living environment for every American family."[20] The goal of providing a decent home for every American is relatively clear and specific, but given the resources provided, it was a symbolic rather than an operational goal, and as such of little use to the organization responsible for enforcing it. In addition to vague and symbolic goals, public agencies are often assigned multiple goals; and even when no conflict exists, priorities are not assigned. The Model Cities Act of 1966 included among its goals rebuilding slums and blighted areas, improving housing income and cultural opportunities of residents, reducing crime and delinquency, lessening dependence on welfare, and maintaining historic landmarks, and Congress assigned no priorities to these diverse and sweeping goals.[21] The Food Stamp Program may have as a primary goal either feeding the poor or improving agricultural income; prisons are supposed to rehabilitate and punish; schools are to educate and provide vocational training and social adjustment skills; social welfare agencies are to ensure that all eligible persons receive benefits and to reduce fraud and abuse in their programs. The examples are endless: public organizations are assigned vague, multiple, and conflicting goals that are often merely symbolic. The consequences for the organizations are similarly multiple and conflicting.

Multiple goals do not necessarily cause dysfunction.

> The need to satisfy multiple goals may be the political price for reorganizing a series of competing ideas to an applicable public policy decision. In point of fact, the Food Stamp Program's success is explained in large part because it met more than one goal: while the program availed foodstuffs to a large segment of the poor at nominal cost, it also provided new price supports and sources of stability for the agricultural community. Given these gains by diverse segments of society, the program met with little resistance.[22]

Further, Etzioni contends that organizations with multiple goals serve all their goals more effectively and efficiently than single-goal organizations. They also have greater recruitment appeal and provide more opportunities for job enrichment for employees.[23]

Vague Goals and Organizational Behavior

Rational bureaucratic theory assumes that organizations have clear operational goals that guide the behavior of the organization as a whole and that are internalized by the members of the organization and applied by them during the performance of their roles.[24] Goals that have no clear or consistent meaning cannot serve as a guide for either the organization or its members. Yet many public organizations have vague and imprecise goals whose actual meaning is subject to endless interpretation and conflict but which nevertheless function and endure. Precisely how organizations with such goals operate is one of the more intriguing questions of public organization theory.

One answer was proposed by Cohen, March, and Olsen, who suggested that such organizations should be viewed as organized anarchies.[25]

Organized anarchies are characterized by three general properties: "vague, unclear goals, unclear technology and fluid participation in the sense that organizational members vary in the amount of time and effort they devote to different domains."[26] Many public organizations exhibit these characteristics and still function as collectivities. Cohen and March use universities as an example. Almost anyone who has spent time in a public university can identify its official goals: education, research, and service, terms which are certainly vague and ambiguous. From Cohen and March's perspective, this means that such organizations cannot be managed according to conventional management theory, which is based on well-defined goals and technology.[27]

The initial problem with the assumption that organizations that have vague goals cannot operate rationally is that the top management and many employees of such organizations would not agree that their goals are vague. A university administrator will be likely to assert that to educate means to recruit a certain number of students, establish a required curriculum for them, provide a sufficient number of required courses necessary for students to graduate and a sufficient number of instructors to teach them, and ultimately to graduate a significant proportion of students admitted. Research means requiring faculty members to be involved in scholarly pursuits, seek grants, and publish. It may certainly be argued that this is neither "education" nor "research" from some grand philosophical perspective (and this is probably true), but it is irrelevant to the leaders and to most members of the organization. From the more limited, but clearer, definition of their goals, these organizations hire, evaluate, and promote employees, allocate financial resources, and establish structures just as if they knew what they were doing—and from their perspective, they do.

A similar situation exists for police departments. As a society, we are ambivalent about the role that we expect the police to fulfill; consequently, the goal of police departments is likely to be stated as "maintaining law and order," or "protecting public safety," or "to promote the safety of the community and a feeling of security among the citizens."[28] The vagueness of these goals has not prevented organized police departments from operating just as if they knew what they were doing, and most police administrators, as most educational administrators, have few doubts about the goals of their organizations. They may be dissatisfied with the extent of goal accomplishment, but they do know what they are trying to accomplish, and police organizations are structured and managed in the appropriate manner to accomplish those perceived goals.

Education and police goals are models of clarity when compared with those of some other public organizations, such as courts, libraries, and recreation departments. The courts, theoretically at least, are supposed to have something to do with "dispensing justice," a term whose definition has intrigued and evaded philosophers since time began. Hatry defines the basic goal of libraries as presenting "library services that, to the greatest extent possible, provide the greatest satisfaction to citizens, including timely, helpful, and readily available services that are attractive, accessible and convenient."[29] Again, from the perspective of an organizational analyst these goals are impossibly vague, but from the perspective of organization management they are clear and basically operational.

Not only do all of these organizations operate similarly to organizations with clearer, more specific goals, they also have formal, bureaucratic structures. They exemplify what Meyer and Rowan termed "institutionalized organizations." They are responses to the "rational myths" society has created that "identify specific social purposes and specify in a rule-like manner what activities are to be carried out . . . to achieve them.[30] Social purposes are defined as technical ones and the myths "specify the appropriate means to pursue these technical purposes rationally."[31] Because goals are vague, "categorical ends are substituted for technical ends. Hospitals treat, not cure, patients. Schools produce students, not learning."[32] Police officers arrest suspects but do not cure crime; courts produce decisions, not justice. Elements of structure are uncoupled from activity: discretion, professionalization, and delegation predominate. Nevertheless "decoupled organizations are not anarchies. Day to day activities proceed in an orderly fashion. What legitimates institutionalized organizations, enabling them to appear useful in spite of the lack of technical validation, is the confidence and good faith of their internal participants and their external constituents."[33] Vague social missions are redefined as specific technical activities, and the organization is structured and run to carry out those activities. Thus goals do not determine structure; society determines structure, and structure defines goals.

From both an organizational and a societal perspective, this method of handling vague goals is usually satisfactory. The major problems associated with vague goals arise in evaluation, if evaluators use definitions of goal achievement that differ from the operative definitions used by the organization, or when societal definitions of goals change. When, for example, society decides that the number of students graduated is not as important as whether those students know how to read and write and possess other basic intellectual skills, it may force educational organizations to redefine, at least temporarily, their goals and modify their behavior.

Vague goals can be redefined into operational goals by dominant coalitions within organizations. These operational goals may be close to the original official mission of the organization, or they may differ considerably. Vague goals are particularly susceptible to goal displacement: the substitution of goals of the organization's choice in place of those that it was created to pursue.[34] Systems goals, such as survival, growth, and control, may emerge as the superordinate goals of the organization, overriding or even obliterating substantive goals. Pursuit of individual members' goals also may submerge substantive goals. Organizations and their members require operational goals to guide their behavior. If the official goals of the organization are vague and if neither society nor organizational power holders redefine those goals into operational terms, other types of goals will emerge as guidelines for behavior.

Vague goals pose other problems for the political system. Vague official goals provide minimal guidance for administrative behavior. As we have seen, the organizations to which these goals are assigned will use various methods to clarify them, and thus the power to establish goals passes to the bureaucracy. The more vague the goals, the more discretion the organization has in deciding how and if to implement them. The greater the discretion vested in the agency, the more subject it is to pressure from and capture by interest or clientele groups.[35] This problem occurs because the organization needs political support in order to survive and thus turns to the groups most active and powerful in its immediate environment for such support. One of the costs of this support, however, is that the organization's goals must be recast to satisfy those groups. With specific goals, this may be difficult or impossible, but the organization can easily adopt the interest groups' interpretation of the meaning of vague goals.

Agency discretion can also increase individual member discretion. Unless the goals are specified by the organization, they will remain vague and subject to interpretation down to the lowest levels of the organization. Finally, vague goals make difficult, if not impossible, effective political control of public organizations. If the political branches who are supposed to control the agencies do not know what the organizations are supposed to be doing or accomplishing, they cannot hold them directly accountable for their performance.

Clear, specific goals have advantages and disadvantages from both organizational and political perspectives. For the organization, clear goals provide unity and coherence in structure and operation. They allow the organization to monitor its performance, and they provide a source of specific behavioral guidance and identification for employees. They make the organization immune, or at least more resistant, to interest group pressure and consequently enhance its power and independence. They also protect the organization from legal challenges over statutory interpretation because clear goals are less subject to displacement at lower levels of the organization. Public agencies with clear goals include fire departments, custodial prisons, the Internal Revenue Service, and the Postal Service. They are characterized by machine bureaucratic structures,[36] though clear goals do not seem to be a prerequisite for such a structure. From a political perspective, organizations with clear goals are easier to evaluate and control than those with vague goals; consequently, accountability and responsibility are enhanced.

Given these advantages, it would seem that one of the solutions to the problem of maintaining effective political control of public agencies would be for statutes to specify clear goals. Unfortunately, the specification of clear goals requires broad social and legislative consensus on the specific purposes agencies are to serve, and for a great many governmental activities, this consensus is lacking. The consensus that does exist is likely to be for some broad, general purpose, and it disappears when specifics are raised; the price of insisting on clear goals may be the failure to create any program or policy at all. Specific goals limit organizational flexibility and, particularly in rapidly changing circumstances, may quickly become archaic and obsolete. When those goals are established with limited understanding of the problem the organization must solve, they may also be unachievable or irrelevant, ultimately guaranteeing their displacement by more realistic goals.

Multiple and Conflicting Goals

All organizations have multiple goals: official goals, operative goals, systems goals, and goals of individual members. Each major category is also likely to consist of multiple goals. Thus organizations attempt to achieve diverse and conflicting goals. Public organizations seem particularly likely to be assigned conflicting substantive goals: the Federal Aviation Administration is charged with "promoting, encouraging and developing civil aeronautics" and with ensuring safety and efficiency in the use of the nation's aerospace.[37] In the interest of safety, the FAA has specific rules concerning required time and distance between airplanes' taking off and landing at airports. In the interests of promotion of commercial aviation, these rules are regularly and necessarily unenforced at major, congested airports. Similarly, most economic regulatory agencies, such as the Federal Communications Commission, the Nuclear Regulatory Commission, and the Federal Energy Commission, are charged with both "regulating and promoting" the industries under their jurisdiction.

The National Park Service has unsuccessfully struggled in recent years to balance its two major conflicting goals: to manage the national park system "for the enjoyment and education of our citizens" and at the same time "to protect the natural environment of the parks."[38] In addition to being in conflict, both goals are also excessively vague, and the Park Service has failed, according to its critics, to operationalize and pursue both goals simultaneously. "How can the same government agency, the Park Service, serve effectively as both a ministry of tourism and protector of wild life and habitat?"[39] The Park Service's response to that dilemma has been to pursue a policy of "natural regulation" of wildlife and habitat in parks such as Yellowstone, minimizing active intervention and allowing nature to take its course while actively promoting recreational use of its facilities. Overall, only 8 percent of the Park Service's budget is allocated to resource management and protection; the majority of its financial resources are allocated to upkeep of roads and tourist facilities.[40] The results have been less than satisfactory and, according to some critics, have nearly destroyed Yellowstone National Park as a wildlife sanctuary. Left unchecked, the elk herds have grown to the extent that they have destroyed habitat essential to other wildlife; the grizzly bear population has declined, and the bighorn sheep herd has diminished to 159.[41]

Recreational use of the parks has increased, putting further pressure on preservation of the natural environment in the park system. Each year approximately 2.2 million people visit Yellowstone National Park seeking a wilderness experience within the comfortable confines of their air-conditioned recreational vehicles and exhibiting an increasing willingness to "sue the government for letting animals run around the forest"[42] if their encounter with nature turns out to be less than perfectly safe. The predictable result is that no one is satisfied with the way the Park Service is managing its dual mission, yet there is no apparent way that these two conflicting goals can be simultaneously maximized.

Several strategies are available to organizations confronted with the need to reconcile conflicting goals. The strategy pursued by the National Park Service is one of the most commonly utilized: one goal is selected for maximization, and the other goal or goals are treated as constraints that the organization "satisfices."[43] For the Park Service, encouraging tourism has emerged as the primary goal that will receive the bulk of its attention and resources, and the goal of providing a wildlife and habitat preservation becomes a constraint to be pursued to a satisfactory, not maximum, level. Although this method may provide an acceptable solution for an organization, organizations with conflicting clientele groups will find that the solution inevitably results in dissatisfaction of one or more of those groups.

An alternative strategy for handling goal conflict is for the organization to attend to goals sequentially. "Organizations resolve conflict among goals, in part, by attending to different goals at different times. . . . [T]he resulting time buffer between goals permits the organizations to solve one problem at a time, attending to one goal at a time."[44]

The Civil Aeronautics Board (CAB), for example, was assigned the dual goals of promoting the development of a sound national air transport system and regulating air carriers in the public interest, including enforcing antitrust laws and encouraging competition. For decades the CAB concentrated on promoting the air transport system, minimizing—and at times ignoring—its mandate to promote competition. The result was the development of a healthy, if noncompetitive and oligopolistic, commercial air transport system that provided national service. In 1976, the CAB turned its attention towards maximizing competition and improving consumer economic treatment by the airlines. It successfully deregulated the major airlines and made the commercial air transport system, at least for the short run, more competitive.

Organizations may also alternate maximization of multiple goals, pursuing them in cycles. A public university may seek to maximize its research goals, devoting an increasing amount of resources and attention to encouraging research for a certain period of time. Resources will be shifted away from the educational function, class size allowed to increase, instruction turned over to graduate students to free faculty time for research, and the performance evaluation system geared toward research contributions. After a time, however, student complaints or adverse publicity or negative legislative reaction may result in a deemphasis of research and an elevation of the education goal. University administration will then shift resources and attention to the educational function until faculty complaints, declining grant money, or declining prestige of the institution becomes noticeable. Then the university may again switch to emphasizing pursuit of research.

When an organization can operationalize only one of its goals, it may choose to emphasize that goal and simply ignore the others.[45] Prisons and mental hospitals have both custodial and therapeutic goals. Regardless of public pronouncements, custodial goals have always been emphasized at the expense of therapeutic goals. This emphasis is attributable partially to technological factors, partially to resource availability, and partially to environmental pressure. Treatment and rehabilitation require far more resources than custodial retention. More personnel, and more highly trained professional personnel, are required in therapeutic situations. Even with a greater commitment of resources, results remain uncertain. The technology for treating and rehabilitating inmates and mental patients remains primitive and uncertain; and even if that goal were to be emphasized, order would still have to be maintained in the institution. Finally, environmental pressures are likely to push towards emphasizing custodial goals. "Organizations have to adapt to their environment. . . . When the relative power of the various elements in the environment are carefully examined, it becomes clear that, in general, the subpublics . . . which support therapeutic goals are less powerful than those which support the custodial or segregating activities of these organizations."[46] Consequently, the most likely organizational response, even for an institution that at least attempts to satisfice on therapeutic goals, is to emphasize the custodial, security, and order aspects of its mission.[47]

Technology and environment are two of the most important factors in determining which of several conflicting goals an organization chooses to maximize. While logically, goals should determine technology, in practice the reverse seems true. Confronted with a goal that cannot be achieved because the means of achieving it are unknown, an organization will redefine the goal or, if another goal exists for which a known technology is available, select that goal for maximization. Environmental factors also play an important role in organizational selection among conflicting goals. Conflicting goals are likely to be the result of conflicting interest groups in the organization's environment.[48] The goal selected for maximization is frequently the goal most compatible with the desires of the most prominent, powerful interest group in the environment. Power shifts in interest group alignments are likely to result in changes in organizational goals. Thompson and McEven contend that goal setting is essentially a problem of defining desired relationships between an organization and its environment. In an unstable environment, goal shifts are frequent, and inconsistency will characterize organizational performance.[49]

Goal conflict is common—even constant—for public organizations. Because their missions are assigned to them by external actors—Congress, the president, state legislatures, governors, mayors, or city councils—the organizations lack control over their initial goal assignment. The political branches assign conflicting goals for political reasons: to placate interest groups, the public, or powerful private organizations or individuals. The result is that the actual, operational goals of policy are determined by the implementing organizations. Responsive to environmental demands and technological realities, these organizations in practice often select goals that ultimately disappoint some of the original proponents of the policy. Specific organizational environments are likely to be very different from the original broader policy environment. Some interest groups will lose interest in or lack resources to remain involved in implementation, and the public's attention span for any given issue is limited. When policy is implemented by a decentralized organization, the result is the selection of goals most supported by powerful *local* coalitions; in a centralized organization the chosen goal will be that supported by the most powerful and vocal actor in the central environment: either way, someone is disappointed. Although this type of outcome is predictable and inevitable, this will not save the organization from criticism from those who believe it is maximizing the wrong goal. The dilemma is unresolvable.

Goal Identification

Since stated organizational goals are likely to be vague, multiple, and conflicting, one of the greater challenges confronting an organizational analyst is to determine what an organization's real, operational goals are. Reading official statements of goals, whether statutes or policy pronouncements issued by top management, is an unreliable and unwise method of goal identification; those pronouncements may have little relevance to actual organizational behavior. Conversely, official statements should not be ignored either, because they may give some clues to the intentions of the organization. Etzioni has suggested that the goals of an organization might be determined by asking organizational members to identify them, but then concedes that this method too is fraught with hazard.[50] Low or mid-level employees may be unaware of what goals are or may repeat the "party" or, in this instance, organizational, line. Top management may also give deceptive answers about actual goals for similar reasons. They may be ignorant of the goals their organization is actually pursuing, but "more commonly, organizational leaders quite consciously express goals which differ from those actually pursued because such masking will serve the goals the organization actually pursues."[51] No top political manager would admit that the real goal of the organization is to increase appropriated funds by 10 percent per year so that it can grow, its personnel can be rewarded, and its power can be enhanced. Instead, the manager will issue public pronouncements of the official goals: "The goal of the Defense Department is to protect the nation from its enemies." But despite the inherent problems in asking participants to identify organizational goals, it remains a standard practice in public program evaluation.[52]

"Goals exist only in terms of the behaviors of organizations, specifically as the intentions that can be imputed to their decisions, and, better, their actions."[53] Thus actual goals can be determined only by examining and analyzing the observable behavior of the organization: how it allocates its resources, how it evaluates performance and gives rewards, and what specific actions the organization takes. Although this method may appear to be more valid than questioning participants or reading policy statements, in practice it is extremely difficult and susceptible to subjective bias on the part of the analyst, particularly with public organizations. Attempting to determine the goals of the Department of Defense by this method will require countless value judgments on the part of the analyst. For example, resource allocation can be calculated by various methods, using various categories. The analyst must determine whether activities should be categorized on the basis of standard budget line items, such as personnel, operating expenses, and capital outlays; by service branch; by comparing expenditures on manpower and equipment; by program category; or by countless other bases. The choice is a value judgment that effectively determines what will be identified as the actual goals of the organization.

Determining outcomes and working backwards towards goals is also unreliable. Goals are related to intentions, but outcomes are frequently unintended. The Interstate Highway Program did not intend to encourage urban sprawl, central city decay, and air pollution, but it did; Medicare was not intended to increase health costs, but it did. Goal determination, it seems, is no easier for analysts than it is for organizations.

GOAL DISPLACEMENT

Displacement of goals occurs when "an instrumental value becomes a terminal value."[54] Goal displacement may take several forms, but in bureaucracies one of the most common forms is a rigid obsession with rules to the point that substantive goals are forgotten or obscured. "Formalism, even ritualism, ensues with an unchallenged insistence upon punctilious adherence to formalized procedures. This may be exaggerated to the point where primary concern with conformity to the rules interferes with the achievement of the purposes of the organization."[55] The result can be brutal and dehumanizing for both bureaucrat and client:

> For two and a half years, I was a social worker for a private child care agency which cared for dependent and neglected children. . . . I had a difficult time adjusting to some of the rules set up by both New York City and the agency that employed me. We always had to become somewhat detached from our clients. . . . Our agency had a rule that the parents could come and visit children every other Sunday. I remember feeling frustrated over this, as I felt that it was hardly enough contact. I remember asking how this decision was arrived at and being told by my supervisor that he didn't know: it had always been that way. . . . There were too many regulations and forms that got in the way of what I considered to be a good relationship based on needs and feelings.[56]

A social worker for Catholic Charities reported a similar obsession with rules in public welfare agencies:

> Still, no one is interested in what your problem is. The case worker screens you like you have applied for a Banker's Trust Loan.
> Eventually, you get pretty tired of all the bullshit questions and ask, Are you so inhuman that you can't deal with the client as a person? Then, being the dedicated caseworkers they are, they'll give you some crap about the manual not allowing for that.
> If you still continue along this line of questioning the caseworker—or as they call it, harassment of the caseworker—they will read you the rules and regulations of the Welfare department.[57]

A related form of goal displacement occurs when the incentive system of the organization rewards performance that is only tangentially related to substantive goal achievement.

> It was found that federal drug control officials spent too much time arresting street pushers and compiling numbers of arrests and too little time searching for major dealers in illicit narcotics. The explanation for this misdirected activity was that the agents of the Federal Drug Enforcement Agency perceived that career advancement was strongly related to the number of arrests they made. Therefore, they de-emphasized the more significant conspiracy cases which could immobilize major drug trafficers and syndicates, but which were also more time consuming and had less chance of leading to arrest.[58]

Federally imposed performance criteria on state administering agencies may have similar effects. When the Department of Labor evaluated manpower training programs on the basis of number of job placements, state agencies responded by "creaming," selecting for training programs those among the unemployed with the best chances for successful placement—the younger, more skilled, and more educated—and ignored those most in need of training. When the Department of Labor attempted to correct this by requiring the state and local agencies to report only on job placement of the hard-core unemployed, the response of some agencies was equally unfortunate. These agencies responded by recruiting drug addicts, convicts, and others whose chances of successful long-run employment was unlikely. One program in Washington, D.C., was composed of more than 50 percent heroin addicts.[59]

Suboptimization of goals is an integral part of the goal achievement process. In this process, broad organizational goals are broken down into subgoals and objectives, and each unit and even each employee is assigned specific goals to maximize, or suboptimize: "to do the best they can on their own goals and forget about the rest."[60] Theoretically, this will result in maximum overall goal achievement. Unfortunately, in practice, component units become so obsessed with their own goals that they lose sight of the overall organizational mission, resulting in goal displacement.

The rivalry among the uniformed services in the Department of Defense illustrates some of the negative consequences of suboptimization of goals. The army, the navy, and the air force have become separate and competitive enclaves. Each pursues its separate goals zealously and, from the taxpayer's perspective, expensively, with considerable duplication of equipment, material, and personnel. Cooperation is difficult and must overcome ingrained institutional loyalties and perspectives.

University libraries occasionally display a similar tendency toward suboptimization of goals. As repositories for a variety of forms of information, libraries are clearly intended to facilitate the accomplishment of the three major missions of universities: education, research, and service. Some libraries come to perceive their goal as protecting books and periodicals from the ravages of excessive use and to believe that books belong on the shelves, not in circulation. They view acquisition budgets as "their" money, to be used on purchases the librarians deem appropriate rather than on books desired by faculty and students. Ultimately, they hinder rather than contribute to the accomplishment of university goals.

Systems goals, particularly growth, survival, and enhancement of the organization's power and status, may also displace substantive goals. Although all organizations experience tremendous pressures to grow, for some growth becomes the overriding goal, absorbing increasing portions of the organization's resources and attention of top management. Again the Department of Defense and the public education system illustrate organizations that seemingly pursue growth with single-minded intensity. For DOD, enough is never enough. From 1980 to 1985, DOD received annual budget increases that ranged from 1.8 percent to 12.7 percent, averaging 7.8 percent.[61] Despite severe pressures at the national level to control the burgeoning federal deficit, the Department of Defense continued to pursue its growth. The success of the Pentagon in achieving this goal may be the source of some of its current management problems. There are real diseconomies associated with size after a certain point, and maintaining control is one of them. Incidents of waste and abuse like the $476 toilet seat may be consequences of an organization grown too large to manage efficiently. Public education is the Department of Defense of state and local governments, at least in budgetary terms. Despite declining enrollments at all levels, educational institutions have pursued budgetary growth with the same zeal as the Pentagon. More money, more hardware, and more staff have not necessarily resulted in better education.

Organizations will also pursue survival as a goal even if there is no longer any substantive purpose left for them to serve. The remarkable tenacity of government organizations has been frequently noticed. "A governmental unit can continue for many years after its utility has passed, or its form of organization or program have become obsolete."[62] By the early 1900s, tuberculosis had become one of the most widespread and feared diseases in the United States. In response to the problem, the states established sanatoria to treat its victims and isolate them from society. By the mid-1950s, effective drug treatment for tuberculosis had rendered the sanatoria unnecessary, but most states continued to maintain them, even though in some cases, Maine for example, the state sanatorium had only six patients. Despite the lack of a valid reason for existence, many state sanatoria continued to operate until the late 1970s.[63]

More recently, Ronald Reagan entered the presidency committed to the abolition of the Departments of Education and Energy. By 1986, both departments were still operating, and it seems likely that both will be part of the federal government long after Ronald Reagan has left it. Suicide appears to be nonexistent among organizations, and when their survival is threatened, most organizations will mobilize their resources to protect themselves. Both the Departments of Energy and Education displayed considerable skill at rallying the support of powerful interest groups and key members of Congress, lending support to Peter Drucker's observation that "the moment government undertakes anything, it becomes entrenched and permanent. . . . A government activity, a government installation, and government employment become immediately built into the political process itself."[64] In fairness to government organizations, it should be noted that business organizations are no more likely to accept demise graciously, as illustrated by the struggles of both Lockheed Aircraft and Chrysler Corporation to avoid dissolution. Similar to public sector organizations, both managed to survive by mobilizing political support that resulted in government intervention to help preserve them.

If failure to accomplish substantive goals may result in the displacement of those goals by systems goals, too much success in achievement of goals also constitutes a serious problem for an organization: "An apparently unanticipated and rarely desired outcome of achieving goals can be the abrupt demolition of the whole organization."[65] The organization, in this situation, has no choice but to displace its original goals. One of the most successful organizations in the United States was the National Foundation for Infantile Paralysis (March of Dimes). The foundation was created for one purpose: to develop methods to control and eliminate poliomyelitis (infantile paralysis). With the development and widespread use of the Salk Vaccine, the goal of the foundation was achieved, and the organization was confronted with a problem: it no longer had any reason to exist. Under such circumstances, an organization has two alternatives: dissolution or succession of goals.[66] Most organizations will, if possible, choose the latter. Thus, the March of Dimes adopted a new goal: the elimination and treatment of birth defects.

Environmental change may make the original goals of an organization irrelevant or inappropriate, presenting a similar choice between dissolution or succession of goals to the organization. Sills documents how several nonprofit organizations survived in a changing environment by modifying their original goals. The Young Men's Christian Association (YMCA) was originally created to "improve the spiritual condition of young men." The secularization of American society made that goal increasingly irrelevant, threatening the YMCA's existence. The YMCA responded by changing its goals to emphasize improving the physical and social conditions of young men by providing activities that met and satisfied its members' interests.[67] Similarly, the American Red Cross expanded its goals from relief of suffering in time of war, calamity, and natural disaster to provision of swimming safety programs and blood donor programs.[68] Blau documents how a federal New Deal agency, having successfully accomplished its original goal of securing acceptance of its laws, similarly sought expanded substantive responsibilities.[69]

All of these organizations might have turned to goal displacement rather than goal succession. Which strategy an organization pursues appears to depend on its relationship with its environment:

> As long as its very survival is threatened by a hostile environment, its officers will seek to strengthen the organization by building up its administrative machinery and searching for external sources of support. This process is often accompanied by a retreat from the original goal. . . . But if the community permits an organization to succeed in achieving its initial objectives, the staff's interest in preserving the organization and expanding its jurisdiction will lead to the advocacy and adoption of more advanced goals.[70]

Goal displacement can also occur in a geographically decentralized organization whose field units come to identify more closely with the values and aspirations of the locality than with the goals of the organization—that is, to "go native." When community and citizen participation is mandated by law, goal displacement is even more likely, because local participants may support local priorities and needs at the expense of central program goals.

Similarly, intended goals may be displaced if the organization lacks the resources to accomplish them. This is a particular peril for public organizations that are supervised and funded by discrete legislative processes. Montjoy and O'Toole found that federal agencies that were assigned mandates (goals) but were provided no resources to implement them tended to ignore them and concentrate on goals for which resources were available.[71] Thus, when the Department of the Interior was instructed to develop a long-term government policy on nonfuel minerals by the Mining and Minerals Policy Act but was provided no additional resources to do so, the General Accounting Office found that the department completely ignored the new goal: "Interior's approach has been to regard the Act of 1970 as a restatement of traditional department responsibilities for such functions as geologic investigations."[72] The new goal was completely displaced by established goals for which resources were available.

A final type of goal displacement occurs when the personal goals of individual members of the organization supersede those of the organization. One manifestation of this type of goal displacement is what Berkeley calls "the pathology of self-service."[73] He cites as one of the most extreme examples that offered by former Attorney General Ramsey Clark of prison wardens who "release the most dangerous criminals before they cause trouble inside and are so relieved to see the dangerous ones go that they disregard the public safety—and the fact that most will be back before long."[74] Another manifestation of individual goal displacement is what Perrow terms "feathering the nest":

> One problem of organizations is that they are very leaky vessels. It is quite easy for a member of one to use some of his or her power and leverage for personal ends rather than the ends of the organization. . . . People tend to act as if they own their positions, they use them to generate income, status and other things that rightfully belong to the organization.[75]

Rare is the organization in which some, most, or all of the members do not come to view the resources of the organization as an additional "fringe benefit," to be used for personal purposes. From personal use of organization stationery, equipment, personnel, or the telephone to use of organization time for the pursuit of personal interests, nest feathering is a common and frequently expensive practice in most organizations.

The causes of goal displacement are varied, but one of the most important factors is vagueness of substantive goals. Vague goals allow members and management of the organization to determine the actual goals the organization will pursue and to structure a performance evaluation and reward system to support that determination. Vague goals may be translated into inappropriate substantive goals, or they may be ignored and replaced by systems goals, the goals of individuals within the organization, or excessive concentration on enforcing rules that have little relationship to the organization mission. Public organizations, particularly prone to vague goals, are also particularly prone to goal displacement. The vagueness of their goals is compounded by the absence of market restraint and, frequently, the lack of any rigorous external evaluation of goal accomplishment. As long as the "goals" selected for maximization are acceptable to the primary components of the organization's environment, the organization will pursue them with minimal interference.

When vague goals are combined with unclear technology, goal displacement is even more likely. "In the absence of unambiguous goals, subunit or individual goals will predominate. In the absence of a reliable technology, there will be heavy reliance on standard operating procedures."[76] That is, not knowing what you are doing or how to do it almost inevitably leads to the wrong thing being done. Adding professionalism—and especially a diversity of professions within the same organization—will further contribute to goal displacement. In the absence of a unifying, clear goal, each profession will pursue the separate goals of that profession. Universities, by all these measures, appear to be particularly prone to goal displacement and to resemble "organized anarchies."[77]

Goal displacement can occur even if an organization has clearly stated goals, if those goals are not communicated to members and the organizational socialization process does not instill commitment to them. Communication is always complex, but geographically decentralized organizations have the most serious problems in ensuring that central goals are communicated and dispersed units are committed to them.

Excessively formalized organizations with extensive written rules and procedures are most likely to develop "means-ends" goal displacement. Consequently, machine bureaucracies are the most likely to develop an obsession with rule enforcement at the expense of accomplishment of organizational goals. The increasing legalism of the public administrative process that has resulted from the "due process revolution" and the increasing number of lawsuits against government agencies could result in agencies' becoming more concerned with following proper procedure and rules than providing services and enforcing the laws.

Environmental hostility frequently forces an organization to displace pursuit of substantive goals with pursuit of systems goals, particularly survival. When the organization's existence is threatened, most of its concern and resources will be diverted to self-preservation. Government agencies that face termination will have little concern for substantive goals, which may have even created the hostility that threatens the organization. Instead, they will try to placate the environment. If those strategies fail and the threat persists, personal goals of members will assume primacy, as individual economic self-preservation needs supersede even those of organizational preservation.

Similarly, lack of resources to pursue substantive goals will result in abandonment of other types of goals. Organizations created primarily for symbolic reasons will almost never be given sufficient resources to pursue their stated goals. Should the organization attempt to pursue its stated goals, it will encounter hostility and frustration. It will probably then resort to systems goals, either organizational—survival, growth, the attempt to secure more resources—or personal, particularly those of top managers, who can use their positions to increase their status and visibility.

Mintzberg identifies still another source of goal displacement in the private sector that is also endemic in the public sector:

> When those who reached the top, as well as most of the managers who reported to them, had no direct experience in the operating core—the place where the mission was carried out . . . the inevitable result . . . was a further loosening of the identification of the managers with the mission of the organization, so that its importance as a goal is further diminished.[78]

Government organizations are commonly headed by political executives who have minimal experience in their organizations or the substantive policy areas entrusted to their organizations. These executives may be unfamiliar with the mission of the organization, or in some instances even hostile to it. The latter situation was illustrated by the Reagan administration's initial appointments to the Environmental Protection Agency and the Department of Interior. Such appointments increase conflict within the organization, rendering impossible the achievement of the organizational mission. The goals of top management emerge as the prevention of substantive goal achievement and the maintenance of political loyalty to the president. The personal goals of lower-level members of the organization, including preservation of their jobs and status and satisfying ideological commitments, come into direct conflict with top management, dividing the organization and diminishing its ability to accomplish its mission.

Where political executives support their organizations but are unfamiliar with their operations, systems goals tend to become dominant.[79] Caspar Weinberger as Secretary of Defense exemplifies this type of goal displacement. With no background or experience in Department of Defense management, he had little familiarity with the complicated technology or organization he was selected to lead. He focused on growth and expansion of his organization, and when that proved increasingly difficult, on maintenance of the organization's size and power.

The evolution of a professional administrative component in the private sector has also been associated with displacement of mission goals by systems goals.[80] The possibility of this occurring in the public sector is enhanced by two separate developments: the creation of the Senior Executive Service by the Civil Service Reform Act of 1978 and the increasing emphasis on professionalization of public administration. The Senior Executive Service concept is that the best managers in all agencies should be identified, rewarded, and then assigned throughout the federal government. This is based on the assumption that a person who has been an outstanding manager in the Department of Health and Human Services would be equally outstanding if reassigned to the Department of Transportation. The ultimate result of the establishment and persistence of such a professional administrative corps, however, could very well be increased goal displacement and concentration on systems goals. Similarly, professionalization of administration enhances the possibility of goal displacement at all levels of government.

Although all organizations have multiple goals (and to a certain extent this is unavoidable and may improve overall organizational performance) this may result in systems goals displacing substantive goals. A proliferation of substantive goals may render organizational mission irrelevant to top management if there are too many missions for any one to become dominant. If top management focuses on only one mission, then others will be neglected or displaced. The most likely outcome appears to be that the primary commitment of top management will be to growth. Conglomerates, multidivisional organizations, typify this type of goal displacement, which is reflected at all levels of the organization: "If any sense of identification is left for the employees of the divisionalized corporation . . . it is not with the mission but with the organization itself, and that means with the systems goals of survival, efficiency, control and especially growth."[81]

Finally, goal conflict is a cause of displacement. If the organization is unable to reconcile its conflicting goals or to develop a consensus on overall goals, either systems goals or personal goals will dominate.[82] Conflicting goals are likely to be reflected by conflict among groups in the organization's environment and to be reflected in groupings within the organization. Both factors pressure the organization to concentrate on survival and growth and to downplay substantive goals.

ULTIMATE GOALS: POLITICAL VALUES AS ORGANIZATIONAL CONSTRAINTS

Goals have been defined both as future states the organization is seeking to establish and as constraints on organization decision making and behavior. For public organizations, the final category of goals that must be considered is the basic values that underlie the political system: responsiveness, representation, responsibility, equity, and due process. Adding these values further complicates an already complex goal situation; ignoring them, however, misses the essence of public organizations. These values are primarily process goals, concerned more with the means the organization uses than the substantive ends it accomplishes (or fails to accomplish). These political values are antithetical to administrative values of efficiency and rationality, and as constraints on behavior they frequently interfere with the accomplishment of substantive goals. The vagueness of the terms and the lack of agreement within society on their meaning make them extremely susceptible to displacement.

Responsiveness can be defined as responding to local needs, to clientele, to interest groups, to the executive, the legislative, the courts, to the public, or to all of the above. Responsibility and representation can be defined similarly. Equity can be defined as treating all equally, treating equals equally, or treating unequals unequally. Due process requires fundamental fairness in the procedures used by the organization, but what may be fair for procedures involving large corporations may be unfair when the poor and the unorganized are the subjects of organization action. These values may themselves also conflict. Due process may impede an organization's ability to be responsive; responsiveness may conflict with equity.

Given the vague and conflicting nature of these ultimate political goals, they will most likely be treated in the same manner as substantive goals that share these same characteristics. Each public organization will handle them as best fits its overall organizational situation. An organization will respond to vagueness by either developing operational definitions at the organizational level or by displacing the vague goal. One organization may define responsiveness as developing cooperative or cooptive relationships with its clientele groups; another may view responsiveness to the wishes of Congress as the most appropriate behavior. An organization that cannot establish operational definitions of these values will allow them to be displaced by other types of goals. Complete displacement of these goals is perilous for public organizations, but as Hoover's FBI illustrated, it is possible.

Organizations will address the multiple and conflicting nature of these values by prioritization, satisficing, or displacement. Thus an organization may determine that one value—due process, for example—is to be maximized. Since maximization of due process is likely to involve the development of legalistic procedures and the proliferation of written regulations, responsiveness and representativeness will probably suffer. Alternatively, an organization may, as Simon suggested, treat all values as constraints, satisficing each and maximizing none. Finally, displacement by other goals may occur.

What determines which of these alternatives an organization selects has not really been explored, though the specific environment appears to be a crucial factor. The demands placed on the organization by that environment include adherence to political values and specific definitions of those values. Changing an organization's response to political goals probably requires a change in its specific environment. The nature of the organization's specific goals may also affect its handling of political values. Clearly, a prison is likely to define, prioritize, and respond to those values very differently than would the Legal Services Corporation. An organization with coercive, punitive goals should respond differently than an organization with redistributive, supportive goals.

Many of the major criticisms directed at public organizations and the bureaucracy have been concerned with their failure to satisfy the critics' perception of how political values should be operationalized. Defending against these criticisms is difficult because the critics are inarguably correct. What the critics overlook is the dilemma that confronts public organizations. It is impossible to maximize all those values simultaneously; to attempt to do so would mean elevating process goals over substantive goals.

CONCLUSION

Goals are central to the operation of an organization; they partially determine its structure, define its technology, establish its legitimacy with its environment, and provide criteria against which to measure its effectiveness. Goals, however, are seldom simple or obvious, and for public organizations especially tend to be vague, multiple, conflicting, difficult to operationalize, and difficult to achieve. As a consequence of these characteristics, goal displacement is common in the public sector. These characteristics have also increased the power of administrative agencies that must give specificity to the goals, resolve conflicts among them, and assign them priorities. Although this increases the power of administrative agencies relative to the legislative branches, it also makes them vulnerable to interest group pressure and to negative reactions if they choose unwisely.

Complicating the goal situation for public organizations are the process goals of the political system as a whole, which must also be incorporated into the organizations' operating procedures. These process goals frequently make substantive goal accomplishment slower and more difficult. To ignore them, however, would result in legal challenges, political retaliation, and a negative public image.

The complexity of the goal problem confronting public organizations exceeds that of their private sector counterparts. However many other goals a private business may have, profit is always its bottom line, and profit is a goal that can be operationalized and measured. In contrast, no single measurable bottom line exists for public organizations. This not only makes management of these organizations more difficult but also makes comparisons among organizations meaningless, and evaluating them objectively nearly impossible.

Understanding the nature of organizational goals of all types is essential to understanding organization behavior. Many of the most commonly criticized aspects of public agencies are a direct consequence of the nature of those organizations' goals. While understanding the problems created by these goals does not negate the criticisms, it does clarify why the problems occur and how they may be alleviated.

NOTES

1. William G. Scott and Terence R. Mitchell, *Organization Theory: A Structural and Behavioral Analysis* (Homewood, Ill.: Richard D. Irwin, 1976), p. 29.
2. Richard Daft, *Organization Theory and Design* (St. Paul: Western Publishing Company, Inc., 1983), p. 82.
3. Amitai Etzioni, *Modern Organizations* (Englewood Cliffs, N.J.: Prentice-Hall, 1964), p. 6.
4. Henry Mintzberg, *Power In and Around Organizations* (Englewood Cliffs, N.J.: Prentice-Hall, 1983), pp. 5–7.
5. United States Department of Agriculture, *Soil Conservation Service Manual*, 1984. (Washington, D.C.: Government Printing Office, 1984). sec. 404.
6. Herbert Simon, *Administrative Behavior*, 3rd ed. (New York: Free Press, 1976), p. 278.
7. Daft, *Organization Theory and Design*, p. 82.
8. Charles Perrow, "The Analysis of Goals in Complex Organizations," *American Sociological Review* (1961): pp. 854–866.
9. *The United States Government Manual*, 1985–86 (Washington, D.C.: Government Printing Office, 1985), p. 488.
10. Murray Edelman, *The Symbolic Uses of Politics* (Urbana: University of Illinois Press, 1964), pp. 22–23.
11. James Anderson, *Public Policy-Making*, 2nd. ed. (New York: Holt, Rinehart & Winston, 1979), p. 156.
12. Mintzberg, *Power In and Around Organizations*, p. 265.
13. Ibid., p. 294.
14. Neil J. Welch and David Marston, *Inside Hoover's FBI* (Garden City, N.Y.: Doubleday, 1984), p. 24.
15. Ibid., p. 26.
16. Petro Georgiou, "The Goal Paradigm and Notes Toward a Counter Paradigm," *Administrative Science Quarterly* (1973): p. 291.
17. Charles Perrow, *Complex Organizations*, 3rd ed. (New York: Random House, 1986), pp. 228–229.
18. Frederick Winslow Taylor, *The Principles of Scientific Management* (New York: W. W. Norton and Company, 1967), pp. 13–14.
19. Terry Moe, "The New Economics of Organization," *American Journal of Political Science* (November, 1984): p. 750.
20. Robert T. Nakamura and Frank Smallwood, *The Politics of Policy Implementation* (New York: St. Martin's Press, 1980), p. 75.
21. Anderson, *Public Policy-Making*, p. 157.
22. Larry Gerston, *Making Public Policy* (Glenview, Ill.: Scott, Foresman and Company, 1983), p. 115.
23. Etzioni, *Modern Organizations*, p. 14.

24. Herbert Simon, *Administrative Behavior*, p. 273.
25. Michael D. Cohen, James G. March, and Johan P. Olsen, "A Garbage Can Model of Organizational Choice," *Administrative Science Quarterly* (March 1972): p. 1.
26. Ibid.
27. Michael D. Cohen and James G. March, *Leadership and Ambiguity*, 2nd ed. (Boston: Harvard Business School Press, 1986), p. 4.
28. Harry Hatry, et al., *How Effective Are Your Community Services?* (Washington, D.C.: Urban Institute, 1977), p. 86.
29. Ibid., p. 67.
30. Richard Scott, "Introduction: From Technology to Environment," in John Meyer and Richard Scott, *Organizational Environments* (Beverly Hills, Calif.: Sage Publications, 1983), p. 14.
31. John Meyer and Brian Rowan, "Institutionalized Organizations: Formal Structure as Myth and Ceremony," in Meyer and Scott, *Organizational Environments*, p. 25.
32. Ibid., p. 39.
33. Ibid., p. 40.
34. Etzioni, *Modern Organizations*, p. 10.
35. See Marver Bernstein, *Regulating Business by Independent Commission* (Princeton, NJ: Princeton University Press, 1955), pp. 263–67, and Theodore Lowi, *The End of Liberalism* (New York: W. W. Norton and Company, 1969).
36. Mintzberg, *Power in Organizations*, p. 332.
37. *The United States Government Manual*, 1985–86, p. 418.
38. Ibid., p. 321.
39. "The Fall of the Wild," *Newsweek* (July 28, 1986): p. 52.
40. Ibid., p. 54.
41. Alston Chase, *Playing God in Yellowstone Park* (New York: Atlantic Monthly Press, 1986).
42. "The Fall of the Wild," p. 51.
43. Mintzberg, *Power in Organizations*, p. 259.
44. R. M. Cyert and James March, *A Behavioral Theory of the Firm* (Englewood Cliffs, N.J.: Prentice-Hall, 1963), p. 118.
45. Mintzberg, *Power in Organizations*, p. 175.
46. Amitai Etzioni, "Two Approaches to Organizational Analysis," in Oscar Grusky and George A. Miller, *The Sociology of Organizations* (New York: Free Press, 1970), p. 218.
47. David Duffee and John Klofas, "Organizational Mandates and Client Careers," in Richard Hall and Robert Quinn, *Organizational Theory and Public Policy* (Beverly Hills, Calif.: Sage Publications, 1983), p. 201.
48. Charles Perrow, *Organizational Analysis: A Sociological View* (Belmont, Calif.: Wadsworth, 1970), p. 137.
49. James D. Thompson and William McEven, "Organizational Goals and Environment," in Amitai Etzioni, *A Sociological Reader on Complex Organizations* (New York: Holt, Rinehart and Winston, 1969), p. 188.
50. Etzioni, *Modern Organizations*, pp. 6–8.
51. Ibid., p. 7.
52. See Harry Hatry, Richard Winnie, and Donald M. Fisk, *Practical Program Evaluation For State and Local Governments*, 2nd ed. (Washington, D.C.: Urban Institute Press, 1981), p. 23, and David Nachmias, *Public Policy Evaluation: Approaches and Methods* (New York: St. Martin's Press, 1979), pp. 14–15.
53. Mintzberg, *Power in Organizations*, p. 248.

54. Robert K. Merton, "Bureaucratic Structure and Personality," in Etzioni, *A Sociological Reader on Complex Organizations*, p. 51.
55. Ibid., p. 52.
56. Ralph Hummel, *The Bureaucratic Experience*, 2nd ed. (New York: St. Martin's Press, 1982), p. 23.
57. Ibid., p. 22.
58. George C. Edwards III, *Implementing Public Policy* (Washington, D.C.: Congressional Quarterly Press, 1980), P. 114.
59. Ibid., p. 113.
60. Mintzberg, *Power in Organizations*, p. 177.
61. Elizabeth Wehr, "Fallout of Anti-Deficit Law Begins to Settle," *Congressional Quarterly* (January 11, 1986): p. 51.
62. Luther Gulick, "Notes on the Theory of Organization," in *Papers on the Science of Administration* (New York: Institute of Public Administration, 1937), p. 43.
63. George E. Berkeley, *The Craft of Public Administration*, 4th ed. (Boston: Allyn and Bacon, 1984), pp. 86–87.
64. Peter Drucker, *The Age of Discontinuity: Guidelines to Our Changing Society* (New York: Harper and Row, 1968), p. 226.
65. C. Wendell King, *Social Movements in the United States* (New York: Random House, 1956), p. 114.
66. Peter Blau, *The Dynamics of Bureaucracy* (Chicago: University of Chicago Press, 1955), p. 195.
67. David L. Sills, "The Succession of Goals," in Etzioni, *A Sociological Reader on Complex Organizations*, pp. 179–80.
68. Ibid., p. 183.
69. Peter Blau, *The Dynamics of Bureaucracy*, p. 196.
70. Peter Blau and Richard Scott, *Formal Organizations* (San Francisco: Chandler Publishing Co., 1962), p. 231.
71. Robert S. Montjoy and Laurence J. O'Toole, "Toward a Theory of Policy Implementation: An Organizational Perspective," *Public Administration Review* (September/October 1979): p. 471.
72. Ibid.
73. Berkeley, *The Craft of Public Administration*, p. 99.
74. Quoted in Berkeley, *The Craft of Public Administration*, p. 99.
75. Perrow, *Complex Organizations*, p. 14.
76. Lee Sproull, Stephan Werner, and David Wolf, *Organizing an Anarchy* (Chicago: University of Chicago Press, 1978), p. 6.
77. Cohen, March, and Olsen, "A Garbage Can Model of Organizational Choice," p. 1.
78. Mintzberg, *Power in Organizations*, p. 284.
79. Ibid.
80. Ibid., p. 286.
81. Ibid., p. 285.
82. Daniel Robey, *Designing Organizations* (Homewood, Ill.: Richard D. Irwin, 1983), p. 219.

4

TECHNOLOGY, STRATEGY, AND SIZE

Although the determination and selection of goals is critical for an organization, it is meaningless unless some means to accomplish these goals exists. The organization's ability to perform effectively and to survive depends on its ability to accomplish or at least seem to accomplish some of its goals. This chapter addresses three crucial variables related to an organization's ability to accomplish its goals: technology, strategy, and size. In organization theory, technology refers to the processes and methods that an organization uses to accomplish its substantive goals. Although it includes automation, computerization, and mechanization, organizational technology is much more comprehensive because for many public organizations particularly, the basic work processes used are based on knowledge rather than machines. Strategy refers to the long-term objectives of the organization and the courses of action that it uses to achieve them. Goals, technology, and strategy are so closely interrelated that organization theorists do not agree on what causes what. We have already seen that an organization that does not know how to accomplish assigned goals because it lacks technology will displace those goals. Goals may determine technology, but conversely technology, and particulary the lack of an effective, appropriate technology, may determine operative goals. Similarly, strategy, rather than being rationally planned and executed, may simply reflect the organization's use of whatever technology is available.

Organization size also emerges as both a cause and effect of goals, technology, and strategy. Broad, encompassing goals, such as to provide for national security, coupled with uncertain technology may cause the organization to burgeon in size as it gropes for certainty in goal achievement. On the other hand, large size can cause the organization to modify its goals, altering its treatment of employees and clients and effectively determining its long-range strategy. Size usually indicates resource availability, which may determine or affect the choice of technology and even the organization's ability to accomplish its goals. Combined, these variables affect every aspect of an organization.

TECHNOLOGY

At the most basic level, an organization receives inputs in the form of raw materials, performs certain actions on those raw materials to transform them, and then releases the changed raw materials into the environment as an output. McDonald's takes ground beef, vegetables, and bread and transforms them into McDLTs; General Motors takes steel, chrome, aluminum, and rubber and transforms them into automobiles. An organization's technology is "the knowledge, tools, techniques and action used to transform inputs into outputs."[1] Thus, while in common usage technology frequently refers to mechanization or automation, in organization theory, automation is only a part, and frequently a minor part, of an organization's technology. Actually, an organization may use several technologies; more precisely, different parts of an organization use different technologies. Maintenance, clerical, budgeting, personnel, and public relations departments each have their own discrete work flow processes, methods, and techniques for performing their functions. Our primary concern in this section is with the technology of the operating core of the organization—that part of the organization directly and primarily concerned with the actual accomplishment of the organization's substantive goals.

In no area of organization behavior are public organizations more likely to differ from private organizations than in the nature of the technologies of their operating cores. The key to the difference is the difference in raw materials that the two types of organizations are expected to transform. The vast majority of public organizations, and particularly the largest in terms of size and resources, have as primary raw material people, paper, or complex social, political, or economic problems. Schools, prisons, mental hospitals, and social welfare agencies have people as their primary raw material, and they are expected to achieve some kind of transformation in them, although, as we have seen in the preceding chapter, frequently little agreement exists as to what that transformation is to be. The Social Security Administration transforms paper—applications for benefits—into benefit payments. Police departments transform reports of crime into arrests; the Department of Defense transforms threats, potential and actual, to national security into non-threats. The Department of Agriculture is supposed to transform a depressed agricultural economy into a healthy one. Even organizations that have clear, agreed on, and relatively specific goals, such as fire and sanitation departments, deal with the transformation of raw materials that are considerably different from most business organizations. Few are the public organizations that transform raw materials into tangible products.

This basic difference in raw material is reflected in basic differences in transformation processes—technology; consequently, much of business organization theory dealing with technology is not relevant to public organizations. For example, the classic study by Joan Woodward that established links among technology, structure, and organizational effectiveness in manufacturing firms (based on whether they used custom, mass production, or continuous process technologies) holds little relevance for public organizations.[2] What business theory does teach us is the importance of technology in organization behavior. Technology affects organization structure, determines the nature of individual jobs, affects employee attitudes and behavior, and controls the informal social structure within the organization and ultimately determines the organization's ability to accomplish its goals.[3]

Perrow's Typology of Organizational Technology

Charles Perrow has provided one of the most useful approaches to analyzing technologies of public organizations. For Perrow, the critical determinant of an organization's technology is "the state of the art of analyzing the characteristics of the raw materials."[4] Two aspects of the raw material are particularly important: the extent to which its basic nature and characteristics are understood, and its degree of variability. When the raw material is well understood and its nature is stable and predictable and shows little variation, standardized, routine procedures for transforming it can be developed.

Any technology requires some knowledge of a nonrandom cause and effect relationship between procedures used, and resulting changes in the raw material and the efficacy of those procedures must be repeatedly demonstrated.[5] Many government organizations rely on basic knowledge provided by the social sciences. The knowledge base provided is notoriously weak, and true cause and effect relationships are few. So weak is the knowledge base that in many instances if a cause results in an effect more than 50 percent of the time, the cause is often considered for operational purposes a proven causative agent. In order to routinize its technology, an organization may treat that knowledge as far more predictive and certain than is warranted. Human nature, human cognitive and emotional processes, and human beings in general are not at all well understood, and people differ tremendously from individual to individual. Many organizations that process human beings—schools, prisons, and mental hospitals, for example—act on the assumption that humans are essentially the same and, for the purposes of the organization, well understood. Thus the perception held by the organization and its members about its raw material is far more important in determining technology than the actual state of knowledge about that raw material.

The technology developed from the knowledge base varies along two dimensions: routineness of procedures and nature of the search procedure used when exceptions arise. Routine procedures are well-established techniques applied with little variability to similar raw materials. Nonroutine procedures are used when no well-established techniques have been developed and methods are uncertain. This is most likely to occur when raw materials are neither well understood nor standardized.[6]

Search procedures for solutions to problems can be classified as either analyzable or nonanalyzable. If the problems or exceptions that arise in the conversion process do not vary and are well understood, the search for solutions will be analyzable and the solution usually found in procedural manuals and rules and regulations of the organization. If the problems that arise are highly variable and unfamiliar, the solutions will not be found in manuals. "The individual must rely upon a residue of something we do not understand at all well—experience, judgment, knack, wisdom, intuition."[7] From these two dimensions, Perrow derives a four-cell typology for organizational technology (See Figure 4–1).[8]

Each of the technologies is associated with a characteristic structural type. Routine technology is most likely to result in a classical machine bureaucratic structure; nonroutine technologies require an organic, flexible structure. Craft technology requires a decentralized structure with lower formalization and more discretion vested in employees than routine technology (professional bureaucracies are likely to be characterized by a

FIGURE 4–1.   Perrow's Technology Typology

VARIABILITY OF RAW MATERIAL

NATURE OF SEARCH		*Few Exceptions*	*Many Exceptions*
	Unanalyzable	Craft	Nonroutine
	Analyzable	Routine	Engineering

Source: From *Organizational Analysis: A Sociological View*, by Robert Perrow. Copyright © 1970 by Wadsworth Publishing Company, Inc. Reprinted by permission of Brooks/Cole Publishing Company, Pacific Grove, California 93950.

craft technology). An engineering technology is best adapted to a structure high on centralization and formalization.

Public Organizations: Raw Materials and Knowledge Base.   Human beings are the raw materials of a variety of public organizations from schools, universities, and hospitals to prisons, parole and probation departments, social welfare agencies, and public defenders' offices. Human beings vary tremendously in abilities, skills, needs, and desires, and despite the systematic efforts of generations of psychologists, psychiatrists, sociologists, and other researchers, we understand relatively little about human behavior. Theories abound on how people learn, why they commit crimes, why they develop neuroses and psychoses, and how to teach them, make them mentally well, reform them, control them, and improve them. In practical application, sometimes the theories work and sometimes they fail badly: children do not learn, criminals become recidivists, the mentally ill never recover. From the standpoint of organizational technology, this perspective on human beings as raw material leads to the conclusion that the people-processing organizations should adopt a nonroutine technology and an organizational structure to match.

Most such organizations do not do that, however. The technology of university teaching illustrates clearly how the opposite perspective on people as raw material dominates most people-processing organizations. First, the overriding assumption in the university is that students are essentially similar. The major relevant distinction among them is whether they are graduate or undergraduate students. Within these two categories, the raw material is treated as essentially stable, predictable, unvarying, and well understood. For the undergraduate students, the transformation process is one of established routine. They are required to take a certain number of classes, in which they are lectured to two or three times a week and given assigned readings and standardized examinations to evaluate their performance. In large public universities, this type of technology is ingrained and institutionalized and in many instances as routine as assembly line production. From the production perspective, the exceptions are few and familiar (students always have had similar problems and exhibited similar behavior), and the appropriate methods of dealing with those problems have long been identified. For graduate students, the mechanics of the technology are slightly different but just as routine in practice. The classes are smaller, frequently a seminar format is used, and examination formats are different. The products emerge, labeled, classified, and graded, just like eggs or beef.

Most prisons make similar assumptions about the basic alikeness of prisoners, although prison personnel most likely take a less sanguine view of their raw material than do university professors. Prisoners are by definition convicted criminals and thus sufficiently similar to merit being treated similarly and routinely: isolated from society, stripped of individuality, confined to cells, guarded, and controlled. Problems or exceptions are usually instances of prohibited behavior on the part of the prisoners, and the solutions to these problems are well understood and routinized: punishment in one form or another, ranging in severity depending on the offense involved.

Examples of people-processing organizations that utilize routine technologies based on perceptions about the similarity and well-understood nature of their raw material abound; the exceptions are few. The reasons for this will be examined later, but at this point recognizing the consequences of accepting the opposite view of human beings is important. If schools were based on the belief that every child is different, then every child would need an individualized educational program. If every prisoner is different, then every prisoner must be treated differently. Exactly how differently children would be educated or prisoners rehabilitated is unclear; what is clear and certain is that the resources needed to implement such nonroutine technologies would be far greater than those for the routine technologies currently utilized, and those additional resources are not easily or readily available in the contemporary political climate.

Organizations that have social or economic problems as their raw material face an equally challenging technological situation. The Office of Economic Opportunity was the lead agency in the 1960s' War on Poverty. Its impossible mission was to solve the problem of poverty in the United States. Theories abounded as to the causes of poverty, but in reality no one really knew or understood what would or would not work as possible solutions. Daniel Moynihan, one of the chief poverty warriors, summarized the knowledge base thus:

> This is the essential fact: the Government did not know what it was doing. It had a theory; or rather a set of theories. Nothing more. The U.S. Government at this time was no more in possession of a confident knowledge as to how to prevent delinquency, cure anomie, or overcome that midmorning sense of powerlessness than it was the possessor of a dependable formula for motivating Vietnamese villagers to fight communism.[9]

Similarly, at the time of creation of the Environmental Protection Agency (EPA) and passage of the Clean Air Act of 1970, no one knew what would work in cleaning the air and water, and the technology for accomplishing those purposes simply did not exist.[10] The EPA was supposed to at least appear to handle a problem no one really understood or knew how to solve.

The National Park Service's problems with managing wildlife in natural parks discussed in Chapter 3 were and are similarly exacerbated by the lack of an agreed on technology to accomplish its goals. The Park Service selected one of several possible wildlife management techniques, "natural regulation," in the early 1970s. At the time of adoption, natural regulation was viewed by the Park Service, many environmentalists, and other involved interest groups as a workable solution. In retrospect, natural regulation has been unsuccessful and possibly even disastrous, but again the fault lies in the lack of the knowledge base needed to develop a successful technology. Despite widespread agreement that the current methods have not worked, no agreed on alternative has emerged.

There are countless similar examples: there is no agreement on how national security can best be protected, how farm surpluses can be controlled and farm income stabilized, how unemployment can be lessened or inflation or acid rain controlled. Yet organizations are created, maintained, and required to deal on a daily basis with these messy problems. In the private sector, an organization that did not know how to accomplish its mission, whether making cars or hamburgers, would most likely not survive. In the public sector, organizations survive, at least partly, because they do not know how to accomplish their missions and consequently cannot solve the problems assigned to them.

Technologically, these organizations operate similarly to people-processing organizations. From the various unproven theories available to them, such organizations select one most preferred by political executives, by the dominant power coalition within the organizations, or by interest groups or politicians in their environment. The theory selected, including a corresponding proposed course of action and methodology, is operationalized, and a corresponding technology is developed and routinized. As long as the technology chosen is not viewed by relevant environmental actors as too inappropriate or too ineffective, the organization will persist in using it.

The operating technology of police departments would be viewed by most private organizations as excessively ineffective. The major inputs to police departments are reported crimes. Yet for every fifty reported crimes only twelve arrests are made, and only half of those end in conviction: a successful "conversion" rate of less than 13 percent. The most appropriate classification of police technology, using Perrow's categories, would be somewhere between routine and craft. Reports of crime are treated as basically similar and trigger a standardized investigatory process. Given the low effectiveness of that process, it might seem that a major change in technology is indicated. Theoretically, crimes might be viewed as essentially different, requiring a nonroutine technology to handle them successfully, but two major factors militate against such a major technological change. First, the knowledge base required to develop an alternative crime-solving technology is notoriously weak, and no superior technology has been developed. Second, treating crimes as distinct events to be handled by nonroutine, ad hoc technology would be prohibitively expensive. Most large police departments are already overloaded and have neither time, resources, nor personnel to deviate significantly from established procedures.

Paper-processing organizations—such as the Social Security Administration (SSA), whose major input is applications, or the Internal Revenue Service, whose input is reports from individuals and businesses—are most likely to develop routinized, automated technologies. For this type of organization, the vast majority of inputs are, in fact, essentially similar and can be handled by computers. The computers are used to identify exceptions that need personal attention, and appropriate treatment of these exceptions is detailed in both agencies' procedural manuals. The Social Security Administration's situation is complicated by the existence of three separate benefit programs to administer: the retirement benefit program, the disability benefit program, and the supplemental security program. Of the three, the retirement program has been most susceptible to routinization, and the disability program least so. Although initial determinations of eligibility for disability benefits are made at the state level, appeals of state decisions are decided by SSA through adjudicatory procedures. For these two programs, SSA has two separate technologies: one a routine and the other an engineering technology. The disability program's adjudicatory procedures are basically an engineering technology. The number of exceptions is enormous, which is why the Social Security Administration has the largest number of administrative law judges of any federal agency. The adjudicative procedures used to resolve these exceptional problems, however, are well understood and for the most part routine.

Organizations prefer raw material that is uniform, stable, and well understood. As the examples presented illustrate, even when the raw material is none of these things, many organizations will act as though it was, developing routine technologies to process that raw material. Public organizations are very likely to have unstable, ill-understood raw material and an insufficient knowledge base for successfully handling that raw material. Rarely do they adopt nonroutine technologies or the structure associated with that technology. The reasons for this will be explored in the next sections.

Environment, Goals, and Technology

The missions of public organizations are determined by actors external to the organization—legislatures, executives, and courts—and are frequently vague, leaving these organizations considerable flexibility in developing their operative goals. The environment is equally important in determining their technology. "Cultural definitions regarding the basic material thus influence technology and are particularly apparent in organizations which seek to change people."[11] Thus, social and cultural beliefs about the nature of children, criminals, the mentally ill, the poor, and social and economic problems determine the methods and procedures used to transform them. This appears to be far more pronounced in the public than in the private sector, and it is almost negligible in organizations that produce material goods, where there are few cultural definitions regarding either the nature of raw material or how it should be treated.

The environmental factors that determine technology also limit the ability of organizations to adapt or alter technologies that are not effective. Nowhere is this better illustrated than in the court system. The adversarial process, with its complex and complicated rules of evidence and procedure that require legal education and trained professionals to operate, is enshrined in our history and culture as the one best way of resolving legal disputes, civil or criminal. It is also a slow, expensive process (or technology), which only uncertainly dispenses justice. Moreover, it alleviates costs by passing a major portion of the expense on to litigants, and the system is overloaded and permeated with delays. In civil cases fees spiral and even when huge monetary settlements are awarded, frequently the only real winners seem to be the attorneys. Thus, in the criminal justice system, the established technology—the required adversarial procedure—has proven so inefficient that it is adhered to in appearance far more than in reality. The main actors in the system—judges, prosecuting attorneys, defense attorneys, and presumably the accused—have long since recognized that if everyone were given a true trial the system would collapse. Maintaining the belief that this is still the reality is, however, mandated by social and political beliefs and expectations. This effectively bars the development of a more effective technology, but it has resulted in an actual technology, plea bargaining, that maintains the image of the right to trial while in reality ensuring that very few actually receive trials.

In plea bargaining, the accused are encouraged to plead guilty to a lesser charge than that originally filed against them. The precise details of the bargain are worked out by the prosecuting and defense attorneys and officially sanctioned by the judge, thus bypassing an expensive and time-consuming trial. This is an "efficient" process but, if justice is the goal, spectacularly ineffective. Neither the guilty nor the innocent receive justice—from a broader public perspective, justice is equally denied. The prevalence of plea bargaining illustrates again organizational pressures to develop a routine process even when cultural pressures mandate a non-routine technology. Ironically, plea bargaining as the primary technology allows the criminal justice system to maintain the image demanded by cultural and constitutional expectations that the accused has the right to trial by jury. Although participants in the process are increasingly expressing dissatisfaction with its operations and outcomes, sociocultural values and professional resistance inhibit the development of alternative and more effective technologies.

Social values and expectations concerning the goals of public organizations may change even though no appropriate technology exists to implement the new goals.[12] Social expectations and beliefs about mental illness and treatment of the mentally ill have changed drastically in the last fifty years. These changes have made primitive, custodial treatment of those suffering from mental illness both socially and, subsequently, legally unacceptable. But despite social and legal preferences for treatment and cure as the goal of public mental hospitals, in reality no appropriate technology was available for the large public hospitals.

These hospitals had developed a routine technology geared towards accomplishing the goal of a custodial organization, emphasizing maintenance of order within the hospitals. From the taxpayers' perspective, this technology also had the advantage of being relatively inexpensive. Changing the goal of these organizations to treatment and cure mandated a switch from routine to nonroutine technology, and even with that switch, goal accomplishment would still remain elusive, since there is no known cure for many varieties of mental illness. One result, however, was certain: extensive additional resources would have to be provided to the mental hospitals. Routine technologies in people-processing organizations may be ineffective, but they enable hospitals to develop standardized procedures that allow fewer and less-extensively trained and educated personnel to be employed. Nonroutine technologies require individualized treatment, usually by highly trained and highly paid professionals. Societal values concerning appropriate treatment of the mentally ill may have changed, but societal willingness to bear the increased costs associated with the new treatment technology was not forthcoming. Public mental institutions found themselves in a difficult situation. They could no longer merely keep the mentally ill in custody, yet they were not provided the resources, either in finance or in knowledge, to treat and cure. Their response was a new technology: deinstitutionalization, or, as its critics have charged, dumping the mentally ill into the community and allowing them to fend for themselves.

Just as public sector organizations often have vague goals, they also frequently must operate without a clear and well-defined technology. Organizational responses to this situation vary. A common response is to turn the organizational process upside down: "The nature of the organizational process should be determined by the purposeful goals of policy; that is, policy precedes process. In fact, process precedes policy or the means shape the ends."[13] In this way, the organization develops its transformation processes based on political and social expectations or historical precedent or in response to environmental pressure. Once adopted and implemented, the technology determines the operative goals: schools may not "educate" students, but they do put them through a specific conversion process; courts may not provide justice, but they do decide cases. Whatever output results from the conversion process becomes the operative goal of the organization, and over time the link between technology and goals is constantly reinforced. An organization may also translate official goals into operative goals and then search for an appropriate technology. If that search results in the discovery that no agreement on how to achieve that goal exists, the organization may either choose, from among competing theories, a technology that fits the preferences of organization members, or it may redefine operative goals. The National Park Service selected its technology for wildlife management based on its acceptability to major environmental actors. When the technology proved unsuccessful and increasingly unacceptable to environmental actors, the Park Service was pressured to change technologies but not goals. Mental hospitals, unable to identify a workable technology for treatment, in effect changed their operative goals. Because custodial goals were no longer acceptable and treatment goals were unoperational, they substituted the goal of quick release of patients.

Technology and Structure

Even in business organization theory, there is no consensus as to whether technology determines structure; there is agreement that a relationship between structure and technology exists, but the strength and direction of that relationship remain arguable. Both Charles Perrow and Joan Woodward support the technological imperative view. Perrow argued that each of his four basic types of technology was associated with a characteristic organizational structure. Routine technologies would lead to a machine bureaucratic structure, both craft and engineering technologies to a professional bureaucratic structure (the primary difference was that craft technologies required a greater degree of decentralization), and nonroutine technologies mandate an organic adhocratic structure.[14]

From one perspective, Perrow's technological imperative seems unassailable. Identifying an organization that has a routine technology but not a machine bureaucratic structure is difficult if not impossible. Similarly, organizations with nonroutine technologies almost without exception have flexible, decentralized structures. The basic problem with technological determinism, particularly as applied to public organizations, is that it presumes that technology precedes structure. This is not necessarily true; in the public sector, structure can be determined by the political branches or by sociocultural expectations with little regard paid to what type of technology might be most appropriate for accomplishing the organization's purpose. In this situation, structure determines technology. An organization compelled to adopt and maintain a bureaucratic structure will find it difficult to develop and utilize a nonroutine technology.

Strong pressures push public sector organizations toward bureaucratic structures and routine technologies. Political values that emphasize control over and accountability of administration create a strong presumption in favor of bureaucracy with its illusion (if not necessarily reality) of centralized authority and responsibility; written, uniform, standardized rules of procedure; and impersonality. Similarly, constitutional and legal requirements for due process of law and equal protection push towards both bureaucracy and routine technology. And although bureaucracy and routine technology both permit unequals to be treated unequally, they leave the burden of proof for justifying that kind of treatment on the administrative agency, and most agencies prefer to avoid having to defend such treatment. Organizations whose primary input is people, or those that must deal with people on a regular basis, have stronger legal and political values pressuring them to treat individuals as a uniform, stable, and predictable input. The lack of consensus on goals reinforces the pressures towards routinization of treatment. We do not agree on what these organizations are supposed to be accomplishing, so it cannot be proven that routinization is hindering goal accomplishment. As Kramer points out, the means not only precede the ends, they supersede them: political and social consensus exists for the means but not the ends.

Increasing scarcity of resources also supports routinization of technology. Nonroutine technologies require both more personnel and more highly trained personnel. The lack of consensus on goals and the uncertain outcomes of nonroutine technologies have little appeal for organizations experiencing a tightening of resource availability. And when the demands on these organizations show little sign of diminishing, the pressure to maintain levels of service increases the need for an inexpensive, routine technology. This is reinforced by the tendency of organizations experiencing resource constraints to centralize, standardize, and reduce unpredictability.

Although professionalism may result in decentralization and a decrease in written standard operating procedures, it is not likely to increase emphasis on nonroutine technologies. Rather, the routine technology will be developed external to the organization; and once a profession has identified a particular technology as most appropriate, it will enforce conformity. The ultimate result is routinization and the professional bureaucratic structure.

True adhocracies are almost inevitably associated with nonroutine technologies. Since adhocracies are created to deal with new problems for which no solution exists, an adhocracy must experiment, exceptions are common, and the search for solutions to those exceptions will be unanalyzable. NASA, particularly in the early years, had little choice but to use a nonroutine technology. Similarly, research and development organizations that deal with a variety of new and unfamiliar problems also have nonroutine technologies, as well as organic structures.

The technology an organization uses influences the organization in many ways. Once adopted, the technology determines the nature of individual jobs, the qualifications needed to perform them, the ability of the organization to accomplish goals; it even affects the structure that the organization must maintain. Although the relationship between technology and individual jobs is clear and well established, the nature of the relationship among technology, goals, and structure is not. Rationally, goals should be established first, then an appropriate technology should be developed to achieve them and a structure adapted to that technology. But for public organizations, this type of rationality is rare. Goals may not be clearly specified or well understood. Structure may precede technology, which may be mandated by laws, or social and cultural expectations may determine goals. Once a technology is operationalized, it tends to become self-perpetuating: "But that's the way we've always done it," whether "it" is educating students, solving crimes, or putting out fires. Resistance to change may be both external, from society and the political system, and internal, from workers. Thus the selection of an organization's core technology is one of the most critical long-range decisions made by or for the organization.

STRATEGY

From the broadest perspective, strategy can be defined as "the determination of the basic long-term goals and objectives of an enterprise, and the adoption of courses of action and the allocation of resources necessary for carrying out these goals."[15] It involves long-range planning based on the outcome of several fundamental decisions, starting with the choice of basic mission. Determination of the basic mission requires identification of stakeholders (claimants on the organization who depend on it and on whom it depends) and their demands, needs, and desires. From this determination, the organization establishes goals for the stakeholders, for social development, and for organizational development; establishes priorities among those goals; identifies and establishes priorities among programs necessary to reach those goals; and determines the appropriate program-service mix and geographic service area.[16] Long-term comprehensive plans to achieve these goals and objectives are then developed and implemented.

This concept of strategy implies that organizational decision makers are rational and have considerable discretion and power. Logically, strategy determination should precede both goal determination and technology selection. As we have seen, however, for public organizations at least, those two strategic decisions are frequently not within the power sphere of organizational decision makers but are determined externally by environmental forces. This definition also assumes that the organization takes planned, intended action and can exercise organizational free will, which is not true for a great many organizations, both private and public.

A more limited definition views strategy as "how an organization defines its relationship to its environment in the pursuit of its objectives."[17]

Strategy formulation involves monitoring, interpreting, and responding to the environment and developing "consistent patterns in streams of organizational decisions (strategies) to deal with it."[18] From this perspective, strategy formulation is a far less rational, comprehensive, intended process than it is from the broader strategic management perspective.

Public organizations are routinely criticized for their failure to develop strategy and to apply the principles of strategic management to their decision-making process.[19] In periods of relative resource abundance, they demonstrate a preference more for incrementalism, and in periods of resource scarcity a preference for decrementalism—small, short-term, marginal adjustments in procedures and programs—rather than for rational, long-term planning. Levine, for example, found in a survey of police departments that have experienced fiscal cutbacks that the vast majority had responded by "muddling through," making short-sighted responses with little attempt at more thoroughgoing, long-range planning.[20] The response of those police departments has been duplicated by a wide range of agencies at all levels of government.

Criticism of public agencies for their lack of strategic management ignores two controversial aspects of strategic management: its possibility and its desirability. Even in the private sector, no consensus exists on those two aspects, and for the public sector the controversies are even more pronounced and unresolved. Strategic choice is based on the assumptions that organizations have goals toward which they drive; that they move towards goals in a rational manner; and that their environment is a given: both demands and resources are controllable. John Child is one of the strongest proponents of the ability of organizational decision makers to make strategic choices. Child believes that organizational decision makers have autonomy, that they are controlled by neither their environments nor their technology because they have the ability to manipulate their environments and modify their technologies. Thus, he believes that organizations have considerable discretion in decision making.[21]

Howard Aldrich represents the opposite view on the limitations on strategic choice. He points out that most organizations are small and have no control over their environments. "Because of the powerlessness of most organizations, barriers to choice because of their interorganizational dependence and problems in perception and information processing, the opportunities for strategic choice are severely limited."[22] If goals, technology, structure, clientele, and resource availability are determined by the environment, an organization's ability to plan and implement strategy is severely restricted if not nonexistent. A dynamic, hostile environment would seem to limit the possibility of strategic choice even more. Developing strategy requires the ability to project environmental conditions accurately, but when the environment is rapidly changing this becomes impossible, and strategic planning becomes a liability, preventing rapid response to change.

Public organizations confront further barriers to strategic management because they are created by political groups and their structure and missions are determined by those groups. They are assigned vague, ambiguous goals, which they clarify only at the risk of disintegrating the coalition that supported their formation. The stakeholders that they must satisfy are likely to be more diverse and in conflict than those of private organizations. The greater openness within which they are compelled to operate—the fishbowl atmosphere—impedes thorough discussion of issues and discourages long-range plans that might alienate stakeholders. The limited perspective of political executives who will rarely stay in office for longer than four years further discourages the development of long-range strategies.[23] Harlan Cleveland aptly described the limits of strategic choice in public management: "We are tackling 20 year problems with five year plans staffed with two year pesonnel funded by one year appropriations."[24]

The middle ground is taken by Jewell Hage, who contends that "sometimes there is a great deal of strategic choice and at others a great deal of environmental constraint."[25] Hage believes that organizations do have opportunities to make strategic choices but that these opportunities are rare and that a critical choice made in one area forecloses other choices. The first and most important choice an organization makes is its stance towards potential clients. For schools, welfare agencies, and prisons, for example, the choice made at this juncture determines much of the rest of the organization's behavior. Once made, choices tend to become a permanent aspect of the organization's behavior. Even though Hage believes organizations do have limited opportunities for strategic choice, he does not believe that most organizations have clear strategies: "Despite all the images of organizations and their leadership as rational, probably few have articulate strategies until some environmental crisis occurs and management finds itself forced to think about survival and search for alternatives. Most organizations do *not* have a conscious, articulated strategy—they muddle through."[26]

The arguments over the possibility, reality, and desirability of strategic management are basically a restatement of the perennial arguments over rational as opposed to incremental decision making. Conscious, intended strategic management is typical rational decision making. It requires that goals be clearly expressed, alternatives be articulated and evaluated, a multiyear time frame be adopted for decision making, and a comprehensive approach to the organization's problems, mission, and structure be taken.[27]

If planned strategy is to be carried out, an effective, well-understood technology is required, as is a manageable environment. Incrementalism, muddling through, takes a short-range perspective. It is "geared to alleviating concrete shortcomings in a present policy—putting out fires—rather than selecting the superior course of action."[28] No attempt is made to specify major goals or to ascertain the best alternative; search and evaluation processes are usually limited to successive comparisons of policy alternatives only marginally different from current policy.[29] "Often decisionmakers have no real awareness of trying to arrive at a new policy; rather, there is a never ending series of attacks on each new problem as it arises. . . . Policy makers take one small step after another."[30] Instead of planning and analyzing to maximize outcomes, decision makers bargain, compromise, and negotiate to satisfice, to determine a policy direction that alleviates conflict with the environment, with stakeholders, and within the organization. Once a satisfactory course of action is determined, the organization will continue to pursue it until a new "fire" or problem situation requires it to modify its behavior. Then the incremental process will be repeated.

Despite the evidence that most organizations, public and private, are muddlers, the critics of incrementalism insist that it is a basically unsatisfactory and potentially disastrous method of decision making and of managing an organization. Clearly, incrementalism favors the powerful—both inside and outside—the organizations: their demands are the ones that must be satisfied if the organization is to survive. Consequently, the politically weak fare poorly in incrementalism.[31] Particularly in the political arena, where decisions can have grave and irrevocable consequences, incrementalism does not seem to provide any guarantee that decision makers will avoid catastrophe as "they stagger through history like a drunk putting one disjointed incremental foot after another."[32] Levine argues that decremental approaches to dealing with resource scarcity will result in human resource erosion, overcentralization, decisional paralysis, and eventually "general service default . . . when the government is no longer capable of delivering services that enhance or protect the quality of life of its residents."[33] Clearly, basic social problems currently remain unsolved because problems are not addressed; the consequences of decades of incremental decision making in the public sector have been constantly increasing public expenditures, with only minimal accomplishments to justify the ultimate size of the public sector and the public debt.

The proponents of incrementalism are equally adamant about its strength and desirability as a form of public decision making. They start with the assertion that complex problems cannot be completely analyzed, nor can clear goals be agreed on, at least in the public sector. Consequently, rationalism is impossible.[33] Futher, incrementalism is more compatible with democratic politics; it permits different values, opinions, and beliefs to be considered and allows for more participation in decision making. Since decisions are arrived at by persuasion and compromise, by "partisan mutual accommodation," rather than handed down by fiat from experts and because power shifts are common, incrementalism prevents any one actor from assuming dominance and prevents overcentralized, undemocratic decisions. Incrementalism recognizes and accepts the impossibility of predicting the future: it assumes that all decisions are tentative and reversible if they do not satisfice. Decisions involve only minor alterations to the status quo, so incrementalism avoids the risks of drastic social changes that "may easily lead to an intolerable increase in human suffering."[35] Incrementalism seems particularly appropriate in a dynamic, uncontrollable environment because it allows far more flexibility and adaptability than rationalism.

Strategy Formulation

Although strategic management requires that strategy be deliberately and rationally planned, an organization may develop a strategy unintentionally and unconsciously. If an organization, over a period of time, makes a sequence of decisions that exhibits consistency in pursuit of goals, allocation of resources, and responses to stakeholders, it has a strategy that can be identified and described. For descriptive purposes, it makes little difference whether that strategy was formed rationally or incrementally.[36] Thus, strategy formulation can be either planned or evolutionary.

Planned strategy formulation involves an ordered, integrated process that results in an intended strategy: a deliberate, conscious, explicit set of guidelines that controls decisions and behavior into the future.[37] Emergent strategy formulation involves making decisions on an individual basis as the result of the interplay between a continuously changing environment and an organizational operating system that seeks to stabilize actions. This results in an emergent strategy, formed unintentionally: a pattern in a stream of decisions. Mintzberg has no doubts about which type of strategy formation is most common or most advisable for organizations:

> The aggressive proactive strategymaker—the hero of the literature on entrepreneurship—can under some conditions do more harm than the hesitant, reactive one. Contingency planning, a popular prescription in times of environmental turbulence, can be risky because the plans may tend to become actualized, whether needed or not. And so too can it sometimes be risky to make strategy explicit, notably in an uncertain environment with an aggressive bureaucracy. In general, the contemporary prescriptions and normative techniques of analysis and planning—and the debate that accompanies them—seem unable to address the complex reality of strategy formation. To tell management to state its goals precisely, assess its strengths and weaknesses, plan systematically on schedule, and make the resulting strategies explicit are at best overly general guide-lines, at worst demonstrably misleading precepts to organizations that face a confusing reality.[38]

Planned strategy formulation can be particularly dangerous for bureaucratic organizations. For once given an explicit, clearly articulated strategy, "bureaucracy runs like an elephant. Once underway, there is no stopping it."[39] Flexibility and adaptability are lost, as is the ability to manage discontinuity, essential in the public sector where "coalitions are unstable, political tenure is brief, and agendas change constantly."[40] Given the hierarchical, centralized nature of bureaucracy, planned strategy would have to be formulated at the top and implemented at the bottom. This would probably result in inappropriate strategy unless two fundamental conditions were met: first, the formulator would need full information; second, the situation would have to be sufficiently stable or predictable to ensure that there would be no need for reformulation during implementation.[41] Unfortunately, these conditions are seldom present.

Strategy in professional bureaucracies is usually determined by actors and circumstances external to the organization. Characterized by vague goals and uncertain technologies determined by professional associations, professional bureaucracies are unlikely to be able to formulate a single, integrated pattern of decisions for the entire organization.[42] Wechsler and Backoff provide an excellent example of strategy formulation for professional bureaucracies with their study of the Ohio Department of Mental Retardation and Developmental Disabilities (DMRDD). In the 1970s and 1980s, DMRDD was compelled to modify its strategy by a variety of environmental pressures and changes, including "fundamental changes in professional opinion regarding appropriate and effective care and treatment for the mentally retarded, the development of new behavioral science technologies for training retarded individuals for normalized living environments, and a national legal rights movement which established basic principles of more humane treatment for the retarded."[43] This combination of environmental pressures left DMRDD with little choice but to modify its long-standing strategy. The new strategy emerged gradually but ultimately resulted in a fundamental change in the goals, procedures, and direction of the agency. The DMRDD function changed from providing a residential, service-delivery system to regulating a community-based care and treatment system.

By definition, adhocracies are the organizations least likely to develop a planned, integrated strategy. When temporariness and innovation are central characteristics of an organization, the organization can neither plan for nor predetermine its long-range direction. Strategy becomes the result of specific decisions made one at a time as particular tasks are attacked and completed.[44] Adhocracies are decentralized, so the formation of strategy is equally decentralized. In NASA, for example,

> while it is clear who has the authority to make, and who announces the final decision (the top administrator of NASA), it is much more difficult to say who, in fact, "makes" the decision. It is the product of a complex process of interaction and confrontation in which technical, administrative, and broader political criteria are applied and in which both technical and managerial personnel participate.[45]

Somewhat ironically, adhocracy, which is frequently praised as the organizational type most suited for a turbulent environment, appears also to be the type least likely to engage in conscious, rational strategy formulation. Instead, strategic planning is

> a rather different function in these large developmental systems where uncertainties predominate. Traditionally, managers are taught to identify their ultimate ends and purposes, set objectives that will help attain these ends, and then develop operational plans. Unfortunately, this comforting and logical sequence gets upset in the real world of large systems. Clear objectives often disguise conflicting purposes. . . . Planning turns out to be a dynamic, iterative process. This inevitably disperses authority, since a small group of expert high-level "planners" cannot define strategy.[46]

The realities of organizational strategy formulation do little to resolve the normative debate over the desirability of rationalism versus incrementalism. Emergent, evolutionary strategy formulation appears to be far more common in organizations than planned, rational formulation. The way things are is not always necessarily the way things ought to be, but the widespread existence and persistence of a particular method may indicate that barriers to radical change are insuperable in the absence of compelling circumstances. Rational, planned strategy does appear to be dysfunctional for both bureaucracies and adhocracies. For in both cases it is likely to result in inflexible adherence to policies that can be rendered obsolete by a rapidly changing environment. From a broader perspective, if rapid environmental change is endemic and unpredictable, rational strategy formulation is not only impossible but also undesirable.

Typology of Organizational Strategies

Whether planned or evolutionary, organizational strategies exist and can be identified and described. Miles, Snow, Meyer, and Coleman identified four basic types of strategies pursued by business organizations.[47] A modified version of their typology will be used to illustrate the strategic types of public organizations.

Reactors.   Although Miles and associates viewed reactors—organizations that lack definite clear strategies and simply react to environmental change—as the least satisfactory of their strategic types, they are very common in both government and business. An organization with a complex, dynamic, and hostile environment that it can neither control nor predict has little choice but to pursue a reactive strategy. Of the four strategy types identified by Wechsler and Backoff for state agencies in Ohio, three were reactive. The transformational strategy pursued by DMRDD was a sequence of decisions and actions taken in response to changes in legal requirements and professional standards. The protective strategy of the

Department of Public Welfare was even more reactive and directed at ensuring organizational survival.

> A hostile and potentially threatening environment, combined with limited organizational capacity, produces the protective strategy. . . . Hostile relationships with legislators and other key stakeholders, nearly continuous media attention, tremendous increases in human service needs, decreased resource availability, and changing federal policy and programs were among the most important variables affecting departmental strategy.[48]

Similarly, the political strategy of the Public Utilities Commission (PUC) was developed in response to a change in the balance of power among environmental actors. The PUC's environment changed from a stable, low-conflict environment dominated by the regulated parties to a dynamic, complex, high-conflict one by the energy crisis and its impact on utility rates. As rates skyrocketed, affected business and consumer interests became active and pressured the PUC to modify its basically pro-utility strategy. The commission responded by altering its regulatory strategy to balance the competing interests of producers and consumers.

It might seem that reactors are ineffective and poor performers, but their strategy exemplifies open-systems behavior. Above all, reactors are creatures of their environment and responsive to changes in that environment: strategy emerges as a result of the organization's responses to environmental change. Reactive strategy is likely to be incremental, as the organization seeks only to satisfice—to determine the least abrupt departure from current operating procedures and goals necessary to restore its equilibrium. However, abrupt and radical environmental change may require an equally abrupt and radical change in organization behavior. Reactive strategy appears to be very common in the public sector, particularly in response to increasing resource scarcity.

Defenders.   Defenders are organizations that have established a stable, supportive niche in the environment and whose basic strategy is aimed at protecting that niche. They have little or no interest in expanding their domain or seeking new power or jurisdiction. Growth is pursued only through expansion of services or benefits provided to existing clientele. Defenders usually operate in an environment that is homogeneous, stable, supportive, and of low complexity, where conflict is either minimal or nonexistent. The organization thus concentrates on providing services to established clientele and protecting its turf from "invasion" by potentially hostile forces. As long as no threats emanate from the environment, defenders adhere to standard operating procedures and maintain the status quo, expending no effort scanning the environment for new opportunities to grow. Almost by definition, the defender strategy is particularly compatible for bureaucratic organizations.

The defender strategy is best illustrated by, and most successful for, federal agencies that administer distributive policy, particularly those characterized by subgovernment dominance. The Agricultural Stabilization and Conservation Service (ASCS), which administers the farm price support program, operates in a tightly circumscribed environment populated by highly supportive actors: the commodity subcommittees of the congressional agriculture committees and the various commodity interest groups, such as the National Association of Wheat Growers, the Soybean Council, and those representing cotton, rice, tobacco, sugar, and corn farmers. All participants share a common understanding of the basic goals to be pursued by ASCS: it should pursue and distribute the most favorable level of price supports obtainable for each and all commodities, separately and collectively. Conflict and competition are avoided, and cooperation and reciprocity are the dominant norms of behavior for all participants. The long-run and short-run strategy of the ASCS has been to protect its programs and clientele and to seek growth only by obtaining higher levels of price supports for the various commodities. Only rarely has its environment been invaded by opponents, and then not only ASCS but its clientele and the congressional subcommittees have united to defend its turf and repel the invaders. In 1981, for example, the Reagan administration failed to cut overall spending on agricultural subsidies when the subgovernment participants closed ranks and bargained among themselves. "After the dust had cleared, all crops received increased price supports, although the increases were, no doubt, less than the subgovernment supporters would have provided in an unchanged decision context."[49]

The Army Corps of Engineers operates in a similar environment and pursues a similar defensive strategy. Its immediate environment is populated almost exclusively by supporters and beneficiaries: the Public Works Committees of the House and Senate, individual members of Congress seeking Corps projects, and representatives of affected local interests and national lobbying associations. Again, consensus prevails among environmental actors and the agency, and decisions are reached by logrolling, bargaining, and negotiation. Decisions on water resource projects are made individually, and overall water resource policy emerges as the aggregate of individual decisions. The Corps' strategy is both emergent and defensive, even more so than that of ASCS because proposals for new projects do not initiate with the Corps but rather with local interests and members of Congress seeking to further those interests. Recent Presidents, Jimmy Carter for example, have tried to intervene and disrupt the water resource subgovernment, as have environmental groups, but the interventions have been successfully repelled; the Corps, with its supportive environment, has rigorously defended its turf.[50]

A defensive strategy is most successful in a stable, supportive environment. When defenders find their environment disrupted by the entrance of competitors or powerful actors hostile to them, they are compelled to switch, at least temporarily, to a reactive strategy. If environmental hostility is prolonged, the defender must continue to react to it until it can once again carve out a safe niche. Both the ASCS and the Corps of Engineers have managed, with a lot of help from their friends, to protect themselves and to continue to pursue a defensive strategy.

From the perspective of the political system, defenders constitute a problem. Even when assigned broad policy responsibility, defenders will approach it piecemeal. Policy decisions will be disaggregated, and no attempt will be made to assess overall policy consequences. Successful defender strategy depends on constantly satisfying the demands of clientele, which in turn means constantly increasing their benefits. The result is a constant increase in expenditures without a corresponding increase in goal accomplishment. The public interest is submerged, ignored, or identified with the interests of clientele groups. The closed environment limits meaningful participation by political executives and potentially competing interests. As a result, accountability and responsibility are diminished.

Prospectors. Prospectors constantly seek new opportunities to expand their power and jurisdiction. For public organizations, this entails scanning the environment for new problems to resolve and then either using existing authority or seeking new legislative authorization to deal with them. The payoff for successful prospectors is increased power and prestige and frequently increased resources and size. This in turn may attract more competent and committed employees; it also allows the organization to provide more rewards to those employees, including more satisfying, challenging work and more opportunities for career advancement. But the risks of prospecting are equally great. Each successful domain expansion broadens the organization's environment and increases its scope and complexity and potentially the level of conflict in that environment. Expansion may activate competitors and opponents, and resentment of the organization may increase. Incessant activity increases the visibility of the organization to the media, the public, and political controllers, which increases the possibility of opposition. As opposition increases, negative political response may occur, and the prospector may eventually be compelled to change strategy, to become either a reactor or a defender.

The Federal Trade Commission (FTC) is a clear example of an organization that switched its basic strategy from that of a defender to that of a prospector and ultimately, after a period of reaction, reverted to being a defender. Created in 1914, The FTC pursued for most of its existence a defensive strategy. Although originally vested with potentially far-reaching power over the competitive practices of nearly every business in the American economy, the FTC exercised that power with great restraint. Such restraint in enforcement muted potential conflict in the FTC's environment and permitted it to carve out a niche that was narrow but secure. Although Congress consistently expanded the FTC's power and jurisdiction, the FTC just as consistently resisted active enforcement of its new statutory authorizations. Subjected to constant criticism for its lack of enthusiastic enforcement, the FTC was secure in its niche because, regardless of its substantive accomplishments, its symbolic importance protected it from any real threat to its survival.

After nearly sixty years of pursuing a defensive strategy, in the mid-1970s the FTC gradually became a prospector, scanning the environment for new opportunities to exercise its power and seeking expanded power from Congress. In its role as prospector, the FTC attempted to apply its power over competitive practices to the legal profession, the medical profession, used car dealers, funeral homes, the insurance industry, the eyeglasses industry, the accounting profession, and advertising on children's television shows. Some of this expansion was undertaken at the agency's own initiative and some in response to demands by various interest groups, but from the early 1970s until the early 1980s the FTC was constantly prospecting for new areas in which it could expand its domain.

As a result of this prospecting, the FTC's environment included several new powerful and hostile actors. Every business, profession, or industry that the FTC attempted to regulate resented and resisted its attempts. Their resistance took the form of both legal battles and political retaliation. Through direct contact and campaign contributions, the FTC's opponents took their case to Congress, and Congress emerged as one of the foremost adversaries of the agency. The FTC's authorizing statute expired in 1977, and Congress refused to renew it for four years. For the FTC, this meant it had to exist on a year-by-year basis, depending on continuing appropriation statutes as its authorization to continue. When Congress did renew its authorization in 1980, it included a sweeping legislative veto provision for FTC rules and proceeded in 1982 to negate FTC attempts to regulate used car dealers. Although President Carter had been quietly supportive of the FTC, the election of Ronald Reagan and the changed political climate added one more adversary to the FTC's already hostile environment. The Supreme Court decision in 1983 declaring all legislative vetoes unconstitutional only increased the turbulence and uncertainty in the FTC's environment because it effectively left the agency again without an authorizing statute.

The drastically changed environment that resulted from the FTC's prospecting eventually forced the agency to change strategies again, first to reactive and then, once it had drastically curtailed its activity, to defensive. The FTC's declining to force the recall of defective underwater survival suits (on the grounds that heirs of victims who drowned could always sue the manufacturer) was an action of an agency that had abandoned prospecting.[51]

The experience of the FTC illustrates not only the use and consequences of a prospective strategy but also the circumstances associated with basic strategic change for an organization. In both instances, the impetus for the FTC's strategic change came from its environment. The switch from defender to prospector began in 1970 when President Nixon selected a new chairman, Caspar Weinberger, for the FTC. The new chairman reorganized the commission, removed over one-third of its employees, and recruited young, consumer-oriented lawyers to the agency. The FTC's prospector strategy accelerated with the appointment of Michael Pertschuk as chairman in 1977. Pertschuk, an outspoken and aggressive consumer advocate, led the agency to take on increasing responsibility. The growing environmental hostility that his activism engendered culminated in the selection of James Miller as chairman by President Reagan; Miller was fundamentally opposed to activist intervention in business practices and he and other commissioners appointed by Reagan gradually succeeded in forcing the agency to change its strategy.

Analyzers.   Analyzers are more cautious than prospectors but more adventurous than defenders. Their basic strategy is to expand into new areas but only after careful analysis has indicated that expansion involves minimal risk of adverse reaction. If an analyzer has overlapping or duplicating functions with a prospector, the analyzer will follow the lead of the prospector, waiting until that organization has entered the new area and has proven it to be safe and rewarding.

To a certain extent, the Environmental Protection Agency (EPA) has pursued an analyzer strategy, frequently following the lead of the more prospector-oriented Occupational Safety and Health Administration (OSHA). Although the EPA has the responsibility of regulating hazardous substances in the environment, if those substances are found in the work place, OSHA has primary jurisdiction. OSHA has led the way in regulation of a variety of hazardous substances, such as benzene, PCBs, and asbestos, and has engendered considerable hostility and conflict through its efforts. The EPA's approach has been far more cautious, and it has expanded its jurisdiction only after OSHA has absorbed much of the hostility. Asbestos regulation imposes high costs on affected industries, which engenders extensive legal and political resistance. The EPA moved extremely cautiously and slowly on this issue, deciding in 1985 that it would refer all asbestos regulation to OSHA and the Consumer Product Safety Commission. When this decision aroused opposition in Congress, EPA reluctantly announced that it would regulate asbestos and attempt to limit its use.[52] EPA's analysis indicated that there was more risk involved in not regulating than in regulating.

The U.S. Postal Service also appears to be an analyzer. The Postal Service went through a long and difficult transition from cabinet department to government corporation. As a cabinet department and monopoly, the Postal Service was clearly a defender; but the switch to corporate status involved a change in orientation from service to efficiency, which resulted in the Postal Service engaging in previously unheard of activities such as advertising and hiring a sales force, which might alone have been sufficient to cause a change in strategy. However, the development of aggressive competitors, such as Federal Express and United Parcel Service, forced the Postal Service to become more aggressive. Although the Postal Service has not initiated new services, it has, in the manner of an analyzer, quickly followed the lead of its competitors when a new service developed by them proves profitable. Thus, Federal Express's one-day delivery was matched by the Postal Service's overnight mail.

Although the preceding typology of organizational strategies is far from comprehensive, it does provide an overview of the basic types of strategies that organizations follow. Whether planned or emergent, every organization does have a strategy, a consistent course of action that it follows in accomplishing its purposes. Environmental conditions are key in determining what type of strategy an organization pursues and what strategic type is effective and compelling in strategic change.

SIZE

Logic, personal experience, and common sense lead one to suspect that large organizations are different from small organizations. A police department that employs 20 people ought somehow to be different from one that employs 20,000; a college with 1000 students will certainly differ from one with 25,000 students; and the Defense Department with its 1.7 million civilian and 1.8 million uniformed employees ought to be unlike any other organization in the United States. "Large organizations . . . are assumed to be more bureaucratic, less responsive to client and member needs, to contain an inordinate number of unproductive staff positions and have less satisfied employees."[53] Unfortunately, using common sense and personal experience to derive generalizations about organizations is nearly as risky as using them to derive generalizations about human behavior and personality. Although organization theorists disagree on almost every aspect of organizations examined so far, the extent of their disagreement on the impact of size on organizational behavior exceeds that on most other aspects they have examined.

The initial point of disagreement is over how size should be determined. The most obvious measure of an organization's size would appear to be the number of employees, but other measures are frequently used: prison size is frequently designated by the number of prisoners; school size by the number of students; library size by the number of books and periodicals; hospital size by the number of patients; and bank size by the value of assets. Fortunately, because the number of employees would appear to have the most significant impact on structure, nature of jobs, and employee satisfaction, researchers have determined that there is a high correlation between number of employees and the other possible measures of size.[54] Still, there are glaring exceptions to this generalization. In employee size, the Department of Defense clearly dwarfs the Department of Health and Human Services (DHHS), which employs approximately 137,000 people; in terms of financial resources, however, DHHS, with a budget of $318.5 billion for fiscal year 1986, is larger than DOD, with its $265.3 billion. Though other measures do exist, number of employees will be used as the measure of size for the remainder of this section.

Size and Structure

J. B. S. Haldane, in his classic essay, "On Being the Right Size," noted, "It is easy to show that a hare could not be as large as a hippopotamus or a whale as small as a herring. For every animal [organization] there is a convenient size, and a large change in size inevitably carries with it a change in form."[55]

If we were to compare a police department with twenty-five employees with one employing twenty-five thousand, we might expect the larger department to have more specialized units, such as a homicide division, a burglary division, and a vice squad, that coordinating these specialized units would require a steeper hierarchy, that the organization would be more geographically dispersed, that control would require more formalization, and that even with increased formalization, the difficulties of direct supervision and control would result in increased discretion and more bureaucratic decentralization. We might even expect this to characterize the differences between large and small organizations generally. Unfortunately, for every researcher who has found these generalizations to be true, another researcher has found them to be invalid.

Supporting the contention that size causes structure are the Aston group, Marshall Meyer, Peter Blau, Henry Mintzberg, and Pradip Khandwalla. The Aston group, led by D. S. Pugh, studied business organizations and concluded unequivocally that size was the primary determinant of structure.[56] Meyer studied the structures of 194 city, county, and state departments of finance and similarly concluded that size was the single most important determinant of structure, especially of structural differentiation, both horizontally and vertically.[57] Peter Blau and associates studied 53 state employment agencies with 387 divisions and 1,201 local offices. They concluded that increased size is correlated with increased specialization, increased spatial dispersion, increased size of individual units, and increased number of hierarchical levels.[58] Mintzberg similarly asserts that increased size is associated with increased specialization, differentiation of units, and formalization and an enlarged administrative component.[59] Khandwalla arrived at similar conclusions.[60]

Walter Boland found a particularly interesting impact of size in universities. In large universities, faculty members were more powerful in controlling educational policy than in small ones; students bore the main brunt of increased bureaucratization as education became more routinized and formalized. Similarly, large universities were characterized by the development of a "center" at the highest organizational level to handle external relations crucial to maintenance and development.[61] Although Boland did not deal with goals, this might indicate that large organizations emphasize systems goals and the goals of members at the expense of substantive goals.

Opposite conclusions about the impact of size and structure were reached by Hall, Haas, and Johnson; Aldrich; and Dewar and Hage. Haas, Hall, and Johnson studied a broad range of organizations, ranging in size from 6 to 9000 members, including a public school system, a post office, a state hospital, and a government regulatory agency. They concluded that "size may be rather irrelevant as a factor in determining organizational structure. . . . [T]he relationships between size and other structural components are inconsistent. Neither complexity nor formalization can be implied from knowledge of organizational size."[62] Dewar and Hage studied sixteen social service agencies and concluded that no relationship existed between size and structure.[63] After reexamining the data of Pugh and associates, Aldrich arrived at a similar conclusion.[64]

Although the conflict between these two points of view appears irreconcilable, a common ground—in this instance, an intervening variable— may provide the key. Aldrich and Dewar and Hage believed, based on their research, that technology was more important in determining structure than was size: routinized, automated technology results in increased formalization, standardization, and centralized control. Hall, for example, asserted that if the technology of an organization is routinized, formalization and complexity increase with size; if the technology is nonroutine, the relationship will not hold.[65] Nonetheless, size may determine technology. The evidence is very strong that size is the best single predictor of computer use and automation.[66] Computerization of tasks is synonymous with routinization. Meyer, in studying the impact of automation in state and local finance departments, found that automation resulted in increased levels of hierarchy, larger individual units, wider span of control for first-line supervisors and narrower spans for top managers.[67]

In people-processing organizations, particularly those with limited ability to control demand for their services, size affects the choice of technology in more than just computerization. The more students that must be educated, the more prisoners housed, the more mental patients institutionalized, the greater the pressure on the organization to adopt a routine technology. Organizations treating a small, limited number of clients may be able to treat them as unique individuals and provide personalized, intensive treatment; large organizations rarely have either the staff or resources to do so. Further, large organizations experience more repetitive behaviors, problems, and situations. There is more predictability and thus enhanced possibility of formulating standard operating procedures to guide member behavior in dealing with recurring problems. Finally, as will be discussed later, large organizations seem to be more subject to dysfunctional behavior on the part of employees. As a result of attempts to control and regulate this behavior, rules proliferate. Thus, when large size is combined with routine technology, increased formalization results.[68]

Parkinson's Law

Work expands so as to fill the time available for its completion. . . . Granted that work is thus elastic in its demand on time, it is manifest that there need be little or no relationship between the work to be done and the size of the staff to which it may be assigned. . . . [T]he fact is that the number of the officials and the quantity of the work are not related to each other at all.[69]

Parkinson expanded his satirical law to "prove" that in organizations, administrators would proliferate far more rapidly than line personnel or, for that matter, work to be done. What Parkinson wrote in satire, organization theorists took seriously, and they attempted to verify his conclusion. Again, personal experience frequently seems to validate the idea that large organizations are top heavy, and anecdotal evidence is easy to come by. George Berkeley lists the following examples of Parkinson's Law in action in the federal government:

During World War II, 12 million men and women were in the military; they were commanded by 139 three and four star generals and admirals. By 1972, the military had decreased to 2.5 million but the number of three and four star generals and admirals had increased to 190. From 1970–73, the Postal Service reduced its work force by 63,000; at the same time, however, the number of assistant postmasters general doubled, going from eight to seventeen.[70]

If Parkinson is correct, large organizations are less efficient than smaller organizations because the more of its resources an organization has to devote to internal administration, the fewer resources available for functional activities.

Although many studies have been undertaken to determine whether the administrative component is proportionately larger in large organizations, the results are inconclusive. Terrien and Mills studied 428 public school districts in California and concluded that the administrative component did indeed increase as the size of the schools increased.[71] A similar conclusion was reached by Raphael in a study of labor unions and by Hinings and Bryan in a study of churches.[72]

The opposite conclusion was reached by Anderson and Warkov after studying forty-nine Veterans' Administration Hospitals, by Daft and Becker in their study of school districts, and by Blau in his study of employment security agencies.[73] Anderson and Warkov found that although administrative intensity was negatively related to size, it was positively related to functional complexity. Blau found counterpressures operating to both increase and decrease the proportion of administrators as the organization grew. Growth was accompanied by increased specialization, which meant that less supervision was needed within units, and consequently, span of control could be considerably increased; at the same time, differentiation also increased, and this required more coordination among departments, and thus more administrators. After reviewing all of the studies on size and administrative intensity, Child concluded that "most published studies have supported the counterhypothesis that the larger the size of the containing organization, the smaller will be the proportion of employees given over to its supportive component."[74]

Reconciling these apparently conlicting research findings may not be as difficult as might be thought. First, Haas, Hall, and Johnson found in their reevaluation of the Aston group's studies that the relationship between size and administrative component was curvilinear—the size of the administrative component was larger for smaller (fewer than 700 employees) and larger organizations (more than 1,400 employees).[75] As size increased, the organization could take advantage of economies of scale: increased computerization and fuller utilization of the capabilities of support personnel. Beyond a certain point, however, diseconomies of scale emerged: difficulty in controlling behavior, communications problems, and coordination problems requiring an increase in administrative and support staff. Second, the research studies themselves are not directly comparable because they use widely differing definitions of the administrative component, ranging from only those personnel who were classified by the organization as administrative (Anderson and Warkov) to all support personnel—clerical, maintenance, and professional staff (Hall, Haas, and Johnson). Thus in reality, the studies were examining two very different phenomena. Finally, one variable almost never completely explains changes in another variable in organization theory, and other researchers have found that the size of the administrative component is partially determined by environmental complexity, technological complexity, and spatial dispersion of the organization.[76]

Child cautions that a final factor that has not been studied may be crucial in determining administrative intensity: organizational politics, which of course brings us back to Parkinson. In the struggle to achieve status, prestige, and power in organizations, administrators may multiply their subordinates: administrative assistants and assistants to those assistants are hired and in turn require clerical and staff support; and, as Parkinson noted, "officials make work for each other."[77]

Size and Member Behavior

Large size also has diverse and conflicting impacts on the individuals who work in the organization. On the positive side, large organizations provide enhanced opportunities for status and power; for professionals they provide more resources to carry out their professions and generally offer more opportunity for career advancement. It seems likely that large organizations also have lower expectations of job performance because the contribution of individual members to goal accomplishment is relatively insignificant and difficult to measure.

On the other hand, size has long been suspected of causing increased worker alienation and dissatisfaction. Partly, this stems from the changed nature of personal relationships on the job and the decreased importance of specific individuals to the organization:

> The loose, flexible, personalized way of conducting affairs diminishes and in its place comes closer control to what must be and what must not be done. Relationships between jobs and people become more formalized, less personal. There is greater emphasis on personal competence and less on personal acceptability. As a result, the organization becomes less dependent on the services of particular individuals. Organization members may come and go or shift locations with less impact on the overall performance of the organization.[78]

This, in turn, results in an increase in certain types of dysfunctional behavior: tardiness, absenteeism, accident rates, turnover rates, and strikes.[79]

Once again, however, research does not provide definitive proof that large size equates with worker dissatisfaction. Meltzer and Salter found that for scientific researchers the relationship between size and job satisfaction was actually curvilinear, with dissatisfaction highest in both small and large organizations.[80] Kahn and associates noted a similar curvilinear relationship between size and stress:

> Stress and organizational size are substantially related. The curve of stress begins to rise as we turn from tiny organizations to those of 50 to 100 persons and the rising curve continues until we encounter the organizational giants. Only for organizations of more than 5000 persons does the curve of stress level off—perhaps because an organization so large represents some kind of psychological infinity and further increases are unfelt.[81]

In seems equally likely that small work groups, which develop in large organizations as well as smaller ones, mitigate the impact of impersonality and alleviate some, if not all, of its negative consequences. The likelihood that large organizations are also usually geographically dispersed into smaller operating units has a similar mitigating impact.

CONCLUSION

This chapter examined three aspects of organizations that are central to their performance: technology, strategy, and size. An organization's operating technology is central to its ability to accomplish its goals. As we have seen, one of the major obstacles to goal accomplishment for many public organizations is the lack of a known technology that successfully converts inputs into desired outputs. One of the ironies of organizational behavior is that this has less impact on day to day activities within the organization than might be expected. The organizations tend to develop a routine procedure and follow it, showing minimal concern about its effectiveness as a technology. As they do with so many other aspects of administration, when faced with choosing a technology, organizations satisfice.

Similarly, strategic choice also appears usually to be a matter of satisficing, or in this instance muddling through. Despite persistent suggestions from decision-making theorists that organizations should rationally determine and follow long-range strategy if they wish to maximize goal achievement, most organization strategy is determined or evolved incrementally. For public organizations in particular, rational strategic planning may be both politically inadvisable and impossible. Vague goals, unclear technologies, and annual, uncertain appropriations by definition eliminate the possibility of rationality. Clarity, specificity, and long-range plans may only serve to mobilize political opposition and undermine the organization's support.

Size, obviously an important characteristic of an organization, appears to have no uniform, universal impact on organization structure, administrative intensity, or employees. It does enhance the organization's power and likelihood of survival, but beyond that its impact appears to be mitigated by a variety of intervening variables, including goals, technology, and environment.

NOTES

1. Richard L. Daft, *Organization Theory and Design* (St. Paul: West Publishing, 1983), p. 159.
2. See Joan Woodward, *Industrial Organizations: Theory and Practice* (London: Oxford University Press, 1965).
3. Arthur G. Bedeian, *Organizations: Theory and Analysis* (Hinsdale, Ill.: The Dryden Press, 1980), pp. 212–214.

4. Charles Perrow, "A Framework for the Comparative Analysis of Organizations," *American Sociological Review* (1967): pp. 196–97.
5. Charles Perrow, "Hospitals: Technology, Structure and Goals," in James G. March, ed., *Handbook of Organizations* (Chicago: Rand McNally, 1965), p. 915.
6. Charles Perrow, *Organizational Analysis: A Sociological View* (Belmont: Wadsworth Publishing Company, Inc., 1970), p. 75.
7. Ibid., p. 76.
8. Ibid., p. 78.
9. Daniel Moynihan, *The Politics of Guaranteed Income* (New York: Vintage, 1973), p. 240.
10. B. Guy Peters, *American Public Policy: Promise and Performance*, 2nd ed. (Chatham: Chatham House Publishers, Inc., 1986), p. 86.
11. Perrow, "Hospitals: Technology, Structure and Goals," p. 914.
12. Ibid, p. 915.
13. Fred Kramer, "Public Management in the 1980s and Beyond," *Annals of the American Academy of Political and Social Sciences* 466 (March 1983): pp. 91–102.
14. Perrow, *Organizational Analysis*, p. 81.
15. Alfred Chandler, *Strategy and Structure: Chapters in the History of the Industrial Enterprise* (Cambridge: MIT Press, 1962), p. 13.
16. Alan Steiss, *Strategic Management and Organization Decisionmaking* (Lexington, Mass.: Lexington Books, 1985), pp. 13–14.
17. L. J. Bourgeois, "Strategy and Environment: A Conceptual Integration," *Academy of Management Review* (January 1980): p. 45.
18. Henry Mintzberg, *The Structuring of Organizations* (Englewood Cliffs, N.J.: Prentice Hall, 1983), p. 25.
19. See M. S. Wortman, "Strategic Management: Not-for-Profit Organizations," in D. E. Schendel and C. W. Hofer, eds., *Strategic Management: A New View of Business Policy and Planning* (Boston: Little, Brown, 1979), pp. 353–381.
20. Charles Levine, "Police Management in the 1980s: From Decrementalism To Strategic Thinking," *Public Administration Review* (November 1985): p. 692.
21. John Child, "Organization Strategic Choice," *Sociology* (January 1972): pp. 1–22.
22. Howard Aldrich, *Organizations and Environments* (Englewood Cliffs, N.J.: Prentice Hall, 1979), p. 136.
23. Peter Smith Ring and James L. Perry, "Strategic Management in Public and Private Organizations: Implications and Distinctive Contexts and Constraints," *Academy of Management Review* (1985): pp. 276–286.
24. Quoted in Ibid., p. 281.
25. Jewell Hage, *Theories of Organizations* (New York: John Wiley, 1980), p. 423.
26. Ibid., p. 435.
27. Levine, "Police Management in the 1980s," p. 691.
28. Irving Janis and Leon Mann, *Decisionmaking* (New York: Free press, 1977), p. 33.
29. See Charles Lindblom, "The Science of Muddling Through," *Public Administration Review* (January/February 1959): pp. 9–99, and "Still Muddling, Not Yet Through," *Public Administration Review* (November/December 1979): pp. 517–526.
30. Janis and Mann, *Decisionmaking*, p. 33.
31. Amitai Etzioni, *The Active Society* (New York: Free Press, 1968), pp. 271–272.
32. Kenneth Boulding, "Review of a Strategy of Decision," *American Sociological Review* (1964): p. 931.
33. Levine, "Police Management In the 1980s," p. 692.
34. Lindblom, "Still Muddling, Not Yet Through," p. 524.

35. Karl Popper, *The Open Society and Its Enemies* (Princeton: Princeton University Press, 1963), p. 158.
36. Henry Mintzberg, "Patterns in Strategy Formulation," *Management Science* (May 1978): p. 935.
37. Ibid., p. 935.
38. Ibid., p. 948.
39. Ibid., p. 947.
40. Ring and Perry, "Strategic Management", p. 284.
41. Mintzberg, *The Structuring of Organizations*, p. 345.
42. Ibid., p. 363.
43. Barton Wechsler and Robert Backoff, "Policy Making and Administration in State Agencies: Strategic Management Approaches," *Public Administration Review* (July/August 1986): p. 324.
44. Mintzberg, *The Structuring of Organizations*, p. 443.
45. M. K. Chandler and L. R. Sayles, *Managing Large Systems* (New York: Harper & Row, 1971), p. 174.
46. Ibid., p. 7.
47. Raymond Miles, Charles Snow, Alan Meyer, and Henry Coleman, Jr., "Organizational Strategy, Structure and Process," *Academy of Management Review* (July 1978): pp. 548–562.
48. Wechsler and Backoff, "Policy Making and Administration in State Agencies," p. 324.
49. Randall Ripley and Grace A. Franklin, *Congress, the Bureaucracy and Public Policy* (Homewood, Ill.: Dorsey Press, 1984), p. 111.
50. The preceding discussion was based on ibid., pp. 113–117.
51. See Kenneth J. Meier, *Politics And Bureaucracy*, 2nd ed. (Monterey, Calif.: Brooks/Cole Publishing Co., 1987), pp. 13–14, and Ripley and Franklin, *Congress, the Bureaucracy and Public Policy*, pp. 161–163.
52. *National Journal*, January 11, 1986, p. 108.
53. Daniel Robey, *Designing Organizations: A Macro Perspective* (Homewood, Ill.: Richard D. Irwin, 1982), p. 196.
54. For example, D. S. Pugh, D. J. Hickson, C. R. Hinings, and C. Turner, "The Context of Organization Structures," *Administrative Science Quarterly* (March 1969): pp. 91–114, found the correlation coefficient between net assets and number of employees to be .78; Theodore Anderson and Seymour Warkov, "Organization Size and Functional Complexity: A Study of Administration in Hospitals," *American Sociological Review* (February 1961): p. 25, found the correlation between patient load and work force size to be .966; and Amos Hawley, Walter Boland, and Margaret Boland, "Population Size and Administration in Institutions of Higher Education," *American Sociological Review* (April 1965): p. 253, found the correlation between student enrollment and faculty size to be .94.
55. J.B.S. Haldane, "On Being the Right Size," in Haldane, *Possible Worlds and Other Papers* (New York: Harper and Brothers, 1982), p. 5.
56. Pugh et al., "The Context of Organization Structures," p. 112.
57. Marshall Meyer, "Size and the Structure of Organizations: A Causal Model," *American Sociological Review* (1972): pp. 434–441.
58. Peter Blau and Richard Schoenherr, *The Structure of Organizations* (New York: Basic Books, 1971), pp. 55–81, and Blau, "A Formal Theory of Differentiation in Organizations," *American Sociological Review* (1970): pp. 201–218.
59. Mintzberg, *The Structuring of Organizations*, pp. 230–233.
60. Pradip Khandwalla, *The Design of Organizations* (New York: Harcourt, Brace, Jovanovich, 1977), p. 297.

61. Walter R. Boland, "Size, External Relations and the Distribution of Power: A Study of Colleges and Universities," in Wolf Heydebrand, ed., *Comparative Organizations* (Englewood Cliffs, N.J.: Prentice Hall, 1973), p. 439.
62. Richard Hall, J. Eugene Haas, and Norman Johnson, "Organization Size, Complexity and Formalization," *American Sociological Review* (December 1967): pp. 911–912.
63. R. Dewar and J. Hage, "Size, Technology, Complexity and Structural Differentiation," *Administrative Science Quarterly* (1978); pp. 328–346.
64. H. E. Aldrich, "Technology and Organization Structure: A Reexamination of the Findings of the Aston Group," *Administrative Science Quarterly* (1972): pp. 26–43.
65. Richard Hall, *Organizations: Structure and Process* (Englewood Cliffs, N.J.: Prentice Hall, 1972), p. 119.
66. B. DeBander, Q. DeSchoolmeister, R. Leyder, and E. Vanlommel, "The Effect of Task Volume and Complexity on Computer Use," *Journal of Business* (1972): p. 56–84.
67. Marshall Meyer, "Automation and Bureaucratic Structure," *American Journal of Sociology* (November 1968): p. 574.
68. Mintzberg, *The Structuring of Organizations*, p. 235.
69. C. Northcote Parkinson, *Parkinson's Law and Other Studies of Administration* (New York: Ballantine Books, 1957), pp. 2–3.
70. George E. Berkeley, *The Craft of Administration*, 4th ed. (Boston: Allyn and Bacon, 1984), pp. 92–93.
71. F. W. Terrien and D. L. Mills, "The Effect of Changing Size upon the Internal Structure of Organizations," *American Sociological Review* (1955): pp. 11–13.
72. E. Raphael, "The Anderson-Warkov Hypothesis in Local Unions: A Comparative Study," *American Sociological Review* (1967): pp. 768–776, and C. R. Hinings and A. Bryan, "Size and the Administrative Component in Churches," *Human Relations* (1967): pp. 457–475.
73. Theodore Anderson and Seymour Warkov, "Organizational Size and Functional Complexity," *American Sociological Review* (1961): pp. 23–28; Richard Daft and Selwyn Becker, "District Size and the Deployment of Personnel Resources," *The Alberta Journal of Educational Research* (1978): p. 181; Blau and Schoenherr, *The Structure or Organizations*.
74. John Child, "Parkinson's Progress," *Administrative Science Quarterly* (1973): p. 328.
75. J. Eugene Haas, Richard Hall, and Norman Johnson, "The Size of the Supportive Component in Organizational Analysis: A Multiorganizational Analysis," *Social Forces* (October 1963): p. 15.
76. I. J. Freeman, "Environment, Technology and the Administrative Intensity of Manufacturing Organizations," *American Sociological Review* (1973): pp. 750–763; Child, "Parkinson's Progress," p. 328.
77. Parkinson, *Parkinson's Law and Other Studies of Administration*, p. 4.
78. Joseph Litterer, *The Analysis of Organizations*, 2nd ed. (New York: John Wiley, 1973), p. 668.
79. Robey, *Designing Organizations: A Macro Perspective*, p. 207.
80. Leo Meltzer and James Salter, "Organizational Structure and the Performance and Job Satisfaction of Physiologists," *American Sociological Review* (June 1962): pp. 351–362.
81. Robert Kahn, Donald Wolfe, Robert Quinn, J. Diedrick Sroek, and Robert Rosenthal, *Organizational Stress: Studies in Role Conflict and Ambiguity* (New York: John Wiley, 1964), p. 394.

5

ORGANIZATIONAL CHANGE

"The more things change, the more they are insane."[1]

Change is inevitable for individuals, organizations, and society. Technology changes, values and attitudes change, goals and needs change, resource availability changes, laws change, political control of government changes. As has been noted in earlier chapters, change is endemic, it is frequently unpredictable and uncontrollable, and the rate of change appears to be increasing. If all of this constant change is unsettling for individuals, it is equally so for organizations. Change disturbs their internal equilibriums and disrupts their relationships with their environment. Change comes in many forms, and not all change is beneficial—it almost always involves costs as well as benefits. Even if change is ultimately beneficial, organizations, like individuals, frequently resist and resent it. The inevitability of change and the necessity for organizations to adapt to it make it one of the most important concerns of contemporary organization theory.

This chapter will examine organizational change: why and when it is necessary, its major types, why it is resisted, and the processes and procedures organizations use to implement it. Three of the most significant types of change that organizations experience, aging, growth, and decline, will be examined separately.

THE MORE THINGS CHANGE, THE MORE
ORGANIZATIONS FIGHT TO REMAIN THE SAME

Organizations are complex social systems with well-defined, established procedures, processes, and patterns of interpersonal relationships. Their established formal structure is supplemented by an equally firmly established informal structure, and both structures allocate power, status, prestige, and satisfaction to members. Though as open systems they constantly receive inputs from their environment and must respond to changes in those inputs (particularly in the form of new personnel who bring new attitudes, values, and behaviors into the organization), organizations are essentially conservative. Evolutionary, incremental change that requires only minor adjustments is most easily handled. As open systems, however, they must remain responsive to their environments, and major, abrupt changes in their environments force organizations to make major internal changes as the price of survival.

For public organizations particularly, the impetus for change usually comes from the environment. New statutes expand or contract jurisdiction or modify their goals. A change in political control of the executive brings in new leadership, new policies, proposals for reorganization, and frequently new management techniques. Changes in the economy or political attitudes result in diminished resources or reductions in force. Changes in civil service laws change recruitment procedures and the type of individuals being brought into the organization. Professions change their procedures and new technologies must be incorporated. Public or client attitudes or needs change and service delivery must be modified to accommodate them. Political, public, judicial, media, or professional evaluation may indicate that the organization is performing inadequately, and demands may be made that the organization improve its performance.

Change for public agencies is dialectical.[2] Demands for change are constant, and responding to those changes frequently triggers demands for further change. Initial goals meet resistance from environmental actors, so new goals are developed; innovations intended to solve one problem often create others. Low productivity frequently leads to automation, which in turn leads to boredom, monotony, and declining productivity. "Problems are endemic and therefore serve as a continual source of change in the system. . . . Final solutions and perfect adjustments are impossible."[3]

Pressures, tensions, and demands on the organization may require change in organizational goals, technology, structure, management style, or personnel. Even in the most loosely coupled organization, a change in any one area triggers or requires changes in others. All too frequently, intended change fails because the agent of change neglects subsidiary aspects involved in implementing a change. Even more frequently, proponents of change underestimate the scope and intensity of the resistance mandated changes will meet, resulting in the failure of the change effort and the loss of intended benefits.

In large part, organizations resist change because people resist change, and people frequently resist change because it is perceived as threatening to some valued self-interest. Structural change, for example, may disrupt established and valued interpersonal relationships or change the status, power, or compensation of individuals in the organization. Similarly, technological change may be viewed as implied criticism, wounding workers' self-esteem. Workers may fear that their skills and abilities will be devalued, that they will be unable to acquire needed new skills, and that new technology will result in less satisfying and more boring or monotonous jobs. Any change implemented in the interest of improving efficiency will raise fears of forthcoming reductions in force and the possibility of unemployment. All of these fears will be compounded if workers lack confidence in the integrity of management or those who are attempting to effect change. From the perspective of rational man theory, change does impose costs; thus many of the fears that workers have of change are valid, and the things they fear most will in fact result from changing the organization.[4] Unless the perceived benefits of the change outweigh the costs, individuals will resist.

Individual tolerance for change varies considerably. For some, "facing the unknown consequences of change is a fundamental threat challenging their sense of adequacy and self-esteem."[5] For others, change is less threatening and may be viewed as challenging and satisfying. One of the crucial factors in determining response to change appears to be how much change an individual is accustomed to experiencing: "Sheer experience with innovation develops a capacity for tolerance of change."[6] From this perspective, the more things change, the more individuals are likely to accept the change; what causes the most resistance is acceleration in the rate of change.

Although individuals within an organization are the major source of resistance to change, individuals external to the organization, particularly clients and consumers, may also resist changes that affect them. College students, welfare recipients, hospital patients, and veterans would be as likely to resist major innovation in the ways that services are delivered to them as would the organizations required to implement the changes. The reasons for client resistance are similar to those for worker resistance: fear of loss of self-esteem, status, or compensation, fear of being unable to understand and adapt to the changed system, and fear of further dehumanization by more efficient technological systems of service delivery.

Ironically, although the environment may be the major source of demand for organizational change, it may also constitute a major barrier to change for some organizations. Social and cultural values and beliefs about how educational institutions, hospitals, prisons, police departments, welfare programs, and countless other public services should be organized and operate may effectively bar innovations that conflict with those values.

Organization structure may constitute an additional barrier to change. Once the organization has become formalized and developed written rules, regulations, and standard operating procedures, change that requires comprehensive revision of those rules becomes difficult. From this it would seem to follow that bureaucracies are the most difficult organizations to change, and this has been one of the most recurrent and vehement criticisms of bureaucracy.

Strangely, the evidence does not support this criticism. Blau, in his study of employment agencies, found no rigid opposition to internal change among civil service officials, noting rather that "bureaucratic conditions engender favorable attitudes toward change."[7] Blau's explanation for bureaucratic receptiveness to change was that the job security provided by civil service eliminated many of the fears workers have about change and that the very routinization of tasks characteristic of bureaucracy creates a desire for challenge and variety. Further, the agencies Blau studied were accustomed to change because their rules and regulations were constantly altered to fit changing statutory requirements.

Hage found that machine bureaucracies are more susceptible to radical change than are organic structured organizations. Organic structures are more suited to evolutionary change because of the decentralized nature of their power structures. "Thus, we are led to a curious paradox—namely that mechanical organizations . . . are also places where radical innovation can occur, because they are more likely to have crises as well as a structure that is more tolerant of dictatorial practices."[8] A final explanation for bureaucracies' ability to implement radical change lies in their propensity "to run like elephants." If the change plan is well developed and clearly articulated, the inherent nature of bureaucracy is to implement it.

The culture, climate, and age of an organization also determine its willingness and ability to change. The culture of an organization comprises the shared beliefs, attitudes, and values of members that determine organizational norms of behavior. The more widely and firmly held a set of values, the more difficult they will be to change. A change that conflicts with basic values about what the organization does or how it should do it will meet strong resistance.[9] Organizational climate refers to levels of satisfaction with and acceptance of the organization culture by its members. High levels of dissatisfaction may either help or hinder change. If members believe that the change will alleviate some of the sources of dissatisfaction, they may welcome it. If the climate of the organization is characterized by mistrust and high levels of conflict between work groups and management, change will be regarded skeptically and generally resisted. Both old and young organizations will resist changes in this task structures—the programs that constitute the means by which they achieve their goals—because this type of change upsets routines and redistributes power. For other types of change, age of the organization helps determine the level of resistance. Old organizations are more likely to resist changes that disrupt established social relations, but they will frequently support changes in goals; young organizations are more likely to resist changes in goals.[10] As organizations age, members develop commitment to the organization rather than to specific goals. Consequently, members are more likely to support goal changes that will enable the organization to survive and grow. In newer organizations, members' primary commitment is to the goals or the purposes of the organization, and they will resist attempts to change the goals.

Although organizational change is possible, it is difficult and demanding. More often than not, change will be resisted and unless special efforts are made to alleviate fears and reduce resistance, change will not occur.

THE CHANGE PROCESS

In 1947, Kurt Lewin described the process of changing individual behavior as involving three steps: unfreezing, moving, and refreezing.[11] The same steps are involved in organization change. Unfreezing behavior means disturbing the equilibrium of the organization sufficiently to make the organization ready and willing to change. The next step, moving, involves the introduction of change; the final step, refreezing, integrates the change into the organization's culture and behavior.

Hage provides a four-step model of the change process for organizations that is basically similar to Lewin's. The first step is evaluation (unfreezing). The recognition by key actors of a performance gap that threatens the organization triggers demands for change, and according to Hage, this is precisely why many public organizations do not change. Performance measurements, particularly for people-processing organizations, are either nonexistent or extremely countroversial, primarily because of the vagueness of the organizations' goals. If there is no agreement as to what schools, prisons, police departments, the Department of Defense, and countless other public organizations are supposed to be accomplishing, measurement of their performance is difficult if not impossible. Without such measurement, however, no information on performance gaps is available, and there can be no impetus to change.[12] Consequently, some type of crisis, financial or otherwise, will be required to convince the organization that change is necessary.

Once the need for change has been recognized, the next step is initiation: development of an idea or plan to change the organization to improve its performance or at least cope with the crisis. The idea is generated either internally or externally, but it requires a clear understanding both of the source of the organization's problem and of what type of change is needed to solve the problem. Public organizations frequently face severe difficulties at this stage. Bureaucracies may be successful in implementing change, but little evidence suggests that they are adept at initiating change. Radical innovation almost always involves technological change, and given the uncertain technologies of many public organizations, such change is unlikely to be developed, and in the rare instances when it is, it meets resistance from the public and clients as well as from the organization. Changes initiated by such bureaucracies are far more likely to be incremental than radical.

Once the desired change has been identified, it must be implemented. Resources—both money and personnel—must be obtained, and the difficult task of convincing organization members to cooperate must be undertaken. Resistance to change takes two forms: passive resistance—reluctance and unwillingness to cooperate—and overt, active conflict—disagreement about the change. The greatest conflict is most likely to occur when those who have proposed the change perceive the performance gap and the other members of the organization do not.[13] Excessive resistance or conflict which is not dealt with successfully may result in the nullification of the change effort.

Once the change effort is implemented, it must be routinized—behavior, attitudes, and values must be refrozen. Because change is disruptive and involves real costs in time and money, the temptation to expect quick and dramatic positive results is strong. Consequently, premature attempts to evaluate the change may be undertaken both to prove its effectiveness and to mute continuing resistance and conflict. Unfortunately, this is usually unwise. First, proving the positive impact of a change is difficult for many public organizations for the same reason that recognition of performance gaps is difficult: the lack of valid output measures makes it extremely difficult to prove a change has had a positive impact; thus, routinization may not occur. Second, the more radical the change, the more disruption it will have caused and the longer the time it will require to become routinized and to result in positive outcomes. The earlier the evaluation is made, the more likely it is that the costs will outweigh the benefits. The longer a change is in effect, the more sunk costs the organization will have in it, and at some point those sunk costs become sufficient to ensure that the organization will be unwilling to abandon it. The possibilities of routinization are enhanced by these sunk costs.

Successful implementation and routinization of change is a complex and difficult process, and a great many changes that are initiated fail to survive the implementation process. One of the ironies of organizational change is that the organization structure most likely to generate innovative ideas is also least compatible with successful implementation and routinization. Organic structures characterized by decentralization, low formalization, and high professionalism are best for generating innovative ideas, but those same characteristics make implementation difficult and resistance easier.[14] This has led some organization theorists to suggest that the most effective and surest way to ensure implementation is to create a new unit with new personnel or an entirely new organization whenever a major change is initiated.[15] Others have suggested that organizations must become ambidextrous, incorporating structures that are appropriate to both initiation and implementation. This requires the creation of parallel organizations, institutionalizing "a set of externally and internally responsive, participatory problem solving structures alongside the conventional line organization that carries out routine tasks."[16] In times of ample financial resources, such suggestions deserve careful consideration, but the current reality for many public organizations is that they have few resources to allocate to new units and many are also forced by circumstances to implement change with existing structures.

OVERCOMING RESISTANCE TO CHANGE: STRATEGIES FOR SUCCESSFULLY IMPLEMENTING CHANGE

Two basically contrasting strategies exist for implementing change: top-down and power equalization. Top-down change strategy is characterized by a unilateral use of power. "Change is implemented through an emphasis on the authority of a man's hierarchical position . . . there the definition and solution to the problem at hand tend to be specified by the upper echelons and directed downward through formal and impersonal control mechanisms."[17] Changes are decreed by those at the top of the organization, and implementation frequently involves the replacement of individuals in key positions and structural modifications that change the relationships of subordinates working in the organization. Power equalization strategies involve either shared power (where authority is still vested in those at the top, yet there is also interaction and sharing of power)[18] or delegated power "where almost complete responsibility for defining and acting on problems is turned over to the subordinates."[19] Obviously, proponents of participatory management are convinced that power equalization strategies, particularly the shared power approach, are more effective than top-down strategy. At least theoretically, the shared power strategy should increase understanding of and commitment to the changes, improve the quality of the changes, enrich workers' jobs, and encourage democracy in the work place.[20]

As is true of so many other aspects of organization theory, which strategy works best depends on a variety of factors. Power equalization strategies are most likely to be successful when there is no time pressure for implementing and routinizing the change, when the problem that has triggered the need for change is not generally recognized throughout the organization, when knowledge required to implement the change is widely dispersed, when members of the organization expect participation, and when the power base of the change agent is small.[21] Changes in technology or in people are also facilitated by power equalization strategies.[22] Top-down strategies are likely to work better when the change must be accomplished quickly, when the need for change is widely recognized, when knowledge about the change is concentrated at the top, when members expect authoritative change, and when the power base of the change agent is great.[23] Structural and administrative changes are facilitated by a top-down process.[24]

Regardless of the strategy selected, resistance to the change must be anticipated and analyzed, and techniques should be selected for minimizing it. The first step involves identifying the likely sources of resistance. Depending on the sources and reasons for resistance, one or more of the following methods should be used to deal with it: education and communication, participation and involvement, facilitation and support, negotiation and agreement, manipulation and cooptation, or explicit and implicit coercion.[25] Education and communication are essential in all change situations; if the people who will be affected and must implement the change do not understand it or have no knowledge of it, little positive change is likely to result. If lack of information, inaccurate information, or misunderstanding is the major source of resistance, education and communication may be all that is required to eliminate resistance.

Participation and involvement is the basic requisite of power equalizing, a method of reducing resistance based on the belief that people who participate in the development, initiation, and implementation of change will be committed to it. Power equalization is also based on the assumption that the members of the system targeted for change "are rational, possess the required expertise to contribute meaningfully and are willing to act in good faith."[26] Facilitation and support involves providing employee counseling and therapy and is particularly useful when resistance is based on fear and anxiety. It helps employees understand the need for change and their feelings about it and then helps them work through these feelings toward support of change. Facilitation and support techniques are expensive, time consuming, and frequently unsuccessful.[27]

Negotiation involves "the sequential exchange of resources, sanctions, accommodations, and rewards, with the intent of reaching some mutually acceptable position."[28] It is most useful in situations "where someone or some group will clearly lose out in a change, and where that group has considerable power to resist."[29] The basic disadvantage of negotiation is that it sets the precedent for bargaining with those who resist, increasing the time and expense necessary to implement the change and running the risk of so diluting the proposed change that it will not accomplish intended results.

All of the preceding methods may be used in both top-down and power-equalizing strategies, but the remaining methods are characteristic of top-down approaches only. Manipulation, which "involves advocating a position through a presentation designed to appeal to the particular interests or sensitivities" of the resisters, may involve selective distortion of information, conscious selection of facts, and emotional appeals.[30] Cooptation is the absorption of key resisters into the power structure; the resisters gain status and prestige in exchange for endorsing the planned change. Both involve potential risks. People frequently resent having been manipulated, and once they realize they have been they may become increasingly uncooperative and hostile. Cooptation carries the obvious risk of reducing the power and discretion of organization decision makers and risks goal displacement as well. Explicit and implicit coercion both involve the use of threats and punitive actions to force acceptance of a change. Punishments for resisters range from transfers, demotions, and loss of promotion all the way to dismissal. To use coercive techniques, the change agent must possess the power to carry out the threats used to gain compliance. Thus, those who use coercion must be prepared to continue using it because it will almost inevitably generate resentment and hostility in those who have been its subjects.

Organization Development

Organization development (OD) is an approach to managing change that has received considerable attention in both the private and public sectors. No single definition for OD exists. Richard Beckhard defined it as "an effort (1) *planned,* (2) *organization-wide* and (3) *managed* from the top, to (4) increase *organization effectiveness* and *health* through (5) *planned interventions* in the organization's processes, using behavioral science knowledge."[31] To this definition must be added that OD is value laden, is consultant and third-party oriented, and relies heavily on human relations techniques.[32] It is also a lengthy and expensive process.

OD can be initiated only by top management, but it requires an OD consultant to act as a change catalyst. Usually, the first phase of OD is diagnosis. Using a variety of techniques, including survey questionnaires, personality tests, and indicators of organizational effectiveness, the change agent identifies the problems of the organization that are preventing it from achieving maximum productivity, development, and satisfaction of its employees. Despite the contention that OD can effect structural and technological change, its primary focus is on people, changing their attitudes, values, and behavior.[33] To do this it relies heavily on T-groups and sensitivity training, in which employees are encouraged—even forced—to explore their feelings, emotions, and impact on others and to assess and improve their interpersonal skills. This phase of OD can be considered the "building better people" phase, inculcating into employees the attitudes and values that encourage them to view people as essentially good, accept individual differences, express feelings, trust others, and be willing to collaborate.[34]

From building better people, OD progresses to building better teams or work groups. Again, sensitivity training and encounter groups are used to teach participants how to be more effective in group situations, to engage in joint problem solving, and to collaborate to achieve common goals. From team building, OD moves to intergroup confrontation, in which overt conflict is encouraged and conflict resolution techniques are taught. Theoretically, this reduces conflict within the organization. In the next phase, top executives review and refine organizational goals and develop a strategic plan. Special problems are identified, and in the next phase special task forces are established to develop solutions and implement plans. The final phase is evaluation and assessment.[35] The organization's progress is tracked on a managerial grid showing its movement toward total development.

Although proponents of OD are convinced of its effectiveness and its superiority over other types of change strategies, certain aspects of it raise troublesome questions. It is unquestionably value laden and based on the assumption that only one right and acceptable set of values exists. If scientific management was authoritarian in its approach, OD is totalitarian. The values underlying it must be accepted by participants; if participants do not accept those values after indoctrination through sensitivity training and encounter groups, they can have no place in the organization. Frederick Taylor was satisfied if he could control the physical movements of the workers; OD wants their hearts, souls, and minds.

Beyond this, there is no empirical evidence to prove that OD works. Even Robert Golembiewski, one of OD's strongest proponents and a practitioner of public sector OD, has been unable to provide convincing evidence that OD has brought about change in the organizations that have attempted to use it.[36] OD lacks specific means for measuring its impact on intended change targets or for identifying unanticipated changes. Its heavy, almost exclusive, reliance on human relations techniques is also troublesome. As Perrow notes, "There is only a little empirical support for the human relations school, . . . extensive efforts to find that support have resulted in increasing limitations and contingencies, and . . . the grand schemes . . . appear to be methodologically unsound and theoretically biased."[37]

McCurdy identified four factors likely to determine whether OD will succeed in an organization: resources, task, social and political setting, and extent of routinization. OD works best when the organization has ample resources, is performing nonroutine tasks, is supported by political and social values, and is experiencing turbulence and change either internally or externally.[38]

Implementing Change in Two Public Organizations

Eastham Prison. Prisons are admittedly different from most other organizations, public and private, and using a prison for an example of a change process is meant to provide not an example of change in a typical organization but rather a worst case scenario for change implementation. Nor is the case selected a textbook example of how change should be implemented; rather, it is a real life example of the costs, the problems, the frustrations and limitations of implementing radical change in an organization.[39]

Eastham prison is a unit of the Texas Department of Corrections and is located in eastern Texas. A maximum security institution, by 1982 it had become the institution where other prisons in Texas sent their worst disciplinary problems. During the 1970s its population had increased from 1,416 to 2,938, without an increase in the number of prison guards. Prisoners were housed three to a cell, and physical conditions in the prison were deplorable. Even its physical design made it an extremely difficult prison to manage: no separate catwalks were provided for the guards to patrol and observe the cell blocks.

The prison was basically unmanageable using conventional corrections methods, but because it still had to be managed, decidedly unconventional methods of management were utilized. To maintain some semblance of order, prison personnel had turned much of their responsibility and power over to "building tenders": inmates, usually the most violent and dangerous inmates in the prison. As a captain of the prison guards explained it, "To put it in sociological terms, we coopted a group of the sub-culture, and through that, we controlled the behavior. We reinforced it with a kick in the ass or a slap upside the head. That was pretty much the philosophy."[40] The tenders maintained order through fear and violence. Most of them carried weapons, and none hesitated to gang up on recalcitrant inmates and beat them. The tenders came to have more power than the guards, and guards who attempted to interfere with them were reprimanded. Eastham evolved into the antithesis of bureaucracy: there was no law, no rules controlled behavior, and the official hierarchy had little control over the organization.

In November 1981 a prison riot developed when six Hispanic prisoners who were being harassed by tenders fought back. The conflict expanded and the inmates got out of control and began burning mattresses. Although prison guards formed a riot squad, they were too few to control either the inmates or the three hundred tenders who united to retaliate against the threat to their authority. Armed with clubs, bats, chains, and knives, the tenders pursued and subdued the rebellious inmates. The tenders formed a gauntlet, a "whipping line," and forced inmates through it. Many were bludgeoned into unconsciousness; blood covered the prison floor. The guards had clearly lost control and did not attempt to intervene. Order, such as it was, was eventually restored by the tenders.

Not surprisingly, the impetus for change came from the U.S. District Court in Houston. The first inmate suit against the Texas Department of Corrections was filed in 1972. For ten years, the state successfully delayed final verdict, denying all prisoner allegations and insisting it ran an efficient, safe and cheap system. The district court judge, William Justice, initially ruled against the state in 1980 and ordered the state to institute sweeping changes, including abandonment of the tender system. The state continued to resist until the attorney general was finally persuaded by the private law firm handling the state's appeal that the charges were true and that further resistance was futile because the state would ultimately lose at the cost of extremely high legal fees. In April 1982 the state finally agreed to obey the judge's order. All that was left to do was to implement the changes.

By any measure or theory, the prospects for successful change at Eastham were dim. The change agent was external to the organization and had little operational power over those who would implement the change. Resistance to the change was widespread and intense: administrators of the Department of Corrections denied that it was necessary, and prison administrators and personnel were adamantly opposed to it. Captain Keith Price, who was appointed compliance officer, described the warden's attitude toward abolishing the tender system: "It was clear in the warden's mind that we just weren't going to do that. . . . Some of the paperwork things, that was fine to go ahead and do. But when it came to anything operational, like pinning the cells shut, that just wasn't going to happen."[41] The guards were without exception opposed to the change, and their resistance was quite justifiably based on fear. The tenders were openly and scornfully resistant and demonstrated that resistance by brutally beating an inmate who made the mistake of telling one of them that he no longer had to obey them.

Given the situation, the most rational and appealing solution would have been to disband Eastham prison, transfer all personnel and all inmates, and create a new facility. That, however, was not possible given the state's unwillingness to appropriate the necessary money. The change had to be implemented in the existing institution using existing personnel. The state's one concession was to provide 140 new guards to replace the building tenders, but the new guards were inadequate substitutes. Most were young, inexperienced, and frightened of the inmates, the tenders, and the situation.

The initial phases of the change process were disastrous. The old order crumbled, and the new one was slow to develop. In the transition stage, no one appeared to be in control of the prison. Judge Justice had warned prison officials that a power vacuum in a prison would "remain unfilled only briefly . . . predatory prisoners, disorganized or otherwise, will seize the opportunity to achieve control. As the experiences of other states have demonstrated, such power structures once they arise defy . . . vigorous efforts aimed at their elimination."[42] The power vacuum at Eastham was filled by the development of prison gangs. Violence in the prison escalated; three inmates were murdered in 1984, three more in 1985. Although an extreme case, Eastham reflected the problems of the entire Texas prison system. Statewide, more than 80,000 incidents of violence occurred in the Texas prison system in 1984-1985.

Chaos reigned in the administrative system. Eastham had four wardens in five years. The official response to the increased violence was a new policy: administrative segregation (ad-seg), otherwise known as solitary confinement, for all troublemakers. Ad-seg cells are 9 feet by 6 feet; once committed to ad-seg, a prisoner frequently spends the rest of his prison sentence there. In ad-seg, prisoners are entitled only to basics—decent food, reading material, and exercise.

> The only thing as bad as being confined to ad-seg is working there as a guard. With nothing but time on their hands, the prisoners craft weapons from available resources. . . . [W]ith little other sport they routinely curse passing guards. And when they're annoyed or go stir crazy, they fling cups of urine or feces or boiling water.[43]

The guards fiercely resented the situation. One of the captains of the guards expressed this resentment:

> "These inmates are getting new rec yards, new towels, food brought to them, and they don't have to work," he says with some bitterness. "It's not right that millions are spent for convicts who refuse to respect anyone. It gets to me that I'm working 12 to 14 hours a day and the inmate is doing nothing. And then he throws piss in an officer's face and I have to tell that officer to bring that inmate his food tray."[44]

The fourth warden appointed was the first to take a positive approach to implementing change. He instituted badly needed programs to improve staff morale, even reconditioning their clubhouse and baseball field. New techniques for controlling inmates were instituted, including the creation of a three-member conciliation team—one male guard, one female guard, and a chaplain—to defuse potentially violent situations before force had to be used. Working with limited resources, he undertook physical improvements in the prison. So change of a sort has occurred at Eastham, but major problems still remain. The prison is badly overcrowded, the system of administrative segregation is dehumanizing and brutalizing, and staff morale remains low.

Change occurred despite the fact that the change process utilized violated practically every recommendation for effective change implementation. The change was externally mandated and imposed on an organization whose members neither recognized nor accepted the reality of the performance gap that led to the mandate. Because the change agent was external to the organization, he provided no guidance on the practicalities of implementing the change. Adequate resources were not provided to carry out the mandated changes. Implementation was left to people who were clearly opposed to the change, and no attempt was ever made to deal with the causes of their resistance. Not surprisingly, the costs associated with the change were enormous. The murder and violence that erupted in the prison, the stress, fear, and frustration that the guards experienced, and the heart attack that the fourth warden suffered are the major non-monetary costs that outweigh the monetary costs of the change. The temptation to conclude that much of what occurred could have been avoided is overwhelming, but hindsight frequently leads to that conclusion. Hopefully, the Eastham experience provides some lessons, if not on how to implement change, at least on how *not* to do so.

The Post Office Department Becomes the Postal Service.   The transition from the U.S. Post Office Department to the U.S. Postal Service was nearly as dramatic and traumatic, if not as physically violent, as the changes at Eastham. Similar to the change at Eastham, the change was "imposed by a coalition of external interests onto a bureaucracy that neither sought nor welcomed the change."[45] In this case, the change was imposed by Congress and the president following recognition of a deterioration in the speed and efficiency with which the Post Office delivered the mail. Critics of the Post Office alleged that the Pony Express had been faster. The old Post Office was both highly bureaucratized and intensely political, one of the few major remaining sources of patronage at the federal level. The mandated change altered the status and structure of the Post Office from that of cabinet department to government corporation, with the clear intention that it should be run like a business, stressing the virtues of efficiency and cost control.

Resistance and open opposition to the change were widespread throughout the organization. The strategy selected by the newly appointed postmaster was clearly a top-down strategy, concentrating on two key targets: changing the ideology of the organization and changing the leadership at all levels. The old Post Office had emphasized and taken great pride in its "neither snow nor rain nor heat nor gloom of night" concentration on service at all costs. A new name, the Postal Service, reflecting the change in status to an independent agency; a new symbol, an eagle poised for flight to replace the colonial rider; and new colors, red, white, and blue to replace drab olive; were the first steps in changing the image and orientation of the organization. *Postal Life*, the internal publication of the Postal Service, was also used to change member attitudes. It changed from a publication that stressed "human interest stories and bits of information about postal history and lore"[46] to one that stressed the new ideology of efficiency and businesslike attitudes. A new publication, *Postal Leader*, directed at middle management, carried the same message. More systematic indoctrination was conducted at the newly established Postal Management Institute, where a staff of seventy-five trainers used a variety of methods to build new attitudes in postal service management personnel.

Not all of the techniques used to effect change were this benign. "In May, 1971, the Postmaster General, in a sweeping move to purge older postal officials, gave regional and headquarters employees a one-time bonus of six months pay if they would leave immediately."[47] Over two thousand accepted the offer, and an additional four thousand were transferred throughout the system. The vacancies were filled primarily by business school graduates whose orientations and commitments were more in line with the new ideology than those of their predecessors. At the same time, more than sixty-three thousand employees were eliminated in the interests of cost reduction.[48]

The Postal Service's change process is generally regarded as having been successful, and in terms of goal achievement it was. A careful examination of that process teaches us not only how change can be implemented but also an equally important lesson: that frequently the fears and anxieties of employees toward change are valid. The implemented changes were, in reality, responses to criticisms of employee performance: demotions, dismissals, transfers, and thinly veiled forced retirement were an integral part of the change process. Too often, employee resistance is believed to be based on misconceptions and misunderstanding of the impact change will have on them. When this is true, power equalization strategies are recommended. When those fears are valid, however, only a top-down strategy will succeed, for it is not only difficult but also cruel to compel people to participate in their own demise.

STRUCTURAL CHANGE: THE POLITICAL
FASCINATION WITH REORGANIZATION

Major structural change is one of the most disruptive types of change that organizations experience because it deeply affects the informal organization, the network of interpersonal relationships and communication that members have established over time. "Major structural reorganization takes several years to shake down. In their first year or two, new departments are likely to be less efficient, not more; to display lower morale, not higher; to afford greater opportunities, not smaller, for error, confusion and scandal."[49] Consequently, it would seem that structural change should be undertaken only rarely and only in response to a severe performance gap.

From an administrative perspective, several circumstances may result in an organization's being compelled to reorganize. The first, most obvious circumstance leading to reorganization is growth. We have already seen that large organizations are different from small organizations, and a structure that was workable for a small organization will not necessarily be effective for it after it has experienced considerable growth. Major changes in goals and objectives may also require structural change to reflect those changes. New technologies, automation, computerization, and new management techniques may require structural modification. Changes in the organization's environment, such as increased hostility, increased or decreased resources, increased clientele demands, or changed social needs may force the organization to modify its structure to respond effectively to those changes. Finally, changes in the work force, increased or decreased qualifications of personnel, or unionization may trigger structural changes. The administrative reasons for reorganization are relatively few, and given the costs involved, reorganization should be undertaken only rarely to address administrative changes.

Politically, reorganization is often regarded as a panacea for curing a variety of administrative and political problems. Rare is the president or governor who can resist the temptation to reorganize the executive agencies he or she nominally heads, and as March notes, these reorganization efforts are almost invariably couched in the rhetoric of orthodox administrative theory: "to facilitate the efficiency and effectiveness of bureaucratic hierarchies."[50] Whether any of the countless reorganizations that have been implemented at the federal level have actually saved money remains unknown, but all the evidence indicates that they do not.[51]

Reorganizations not justified in administrative terms may be justified in political terms. March and Olson suggest that in the rhetoric of realpolitik reorganization is a political struggle among contending interests: "fundamental political interests, within the bureaucracy and outside seek access, representation, control and policy benefits."[52] Presidents may seek reorganization to break up subgovernments, to bypass troublesome committee and subcommittee chairmen in Congress, to dump unwanted officials, to provide the appearance of decisive action, to kill an unwanted program, or to reward a supportive interest group.[53] Thus, political reorganizations become "garbage cans" into which groups and individuals dump their preferred solutions to poorly defined problems.[54] It is not surprising then that the results of reorganization are frequently so disappointing. "Few efficiencies are achieved, little gain in responsiveness is recorded; control seems as elusive after the efforts as before."[55]

THE AGING OF ORGANIZATIONS

The change processes examined so far have been those used for intended interventions in the organization's operations undertaken in response to perceived performance gaps. Organizations experience other types of change, such as aging, which is inevitable. Whether organizations go through an identifiable life cycle similar to that of people remains controversial, but almost all organization theorists agree that old organizations are different from new ones.

> Like people, organizations show the characteristics of age. Old organizations find their niche in the world. They learn to cope with their environment as well as with the needs and idiosyncrasies of their members. They reduce to a routine the solution of most of their operating problems. They also become conservative, as old folk do. They often resist innovations.[56]

New organizations have vague task definitions and uncertain and unclear work processes and procedures. Their environments are likely to be hostile and their understanding of those environments limited. As organizations age they learn more about how to cope with the environment, and the environment thus becomes safer, more predictable, and more stable. As they age, the "we've seen it all before syndrome" develops, and procedures and behavior become more formalized and routines and standard operating procedures are established.[57] Both complexity and centralization are likely to increase.[58] Goals may be scaled down, and goal commitment of members declines as their primary commitment is switched to the organization itself.[59]

Life cycle theories are based on the premise that as organizations age, they pass through identifiable stages, each of which is characterized by specific types of behavior and structure. The stages are analogous to those of the human life cycle: birth, youth, maturity, and old age. Political scientists are most likely to be familiar with the life cycle theories of Marver Bernstein[60] and Anthony Downs,[61] but business organizations theorists, such as Larry Greiner,[62] have also developed similar theories for business organizations. Although the theorists tend to agree on the specific organizational characteristics evidenced at each stage, they differ in their explanations of what causes these characteristics to emerge. For Downs, the explanation lies primarily in the personality types that are dominant in the organization at each stage; Bernstein takes more of an environmental change approach; and for Greiner, the changes are viewed as consequences of actions the organization takes to resolve the major crises it faces as it grows and ages.

Birth

Organizations are created for various reasons and by various processes. In the private sector, they are normally the creation of an entrepreneurial individual or group of individuals who have developed a product or service that they believe they can market successfully. Public organizations are also frequently the creations of entrepeneurs—the Peace Corps and VISTA, for example, were created as organizations because a small group of individuals had an idea, a policy, that they believed should be institutionalized. Organizations may also be created at the urging of groups who believe they will benefit from the organization's activities. Consumers, business interests, agricultural interests, educational interests, and environmental interests have all at various times successfully pressured Congress to create organizations to protect and promote their interests. Organization birth, the entrepreneurial stage, is marked by innovativeness and creativity. Once born, an organization's primary concern is survival. Similar to humans, organizations face a real and constant danger of infant mortality. For public organizations, the environment is frequently unstable and hostile, and those who opposed their creation still attentive and involved.

Youth and Organizational Quest for Growth

Youth is typically characterized by rapid growth and by idealism, informality, and commitment to goals. Downs contends that in youth, organizations are dominated by zealots and advocates, the entrepreneurs who created the organization because they believed in the importance of the policy goals that the organization is pursuing. The environment becomes more predictable and more stable as the organization begins to develop methods of relating to it. As the organization grows, however, it begins to attract a new type of personnel: climbers, who are mainly interested in power, status, prestige, monetary reward, and career advancement. Although they initially contribute to the organization's quest for growth, their loyalty, other than to themselves, is to the systems, not the substantive goals of the organization.

Organizations pursue growth for a variety of reasons. First, and perhaps most important, growth is sought to ensure organizational survival. Large, complex organizations survive; smaller, simpler organizations have a much higher mortality rate.[63] Environmental uncertainty is a major cause of organization mortality, and size gives the organization more control over its environment. From an organizational perspective, growth is spurred by a desire for organizational self-realization. In the American value system, growth is regarded as a sign of success; growth is proof that the organization is progressing and doing a good job.

In some ways growth does contribute to organizational effectiveness. It allows the organization to take advantage of economies of scale, increasing the organization's power. For public organizations, growth provides proof that the organization is providing a needed service and justifies increased revenues, which fuel more growth. For individual members of the organization, growth is equally important. It provides opportunities for executive mobility, greater prestige, power, monetary compensation, and job security. Growing organizations are more exciting to work in and offer challenge, risk, and adventure.[64]

As the organization ages, its growth rate declines. It must continually compete with other organizations for social attention and resources, and it encounters more and more resistance to further growth. Hostility and antagonism from competitors—organizations with similar functions—develop and increase. Unable to continue producing impressive substantive results, the organization cannot generate external support. Increased size brings increased complexity and larger problems of planning and coordination. Zealots and advocates, disappointed with the inability to produce results, depart.

Maturity

As the size of the organization stabilizes, the climbers also become increasingly restless. The opportunities for rapid promotions disappear, and the climbers move on to more promising, still growing organizations. Conservers, individuals primarily interested in job security, routine work habits, stability, and convenience, predominate in the organization.[65] Many of the conservers join the organization during its growth phase, and as the growth rate declines and stabilizes, the organization experiences the "age lump phenomenon." The average age of its membership increases, and the hierarchical ladder is more or less blocked to those who might wish to climb it. Formalization increases, and the rules and administrative machinery become more complex and demanding.

Mature public organizations find their environments more stable and predictable and less populous. Frequently, all but those who are directly affected by the organization—its clientele and the interests groups representing them—lose interest in the organization's activity; even the political branches pay it only sporadic attention. As long as the organization creates no serious conflict or opposition, it may continue to operate comfortably in its established environmental niche. Dominated by conservers, the organization is unlikely to take risks or engage in activities that will create opposition.

Old Age

Bernstein describes old age as a period of debility and decline. The organization becomes passive and stagnant; frequently, goal displacement occurs, and fixation with rules and procedures may develop. The organization's environment has become similarly stagnant and restricted; its domain is strictly limited, and it displays no interest in expanding that domain. Conservers clearly dominate, and they enforce the propensity of the organization to avoid risk, which for regulatory agencies means taking no action that would antagonize regulated interests, Congress, or the president.

It might seem that once the organization reaches this point, it should eventually run out of gas and expire, but this is not necessarily true. Organizational death and decline will be examined more thoroughly later, but at this point it should be noted that all old public organizations do not die. Old organizations may well have reached a stable and satisfactory equilibrium with their environment, satisfying the major actors in that environment and encountering little opposition or competition. As long as the organization successfully maintains some supportive clientele to protect it, it may continue to exist for an extremely long period of time. Rejuvenation is also always a possibility.

Conservers eventually retire and may be replaced by a new round of zealots or climbers. Scandal, crisis, or change in the political and economic environment may bring new attention to the organization and introduce new actors into its environment, disturbing the equilibrium and forcing change in personnel, goals, and procedures. Environmental turmoil may result in the agency gaining new responsibilities and powers, and this may in turn fuel a new wave of growth, changing the internal environment of the organization.

Greiner's Phases of Organizational Growth

One of the more troublesome aspects of using conventional life cycle theories to explain organizational behavior is their assumption that the organizational development process can be equated with the human developmental process. Although they are composed of human beings, organizations are not really that similar to individuals. They are complex social systems, and the changes they experience as they age are likely to be more complex than those of humans.

Larry Greiner provides a different perspective on how organizations behave as they age and grow. His perspective avoids the temptation of equating the organizational development process with that of humans. His model describes five major phases an organization experiences as it grows and develops. Each phase consists of an evolutionary period, marked by relative calm, during which the organization develops and accommodates changes in size, followed by a revolutionary period spurred by a management crisis.[66] Phase One is the period of creativity. The organization is informal and nonbureaucratic and dominated by entrepreneurs—in Downs' terms, advocates and zealots. The skills and abilities that make for a successful entrepreneur, however, are not usually the skills and abilities required to manage a complex organization. So the first crisis the organization experiences is a crisis of leadership. The crisis is frequently accompanied by a power struggle between entrepreneurs and professional managerial personnel. The professional managers (climbers) prevail, and the organization enters Phase Two, growth through direction.

Under the guidance of the managers, the organization becomes more formalized, specialized, and centralized. Top managers centralize power and do not want to give it up. Expertise, however, is increasingly found at the lower levels of the organization, and members become restive and dissatisfied with overly centralized management. This results in the crisis of autonomy, which is resolved by increased delegation and decentralization.

Phase Three is growth through delegation. The organization continues to grow larger, more geographically dispersed, and more decentralized. As the units of the organization become more autonomous, the organization seems to lose its sense of direction and to be pulled in several different directions. This leads to a crisis of control, which is solved by the introduction of systems of formal control and sophisticated techniques of coordination.

Phase Four, growth through coordination, is marked by increasing bureaucratization and formalization. Rules and regulations proliferate, a lack of trust between headquarters and field units develops, and ultimately resentment to increased paperwork appears. Line-staff conflicts emerge, and complaints about the bureaucratic maze become common. The crisis of red tape occurs; bureaucratization has reached its limits. This crisis is met by decreased reliance on formal controls and increased reliance on informal social controls.

The final observable stage of organization development, Phase Five, is growth through collaboration. The organization turns to new methods of cooperative and participatory management. No organizations have been observed to have passed this phase, so the nature of the crisis the organization will encounter is unknown.

ORGANIZATIONAL DECLINE AND DEATH

Organizational decline, "a cutback in the size of an organization's workforce, profits, budgets or clients,"[67] received relatively little attention from organization theorists before the late 1970s. Although life cycle theories included old age in the organizational maturation process, old age was considered not necessarily a period of decline but more a period of stability, conservatism, and steady state equilibrium. Growth was considered the norm, and decline a deviation of little theoretical interest. A deteriorating economic situation characterized by stagflation, increased foreign competition, and increased unemployment resulted in serious problems for organizations in key industrial sectors: the steel, textile, aluminum, and automobile industries. Decline (or negative growth, as some theorists prefer to call it) began to appear as an inevitable phenomenon that organizations were going to have to learn to manage or at least understand. "There are limits to growth and there will be times when growth is not possible. The life span of many long-lived organizations includes intervals of nongrowth . . . and even prolonged periods of contraction."[68] As the economic situation deteriorated and failed to improve into the 1980s, business organization theorists came to realize that decline was a reality confronting all organizations.

In the public sector, the deteriorating economic situation was equally or even more dismal. The general economic situation had a severe impact: it increased both the demand for certain government services and the costs of providing those services without a commensurate increase in revenues. In 1978, the passage of Proposition 13 in California, limiting property tax revenues, was the first of a series of tax or expenditure limitations that would decrease the financial resources available to state and local governments. Shifting population patterns, from the Frost Belt to the Sun Belt, from the cities to the suburbs, caused many state and local governments to suffer additional declines in resource availability. A political climate of increasing conservatism culminated in the election of a president committed to reducing the size of government at all levels, starting with the federal government. Budget cuts initiated at the federal level trickled, or in some instances, flowed, down to the lower levels of government already struggling to maintain levels of service in the face of declining revenues. The rapidly expanding federal deficit spurred more rounds of budget cuts as Congress and the president tried to control its growth. The sharp decline in petroleum prices brought the realities of financial scarcity even to areas previously spared the financial difficulties. Public organizations had to and still must face the same reality as their private counterparts: decline as a continuing phenomenon.

Whetton identified four general reasons for organizational decline: organizational atrophy, vulnerability, loss of legitimacy, and environmental entropy. Atrophy is a consequence of organizational aging. The organization becomes stagnant and loses its ability to adapt to changing circumstances. Vulnerability is more characteristic of young or small organizations that have not yet established an environmental niche and have not learned how to manipulate their environment or adapt to it. Loss of legitimacy occurs when public values and attitudes change and certain services lose favor and support. Environmental entropy results from the reduced capacity of the environment to support the organization.[69] All of these factors have been present in the current decline of public organizations. The most serious of the reasons, environmental entropy, is the one least susceptible to organizational control and the one most likely to continue for the foreseeable future.

Robbins identified three stages in organizational response to decline.[70] The first stage is denial: organization management either denies that a problem has arisen or else ignores it. The initial reaction of the public sector collectively to the end of the growth period of the 1960s and 1970s was one of denial, a refusal to accept the reality of changed circumstances. From New York City teetering on the edge of bankruptcy to California in the pre-Proposition 13 era to the federal government generally, refusal to recognize that public attitudes were changing and that resources were becoming more scarce and likely to remain so was the dominant attitude and one that effectively blocked any early attempts to manage decline.

The second stage of organizational reaction is to view decline as a temporary crisis. The reaction of the higher education system in the state of Idaho typifies this reaction. Although the state has had a property tax limitation imposed by the voters, has suffered an economic recession of ten years duration, and has had repeated budget crises over the last six years, the management in the university system has continually assumed that although the situation is bad one year, the next year everything will be improved; in its insistence on this temporary perspective, it has regularly requested large budget increases, which have just as regularly been denied. Viewing decline as a temporary phenomenon appears to be widespread in the public sector, and the majority of public organizations faced with decline have not moved beyond this stage. The basic problem from an organizational perspective of viewing decline as a temporary crisis is that it forestalls any attempt to develop and implement intelligent management responses to the problem. Other than increased centralization, management does nothing but conduct business as usual, ignoring the problems that beset the organization. Organizational atrophy may accelerate as a consequence, making the organization increasingly incapable of responding to changed demands. Only in the third stage, acceptance, can management begin to make decisions and take actions to maintain organizational ability to function.

Even though management may ignore or refuse to deal with decline, the organization and its members respond to it. As salaries are frozen, appropriations decrease, and layoffs are required, the climate within the organization changes drastically. Voluntary turnover rates begin to increase as those who have mobility leave for more promising organizations. Usually, the organization loses its best and brightest first because they have the greatest career mobility. Rumors are likely to replace the formal communication system, and uncertainty about the future spreads throughout the organization. Employees experience increased feelings of fear, anger, depression, disappointment, and emptiness; stress increases, morale plummets, absenteeism increases, and productivity decreases, and the level of conflict within the organization among units, groups, and individuals accelerates. Political struggles, for power and position, become more intense.[71] The organization enters what Easton calls "the ever descending spiral."[72] Discontent grows and is quickly communicated throughout the organization, positively reinforcing itself, and further weakening the organization.

As layoffs, reductions in force, and voluntary departures occur, the organization begins to experience even more negative consequences. The combined impact of personnel reductions is likely to result in an increase in the proportion of total resources devoted to personnel. The vast majority of layoffs are conducted on the basis of seniority—last hired, first fired—so the older, most senior members, who are usually also the most highly paid, remain. The younger, less highly paid employees depart.[73] Ironically, Parkinson's Law finally triumphs. As the organization shrinks, the administrative component does become proportionately larger, partially because of the political position and power of the administrative component within the organization. In the power struggles that develop, the political position of administration becomes more dominant, and it is able to resist shrinkage.[74] The administration determines where cuts will be made, so it protects itself. In some instances, the administrative component may actually increase as organization size decreases.[75] This may occur because top management feels that more management advice and assistance is needed to deal with the chaos developing within the organization. Alternatively, it may result from management's refusal to accept decline and to instead increase the size of boundary-spanning units, such as public relations and legislative liaison units.

Decline is also likely to result in goal displacement and decreased specialization. Clearly, substantive goals become less important than systems goals and individual member goals as the organization attempts to cope with decreased resources. Rules and regulations already in effect are unlikely to diminish or change; they may become the only certain things in an increasingly uncertain situation, and members will adhere to them even though they become increasingly irrelevant to the current situation. As the organization declines, "most of the functions performed when it was larger still remain to be done, but they are combined into fewer and fewer positions."[76] Despecialization occurs and the organization's effectiveness is likely to be further reduced.

Rubin examined how budget cuts had affected several federal agencies. She found that the "overall impact of cutback on federal agencies was a deterioration of management and productivity."[77] Uncertainty negatively affected the quality of decision making, planning was ignored, and hard decisions were avoided. Agencies operated in an atmosphere of chaos as RIF (reductions in force), relocations, and reorganizations "left employees in the wrong places at the wrong times with the wrong skills."[78] Morale and productivity plummeted, and agencies became polarized as "old conflicts between males and females, whites and blacks" resurfaced.[79] Quality of work life deteriorated, and in general the federal work force became older and more homogenous—more white and more male.[80]

Decline cannot be managed as long as the organization's management refuses to accept it as a continuing reality. Whether it can be managed effectively even with such acceptance is far from certain; what effective management of decline means, and what goals the organization should pursue during decline, are far from clear. Substantive goals appear to need modification and scaling down, but for public organizations, the authority to do this resides in the legislature. If the organization attempts to do this overtly on its own initiative, it will probably encounter severe political criticism. Decline is accompanied by an increase in uncertainty: inability to predict resource availability or what demands will be put on the organization. Rational management requires planning, but planning becomes more difficult, if not impossible, in the face of increasing uncertainty.[81] There is a definite lack of skilled, experienced managers of decline, although that problem may be solved if the era of decline lasts much longer. Somehow, Downs' personality types do not seem to include any that would accept the management of decline as compatible with their self-interest. Perhaps a new personality type based on David Stockman, the political hit man, will emerge to preside over declining organizations. Managing decline is managing change, which is never easy, but in decline resistance to change is extremely high, and unfreezing becomes particularly difficult because all of the normal human reasons for resistance are well justified.[82]

Managing decline may be easier in the private sector than in the public sector. "Turnaround management" can be successful when the basic cause of decline is poor management—organizational atrophy. New management can be brought in to eliminate unprofitable product lines, cut costs, implement merges, or seek governmental assistance. Public sector organizations do not have as much flexibility, and crucial management decisions, such as which programs to cut or how to distribute cuts, are not within the power of top management but rather are made by legislatures or elected executives. These decisions will thus reflect political rather than administrative values.

Organizational Death

Organizational death, the final dissolution of an organization, is a more common occurrence than is usually recognized. As Kaufman notes, relatively few organizations survive long enough to go through the life cycle; most organizational deaths occur among younger organizations.[83] Unlike human beings, the longer an organization has survived, the greater its life expectancy. Young organizations suffer from "the liability of newness."[84] They lack an established clientele, frequently must compete with larger, more powerful organizations, and may be handicapped by inexperienced management.

The major cause of organizational death appears to be resource scarcity: "Most of the organizations that die are done in by the interaction of two factors: one is the incessant change, the turbulence of their environment. The other is their difficulty in adjusting to this volatility. The combination causes them resource problems" that result in their demise.[85] All organizations may encounter such problems at various times in their existence; some will adjust successfully and others will not. Kaufman sees survival as not a matter of skill or good management but a matter of luck: comparisons between organizations that survive and those that fail "disclose no significant differences in levels of ability, intelligence, or leadership talents."[86] Nor does he believe that flexibility is the solution, because flexibility involves costs that require the organization to divert resources from more productive activities. Maintaining flexibility requires the organization to maintain a state of constant change, which increases disunity and weakens bonds within the organization.[87]

From a rational perspective, it is somewhat disconcerting for luck to be the critical variable in determining organizational survival. Comparing agencies and programs that have been threatened with termination with programs that have avoided such threats does not seem to uncover an underlying organizational logic. Many programs that appear to be guaranteed existence are more inefficient, poorly managed and ineffective than those targeted for extermination. Certainly, the political power of supporters is crucial to organizational survival in the public sector, but in large part that too, from the organization's perspective, is a matter of luck.

Ironically, managing the death of an organization is easier than managing its decline. Once death is certain, the major problem involved in managing decline—uncertainty—is removed, and plans can be made and implemented. Even so, presiding over the death of an organization is one of the most unpleasant assignments that management can be given. Employee reaction to the announced demise of their organization is the first and most difficult problem that must be handled. Their reaction resembles the reaction of individuals who have been informed that they are dying. They go through the same psychological stages that Elizabeth Kubler-Ross described in *On Death and Dying*. First comes denial: "It's not really going to happen. This is all a mistake." Denial is followed by anger: "Why this organization? We're doing an important job. Why not some other useless, more inefficient organization?" Bargaining, or attempts to bargain, follows. "If they will just give us one more year to prove our worth," or "let them impose cuts but just save the organization." When the situation remains unchanged, depression emerges. "Employees become demoralized. . . . [They] fear not just for their jobs but also their careers; a sense of desperation colors their interactions with superiors, subordinates and clients."[88] Finally, comes acceptance and hope.

While managing an organization through its death throes may seem an exercise in futility, it still has to be done. Certain tasks have to be completed to close out programs and dismantle the organization. Physical holdings of the organization must be inventoried and properly dispersed, clientele informed, the books put in proper order and closed; some projects may need to be transferred to other organizations.

Successful and humane "cutout" management seems to follow certain basic principles. First, employees should be allowed to pass through all the psychological stages. They should not be offered false hope, bullied, or threatened.[89] Secondly, an outplacement program should be initiated. Employees should be actively assisted in finding future employment, and their rights should be scrupulously respected. Decision making should be centralized immediately, and a plan of action should be developed. Direct face-to-face communication between management and employees should be used to explain the termination process.[90]

Greiner, in his discussion of organization development, after identifying the five major stages of growth, was unable to predict the inherent crises of the fifth stage. Perhaps the luck that accompanied the organization as it progressed through those stages finally runs out, and the final crisis is death.

CONCLUSION

Organizational change is caused by many factors and takes many forms. Organizations and their members welcome some changes, resist many others, and fight and bitterly resent certain types of change. Planned change to improve organizational performance requires resources, skilled management to reduce resistance, and considerable time and commitment to be successful. Unfortunately, many changes attempted in public organizations, from zero-base budgeting to the Civil Service Reform Act of 1978, have had disappointing results and fallen far short of the change agents' goals, primarily because of improper implementation. In public administration generally the dominant attitude appears to be that proposing and enacting change is sufficient; little attention is given to the necessities of implementing the changes, particularly the provision of adequate financial and human resources.

In our society, we tend to equate change with progress and to have strong positive orientations towards both. Those who oppose change are criticized as too conservative and antiprogressive. The irony in this attitude is that most people are conservative in the sense that they do resist change and frequently for good reason. This attitude may explain why management tends to underestimate the strength of resistance that organizational changes encounter and its failure to deal effectively with that resistance. This chapter has covered the negative aspects of change. These negative aspects should not be ignored by change agents, because they constitute the major reasons change is resisted. Unless they can be muted or overcome, change will likely not occur; if it does, its costs may outweigh its benefits.

Organizations undergo many changes throughout their existence that are an unavoidable part of organizational evolution. They increase in size; they grow older; personnel attitudes and values change; goals are modified, displaced, and replaced. Increasingly, we have come to realize that organizational decline may also be inevitable. Sound theoretical or practical principles for the successful management of decline remain elusive. Both public and private organizations seem at this point to be unable to manage decline, perhaps because no one really knows what the "appropriate" organizational response should be. The most common organizational response seems to be to fight, but fighting the inevitable is usually futile. Accepting decline, however, runs counter to every organizational goal or principle of behavior. Rational planning seems unlikely and difficult, if not impossible, and muddling through once again emerges triumphant.

NOTES

1. Frustrated federal employee cited in "To Cope or To Manage? Organizing for Change," *Management* (Spring 1980): p. 8.
2. Peter Blau and Richard Scott, *Formal Organizations* (San Francisco: Chandler, 1962), p. 250.
3. Ibid., p. 222.
4. Jerald Hage, *Theories of Organization* (New York: John Wiley, 1980), p. 234.
5. Arthur Bedeian, *Organization: Theory and Analysis* (Hinsdale, Ill.: Dryden Press, 1980), p. 297.
6. Hage, *Theories of Organization*, p. 233.
7. Peter Blau, "Bureaucracy and Social Change," in Oscar Grusky and George Miller, *The Sociology of Organizations* (New York: Free Press, 1970), p. 249.
8. Hage, *Theories of Organization*, p. 243.
9. Debra Stewart and G. David Garson, *Organizational Behavior and Management* (New York: Marcel Dekker, 1983), p. 179.
10. Pradip Khandwalla, *The Design of Organizations* (New York: Harcourt, Brace, Jovanovich, 1977), p. 301.
11. Kurt Lewin, "Frontiers in Group Dynamics," *Human Relations* (1947): pp. 5–41.
12. Hage, *Theories of Organization*, pp. 212–217.
13. Ibid., pp. 220–226.
14. James Q. Wilson, "Innovation in Organizations: Notes Toward a Theory," in James D. Thompson, *Approaches To Organizational Design* (Pittsburgh: University of Pittsburgh Press, 1966), pp. 193–218.
15. Hage, *Theories of Organizations*, p. 244.
16. Barry Stein and Rosabeth Kanter, "Building the Parallel Organization: Creating Mechanisms for Quality of Work Life," *Journal of Applied Behavioral Science* (1980): pp. 371–388.
17. Larry Greiner, "Patterns of Organization Change," *Harvard Business Review* (1967): p. 120.
18. Ibid., p. 121.
19. Ibid.
20. Daniel Robey, *Designing Organizations* (Homewood, Ill.: Richard D. Irwin, 1982), p. 450.
21. Cyrus L. Gibson, *Managing Organizational Behavior* (Homewood, Ill.: Richard D. Irwin, 1980), p. 177.
22. Richard Daft, *Organization Theory and Design* (St. Paul: West Publishing, 1983), p. 273.
23. Gibson, *Managing Organizational Behavior*, p. 177.

24. Daft, *Organization Theory and Design*, p. 273.
25. J. O. Kotter and L. A. Schlesinger, "Choosing Strategies for Change," *Harvard Business Review* (March/April 1979): p. 111.
26. R. J. Patti and H. Resnick, "Changing the Agency from Within," *Social Work* (1972): p. 50.
27. Kotter and Schlesinger, "Choosing Strategies for Change," p. 111.
28. G. A. Brager and S. Halloway, *Changing Human Service Organizations: Politics and Practices* (New York: Free Press, 1978), p. 132.
29. Kotter and Schlesinger, "Choosing Strategies for Change," p. 111.
30. Brager and Halloway, *Changing Human Service Organizations*, p. 132.
31. Richard Beckhard, *Organization Development: Strategies and Models* (Reading, Mass.: Addison-Wesley, 1969), p. 9.
32. Gerald Gabris, "Organizational Change," in Thomas Lynch, ed., *Organization Theory and Management* (New York: Marcel Dekker, 1983), p. 179.
33. Daft, *Organization Theory and Design*, p. 282.
34. Robert Tannenbaum and Sheldon Davis, "Values, Man and Organizations," *Industrial Management Review* (Winter 1969): pp. 67–86.
35. For a thorough discussion of OD see Robert B. Blake and Jane Mouton, *The Managerial Grid* (Houston: Gulf Publishing Co., 1964), and Robert Golembiewski and William B. Eddy, eds., *Organization Development in Public Administration*, 2 vols. (New York: Marcel Dekker, 1978).
36. Gabris, "Organizational Change," p. 182.
37. Charles Perrow, *Complex Organizations: A Critical Essay*, 3rd ed. (New York: Random House, 1986), p. 114.
38. Howard E. McCurdy, *Public Administration: A Synthesis* (Menlo Park, Calif.: Cummings Publishing Co., 1977), p. 294.
39. The case is based on "Inside America's Toughest Prison," written by Aric Press and reported by Daniel Pederson, Daniel Shapiro, and Ann McDaniel, *Newsweek* (October 6, 1986): pp. 46–61.
40. Ibid., p. 49.
41. Ibid., p. 52.
42. Ibid., p. 53.
43. Ibid., p. 56.
44. Ibid., p. 58.
45. Nicole Woolsey Biggart, "The Creative-Destructive Process of Organizational Change: The Case of the Post Office," *Administrative Science Quarterly* (1977): p. 411.
46. Ibid., p. 420.
47. Ibid., p. 422.
48. George E. Berkley, *The Craft of Public Administration* (Boston: Allyn and Bacon, 1984), p. 93.
49. Peter Szanton, "So You Want To Reorganize the Government?" in Szanton, ed., *Federal Reorganization: What Have We Learned?* (Chatham, N.J.: Chatham House Publishers, Inc., 1981), p. 19.
50. James G. March and Johan P. Olson, "Organizing Political Life: What Administrative Reorganization Tells Us About Government," *American Political Science Review* (1983): p. 282.
51. Harold Seidman, *Politics, Position and Power*, 4th ed. (New York: Oxford University Press, 1986), p. 13.
52. March and Olson, "Organizing Political Life," p. 283.
53. Seidman, *Politics, Position and Power*, pp. 25–27.
54. March and Olson, "Organizing Political Life," p. 286.
55. Ibid., p. 288.
56. Khandwalla, *The Design of Organizations*, p. 299.

57. Henry Mintzberg, *The Structuring of Organizations* (Englewood Cliffs, N.J.: Prentice-Hall, 1983), p. 227.
58. Herbert Kaufman, *Time, Chance and Organizations* (Chatham, N.J.: Chatham House Publishing Inc., 1985), p. 141.
59. Khandwalla, *The Design of Organizations*, p. 301.
60. Marver Bernstein, *Regulatory Business by Independent Commission* (Princeton: Princeton University Press, 1955).
61. Anthony Downs, *Inside Bureaucracy* (Boston: Little, Brown, 1967), pp. 5–23.
62. Larry Greiner, "Evolution and Revolution as Organizations Grow," *Harvard Business Review* (1972): pp. 37–46. See also G. Lippitt and W. H. Schmidt, "Crises in a Developing Organization," *Harvard Business Review* (November/December 1967): pp. 26–47 and A. D. Chandler, *Strategy and Structure: Chapters in the History of the American Enterprise* (Cambridge, Mass.: MIT Press, 1962).
63. Marshall Meyer, with William Stevenson and Stephen Weber, *Limits to Bureaucratic Growth* (New York: Walter de Gruyter, 1985), p. 12.
64. W. H. Starbuck, "Organizational Growth and Development," in James G. March, *Handbook of Organizations* (Chicago: Rand McNally, 1965), pp. 451–533.
65. Downs, *Inside Bureaucracy*, p. 96.
66. Greiner, "Evolution and Revolution as Organizations Grow," pp. 37–46.
67. David A. Whetton, "Sources, Responses and Effects of Organizational Decline," in John R. Kimberly and Robert Mills, eds., *The Organizational Life Cycle* (San Francisco: Jossey-Bass, 1980), p. 345.
68. Alan Easton, *Managing Negative Growth* (Reston, Va.: Reston Publishing Co., 1976), p. 4.
69. Whetton, "Sources, Responses and Effects of Organizational Decline," p. 345.
70. Stephen Robbins, *Organizational Theory* (Englewood Cliffs, N.J.: Prentice-Hall, 1983), p. 117.
71. John Freeman and Michael Harmon, "Growth and Decline Processes in Organizations," *American Sociological Review* (1975): pp. 215–228.
72. Easton, *Managing Negative Growth*, p. 20.
73. Ibid., p. 21.
74. Freeman and Harmon, "Growth and Decline Processes in Organizations," p. 225.
75. Jeffrey Ford, "The Administrative Component in Growing and Declining Organizations," *Academy of Management Journal* (1980): pp. 615–630.
76. Easton, *Managing Negative Growth*, p. 102.
77. Irene Rubin, *Shrinking the Federal Government* (New York: Longman, 1985), p. 200.
78. Ibid., p. 202.
79. Ibid., p. 203.
80. Ibid., p. 204.
81. Easton, *Managing Negative Growth*, p. 7.
82. Robbins, *Organization Theory*, p. 21.
83. Kaufman, *Time, Chance and Organizations*, p. 25.
84. A. L. Stinchcombe, "Social Structures and Organizations," in March, ed., *Handbook of Organizations*, p. 148.
85. Kaufman, *Time, Chance and Organizations*, p. 35.
86. Ibid., p. 69.
87. Ibid., pp. 72–75.
88. Irene Rubin, "Managing the End: Death and Dying in Public Organizations," *Public Management* (March 1982): p. 19.
89. Ibid., p. 19.
90. James E. Colvard, "Cutout: The Ultimate Cutback Management," *The Bureaucrat* (Spring 1986): p. 6.

6

POWER, POLITICS, AND CONFLICT IN ORGANIZATIONS

Rational bureaucratic theory portrayed organizations as entities that have clearly articulated, agreed on goals and are structured to maximize specialization and efficiency in the attainment of those goals. Control over the organization was maintained by a hierarchical system in which authority was vested in positions, not persons, and ultimate authority resided at the top of the hierarchy. Within this orderly system, conflict was a deviation, an aberration resulting from incompetent management; power not correlated with formal authority was dysfunctional, illegitimate, and unlikely. Organization participants were unlikely to engage in politics or use political methods, tactics, and games to enhance their power; therefore politics was not a subject of concern for theorists, managers, or employees. Almost all major schools of organization theory—classical, human relations, humanism— accepted the basic tenets of rational theory: that organizations were rational systems for the attainment of specified goals and that conflict, politics, and power struggles within the organization were diseases for which cures must be developed.

Currently, the emphasis on rationality within organizations remains central in most management training. In both business and public administration, great emphasis is placed on rational techniques to improve the management of organizations: strategic planning, policy analysis, program evaluation, program-planning budgeting, and zero-base budgeting are pressed on managers as rational methods that will ever improve the functioning of organizations. Personnel administration stresses rational techniques for selecting, evaluating, and promoting the best candidates, and OD (organization development) and a vast variety of human relations techniques convey the message that conflict is not rational and can be eliminated.

Nonetheless, many of the aspects and processes of organizations that have been examined to this point refute the rational organization concept. Goals, as we have seen, are multiple, vague, and conflicting. Even clear and specific goals are often displaced, suboptimized, and ignored. Technologies to achieve those goals are frequently uncertain and are chosen for reasons other than maximum attainment of goals. Conflict appears to be endemic in organizations composed of individuals and groups with diverse and conflicting interests: professionals versus administrators, lower versus higher levels, clients versus bureaucrats, civil servants versus political executives, line versus staff. Power clearly exists in unexpected places within organizations, from the inmates at Eastham Prison to lower-level employees who successfully resist changes attempted by those in authority.

That rationality remains the central norm in management theory despite all the evidence against its possibility or desirability is not all that surprising. First, rationality is a deeply rooted social value in America, and values are not subject to empirical testing. Second, rationality serves a variety of purposes for individuals and organizations that make the myth well worth perpetuating.

> It is certainly much more noble to think of oneself as developing skills toward the more efficient allocation and use of resources—implicitly for the greater good of society as a whole—than to think of oneself as engaged with organizational participants in a political struggle over values, preferences and definitions of technology.[1]

The preceding quote is valid for people entering business organizations, but it is even more so for those entering public administration. The rational myth also underlies the merit system and the career progress (or lack thereof) for individuals within organizations. Advancement is supposedly based on competence and contribution to achievement of organizational goals, not on one's political skills and abilities. The rational myth also assures the "public that the vast power and wealth controlled by organizations is being effectively and legitimately employed."[2]

Two current approaches to organization theory take very different perspectives on conflict and power within organizations. The interactionist approach to conflict views organizational conflict as not only natural but also desirable, something to be encouraged. The power school of organizational theorists views organizations as pluralistic political systems, "complex systems of individuals and coalitions, each with its own interests, beliefs, values preferences and perceptions, which compete with each other to protect and advance their own interests."[3] From this perspective, conflict and political struggles become integral and inevitable aspects of organization behavior, and the resolution of these conflicts and political struggles reflects the relative power of the participants in the struggles. The power approach to organizations is relatively new and definitely unsettling to those who prefer rational bureaucratic theory. It makes organization behavior (or misbehavior) more comprehensible, but management more incomprehensible and, from the public administration perspective, raises again the questions of the accountability, responsibility, and control of bureaucracy.

ORGANIZATIONAL CONFLICT

Conflict is a social process involving two or more parties that begins when one party (individual or group) perceives that another is preventing the attainment of some goal. This blockage results in frustration, which leads to conceptualization: each party forms its own interpretation of the situation, including a definition of the conflict issue and attributions of the other's intent. Conceptualization is followed by some behavioral response, which may or may not involve interaction with the other party. If the outcome of that response is satisfactory to both parties, the conflict ends. Otherwise residual frustration will trigger continuing or future conflict.[4] In addition, one conflict between individuals or groups sets the stage for the next conflict: "The more sensitive people become to repeated conflicts, the more subsequent conflict is likely to occur."[5]

Individual reactions to conflict vary along two dimensions: cooperativeness (willingness to try to satisfy the other parties' wishes) and assertiveness (refusal to allow denial of one's own wishes). Based on those two dimensions, Thomas identifies five major reactions to conflict: competing, accommodating, avoiding, compromising, and collaborating. Competing emphasizes attempting to satisfy one's own concerns at the other party's expense using argument, threats, force, authority, or power. Accommodating involves giving in, acceding to the other party's demands without protecting one's own interest. Avoiding is ignoring the conflict and sidestepping it. Compromising is the use of bargaining and negotiation to arrive at a solution that partially satisfies both parties. Collaboration involves the use of problem-solving techniques to arrive at an integrative solution that satisfies the interests of both parties.[6] Only collaboration fully resolves the conflict and does not result in residual frustration.

Conflict makes many, perhaps most, people uncomfortable; particularly within organizations, conflict has been viewed negatively, as something to be avoided or eliminated. This aversion to conflict results partially from the preponderance of the rational-bureaucratic model, in which conflict within the organization indicates improper management. If goals are clear and uniformly accepted by all members (as they are supposed to be), if technology is chosen because it is the one best way to achieve goals, if resources are allocated rationally, and if merit and objectivity permeate the personnel system, conflict is deviant and dysfunctional. Although in most organizations none of these conditions is met, the theoretical bias in management theory still favors harmony within the organization.[7] Most managers are evaluated on that basis and are likely to receive negative evaluations if they or their subordinates are involved in conflict.[8]

Aversion to conflict is also partially rooted in American social values. In the home, schools, and churches, considerable stress is placed on being cooperative and agreeable—getting along well with others. The child or adult who does not get along with others is likely to be punished, formally or informally. Pressures to conform are pronounced in American society, with the result that, according to A. H. Maslow, we have a "fear of conflict, of disagreement, of hostility, antagonism, enmity" and of not being liked.[9] Conflict is bad and something that should be suppressed, avoided, or ignored.

These attitudes cause problems in two ways. First, conflict is an inevitable part of life in organizations, in personal relationships, in society, and among societies. Consequently, learning to manage and resolve conflict is essential; but as long as conflict is viewed negatively, we can never learn to deal with it constructively. The second part of the problem with negative attitudes about conflict is that they ignore the benefits and functions of conflict. Dissension and dissatisfaction that are hidden and unexpressed are more psychologically damaging than overt conflict, and frequently the longer they are suppressed and ignored, the worse they become. Conflict allows individuals to express anger and satisfy aggressive urges; it clarifies problems, enabling individuals to understand their own positions and attitudes.

In organizations, conflict is especially functional. A tranquil, harmonious organization may very well also be an apathetic, uncreative, stagnant, inflexible, and unresponsive organization. Conflict challenges the status quo, stimulates interest and curiosity. It is the root of personal and social change, creativity, and innovation.[10] Conflict encourages new ideas and approaches to problems, stimulating innovation. If handled properly, conflict may reduce latent dissension within the organization, ultimately increasing unity, and may encourage managers to question, modify or replace irrelevant goals. Conflict, and the competition frequently associated with it, promotes circulation of leadership and helps equalize power within organizations. When a group is involved in a conflict, it becomes more cohesive and more task oriented. The group structure tightens, and group climate becomes more formal.[11]

Nonetheless, conflict, particularly intense and prolonged conflict, may truly be dysfunctional; it may diminish coordination and reduce teamwork and cooperation. Energy may be diverted from accomplishing the task to winning the conflict, and in the ensuing struggle organizational resources may be similarly disallocated. Hostility between combatants may escalate and, if allowed to continue for an extensive period, may permanently damage relationships between individuals or groups whose cooperation is essential for organizational function. And even an immediate conflict that is resolved sets the stage for repeated conflict between the participants. The stress involved in a conflict situation may have an adverse effect on the mental and physical health, and consequently on the job performance and productivity, of individuals who are particularly averse to conflict.[12] Finally, because of conflict, goals may be distorted or suboptimized.

Groups engaged in conflict also experience dysfunction. Leadership becomes more autocratic, and as group cohesion increases, so do "we-they" feelings. Judgment is altered, perception is distorted, and the group may develop a superiority complex, overestimating its capabilities and developing unrealistic expectations. Stereotyping of opponents occurs, and their motives and capabilities are likely to be misunderstood. Communication between groups decreases, making successful conflict resolution unlikely and coordination impossible.[13] If the conflict is terminated with one group as the clear winner, the losing group will experience dissension and will frequently seek scapegoats. Obviously, its function will be, at least temporarily, diminished.

From a management perspective, conflict presents a challenge: too little conflict is unhealthy, but too much conflict, or conflict that is not properly managed, is equally so. Consequently, management should create an environment in which conflict is encouraged but not allowed to develop to pathological extremes.[14] Conflict of some sort is inevitable in organizations, so at a minimum, managers should learn to accept conflict and to manage it productively.

Sources Of Organizational Conflict

The basic nature of organizations, which bring together individuals with different values, attitudes, motivations, education, and skills, forms the preconditions for ongoing conflict. Individuals are grouped in units wth varying responsibilities and required to interact and coordinate their activities. Units are arranged into a hierarchy with clear differences of authority, status, and prestige. The ambiguity that exists in all organizational situations fosters and encourages conflict: "However well defined official tasks may be, and however neatly we think we have fitted our personnel to these roles, the inescapably fluid daily situation distorts expected working conditions. Circumstances require various out of role and unplanned actions."[15]

One of the most basic sources of organizational conflict is the conflict between the goals and needs of individuals and the goals and needs of the organization.

> Organizations and their membership, including the elites, do have an inherent conflict of interest. What is best for the collective is not best for the individual. Organizations are asked to produce the best medical care, education, material goods, external security, and the like at little cost. . . . But these are not free because the workers are unwilling to give their work free of charge. We all want interesting work, with job automony and high pay.[16]

This problem is particularly severe in contemporary public organizations. The public—taxpayers—have clearly expressed a desire to hold taxes at their current level, while maintaining current levels of service. For public organizations, this has meant diminished resource availability with little accompanying reduction in their responsibilities. A large part of this burden has been passed to public employees, who have seen their wages frozen, their chances for career advancement diminished, their job security undermined, and their job satisfaction decreased. In other words, attainment of their interests has been frustrated; and in many instances, potential conflict between organizations and their members has become overt conflict. The most visible manifestations of this conflict have been union-management disputes, strikes, and increased rates of voluntary turnover.

Vertical conflict (conflict between different hierarchical levels of the organization) usually develops over issues of control, power, and the incentive and reward system. Conflict between political executives and permanent civil service employees is likely to be exacerbated by differences in personal background and experience, loyalties, and goal commitments. Political executives frequently lack substantive experience in or knowledge of the organizations or programs they are selected to administer. Their primary loyalty is to the appointing official, and they are likely to perceive goals as being whatever that official desires. The permanent employees are likely to have spent most of their careers in the same organization, or at least the same substantive policy areas, and to have developed loyalty to the organization and to the goals as they have been operationalized by that organization.

Structural differentiation is an additional source of organizational conflict. Dividing the organization into units based on different specializations or professions fosters conflict. Each specialization has its own work methods and time perspectives and is likely to develop its own definition of organizational goals. Specialists are likely to develop their own language (jargon) and to view their unit as being the most essential to proper functioning of the organization. When they must coordinate and cooperate with other units, conflict can easily result. Similarly professionals, whether they are doctors, lawyers, engineers, or scientists, are likely to resent and have conflicts with generalist administrators.

The likelihood of organizational conflict is increased by low formalization and task interdependency. Rules reduce conflict by minimizing ambiguity and by clearly defining responsibilities, procedures, and authority; ambiguity and vagueness encourage jurisdictional disputes and power struggles.[17] Task interdependence occurs when one unit is dependent on another for materials, resources, or information necessary to carry out its tasks. In the criminal justice system, for example, prosecutors depend on the police to investigate crimes, collect evidence, and arrest suspects; the police depend on prosecutors for guidance on what evidence is needed and to successfully prosecute offenders. Police and prosecutors are likely to have very different goals, attitudes, values, and education. The result of this reciprocal task interdependence is considerable conflict between police and prosecutors. Similarly, in many organizations, separate purchasing departments procure all supplies used by the organization. Government purchasing departments, particularly, have their own set of rules and laws with which they must comply and their own set of priorities and time perspectives that guide their behavior. From the perspective of a department that must wait for a needed piece of equipment, these rules often appear arcane, the priorities perverted, and the time perspective glacial.

By definition, participative decision making also promotes conflict. Unless participants have and express differing ideas and opinions, little is to be gained by having them participate in the decision-making process. These differences constitute the basis for likely conflict. Participation results in the open expression of differences and makes participants more aware of their differences. Conflict that may have been latent becomes active, and once activated may become persistent.[18]

One of the perennial conflicts in organizations has been the conflict between line and staff agencies. Staff agencies provide support services for line agencies: those units that actually provide the services or make the products of the organization. Personnel, budgeting, purchasing, planning, and legal advising are staff functions. According to classical organization theory, staff advises, it does not command, and consequently, conflict between line and staff is minimal. In reality, the potential for conflict between the two is high. As the example of the purchasing office illustrates, the two types of units are linked by task interdependency, a primary source of organizational conflict. Realistically, staff agencies do command: when the budgeting office determines and allocates financial resources, or when the legal office determines that a proposed action is impermissible, control has been exercised over the line unit, and the basis for conflict and power struggle has been established. The potential is increased by the frequent ambiguity concerning the specific authority and responsibility of the two types of agency. When differences in educational background, professional and programmatic commitments, age, and access to the chief executive are added to the other sources, conflict between line and staff seems inevitable.[19]

The perennial conflict between the president's Executive Office staff and the cabinet departments is a classic example of line-staff conflict. Executive Office agencies such as the Office of Management and Budget, the National Security Council staff, and the White House Office have long been resented and resisted by the line departments. "The relationship between presidential staff and departmental officials has been shown to be almost inevitably adversary in character and conducive to considerable conflict."[20] The conflict has escalated to a full-fledged power struggle, with the knowledge and frequently the encouragement of the president, and in the Nixon, Carter, and Reagan presidencies the balance of power has shifted to the Executive Office of the President. Particularly as budgetary and fiscal problems assumed ascendancy and became the primary strategic contingency facing the federal government, the Office of Management and Budget increased both its power and its level of conflict with the line departments.

Two other major sources of organizational conflict have been covered in previous chapters: the introduction of change and increasing resource scarcity. Change causes conflict when those affected by it perceive it as threatening and react by resisting it. Competition for scarce resources is also a continuing source of conflict in all organizations, as each unit seeks to maximize its share of resources. In a growing organization this conflict may be muted, but when resources are diminishing the stakes are much higher, in some cases survival of the unit, and the conflict escalates. Management of declining organizations usually requires increased centralization and control, which results in a loss of autonomy for members, increasing their general frustration with the organization.

Conflict between individuals, interpersonal conflict, can develop from all of the general sources of organizational conflict. It may also occur because of personality conflict. Although the more optimistic psychologists and organizational humanists appear to believe that everyone can get along with everyone else, reality suggests otherwise. Some individuals are basically incompatible; their personalities are so contrasting or their attitudes, values, and behaviors are so different that they simply do not like each other and cannot get along with each other. Will Rogers may well be the only person who never met somebody he did not like. In social relationships, this problem can be solved by avoidance. In organizations, avoidance may be impossible and interaction required; and the result of required interaction is likely to be continuing conflict.

Conflict Management

Conflict presents a difficult challenge to managers. They must learn to distinguish between functional and dysfunctional conflict, to eliminate and control dysfunctional conflict, and to maintain a functional level of conflict.[21] Unfortunately there are no clear distinctions between functional and dysfunctional conflict and no quantitative measures of the appropriate level of healthy conflict. Consequently, there is no one right way to manage conflict.

Earlier in this section, five individual behavior reactions to conflict were identified: competing, collaborating, compromising, avoiding, and accommodating. Each of those reactions may be appropriate, depending on the situation. Avoidance is most appropriate when an issue is trivial or when there is no chance of prevailing. All-out competition is best reserved for important issues when the manager is convinced he or she is right or in situations involving people who take advantage of noncompetitive behavior. Accommodation is most useful for participants who realize they are wrong or losing or when the issue is more important to the other party and accommodation will help maintain cooperation and build credit for later issues. Compromise may be the only sensible response when opponents are of equal power and equally committed to opposing goals. Collaboration is best for situations calling for an integrative solution to an important concern or when feelings have interfered with a relationship.[22]

Satisfactory organizational responses to conflict depend on the type of conflict involved and the cause or source of the conflict. Because a major source of organizational conflict is ambiguity and lack of clarity about responsibility, duties, and authority, one solution is increased formalization: written specification of the domains of the conflicting parties. This solution involves the obvious risk of excessive bureaucratization and all the problems entailed therein. All contingencies and all ambiguities can never be completely identified, and once the organization begins to rely on formalization, rules proliferate. But despite the risk of excessive formalization, many conflict situations could be alleviated if authority and responsibility were clarified.

The basic sources of conflict between the organization and its members can never be completely eliminated, and such conflict is healthy for organizations, society, and individuals. The elimination of this conflict would imply that individuals had totally internalized the organization's values and goals and would adhere to its expectations. The total subjugation of individuality to the organization and the inculcation of a "my organization right or wrong" mentality are not compatible with democratic values and can result in the elimination of internal checks on unwarranted, improper, or illegal behavior by organizational participants and leaders.

Conflict resulting from inadequate compensation, unfair treatment, or unnecessary deprivation of individual autonomy can be alleviated.

Clearly, organizations should provide fair compensation to their members and should also provide an appeals system for resolving employee grievances. Individual needs for autonomy may be partially met through participative management, although it should be recognized that this may actually increase conflict within the organization.

Similarly, conflict between political executives and civil servants is both inevitable and beneficial. The Constitution and the laws of the United States, not elected or appointed officials, are the "supreme law of the land." And the conflict between the two categories of executive employees serves as an additional check to ensure that competing views of the law are raised and resolved. The conflict also ensures that both the needs for stability and continuity and the needs for innovation are at least considered on a regular basis. The conflict becomes dysfunctional only when it results in prolonged antagonism and hostility, which prevents organizations from providing essential services. In reality, it rarely reaches that point, but when it does, the conflict needs to be resolved. Among the tactics that might be used are confrontation and negotiation (compromise), collaboration, or dismissal.

Conflicts between specialists or between specialists and generalists are prime candidates for the use of intergroup confrontation techniques.[23] In this process, the conflicting groups are assembled and made to recognize that they are in conflict and that it would be helpful to reduce the level of conflict. The groups are then separated, and members are asked to prepare a self-image and an image of the group, to list their attitudes towards the other group, and to describe the characteristics of that group. Then each group selects a representative to present the lists to the other group. Separately, the groups discuss the lists they have been presented, arrive at written conclusions, and prepare a list of issues that should receive priority attention from both. In the final step, the groups are brought together to compare lists, agree on a final list of issues to be resolved, and proceed to resolve them.

Structural change may also be used to reduce conflict. Task interdependence can be reduced or eliminated by making each unit self-sufficient. This is an expensive solution for the organization because it results in duplication of materials, equipment, and personnel. As an alternative, groups can be disbanded and members reassigned to other units, or one group's authority can be adjusted so that it is clearly dominant over the other group. Buffer departments to separate conflicting groups can also be created, or liaison agents can be appointed to handle relationships between groups.

Line-staff conflict can be mitigated, if the chief executive really wants to mitigate it, through many of the preceding tactics. Line-staff conflict, however, is frequently viewed as functional and encouraged by chief executives, primarily because it increases executive power. If the troops are fighting each other, they cannot fight the general, and the general can always use the conflict as grounds for intervening and resolving the issue.

Franklin Roosevelt has frequently been praised by presidential scholars for encouraging conflict among subordinates. Line-staff conflict allows the chief executive to bypass both groups and to centralize power in her- or himself. If it is viewed as desirable to reduce the conflict, responsibilities should be clarified and respected, communication between the two groups improved, superordinate goals established, and personnel interchanges implemented.

Personality conflicts between individuals are difficult to resolve, and it is always tempting for managers to ignore them. Sometimes this is successful; either the individuals work out a solution (avoidance, or limiting interaction to those issues where contact is required) or one or the other requests a transfer or quits. If the conflict cannot be ignored because it is disrupting work activities, the easiest solution is physical separation of the two individuals, either by transferring or dismissing one or both. If both are indispensable, psychological counseling might be suggested or required.

Conflict in organizations can be managed, but it can never be eliminated. To this point, conflict has been viewed as the natural result of individuals and groups having different interests. In the attempt to satisfy those interests, one interferes with the other, causing frustration. Though many of these conflicts can be resolved to the mutual satisfaction of both parties, many cannot. Many organizational conflicts are in fact power struggles, part of the ongoing political process of organizations. Power and conflict are always closely related. Conflict can only occur if someone blocks someone else from achieving his or her interests. Successful interference is possible only if the interferer has some power.[24] Some conflicts occur primarily to determine who has the most power and because one or both parties are attempting to increase their power. Power struggles are both a cause and a result of organizational conflict, and politics is the process by which those struggles are settled.

POWER IN ORGANIZATIONS

Power has long been one of the central concepts in political science, so it is not too surprising that no single universally accepted definition of the term exists. William Riker noted in 1964 that "we are not at all sure of what we are talking about when we use the term,"[25] and writers continue to develop individual definitions of the term. Despite the proliferation of specific definitions, the underlying commonality is that power is the ability of individuals or groups to get what they want despite opposition. Dahl, for example, defined power as a social relationship in which one actor, A, can get another, B, to do something that B would otherwise not have done.[26] A more useful definition from an organizational perspective is provided by

Kanter: "Power is the ability to mobilize resources, to get and use whatever it is that a person needs for the goals he or she is attempting to meet."[27] Power is specific to situation: a group or individual may be very powerful in one context or at a given time but unable to prevail in other situations or at other times. Thus a staff budget agency may succeed in persuading top management to adopt a new budget system (have power) but be unable to persuade or compel line agencies to use it (be powerless).

Power is difficult to measure and at times even to identify. Some presidents, in some situations, have some power over Congress. The passage of the 1986 tax reform measure by Congress probably involved the exercise of presidential power by Ronald Reagan, but to assess that power, it would be necessary to determine "a) what would have happened in the absence of the exercise of power; b) the intentions of the actor attempting to exercise power; and c) the effect of actions taken by that actor" on what in fact occurred.[28] Similarly, in intraorganizational budget conflicts, when one unit emerges victorious (that is, gets all or most of what it wanted at the expense of other units), power is involved but still very elusive and difficult to prove or measure empirically.

Power is clearly distinct from authority. Authority is legitimated power. When norms, values, rules, or laws support the right of a person to exercise power, that person has authority. In organizations, authority is hierarchical and vested in positions. Organization charts, position descriptions, and rules specify the scope and magnitude of authority vested in specific positions. The occupant of the position is heir to the authority vested in the position he or she occupies. Distribution of authority seldom parallels distribution of power in organizations, and those with no authority at all, if they are skillful at the game of politics, may exercise considerable power within organizations. The Iran-Contra arms deals well illustrate how power exists very separately from authority. Although no one in the executive branch had the authority—the legal right—to use the money from the sale of arms to Iran to support the Contras in Nicaragua, somebody, even if we are not sure who, clearly had, and exercised, the power to do so.

The orders of those in authority are frequently complied with automatically as long as those orders are viewed as falling within the legitimate sphere of command of the person issuing them, though the power of authority in organizations is usually supplemented by control over two additional bases of power: rewards and punishments. Favorable performance evaluations, promotions, assignments to desired tasks or locations, praise, and overt recognition may be used by those in authority to reward the compliant. Similarly, transfers to undesirable locations or tasks, criticism, disciplinary actions, demotions, and even dismissal may be used to ensure obedience to authority.

The ability to reward and punish also constitutes an important base of power for those in positions of limited or no authority. A reward is the provision of something valued or desired; a punishment is a deprivation of things of value or the infliction of penalties or pain. As the human relationists and Maslow established, individuals desire a great many things in addition to the formal rewards provided by the organization. High on the list of desires for most people is belongingness, the need to be accepted and approved by their work associates. Almost everyone prefers to have pleasant social relationships on the job and to be liked. This need for belongingness constitutes an important basis of power for work groups over their members. The reward for accepting group norms, even if they conflict with the desires of those in authority, is to be accepted; the punishment for violating norms is ridicule, criticism, humiliation, and ostracism.

Street-level bureaucrats also use their ability to reward and punish as a basis of power over clientele. The amount of discretion vested in police, caseworkers, and teachers magnifies their formal authority. Clients may desire informal rewards or fear informal sanctions as much as formal ones and learn that behaving properly (the way the bureaucrat desires) and affecting the appropriate attitude (usually one of submission) is necessary to avoid punishment.

Control of scarce resources, money, materials, knowledge, and information constitutes a major source of organizational power. In any situation in which one unit of the organization depends on another unit for needed resources, equipment, or personnel, the controlling unit has power. One of the more expensive outcomes of organizational power struggles is the unnecessary duplication of resources that occurs as each unit attempts to establish its independence. The realization that money is power intensifies conflict over budgetary allocations within organizations. The more monetary resources a unit within the organization controls, the greater its power. Salancik and Pfeffer, for example, found in a study of university budgeting that departments that brought in the most outside funding were regarded as most powerful and received a greater share of internal resources regardless of size or student loads. "Power derived from acquiring resources is used to obtain more resources, which in turn can be employed to produce more power—the rich get richer."[29]

Information is another valuable resource and constitutes an important power base for those who control it. Secrecy flourishes in many organizations partly because those who control information realize that secrecy magnifies their power over the uninformed. Secrecy also prevents the formation of coalitions among those who might oppose a proposed action and makes blocking a proposal more difficult. "Gatekeepers," such as secretaries and those who control channels of communication, have a potent source of power if they choose to use it.[30] Expertise and control of the organization's technology have long been recognized as sources of power. For expertise to constitute a power base, it must be recognized and accepted as valid and necessary to the functioning of the organization or one or more of its units. Thus, hard scientists and engineers are likely to have a better power base than social scientists, whose theories are likely to be challenged and are difficult to verify. Control of the core technology constitutes an ability to control the outputs of the organization and to determine structural relationships. It is the power to determine how things are done in the organization and who does them. This is one of the reasons that the dominant coalition is likely to prefer routine technologies. Routine technologies eliminate expert power, make individuals more replaceable, and facilitate centralization of power.[31]

Although rules and regulations are initially created to control the behavior of members of the organization and to protect clients, they may eventually constitute a source of power for those they intended to control. Rules have a tendency to proliferate and become more complex and complicated as the organization matures. As the rule book grows thicker, fewer people in the organization are familiar with its contents, and those who are willing to learn and use the rules have a potential power base. In Congress, for example, the rules of procedure and the multivolume interpretations of those rules have long exceeded the interest and understanding of the vast majority of members. A small minority, however, have familiarized themselves with those rules and learned when and how to evoke them to enhance their power, frequently to prevent action by the majority.

Too many rules, some of which conflict and some of which are no longer appropriate to changed situations, makes "going by the book" impossible if anything is to be accomplished and enhances the power of lower-level participants both over clients and within the organization. In regulatory agencies, for example, the proliferation of rules, many of which are vague and contradictory, has enhanced the power of inspectors over regulated groups. Inspectors determine which rules are to be enforced and when and how they are to be enforced—rules were made to be broken or ignored, but only if the employee chooses to ignore them; the power to decide what the rules actually are for enforcement purposes is thus pushed down the hierarchy. Similarly, within the organization, rules may be used as a power base for lower level employees. "Working to rule," the meticulous enforcement of and obedience to all the rules, is frequently capable of stalling the organization and preventing it from accomplishing anything, putting pressure on management to accede to the desires of employees.

At various times during its existence, the organization may face critical problems, either external or internal, that threaten its ability to function. These "strategic contingencies" constitute a power base for individuals or units in the organization that can successfully handle them. "Those subunits most able to cope with the organization's critical problems and uncertainties acquire power. In its simplest form, the strategic contingencies theory implies that when an organization faces a number of lawsuits that threaten its existence, the legal department will gain power and influence."[32] As more and more lawsuits have been filed against governmental entities, their legal departments have become increasingly powerful not only by demanding an increasing share of resources to defend the entities but also by insisting on being consulted before any significant action is undertaken and being given veto power over actions that might constitute grounds for additional lawsuits. Resource scarcity has shifted organizational power to those who allocate resources and those who have responsibility for maintaining relationships with the providers of resources. As universities confront the problem of declining enrollment, power is likely to shift to those who control recruitment and retention of students. Power is dynamic and shifts within the organization as problems change.

If an individual lacks a power base of his or her own, the next best thing is to gain access to and support from those who do have power. Thus the advice to find a mentor, a sponsor, a patron, to succeed and advance in an organization is based on the recognition that being competent at a job is rarely sufficient for those who desire to enter the inner circles of power in an organization. "Old boy networks" have been replaced by gender-neutral "networking," establishing alliances with upwardly mobile peers and power brokers as a way of increasing influence and power. Having the recognized support and backing of a powerful person creates its own aura of power, which others accept and are usually reluctant to challenge, at least openly.

Power may also flow to those who control "counterorganizations," the most obvious of which are unions.[33] Union membership itself is a source of power for employees, and one of the primary reasons people join unions is to overcome the powerlessness that they experience in the work situation: "Oh no you can't scare me, I'm in the union" symbolizes the power and protection that unions convey to their members. The union also offers an alternative power hierarchy to that of the organization, and those who choose it are less subject to organizational power than their peers. Union power within an organization may be based on any of the bases of power described previously. Where unions have the right to strike, they have the ability to both create and control a strategic contingency. Without that right, their power can best be enhanced by relying on other bases. As PATCO (the professional air traffic controllers organization) and its union leadership learned, trying to exert power based on a nonexistent resource can be fatal.

Personality or charisma may also be a base of power. Although no one has ever succeeded in specifically identifying what charisma is or how to acquire it, no one doubts that it exists. Max Weber defined it as "an *extraordinary* quality of a person" that causes "others to submit to them."[34] Ronald Reagan has charisma for the vast majority of the American public; Richard Nixon did not, which may be why he resorted to illegal means to enhance his power. Reputation for power is a basis for acquiring more power. Once people are convinced that you are powerful, they are more likely to defer to your wishes automatically. This enhances your power as well as your reputation for power. The "honey pot" characteristic of power also attracts followers: those who are seeking mentors, those wishing to make alliances and contacts, those who like to associate with the powerful, and those who desire the rewards that the powerful control will be drawn to persons with power.[35]

The bases for power in organizations are multiple and are not solely controlled by those in high-ranking positions in the official hierarchy. Lower-level employees can gain and exercise considerable power in organizations. Scheff detailed how ward attendants in a state mental hospital blocked the transition from custodial to therapeutic social treatment supported by both the hospital administration and the attending physicians, thereby in effect determining both the organization's goals and its technology. The staff attendants, nurses, orderlies, and aids regarded the announced change in policy as "impractical, fraudulent and immoral."[36] Their objections were quickly translated into action (or inaction), and in the ensuing power struggle between them and the physicians, most of the advantages accrued to the staff. The ward physicians were overworked and had short tenure on specific wards and little training or interest in admin- istration. The staff had permanent tenure on the wards and knew that the physicians depended on them to carry out their duties. The staff made excellent use of their power resources. They withheld information on patients, manipulated the patients against the physicians, allowed the patients unlimited access to physicians, ceased to perform any duties not strictly authorized, and in general withheld cooperation. They maintained group solidarity through the use of informal sanctions on any group mem- bers inclined to support the change. The result was victory for the staff: after two years, the administration officially abandoned the attempted change.

The same power resources used by the mental hospital staff are also available to the permanent bureaucrats in a power struggle with political appointees. Civil servants' permanence and tenure in the organization provides them with a familiarity with and knowledge of the organization's laws and policies seldom matched by political appointees. They possess expertise and control information vital to the functioning of the organiza- tion and to the political officials who wish to control the agency. The top-level bureaucrats are also likely to have access to important, powerful individuals external to the organization (congressional committee members and staff, interest groups, and the press) and can form coalitions and alliances with them in opposition to the executive hierarchy of authority. Established social groups within the organization can provide solidarity and support. In an actual power struggle between the politicians and the civil servants, most of the advantages reside with the civil servants. Nonetheless, having power resources is not the same thing as exercising power, and the use of power by the bureaucracy to thwart the authority of political executives is more rumored than proven.

Ironically, those lower-level participants outside the managerial-professional hierarchy—the secretaries, clerks, typists, receptionists, janitors, and blue collar workers, the GS 1–4's of the work force—have by virtue of their dead-end jobs an additional source of power.

> The four basic motivating tools of management are missing: pay, promotion and interesting work. Oh yes, four. Well, they could fire you, but that's hard to do. . . . The organization offers very little to its lower participants and so it has little to take away: Hence, lower participants are difficult to control.[37]

All of which means that basically, within certain parameters, they can—and do—do things their way; and because managers and professionals depend on them to accomplish their jobs, the professionals and managers are frequently in a "subordinate" position. Similarly, those who for various reasons have rejected the pay, promotion, incentive-reward system of the hierarchy are equally difficult to control and thus powerful in their own right. Tenured faculty members who have little interest in the specific university or departments that employ them, and bureaucrats satisfied with their current job, position, and location are not vulnerable to the usual manipulation of rewards that organizations use to gain compliance.

Lower-level participants only rarely exercise the full power that they possess. David Mechanic contends that lower-level participants circumvent higher authority only under specific circumstances. First, as the mental hospital attendants showed, when the mandates of authority are regarded as illegitimate, they will be resisted or ignored. Second, when members become alienated from the organization, they may retaliate by withholding cooperation and exercising their own power.[38]

Power may also be assumed by lower-level participants when those in authority abdicate their responsibility or when they attempt to co-opt resisters to maintain at least the appearance of control. The administration at Eastham Prison allowed and encouraged the development of the tender system, initially in an attempt to maintain order by co-opting the most dangerous inmates. Once the tenders had gained power, they gradually completely usurped the system of authority. Unable to control the prison or the tenders, those in authority ultimately abandoned any attempt to maintain or exercise power. Prison guards frequently allowed prisoners to disobey them and break rules because they lacked the power to enforce rules. Rather than engaging in unsuccessful attempts to compel obedience, which would even further undermine their authority, guards allowed the prisoners considerable freedom in ignoring regulations.[39] Organizations other than prisons frequently allow lower-level participants to exercise considerable power in determining what, when, and how things are done. "When an organization gives discretion to lower level participants, it is usually trading the power of discretion for needed flexibility. The cost of constant surveillance is too high; the effort required too great."[40]

Possessing a base of power does not necessarily translate into exercising power. The exercise of power requires in addition desire to exercise power, the expenditure of time and effort, and skill at using the resources one possesses. "Power flows to those willing to spend the energy to acquire and exercise it."[41] Individuals differ considerably in the strength of their power motives: some individuals are motivated primarily by a need to achieve, some by a need to be liked; for these individuals power is neither sought nor valued. Other individuals have a strong desire to be influential, to control others, to prevail against opposition. This inner drive for power is essential for an individual to play the power game successfully.[42] Americans have always had ambivalent feelings about power and those who seek it. We tend to fear and mistrust those who pursue power at the same time that we admire their success and regard with contempt those who do not use or seek power. This ambivalence applies to those who seek power within organizations, and many organization theorists view the quest for power as an illegitimate activity. David McClelland, however, contends that the most effective managers are those who are primarily motivated by a need for power. The achievement-motivated individual is most concerned with doing things alone, of accomplishing something worthwhile. The affiliation-motivated individual is most concerned with being liked and accepted by peers. The job of management, however, is to influence people, to get them to behave and perform as the organization wishes, and only someone with a strong power motive is capable of doing that.[43] The problem from an organizational perspective and a societal one as well, lies in what McClelland terms the two faces of power. The negative face of power is found in those who seek power for power's sake, to use it to their own advantage. These individuals see power as a zero-sum game and operate by the law of the jungle. The positive face of power is found in the socialized face of power: power sought and exercised to accomplish legitimate goals.[44] Unfortunately, distinguishing between the two types of power motivation is difficult, and organizations attract individuals seeking both types.

An individual who desires power will be willing to devote considerable time and energy to its acquisition. Success, however, depends on political skill.

> Two individuals with access to approximately the same resources may not exercise the same degree of power. . . . A critical factor, one given particular prominence by Machiavelli, is political skill. . . . It is generally thought to be of critical importance in explaining differences in the power of different leaders—different presidents for example. . . . However, despite many

attempts at analysis, from Machiavelli to the present day, political skill has remained among the most elusive aspects in the analysis of power.[45]

The elusiveness of political skill has not prevented many authors from trying to identify it and explain it to potential organizational politicos. Anthony Jay, in *Management and Machiavelli*, urged executives to study and follow the advice of Machiavelli in managing organizations.[46] Mintzberg defines political skill as

> the ability to use the bases of power effectively—to convince those to whom one has access, to use one's resources, information and technical skills to their fullest in bargaining, to exercise formal power with a sensitivity to the feelings of others, to know where to concentrate one's energies, to sense what is possible, to organize the necessary alliances.[47]

Political skills, similar to leadership, seem to involve a combination of both learned and inherent behavior.

The authority structure of an organization is usually easy to identify and relatively stable, changing only as a result of formal reorganization. The power structure is very different. No organization chart identifies who actually has power, and in many organizations multiple power structures exist. Who actually controls what is done depends on the issue involved and the time a decision is made. The power structure may be stable over time or it may change rapidly depending on the amount of uncertainty, internal and external, that the organization is experiencing and the personnel composition of the organization. At some times, an organization may be dominated by its external coalition (those influences of the organization who are not members but who have control over it), which for organizations comprise political institutions (executive, legislative, judicial) that oversee it; clients; and public and professional associations. At other times, the external coalition may have little interest or involvement in the activities and decisions of an organization and one or another of various internal coalitions will be in control.

Mintzberg contends that the external coalition is most likely to be dominant in organizations that have clear goals, stable environments, and unskilled work forces, and he offers police and fire departments as examples.[48] Unfortunately, his examples do not prove his point. With the police, goals are not that clear; prioritization of the multiple goals of police departments forms the basis for political struggles within and external to the organization. Actors in the external coalition—mayors and council members particularly—have multiple concerns and issues vying for their attention, and as long as these organizations are not creating public controversy, they are likely to be left to manage themselves. Because both fire and police departments are often unionized, it is likely that internal power struggles are frequent. As long as the organizations can contain the conflict without disrupting public service, the external coalition will remain uninvolved.

It seems more likely that external coalitions will dominate public organizations in three situations. In agencies that have a single, powerful, well-organized, and active clientele (e.g., economic regulatory agencies and the subgovernments), external actors appear to be dominant. Environmental turbulence, particularly hostility or scarcity, is also likely to result in at least temporary external dominance. And internal turbulence that cannot be contained or controlled—labor-management disputes, strikes, reported incidents of scandal and corruption—are also likely to spill over the boundaries of the organization, attract the attention of political actors, and ultimately be resolved by them.

When power resides within the organization, identifying its locus is difficult. One of the continuing fascinations of the American presidency is attempting to determine who really has power in the White House. Contenders range from the president's chief of staff, certain cabinet members, the director of the Office of Management and Budget, the national security advisor, to old friends and his wife. No one is ever really sure, and the only certainty appears to be that those who state publicly that they are the most powerful usually are not. Which of the many internal coalitions actually is the most powerful depends on the strategic contingencies facing the organization and the resources and skills of those who become involved in the organization's political process.

ORGANIZATIONAL POLITICS

"Politics is the process of gaining, maintaining, and exercising power. Organizational politics involves those activities taken within organizations to acquire, develop and use power and other resources to obtain one's preferred outcomes in a situation where there is uncertainty or dissensus about choices."[49] Just as the rational and bureaucratic models of organization ignore the phenomenon of power, they also ignore the reality and effects of politics in organizations. In rational, bureaucratic organizations there is no uncertainty or dissensus. Goals and criteria are clear and shared by all participants; the choice of technology is unarguable; structure is designed in accordance with goals and technology; problems are solved rationally; and authority resolves all conflict.

In reality, however, goals are not clear, they are multiple and conflicting, and participants have their own goals, which may be more important to them than organizational goals. The most appropriate technology is seldom a clear-cut, unambiguous choice. Structure too is a political choice, and an organization's structure at any given time is the result of a power struggle frequently involving both internal and external coalitions. Problems are complex, ill-defined, and poorly understood, and solutions are frequently unknown. Conflict over these issues is resolved, if at all, through the organization's political process. Only in completely stagnant, homogeneous, and totalitarian organizations are political struggles nonexistent.

The structure of organizations encourages politics because it creates units or departments, frequently organized around occupations or professions, which function as interest groups.[50] Each unit acts to protect and promote its collective interest and the interests of individual members: increasing their power, prestige, resource allocations, material incentives, and physical status symbols. Individuals acting on their own also attempt to advance their interests: career advancement, pay, prestige, satisfaction, and power. From this diversity of interests and attempts to protect them come the "wheeling and dealing, negotiation, and other processes of coalition building and mutual influence," that characterize organizational politics.[51] Somewhat ironically, since surely it is an unintended consequence, the emphasis on democratic, participatory management style has further encouraged politics in organizations.

Individuals are also encouraged by management practices to engage in politics to protect their interests. Many employees mistrust the fairness and objectivity of the performance evaluation system on which career advancement is theoretically based. Particularly when performance is difficult to evaluate quantitatively, as is true with many public service occupations (and particularly with managerial performance), employees who wish to get ahead may resort to political games and strategies. Management policies that involve rapid promotion or frequent transfers also tend to increase employees' lack of confidence in their own skills and encourage them to resort to political maneuvering.[52] Individuals with a strong power motivation are also unlikely to rely on the authority system to satisfy their need for rapid advancement and power.

The combined impact of all these factors makes politics within organizations inevitable. Uncertainty and ambiguity are the necessary conditions for political struggles; political behavior does not emerge for routine, clear-cut decisions for which specific, known rules exist and are followed.[53] The major domains of political activity in organizations are determination or change of goals; determination or change in technology; structural change; interdepartmental coordination; personnel actions; and resource allocation. These are all high-stakes areas for the organization, its units, and its individual members, and all are characterized by uncertainty and ambiguity.

Graham Allison characterized the political maneuverings that occur in bureaucracies as games, interactions among players guided by rules:

> Some rules are explicit, others implicit. Some rules are quite clear, others fuzzy. Some are very stable; others are ever changing. But the collection of rules, in effect, defines the game. First, rules establish the positions, the paths by which men gain access to positions, the power of each position, the action channels. Second, rules constrict the range of . . . decisions and actions that

are acceptable. . . . Third, rules sanction moves of some kinds—bargaining, coalitions, persuasion, deceit, bluff and threat—while making other moves illegal, immoral, ungentlemanly or inappropriate.[54]

Many of the political games in organizations are familiar to anyone who has observed or worked in large organizations. The empire-building game, where managers attempt to expand the size of their units through either growth or the takeover of other units, is played using all the power resources and political strategies at the disposal of the participants. The budgeting game, which was described by Wildavsky, appears to be universal in organizations. Every unit always wants more financial resources and, in its quest for more, uses every ploy and tactic it can envision: always asking for more than it needs, using clientele to support its case, spending to save, emphasizing sunk costs, even resorting to deceit and manipulation of figures.[55] The expertise game, played by professionals in their power struggles with each other and with generalist administrators, uses the mystique surrounding the profession to acquire autonomy and control.[56]

The lower levels of the organization play their own games. The most unsettling from the organization's perspective is the insurgency game, which involves overt resistance to authority. Sometimes insurgency is successful, as it was for the mental hospital attendants, but it is always a game with considerable risk if the authority structure decides to play counterinsurgency. PATCO, the air traffic controllers union, and its unsuccessful attempt in 1981 to force the president and the secretary of transportation to accede to its demand for improved working conditions and increased compensation illustrates the dangers of insurgency against a more powerful actor who is willing to use all his or her power and authority. The controllers believed that they had a number of legitimate grievances about their working conditions, and they had attempted unsuccessfully to resolve the problem through the established structures. Although PATCO had union status, unions in the federal government are strictly limited in terms of their legal bargaining rights: wages and fringe benefits are specifically excluded from the scope of bargaining permitted, and strikes are illegal. Federal law provides that any federal employee who strikes against the government may be immediately dismissed, barred from any further federal employment for three years, and subject to fines and imprisonment. Still, the postal unions had gone on strike in 1971 and won practically everything they demanded without penalty, so mass mutiny, an extreme form of the insurgency game, did sometimes succeed.

PATCO had several power bases on which to base its political game. Expertise and performance of a clearly essential function were the controllers' major power resources, but ones they overestimated. They believed that their expertise and training made them irreplaceable and that in a head-on power struggle they could go out on strike and essentially close down the air transport system of the United States. Solidarity of the membership also constituted an important power resource, and the members unanimously backed the leadership. Two other expected power resources, however, never materialized. PATCO leadership expected support from other labor unions, a coalition which would have vastly magnified its power, and they anticipated that the public would put pressure on the president to end the strike quickly and restore air traffic systems to normality. Neither of those contingencies occurred. The leadership not only badly misread its power situation but also failed to understand its opponent—a crucial error in any game situation.

The union's opponent, President Reagan, was relatively new to the presidency, a conservative, and basically antiunion. An executive new to the position is likely to have less self-confidence than one who has an established power or authority position. Consequently, he or she is more likely to react forcefully to overt challenges to authority and prestige. That type of reaction is even more likely if the executive is unsympathetic to the demands of the insurgents. The president's reputation for power and his ability to lead were directly threatened by the strike—and authority and the law were on his side. He fired all the striking controllers, and the Justice Department moved quickly to begin prosecution of PATCO leaders.

Other labor unions refused to back PATCO, and some labor leaders openly criticized the strike. Although chaos initially prevailed in the air transport system, neither the public nor airlines backed PATCO or favored concessions to it. The controllers learned that their expertise was not quite as exclusive as they had presumed, as controllers from the military were shifted to civilian duty. Ultimately, the controllers also learned an additional fact about their expertise, which perhaps they should have realized and weighed into their decision to strike. When it comes to air traffic control, government is a monopsony: the only buyer of the skills and expertise of air traffic controllers. Their skills turned out to be more substitutable than their careers.[57]

Why the union leadership so badly miscalculated and played the game so disastrously is unclear. Lack of political skill seems obvious, and they also displayed many of the symptoms of groupthink: an illusion of invulnerability; efforts to rationalize in order to discount warnings; an unquestioned belief in the group's inherent morality, ignoring the ethical or moral consequences of their action; stereotyped views of rivals as too evil to warrant genuine attempts to negotiate or too weak to counter their attempts; and a shared illusion of unanimity.[58] The result was a failure to use one of the more potent and legal power resources of the controllers, the rules and the working to rule game, which might have been far more successful.

The lording game is one of the most unpleasant games played by the powerless, and to play it they must find someone even more powerless.

> When a person's exercise of power is thwarted or blocked, when people are rendered powerless in the larger arena, they may tend to concentrate their

> power needs on those over whom they have a modicum of authority. There is
> a displacement of control downward. . . . People will boss those they can, . . .
> if they cannot flex their power muscles more constructively and if, moreover,
> they are afraid they are really powerless.[60]

Lording is the exploitation of legitimate power in illegitimate ways. The low-level and frequently insecure executive lords it over his secretary, treating the secretary in a demeaning manner, forcing him or her to perform meaningless and useless tasks and unfairly criticizing his or her performance. Street-level bureaucrats lord it over clients, from the police officer who hassles suspects because they have the wrong attitude to the welfare caseworker who makes applicants appear for appointments at set times and then keeps them waiting for hours.

For the individual, the rapid career advancement game may be the most important game of all, and the political tactics that may be used are numerous. Political tactics are "those sets of behavior in addition to job competence, hard work and fortuitous circumstances that are intended to accelerate one's career or to acquire additional power within the organization."[61] Finding a mentor and networking appear to be essential first steps. As with any other political games, there are risks involved. If you pick the wrong mentor, one who leaves the organization or turns out to be relatively powerless, you have delayed your career progress. Similarly, if for some reason you alienate your mentor, your career progress may be stymied or reversed. If the mentoring situation becomes too obvious, it may create jealousy and suspicion, and rivals may form alliances against you. Women continue to. have a particularly difficult problem playing the mentoring game, given the fact that most power or authority holders in organizations are men, and gossip and rumor develop quickly and spread even more quickly about such relationships. Helping your boss look good and apple polishing are also recommended tactics.[62] Angling for visibility and looking good, literally and figuratively, when you have achieved it is an extremely important maneuver. Documenting accomplishments, keeping a "hero file" of letters and memos from others praising yourself (which can be used to strengthen credentials for promotion or transfer) is recommended by many consultants in the rapidly growing field of teaching people to play the office politics game.[63]

The portrait of organizational life that emerges from these political games and struggles is far removed from the rational bureaucracy of Max Weber, from the tenets of the merit system, or for that matter from the benevolent organization of the human relationists and organizational humanists. Politics has always been part of organizational life, but it may be increasing and becoming more intense. This is partly attributable to the post–World War II baby boom and to changed attitudes of young upwardly mobile persons. The baby boomers impact on the job market has been extensive, contributing not only to unemployment, but also to increasing competition within organizations for upward mobility. The ultimate result is hierarchical gridlock—all the positions in the hierarchy will be blocked because they are held by relatively young workers who will neither resign nor retire. Climbing the hierarchy under such circumstance requires more than competence; it requires skillful political maneuvering and a willingness to step over or eliminate those who block mobility. The changed attitudes of the 1980s, which emphasize success, power, upward mobility, and material acquisitions, the "yuppie" mentality, further intensify the political maneuvering within organizations. Retrenchment and fiscal scarcity exacerbate the situation. "Office politics really accelerates when you're wondering who's going to get thrown from the airplane."[64] When survival, rather than career advancement, depends on political ability, everybody starts playing politics.

CONCLUSION

In this chapter organizations were portrayed as entities beset by a variety of internal conflicts that cannot be and are not resolved by the system of formal authority. Power struggles and politics emerge as inevitable organizational processes that frequently subvert the nominal authority relationships defined by job descriptions and organization charts. David Easton defined politics as the authoritative allocation of values, and by this definition, organizations are inherently political institutions. Organizations allocate for both their members and their clients things of value: money, status, prestige, job satisfaction, career advancement, property, and symbolic rewards. The composition and structure of organizations fosters the development of politics. Bringing together individuals with diverse backgrounds, education, values, and goals and combining them in units and then encouraging them to compete for the things of value the organization provides makes conflict and politics likely, if not inevitable. The vagueness that characterizes organizational goals, the uncertainty surrounding choice of technology, and the difficulty, if not impossibility, of establishing a clear, objective, uniform, performance evaluation system provide further impetus for those who hold diverse interests to attempt to protect and advance those interests and undermine the ability of those in positions of authority to impose their perceptions and values on dissidents. When individuals whose primary motivation is power are added to this volatile situation, politics is even more certain.

Politics and power may be inevitable in organizations, but whether they are beneficial or detrimental in public organizations is far from clear. One of their most important negative aspects is the extent to which organizational politics complicates, if not undermines, external political control. One of the major theoretical advantages of bureaucracy has always been its clear authority structure, which made it possible to determine responsibility and to hold individuals and organizations accountable for their actions. Power separate from authority is illegitimate and difficult to identify. When politicians or courts must ask "Who's really in charge here?" their control has been seriously weakened. American constitutional theory only unwillingly accepted that administrative agencies, not legislatures, determine operative public policy goals, and still accepted the theory on the presumption that at least the agencies determined these goals rationally. That goals emerge as the outcome of internal agency political struggles stretches the theory to the breaking point. Political struggles also increase the probability that goal displacement will occur in organizations.

Recognizing that career advancement depends as much on willingness and ability to play politics as on skills, abilities, and job performance does severe damage to the credibility of the merit system and may negatively affect overall organization performance. Despite McClelland's assertion that those with strong power motivations make the best managers, the case is far from proven that those most adept at political maneuvering are also the best managers. Preoccupation with political games and power struggles distracts attention from substantive work, may undermine morale, and decreases productivity.

On the positive side, organizational politics may prevent the organization from becoming stagnant and inflexible. It should also be highly evaluated by those who believe in the benefits of incrementalism. If goals cannot and should not be made clear, if there are no final, right solutions to problems, then politics rather than rationalism is the most appropriate process for organizations. The continuing power struggles help ensure that the organization remains flexible and adaptable to both internal and external changes. Organizational politics helps to counter the authoritarian tendency of bureaucracy and may provide individuals with the remedy for that "midmorning sense of powerlessness" they suffer in large, impersonal organizations. Power in organizations, like power in the political system, has many bases, and those who lack formal authority may counter this loss of autonomy by astute use of their power. Political games and power struggles do make work life more interesting, and given the uninteresting nature of many jobs this is not a small contribution. Further, just as conflict and competition in the political system is necessary to prevent the centralization of power in one group or individual, conflict and competition also serve as a check on excessive accumulation of power in authority holders in organizations. Finally, the exercise of power by low-level participants is frequently essential to organizational function. When the rules are too numerous and too conflicting to be enforced, when those in authority lack competence or experience, if the lower levels did not take power, many organizations would collapse under their own bureaucratic weight.

NOTES

1. Jeffrey Pfeffer, *Power in Organizations* (Marshfield, Mass.: Pitman Publishers, 1981), p. 17.
2. Ibid., p. 18.
3. Jay Shafritz and J. Stephen Ott, *Classics of Organizational Theory*, 2nd ed. (Chicago: Dorsey Press, 1987), p. 304.
4. Kenneth Thomas, "Organizational Conflict," in Steven Kerr, ed., *Organizational Behavior* (Columbus, Ohio: Grid Publishing Co., 1979), p. 162.
5. Donald White and H. William Vroman, *Action in Organizations*, 2nd ed. (Boston: Allyn and Bacon, 1982), p. 313.
6. Thomas, "Organizational Conflict," pp. 155–156.
7. William Scott and Terence Mitchell, *Organization Theory* (Homewood, Ill.: Richard D. Irwin, 1976), p. 246.
8. James Gibson, John Ivancevich, and James Donnelly, *Organizations: Behavior, Structure and Processes*, 3rd ed. (Dallas: Business Publishing, Inc., 1979), p. 165.
9. A. H. Maslow, *Eupsychian Management* (Homewood, Ill.: Richard D. Irwin, 1965), p. 18.
10. Daniel Robey, *Designing Organizations: A Macro Perspective* (Homewood, Ill.: Richard D. Irwin, 1982), p. 149.
11. Edgar Schein, *Organizational Psychology*, 2nd ed. (Englewood Cliffs, N.J.: Prentice Hall, 1970), p. 97.
12. Andrew Dubrin, *Fundamentals of Organizational Behavior*, 2nd ed. (New York: Pergamon Press, 1978), p. 360.
13. Schein, *Organizational Psychology*, p. 97.
14. Stephen Robbins, *Organization Theory* (Englewood Cliffs, N.J.: Prentice Hall, 1983), p. 291.
15. Melville Dalton, *Men Who Manage* (New York: John Wiley, 1959), p. 215.
16. Jerald Hage, *Theories of Organization* (New York: John Wiley, 1980), p. 301.
17. Robbins, *Organization Theory*, p. 296.
18. Meyer Zald, "Power Balance and Staff Conflict in Correctional Institutions," *Administrative Science Quarterly* (June 1962): pp. 22–49.
19. Gibson et al., *Organizations: Behavior, Structure and Process*, p. 169.
20. Thomas Cronin, *The State of the Presidency* (Boston: Little, Brown, 1975), p. 155.
21. Gareth Morgan, *Images of Organization* (Beverly Hills, Calif.: Sage Publications, Inc., 1986), p. 191.
22. See Kenneth W. Thomas, "Toward Multi-Dimensional Values in Teaching: The Example of Conflict Behavior." *Academy of Management Review* (1977): pp. 484–490.
23. See Robert Blake, Herbert Shepherd, and Jane Mouton, *Managing Intergroup Conflict in Industry* (Houston: Gulf Publishing, 1964).
24. Robey, *Designing Organizations*, p. 145.
25. William Riker, "Some Ambiguities in the Notion of Power," *American Political Science Review* (1964): p. 341.
26. Robert Dahl, "The Concept of Power," *Behavioral Science* (1957): pp 202–203.
27. Rosabeth Moss Kanter, *Men and Women of the Corporation* (New York: Basic Books, 1977), p. 166.
28. Pfeffer, *Power in Organizations*, p. 11.
29. Gerald R. Salancik and Jeffrey Pfeffer, "The Basis and Use of Power in Organizational Decisionmaking: The Case of a University," *Administrative Science Quarterly* (1974): p. 470.

30. Morgan, *Images of Organization*, p. 167.
31. Robbins, *Organization Theory*, p. 181.
32. Gerald R. Salancik and Jeffrey Pfeffer, "Who Gets Power and How They Hold on to It: A Strategic Contingencies Model of Power," *Organization Dynamics* (1977): pp. 4–5.
33. Morgan, *Images of Organization*, p. 175.
34. Max Weber, *Max Weber: Essays in Sociology*, trans. H. H. Gerth and C. Wright Mills (New York: Oxford University Press, 1958), p. 295.
35. Morgan, *Images of Organization*, p. 184.
36. Thomas G. Scheff, "Control over Policy by Attendants in a Mental Hospital," in Oscar Grusky and George Miller, eds., *The Sociology of Organizations* (New York: Free Press, 1970), p. 330.
37. R. Richard Ritts and G. Ray Funkhouser, *The Ropes to Skip and the Ropes to Know* (Columbus, Ohio: Grid Publishing, 1982), p. 206.
38. David Mechanic, "Sources of Power of Lower Participants in Complex Organizations," *Administrative Science Quarterly* (December 1962): pp. 349–364.
39. Gresham Sykes, "The Corruption of Authority and Rehabilitation," in Amitai Etzioni, *Complex Organizations* (New York: Holt, Rinehart and Winston, 1961), p. 192.
40. Mechanic, "Sources of Power of Lower Participants in Complex Organizations," p. 360.
41. Mintzberg, *Power In and Around Organizations* (Englewood Cliffs: Prentice Hall, 1983), p. 25.
42. David McClelland, *Power: The Inner Experience* (New York: Irvington Publishers, 1976).
43. David McClelland and David Burnham, "Power is the Great Motivator," in Donald White, *Contemporary Perspectives In Organization Behavior* (Boston: Allyn and Bacon, Inc, 1982), pp. 96-100.
44. David McClelland, "The Two Faces of Power," in Paul Laurence, Louis Barnes, and Jay Lorsch, eds., *Organizational Behavior and Administration*, 3rd. ed. (Homewood, Ill.: Richard D. Irwin, 1976), p. 312.
45. Robert Dahl, "Power," in Aaron Wildavsky, *The Presidency* (Boston: Little, Brown, 1969), p. 157.
46. Anthony Jay, *Management and Machiavelli* (New York: Holt, Rinehart and Winston, 1967).
47. Mintzberg, *Power In and Around Organizations*, p. 26.
48. Ibid., p. 320.
49. Pfeffer, *Power in Organizations*, p. 13.
50. Hage, *Theories of Organization*, p. 57.
51. Dubrin, *Fundamentals of Organizational Behavior*, p. 159.
52. Ibid., pp. 158–159.
53. Richard Daft, *Organization Theory and Design* (St. Paul: West Publishing Company, 1983), p. 406.
54. Graham Allison, *Essence of Decision: Explaining the Cuban Missile Crisis* (Boston: Little, Brown, 1971), pp. 170–171.
55. Aaron Wildavsky, *The Politics of the Budgeting Process*, 4th ed. (Boston: Little, Brown, 1984).
56. Mintzberg, *Power In and Around Organizations*, p. 199.
57. For a full account of the PATCO strike see Melinda Beck and William J. Cook, "Who Controls the Air?" *Newsweek* (August 17, 1981): pp. 18–27.
58. Irving Janis, *Victims of Groupthink* (Boston: Houghton-Mifflin, 1972), pp. 197–198.

59. Mintzberg, *Power In and Around Organizations*, p. 200.
60. Moss Kanter, *Men and Women of the Corporation,* p. 189.
61. Dubrin, *Fundamentals of Organizational Behavior,* p. 154.
62. Ibid., p. 162.
63. Ibid., p. 167.
64. Robert Decker, director of the Palo Alto Center for Stress Related Disorders, quoted in E. Gelman, B. Powell, P. Abramson, V. Quade, J. M. Harrison, and P. McAlevey, "Playing Office Politics," *Newsweek* (September 16, 1985): p. 55.

7

ORGANIZATIONAL CULTURE

If organizations can and should be viewed as political systems, they can also be viewed as miniature societies, each with its own distinct and identifiable culture. The complete organization is an extremely complex social entity consisting of formal structure and all the informal relationships that occur within that structure, of the formal rules and the informal rules that guide and control the behavior of individuals and groups within it. One of the greatest challenges facing organization management is ensuring that individuals within the organization have accepted, and hopefully are committed to, the dominant values, norms, and culture of the organization. Some contemporary organization theorists would go one step further and contend that managing culture is the single most important responsibility of organization leadership. To them, managing culture means controlling and manipulating the culture of the organization so that productivity and organizational commitment are emphasized as central values and internalized by all workers.

Although the cultural approach to organizations is one of the newest theoretical approaches, it has antecedents in earlier organization theories. Its clearest precursor is found in the Institutional School, best represented by Philip Selznick. Institutionalists stressed that to understand and analyze organizations it was essential to view them as minisocieties. An organization needed to be viewed as "an organic, declining, evolving whole, with a natural history."[1] In Selznick's view, the key task of organization leaders was to guide the process of institutionalization whereby the organization is transformed "into a 'committed polity' with a high sense of identity, purpose and commitment."[2] That prescription is remarkably similar to that of the cultural approach, just as Selznick's institutions are similar to the most admired organizations of the culturalists: the corporations lauded in Peters' and Waterman's *In Search of Excellence* and Ouchi's *Theory Z*.[3]

From both the rationalist and the individualist perspective, the view of organizations as culture-bearing entities is unsettling. As cultures, organizations are replete with myths, ceremonial rites and rituals, norms, and internalized values whose origins are long forgotten; but these are far more important in shaping and controlling behavior than rational, planned decision making and controls, and they frequently nullify attempts to implement rationally determined changes. As cultures, organizations attempt, with varying degrees of success, to socialize their members, encouraging them to abandon previous identities, values, and behaviors in favor of those mandated by its culture. For some, the prospect of Matsushita Electric Company's 87,000 identically uniformed employees beginning their workday by singing together and reciting the company's code of values is inspiring.[4] To the individualist it is chilling.

Regardless of one's perspective, the evidence that organizations do develop their own cultures and socialize their members into it is persuasive. To understand and perhaps to manage an organization successfully requires that its culture be identified and understood. This chapter examines the concept of organizational culture, describing how it is formed and how it is transmitted to the members of the organization.

ORGANIZATIONAL CULTURE

"Culture is the basic assumptions and beliefs shared by members of the organization that operate unconsciously and that define in a basic taken for granted fashion an organization's view of itself and its environment."[5] Culture is intangible, rarely written down or discussed but still a potent force in shaping and controlling behavior: it is an observable and palpable phenomenon, reflected in the shared philosophies, ideologies, myths, values, beliefs, assumptions, and norms of the organization.[6] Anyone who has practiced the same occupation or held an identical job title in different organizations can attest to the different "feel" of different organizations. For example, an elite private college, such as Reed, Antioch, or Swarthmore, has a distinctive ambience that is drastically different from that of an urban public university even though their basic missions are similar.[7] Even though such cultural differences are apparent to participants and outsiders, defining the culture of an organization is a difficult task. The intangibility of culture makes it extremely difficult to isolate and observe. Quantitative methodologies are nearly useless in attempting to identify unconscious, internalized values. Studying organizational culture requires the use of qualitative research methods, which adds to the controversy over the cultural approach to organizations.[8]

Culture forms and develops gradually as a result of shared group experiences. To survive and function, a group must develop a common language; a way of defining boundaries and selecting members; a way of allocating authority, power, status, and resources; norms for handling interpersonal relationships and intimacy; criteria for dispensing rewards and punishments; and some way of coping with unmanageable, unpredictable, or stressful events.[9] Values and beliefs of early leaders and members of the organization and procedures and methods that initially developed and proved functional and successful become accepted, internalized, and passed on to subsequent generations of organization members. Although culture changes, it does so gradually and frequently imperceptibly:

> The Royal Artillery were giving a demonstration to some visiting Europeans on Salisbury Plain in the 1950s. The visitors were most impressed with the speed and precision of the light artillery crew, but one of them asked what was the duty of the man who stood at attention throughout the whole demonstration.
> "He's number six," the adjutant explained.
> "I too can count. But why is he there?"
> "That's his job. Number six stands at attention throughout."
> "But why then do you not have five?"
> No one knew. It took a great deal of research through old training manuals, but finally they discovered his duty. He was the one who held the horses.[10]

Organizational culture manifests itself in a variety of ways. One of the most important is myths, stories, and legends that glorify the organization and its members and exaggerate their virtues. The myths are usually replete with heroes, villains, and occasionally even heroines. Although organizations such as the marines, the FBI, and the police come most readily to mind as organizations that have elaborate myths that they systematically perpetuate, all organizations with an identifiable history glorify their past. Important events are told, embellished, and retold. Richard Harris, in describing socialization at a police academy, presented the following example of a story told recruits that has all the characteristics of a myth:

> We had one time when things were bad in the community, so we brought in all the drunks, or people with bottles in their hands. All the people were happy; the problems were decreased significantly. The community was satisfied and we stuck out our chests. What happened? Some lawyer was crying "unconstitutional," and now everything is as bad as it was.[11]

Myths create a sense of purpose among members, strengthen commitment and loyalty, and unify the organization.[12] Like ancient Greek myths, contemporary organization myths help make the incomprehensible if not comprehensible at least acceptable by providing some fanciful explanation that expiates the organization and its members from their failings. (In the old days, before Miranda . . .; in the old days before federal intrusion . . . .)

Primitive cultures also had shamans, priests, prophets, and medicine men who helped deal with uncertainty and thus reduced if not actual risk at least the perception and fear of it. Morgan contends that modern organizations have created their equivalents in forecasters, planners, and policy analysts. Their highly quantitative and computerized methods resemble magic and divination, and like their primitive predecessors they are occasionally correct in their predictions but more frequently wrong. Also like their predecessors, despite their mistakes, neither they nor their magic is discredited. Instead their failures are usually attributed to an imperfection in execution or intervention by a more powerful hostile force.[13] For government organizations and their analysts, the hostile higher power is usually the economy; business organizations frequently invoke the government as the uncontrollable force.

Culture is also manifested in the underlying assumptions, the unconscious core beliefs, of the organization: the sense of what ought to be, beliefs about human nature, the nature of human relationships, and the nature of the environment.[14] Schools and universities have their core beliefs about the nature of students and the way they should be educated; welfare agencies have core beliefs about the poor and the way they should be treated; the police have core beliefs about criminals and the proper ways of handling them. Similarly, management beliefs about employees become unspoken and unproved assumptions about the proper way to deal with subordinates. Public organizations develop assumptions about relevant actors in their environment: the legislatures, the courts, the chief executive. For example, the police (and one suspects many other public organizations) tend to view politicians as "an out group . . . unwilling to support them in controversial matters if it was politically expedient not to do so . . . [and] likely to make unwise decisions regarding police affairs."[15] The courts fare even worse: "Did you ever see that lady blindfolded, holding the scales in District Court? If she ever saw what went on in District Court, she'd throw away the scales."[16]

Physical manifestations of culture are found in the symbols, slogans, and logos that embody the essence of the organization as it wishes to be portrayed. The Postal Service's eagle poised for flight; the Forest Service's Smokey the Bear; the red, white and blue logo of the Job Service; and police departments' "To Protect and Serve" are symbols intended to convey to the public and the organization's members an image of the organization. For members, such symbols increase identification with and commitment to the organization. When combined with distinctive uniforms, they serve to distinguish members from nonmembers and create "we-they" feelings that intensify group cohesion. Slogans can also be used to recruit new members as well as to inspire current members. The Peace Corps' "The Toughest Job You'll Ever Love," or the Army's "Be All That You Can Be" may not be accurate portrayals of actual life in those organizations, but they are accurate representations of how organizations wish to be perceived.

Similarly, physical layout and furnishings are frequently manifestations of the organization's culture. Organizations whose cultural values emphasize openness and equality frequently represent this symbolically by not having closed offices but rather using open cubicles with identical furnishings. Conversely, an organization with a highly differentiated status system not only will have private offices but the size of the offices and the quality and type of furnishings will clearly reflect the status of the individuals who occupy them.

Norms are "the unwritten rules of the game . . . the behaviors and attitudes that the members of a group or organization pressure one another to follow."[17] What to wear, how to treat clientele, how to treat subordinates, whom to speak to and what to say, even how hard to work are all frequently regulated by the norms of the organization. When combined with internal status symbols, these norms provide unmistakable cues to organization members about what kinds of behavior and values are acceptable in an organization. They help simplify life for both organizational participants and the public.

> In organizational life, judgments about others have to be made that are woefully uninformed . . . and here is where speech, dress and manner come in, and why symbols and symbolic activities are so important . . . why people attach so much importance to symbols of high status—the rug on the floor, the window, the corner office.[18]

Organizations with uniforms with identifiable rank symbols make it easy to know how to react to an unknown member of the organization. A former student of the author who became an officer in the army and was assigned to the Pentagon described how chance meetings in the halls were handled: "Nobody ever looks at anybody's face or speaks first. Instead, they look first at the shoulder or the collar of the person approaching for the bar, the eagle, the star, or whatever. The actual greeting that follows depends on what they find there, and what their own rank is."

Organizations without uniforms make it more difficult, but they are likely to have subtle and not-so-subtle distinctions in their unwritten dress codes and informal rules of behavior that help members differentiate. Many universities are characterized by a culture and status system so rigid that to lower-level participants it appears to be a caste system:

> Higher education, like every field, has its acculturation process, through which neophytes learn the requirements for survival and advancement. New

junior faculty members quickly adapt to the intricacies of the campus caste system and discover the role and activities that separate them from the non-teaching staff.

Considering that the caste system works entirely to the advantage of professors, it is not surprising that they learn so fast. What is surprising is that most of them are (or pretend to be) ignorant of the system's existence—in spite of such obvious evidence as gross inequities between faculty and staff members in pay and in the amount of time worked. . . .

The caste system has many customs. From the perspective of the faculty, the list includes, but is not restricted to, the following:

—If staff members accept an open invitation to a departmental or college social function, never talk to them, no matter how chatty you are at the office.

—When applying for a grant, do not include extra pay for the secretary in your proposal. . . . Faculty members are paid for extra work; secretaries are not.

—Feel free to regale your secretary with examples of conspicuous consumption: "I'm leaving now to take my son to his skiing lesson and may not be back." . . . "Let me know when the Mercedes dealer calls to say the car is ready." Such statements are a great way to emphasize the social and financial gap between you and her.

—Rub in the fact that you get a midterm break but she does not.

—Call attention to the privileges accompanying your superior status.[19]

Although the status system and norms may be discomforting for the staff, they are clearly functional for both faculty members and the universities. Professors frequently believe themselves to be underpaid, but their superior status and the norms that permit them to flaunt it provide psychological benefits that at least partially make up for their inadequate monetary compensation. The universities save money by being able to undercompensate both higher- and lower-level caste members.

Cultures also have taboos, forbidden forms of behavior, such as "those items people are forbidden to eat, to touch, to discuss, to study and research, places they are generally forbidden to enter, those persons with whom it is generally prohibited to have a sexual relationship.[20] Officers may not fraternize with enlisted personnel; students may not enter faculty lounges; computers and office equipment may be used by authorized personnel only; obvious mistakes made by high-status members are not to be pointed out or discussed. Every organization has its own taboos that establish clear boundaries of permissible behavior.

Rites are elaborate and dramatic events that "consolidate various forms of cultural expression into one event."[21] Ceremonial rites are extremely important in transmitting and maintaining culture. They help socialize new members, reinforce the loyalty of all members, reaffirm the importance of pivotal values, increase identification with the group, and bolster group solidarity. Rites of passage facilitate transition of people into new social roles and include both initiation rites and ceremonies carried out when a member retires or is promoted, demoted, or fired. Initiation rites introduce new members to the organization and start their socialization into its culture. Initiation rites frequently involve hazing, teasing, and ridicule, which demonstrates to new members their inferiority and ignorance in relation to the superior group members. The humiliation and cruelty inherent in initiation rites test the new members' attitudes towards the group and the strength of their desire to become members. It carries the implication that if full membership of the group were too easily attained it would not be worth having.[22] Although military and paramilitary organizations have the most severe and dehumanizing rites of initiation, all organizations put new members through some type of initital rites of degradation. If recruits survive the initiation rites, their full acceptance into the organization will be marked by some form of rite of passage, ranging from the formal graduation ceremonies characteristic of the military and the police to a more simple notification that they have survived the probationary period. Universities have the lengthiest initiation period, ranging from five to seven years before the rite of passage, the granting of tenure, occurs. That rite of passage is in many respects more humiliating than anything that occurs in boot camp, as the members are required to prove formally their worthiness to belong to an organization for which they have worked for five or more years.

Rites of passage also mark significant changes in the status of members. Promotions are marked by a variety of ceremonial events, from announcement in newspapers and at staff meetings to formal lunches or dinners. Such rites provide an opportunity for manifesting group loyalty and identification, provide recognition of individuals for their accomplishments (thus strengthening their commitment), and also serve to motivate and increase commitment of all group members. Demotions and the rites accompanying them serve as a warning to members of the perils of nonconformity and simultaneously reaffirm the importance of the position involved as well as the importance of remaining a member of good standing within groups. Rites of separation for members who retire or voluntarily resign from the organization serve functions similar to funerals and from the organization's perspective are more important for those who remain than for those who are departing, who after all are of no real further importance to the organization. The farewell party or retirement dinner emphasizes the finality of the social rupture, eases the process of separation from the group, and manifests once again group loyalty and identification.[23] Dismissals or firings are accompanied by rites of degradation. "The collective attention is focused on the people being degraded and their behaviors are publicly associated with failures and problems. . . . The degraded people are stripped of their positions and statuses."[24] Such rites do not communicate what behavior is desired; rather they indicate clearly what types of behavior are likely to lead to public humiliation and expulsion from the organization.

Rites of intensification are intended to increase belongingness and pride of membership. They are ceremonial events that demonstrate the solidarity of the group: the office Christmas party, the annual picnic or barbecue, the traditional softball game between officers and enlisted personnel, the annual meeting for the "state of the agency" address by the secretary, are all forms of reaffirmation of the oneness of the group. Ceremonies are also occasions where leaders like to make ritual statements not intended to be taken seriously, and status differences may be temporarily ignored. High-ranking officials are given to saying things like "My door is always open to any employee who wants to talk to me," or "I want anyone in this organization who has a problem to feel free to come in to talk it over with me." Seldom, if ever, do they really mean that, and any low-ranking employee who subsequently attempts to avail him or herself of the opportunity presented is likely to find the way blocked by a series of receptionists, secretaries, and administrative assistants. Ritual social occasions frequently permit employees to engage in behavior that is otherwise prohibited by norms. Dress codes are relaxed or ignored; high-ranking members may be called by their first names, restrictions on who may fraternize with whom are relaxed or ignored. Emotions are vented, feelings of camaraderie encouraged, and ironically the rectitude and importance of the norms that have been relaxed are reaffirmed. In some organizations, staff meetings also become ceremonial rituals held primarily to communicate and reinforce norms of passivity, fear, and respect.[25]

A common language is a requisite for any culture, and frequently organization members will invent a new language, familiar only to those who are members. Bureaucratese has long been condemned and lamented by outsiders, clients, the press, the public, and English professors. Depending on the agency, bureaucrats speak and write of "transitionalizing," "prioritizing," and "interfacing" and develop acronyms—POSDCORB, PPBS, GAAP—that confuse and irritate outsiders. Ironically, from a cultural perspective, that is precisely what language is supposed to do: to establish boundaries, to exclude outsiders, to strengthen bonds among members, and to serve as a means of identifying members.[26] Professional groups develop technical jargon easily understood by members but mystifying to nonmembers. For many professions, this also serves to establish the superior status of members of the profession over nonmembers, especially clients. Argot, the use of substitutes for words in daily use, serves similar purposes for many occupational groups. Sailors speak of "starboard" and "port" when they could just as easily say the right or left side.[27] Police officers commonly use the numerical language of the penal code and the police radio in everyday conversation, effectively excluding outsiders and increasing their own sense of solidarity.

Whether leaders can change the culture of an established organization is debatable, but they clearly play an important role in maintaining that culture. The upper ranks of the organization, the members of the "Men's Hut," are guardians of the organization's culture. The Men's Hut "is a place of taboo, a repository of arcane and secret lore . . . a symbol of, and a medium for, maintaining the status quo and the good of the order."[28] It is to the members of the Men's Hut that other members of the organization look for behavioral cues and guidance as to what is acceptable and what is unacceptable behavior. Membership is restricted and, equal employment opportunity notwithstanding, in most organizations it is a *Men's* Hut or, as a disgruntled female executive once remarked, a little boy's room. Gaining membership is a rite of passage gained only after considerable testing and repeated demonstrations of one's worthiness—the ability to fit in, the willingness to conform. Lower-level members of the organization are likely to impute special and extraordinary qualities and abilities to those in higher ranks, even if in reality they are rather ordinary individuals.

> Incumbents of high office are held in awe because they are in touch with the mysteries and magic of such office. . . . Since one knows less and less about the activites of superordinates the farther away in the hierarchy they are, the greater is the awe in which he holds them. . . . There results an increasing vagueness as to the activities at each level as one mounts the hierarchy and this vagueness supports the prestige ranking which we call the status system.[29]

Thus, the administration becomes an almost mystical and occasionally incomprehensible group that embodies the culture of the organization and sets standards for other members to follow. But the leaders themselves are limited by the culture they guard. They are no more free to deviate from its norms than are ordinary members. Frequent and blatant violations of pivotal norms will result in the leaders being discredited, losing the respect and support of group members and ultimately being replaced or at best ignored. The unhappy and unsuccessful experience of James Watt as secretary of the interior during the early years of the Reagan administration was at least partially attributable to the wide discrepancy between his expressed values and the core values of the members of the Department of Interior.

Changing Organizational Culture

Values that are internalized and frequently operative only at the subconscious level are extremely difficult to change. In organizations, the unconscious, underlying values that shape "the way we do things" are equally difficult to change. Managing culture is likely to be far more difficult than some of its proponents recognize; radically changing the culture of an entire organization may be impossible without massive purges of organization membership, and even then it is likely to be a slow and painful process. Cultural purists argue that culture emerges and is created by members, not leaders.[30] The optimism of the cultural management approach is reminiscent of the optimism of reformers of the past who believed that native Americans should and could be turned into white

Americans or that the "American way" would be easily transplanted to radically different cultures.

Changing organization culture is also complicated by the tendency of complex organizations, like complex societies, to be characterized by a proliferation of subcultures. Both professionalization and differentiation cause subculture formation. Subcultures develop as groups with occupationally specific cultures—doctors, lawyers, planners, foresters, engineers—are included in the organization.[31] Each profession has its own set of internalized values and norms that members can carry with them into the organization; and because professionals are usually grouped together within the organization, they perpetuate and reinforce their own subcultures. Differentiation, even in the absence of diverse professions, also results in subculture formation. As police departments were compelled to devote more resources and attention to illegal drug problems, they created undercover narcotics units. The members of those units were required to develop very different norms from their "straight" colleagues as a price of survival. Their appearance and their behavior, which are at times almost shockingly different from that of the overall police culture, increases group cohesion and has become a badge of pride that distinguishes them from ordinary police officers. As subcultures develop and proliferate within an organization, the more disunified the organization becomes and the more conflict is likely to develop. Changing culture requires, at this stage, changing not only the dominant cultural values but also those of subcultures. The more subcultures there are in the organization the more difficult and time consuming the cultural change process becomes.[32]

Changing culture seems to be most feasible at times when the organization is undergoing transition—for example, when it is moving from one phase of its life cycle to the next.[33] Similarly, periods of environmental or internal crisis are also excellent opportunities for planned cultural change. Old values and norms appear archaic and no longer sensible; the old ways of doing things appear unsuccessful. A skilled and inspiring leader may succeed in instilling a new sense of values and behavior if they appear likely to solve the crisis facing the organization.

Recognizing that organizations develop distinct cultures helps explain many of their behavioral peculiarities: why they are so resistant to change, why reorganizations and merges fail, why new technologies are rejected, and why new, dramatically different leaders do not often succeed. It also helps explain why cabinet officers and political executives so frequently "go native," abandoning the values of the chief executive who appointed them in favor of the dominant values of the organizations they must lead: it is the price they must pay to enter and remain in the Men's Hut. Organizations value stability, and culture is a stabilizing influence. Imparting that culture to new members is essential if the organization is to continue. From an organizational perspective the basic problem in managing culture is ensuring that it is faithfully and systematically transmitted to new employees.

ORGANIZATIONAL SOCIALIZATION

Socialization is the process by which an organization transmits its culture, instilling in new members the values and norms of the organization, transforming an outsider into an insider. Socialization is a continuous process that begins before the individual enters the organization and ceases only when that individual leaves. The efficacy of the socialization process is determined by the depth of commitment to the organization of individual members. Organizational commitment, the individual's psychological bond to the organization, includes organizational identification (the extent to which the individual identifies with the organization), organizational loyalty (my organization right or wrong), and job involvement. Total organizations (e.g., the military, IBM, Hewlett-Packard, many Japanese corporations) seek total commitment; other organizations, though they might prefer total commitment, are generally willing to settle for considerably less.

Preliminary Considerations: American Social Values and Organizational Cultures

New members do not enter the organization as tabulae rasae; they have already been subject to a prolonged socialization process into American culture. In their homes, in the schools, by their peers, and by the mass media, they have been constantly exposed to and pressured to accept the dominant values of American society. Most of those values are quite compatible with basic organization values. Growing up in America, one learns to respect authority and to obey it, to respect and desire material possessions, and to judge oneself and others by how much they have accumulated. Individuals are taught to conform and to be apprehensive, if not suspicious, of those who do not. The need to be liked—to be popular, to be one of the crowd, and to avoid conflict—is instilled early and reinforced constantly throughout the socialization process. A respect for size (bigger is better) and the importance of being number one are also deeply rooted in American values.

Cultural myths have also been imparted and their basic precepts internalized. The myths of rationality and of individualism, the American dream, help prepare us to accept the legitimacy of work organizations and the demands they will put on us. The myth of rationality has been discussed in preceding chapters, and it is one of the central beliefs in American society. Like most myths, it is comforting to believe even if it is not true. It convinces us of our ability to control events, and because organizations are rational problem-solving entities, the myth of rationality ensures their legitimacy and the legitimacy of the demands they place on us. The myth of individualism teaches us that we are responsible for our own destiny. Individuals are taught that they must have goals but that not just any goals will do. The preferred goals are those associated with occupational success and material acquisition. People with goals work harder and and are more suitable for organizational life and its demands. If we succeed (and we will if we work hard and really want to), it is because of our own efforts. Conversely, if we fail, the fault lies not with the system or the organization or others but solely with ourselves. The myth of meritocracy reinforces individualism. People get ahead because of ability and hard work, and by logical extension, those who have succeeded are people of merit. Through merit and hard work the American dream may be realized: upward mobility, the house in the suburbs, two cars, and the endless array of consumer products that one is taught to want come to the deserving. And making it in American society usually means making it in organizations.

Other social norms are also carried into and incorporated by organizations. Norms about women and minorities are instilled long before individuals become workers, and those norms are incorporated in dominant organization norms, complicating the attempt by women and minorities to succeed in organizations. According to stereotype, women are emotional, passive, and nurturing; both men and women are socialized to accept this. Within work organizations, men assume that women will behave accordingly, and lacking alternative role models, women frequently fulfill the assumption. When they do not behave in accordance with these expectations, men and frequently other women become uncomfortable and either seek explanations for this inappropriate behavior or pressure the women to conform.[34] The explanations are rarely pleasant; social deviants are rarely treated fairly. Although these norms have been frequently challenged, like all norms they change at glacial speed, if at all, and both the tightening job market and hierarchical gridlock serve to reinforce them. White men nurtured on myths of individualism, meritocracy, and materialism and their own superiority are likely to resent women and minorities who compete against them and frequently beat them. Already the myth of affirmative action has taken root to placate the injured male ego: "He/she got the job/promotion only because he/she is a woman/minority and AA/EEO required it."

Professionals are subjected to a prolonged and distinct socialization process into the values of their profession before entering their work organizations. During their education and training they are exposed to and indoctrinated with the distinct values of the profession, and while each profession has its own separate culture, all share certain common values: the need to accept authority, to conform, to exercise self-discipline, to work hard, to view one's profession as an autonomous and self-governing entity, to be rational, and to control one's emotions.

Although every organization has a separate culture, a generic organizational culture exists. All organizations value hard work, order, predictability, conventionality, discipline, status, and commitment. Fortunately for organizations, these general values are compatible with basic social values, and new members are already thoroughly exposed to them. Basic American social values fit neatly with basic organizational values and thus a major portion of socialization is completed before individuals enter specific work organizations. From the organizational perspective, socialization is simplified. Basic values need only be reinforced and values specific to the organization can be concentrated on in the socialization process.

Recruitment and Selection

The recruitment and selection process allows the organization to winnow out those who are prima facie undesirable—that is those who clearly will not fit into the organization's culture. The selectiveness of the recruitment process determines how much effort must be invested in socialization. Recruitment tactics are geared toward attracting those who are predisposed to the organization's values and missions. The Army's "Be All That You Can Be" may be an inspiring slogan, but watching the television commercials and reading the posters communicates clearly that being all that you can be is going to require working around tanks, guns, airplanes, and missiles; having short hair; and wearing a uniform. Similarly, many organizations, public and private—police departments, fire departments, the Forest Service, universities, welfare agencies—have clearly developed public images that are used to recruit those already committed to the organization's goals and values.

For many organizations and individuals socialization begins before entry into the organization. "Anticipatory socialization" begins even before one definitely selects a career or occupation. When children express desires to be firefighters or doctors or police officers they have already begun to identify with the image of those occupations. When the choice of occupation becomes more definite, anticipatory socialization intensifies. Through interaction with friends, relatives, and teachers and contact with and observation of those already in the occupation, behavioral expectations and values are communicated, clarified, and internalized.

The selection process allows organizations through their boundary guards, recruiters, and personnel specialists, to examine potential members personally to determine if they will fit in. The Forest Service, for example, screens carefully to select only those who already have a strong public service orientation.[35] Organizations also often give psychological tests, the MMPI (Minnesota Multiphasic Personality Inventory) for example, to prospective employees, the basic purpose of which is to determine how well the applicants fit the personality profile desired by the organization. Similarly, lie detector tests, which are mandatory for employment with law enforcement agencies, in many states have become increasingly probing, seeking in-depth information about applicants' personalities, values, and beliefs to ensure that those who do not fit in do not get into the organization. The personal interview is the final step in assessing recruits and determining whether they will successfully accommodate themselves to the demands of the organization. Appearance, attitude, approaches to interpersonal relationships, and reactions to stress are assessed and compared with the norms of the organization. If the organization decides to hire and the individual accepts, a significant part of the socialization process has thus already occurred. The recruit has already demonstrated at least a superficial, and sometimes considerably deeper, willingness to conform to the organization's expectations. Acceptance of membership signals to the organization a desire to participate and a willingness to acquire a new role.[36]

The Psychological Contract

When individuals accept a job with an organization they enter into a psychological contract with the organization. Much of this contract is unwritten and unverbalized and consists of "the mutual expectations of the individual and the organization . . . of what each will give and receive."[37] For both parties, the expectations may be vague, and how they should be fulfilled is not specified or clear. Frequently, because the full range of expectations is never verbalized, both parties may be unaware of some of their own expectations as well as the expectations of the other party.

The precise contents of the psychological contract vary from individual to individual and organization to organization. The expectations of college graduates and professionals are usually higher than those of high school graduates—so high in many instances that they are unrealistic and destined never to be fulfilled.[38] Generally, these individuals expect that they will be paid a good salary, have the opportunity for personal career development and promotion, receive recognition and approval for good work, be treated fairly, have security in their positions, be able to work in a friendly, supportive environment, and be given meaningful work. Specific professional groups are likely to have even higher expectations: social workers that they will be able to help people; teachers that they will be able to educate and shape the minds of their students; police officers and firefighters that their jobs will be exciting, glamorous, and full of adventure; public defenders that they will be assisting the poor to receive justice; MPAs that they will be able to practice all the fancy techniques and theories that they have been taught. Many people entering the public service generally expect that they will be appreciated not only by their organizations but by the public as well. The source of these expectations is the general educational process, the method by which as a society we collectively con "the marks," and the explicit and implicit statements made by organizational recruiters.

As the preceding statement implies, the process of educating, training, and recruiting people into the work force generally and into specific organizations is similar in some respects to a con game.[39] The mark is the individual in whom expectations about high payoffs for participating are instilled. The con artists, and in this instance that includes educators and trainers as well as organization recruiters and managers, explicitly and implicitly hold out the promise of big payoff if the individual participates and does what is expected of him or her. The sting, when it comes, is when individuals finally realize that despite all their efforts, the expected payoff is not coming; they have been suckered. Fortunately, for organizations, this realization is slow to develop; and when it does, organizations have developed methods for handling it.

Con game or not, the recruitment process provides the basis of the psychological contract, and that contract is not one sided. The organization and its managers have their expectations as well, which may frequently be as unrealistic as those of the recruits. Generally, organizations expect that new members will be loyal to the organization, conform to its norms, work hard, and be effective, flexible, and willing to learn.[40] Specific organizations have additional specific expectations. Does the con game work both ways? With some individuals it probably does. During the hiring process and throughout the probationary period, these employees give every indication that they are going to pay off generously for the organization; for various reasons, some of which will be explored subsequently, once tenure or permanent status is granted, they then sting the organization.

Usually none of this is recognized by either party at the time the psychological contract is negotiated and finalized. Those mutual expectations facilitate the socialization process. Individuals realize that to get what they want out of the organization they must buy into it, accept its expectations, try to fulfill them, and most of all fit in, be accepted by the other members of the organization. From the organization's perspective, the socialization process clarifies its expectations of new members, communicates to them what it actually expects, and instills sufficient loyalty and commitment in them so that they will eventually revise their expectations to a more realistic level and still produce for the organization.

The Socialization Process

The Entry Phase. The first days, weeks, and, in some cases, months on the job are times of extreme anxiety for most individuals. The newcomer to the organization experiences disorientation, foreignness, sensory overload, and "reality," if not culture shock.[41] This is frequently intensified by the initiation practices of peers. The more unrealistic the expectations of the new member, the greater the shock and the more anxiety the individual experiences. The stress and anxiety experienced by new members is useful from the organization's point of view because culture is learned through reduction of anxiety and pain.[42] The entry experience is one of change, contrast, and surprise. Old roles and the behaviors associated with them must be abandoned, whether they be those of student, civilian, or member of another organization. Requirements of the new role must be identified, understood, and internalized. Differences from previous experiences are marked: the way people talk, dress, and behave; the way they treat and respond to the new member; new physical settings; and new ways of doing things all inundate the individual.

Surprise occurs when the new member notes the difference between his or her expectations and the actual experience of organizational membership. The first surprise occurs when expectations about the job are not fulfilled, when the welfare worker realizes that more time is spent filling out forms and processing work than helping clients, when the budget analyst realizes that the agency uses straight line-item budgeting rather than the new sophisticated techniques, when the teacher realizes that students are not empty vessels enthusiastically waiting to be filled with knowledge. The second surprise occurs when expectations about oneself are unmet, when the individual who thought he could easily handle the rigors of basic training discovers that it demands more physically, mentally, or emotionally than he seems to be able to handle or when the professional discovers that all those years of professional training did not really prepare her for the seemingly endless demands put on her time, ability and patience. The third surprise is when one's reactions to new experiences are unanticipated, and anger, boredom, anxiety, or dislike are experienced instead of the anticipated excitement, enjoyment, or pleasure. Another surprise may occur when assumptions about the organization prove erroneous. Similar to anxiety, surprise requires adaptation; expectations are reoriented, and attitudes and behavior adjusted to the newly recognized reality.[43] The stressfulness of the situation motivates the new members to abandon old roles and behaviors, to unfreeze them and search for information and identification models to help relieve the stress they are experiencing.

Groups play an important role during the entry phase as well as throughout the individual's tenure in the organization. The precise role of the group depends on whether the organization hires and trains employees singly or in groups. Many public organizations hire on an individual basis; in this situation, the primary training and socializing agent is the immediate work group to which the individual is assigned. The work group will initiate the new member into the organization's ways, its norms, rules, and procedures. Formally and informally, the group will teach the individual what constitutes proper and improper behavior. Teasing and ridicule are standard aspects of group treatment of newcomers. Anxiety and the desire to be accepted encourage the newcomer to abandon old values and behaviors and adopt the expectations of the group. The influence of the group increases as its homogeneity and isolation increase and its size decreases.[44] Frequently a coach, a specific person, will either be assigned or assume primary responsibility for grooming, instructing, and advising the individual during the break-in period.

The socialization process is far more intense in organizations which recruit and hire in groups, or "classes." Japanese corporations, the police, and the military are prime examples of such organizations. Thomas P. Rohlen described the socialization process in a Japanese bank in *For Harmony and Strength*. Employees are hired, trained, indoctrinated, and initiated in classes. The initial break from past associations is complete and marked by a formal entry ceremony. The recruits are housed in all-male company-provided dormitories, which are self-contained facilities providing the recruits with all the necessities and amenities of life. External social relationships are discouraged, and participation in group social activities like baseball and martial arts is required. Indoctrination into the company's ideology is pervasive: the company creed must be memorized and recited and the company song sung at the start of every day. Rites of degradation include the *roto* and a twenty-five-mile endurance walk. In the *roto*, the trainees must each go door to door in a residential neighborhood, offering to work free of charge for the householders. For the Japanese, who rarely approach strangers, this experience is emotionally demanding and humiliating. The endurance walk matches in physical punishment the demands of basic training for military recruits. The first nine miles are walked individually; the second nine are walked in groups; the remaining seven are again walked individually. The end of the initial socialization process is marked by a formal graduation, comparable in scale and seriousness to a college graduation.[45] The socialization thus begun continues throughout the work life of the employee. Class members remain together throughout their careers, solidifying the all-important group bonds that are so important in maintaining conformity.

The initial socialization into the military follows a similar pattern. A clean break with the past is achieved quickly as recruits are physically and socially isolated from civilian contact. Uniforms, identical haircuts, and identical living quarters strip away outside social status and past identity.[46] Mortification procedures undo old values so that recruits are receptive to new values, and the formation of peer groups of novices alleviates the problem of defense against the organization and enhances socialization.[47] "The union of sympathy" shared by the recruits strengthens esprit de corps and makes the demanding and degrading socialization process tolerable and more effective.[48]

Socialization of police officers usually begins at the police academy, once again in a group setting marked by harsh discipline, degradation, and required uniformity of appearance and behavior.

The newcomer—surrounded by 30 to 40 contemporaries—is introduced to the often arbitrary discipline of the organization. A man soon learned that to be one minute late to class, to utter a careless word in formation, to relax in his seat or to be caught walking when one should be running may result in a "gig" or demerit costing him an extra day of work or the time it may take to write a long essay on, say, "the importance of keeping a neat appearance." Only the recruit's classmates aid in the struggle to avoid sanction from a punitively-oriented training staff and provide the recruit with the only rewards available. Yet, these rewards are contingent upon his internalization of the "no rat" rule which protects fellow-recruits and himself from departmental discipline.[49]

Through lectures, drills, and informal conversations with instructors, the recruits are introduced to and indoctrinated into the culture of the police department. By the time the recruits graduate from the academy, they have had instilled in them the major themes and values of police work: defensiveness, professionalization, and depersonalization.[50] Equally important, feelings of solidarity have been instilled in the recruits; "consensus, integration, friendship, personal intimacy, emotional depth, moral commitment and continuity in time . . . a subjective feeling of belongingness and implication in each other's lives has been created."[51] It is a feeling that will endure and become a continuing part of the police officer's basic orientation towards other officers and towards outsiders.

Continuance: Metamorphosis.   Although socialization is a continuous process that ends only when the individual leaves the organization, early organizational experiences are a major determinant of later beliefs and behaviors. Whether marked by an informal or formal ceremony, the end of the entry phase is a significant rite of passage, from the status of novice to full-fledged employee. At this point socialization becomes even more the task of the work group. In effective socialization processes, the recruit has become an accepted member of the group, and the desire to maintain that acceptance is a powerful force for conformity. Through constant face-to-face interaction, the group monitors and controls the behavior of the members. At some point, the metamorphosis is complete, as the recruit's job-related attitudes come to approximate those of the more experienced members.

The organization reinforces early socialization through performance evaluations, ceremonies and rituals, and the rewarding of the faithful through promotions and increased status. Continued training, retreats, and workshops are formal socialization techniques that reinforce early socialization. Human relations techniques, organization development, and sensitivity training are similar socialization methods aimed at instilling or reinforcing the proper attitudes and behaviors in employees.

Effective Socialization

Successful socialization provides the individual with a new self-image, new involvements, new values and accomplishments, and the knowledge, ability, and motivation to play an organizationally defined role. It creates a bond between the individual and the organization and among the members of that organization. Ideally, it results in the creation of organizational commitment and loyalty.

Some socialization processes are more effective than others. Van Maanen has identified five characteristics that influence the effectiveness of socialization: the formality of the setting, the individuality or collectivity of the process, the serial or disjunctive character of the process, the length of the entry phase, and the presence or absence of a "coach."[52] In formal settings, the recruit's role is strictly separated from other organizational roles, and primary emphasis is placed on internalization of organizational perspectives: the initial concentration is on attitude, not job or task performance. Collective socialization results in far more homogeneous attitudes than individual socialization, and serial socialization is most effective in ensuring long-range organizational stability. The longer the initial socialization process, "the more demanding, degrading and perhaps frustrating the process is likely to be" and the more intense and enduring the bonds of fellowship created.[53] Finally, the presence of a specific coach leads to an intense socialization process, which is likely to be extremely effective.

Two qualifiers need to be added to these determinants of successful socialization. First, groups are extremely important and effective socialization agents, but as has been recognized at least since Mayo's Hawthorne experiments, groups have a tendency to develop their own norms, which may or may not be compatible with the norms and values of the overall organization. If the norms of the socializing group diverge from those of the organization, the group norms will prevail. Similarly, if the coach's norms vary from those of the organization, the recruit will more likely be concerned with satisfying the coach than the organization.

Second, professionals constitute a challenge to organizational social processes. They are socialized into the norms of their profession before they join the organization, and this presocialization process has likely been lengthy and demanding. Professional norms do not necessarily conflict with organizational norms, but the potential for conflict does exist. Personal success is frequently equated with success within the profession, not within the organization; thus primary loyalty may be to the profession and its standards. The quest for professional success may result in considerable organization switching as the upwardly mobile professional seeks the organization that will provide the best resources for practicing and excelling in the profession. Loyalty to a specific organization is likely to be superficial at best. Nonetheless, this conflict should not be overstated. Professionals do need organizations to provide them with jobs, resources, status, and monetary rewards. Professional recognition is important, but so are the rewards the organization provides. Dependence is the basis of most effective socialization, and very few professionals are independent. Further, the majority of professionals are what Gouldner termed "locals," individuals committed to success in their organizations and thus very susceptible to its influence. "Cosmopolitans," whose primary reference groups are external to the organization, are a minority but are decidedly more resistant to organizational socialization efforts.[54]

Individual Patterns of Accommodation

In all organizations, even those with the most rigorous and intense socialization processes, the efficacy of that process, the extent to which members accept and internalize the norms and values of the organization, varies considerably. The acceptance levels of members range from total acceptance and conformity to total rejection and rebellion. The failure is partially attributable to the disillusionment experienced when reality shock occurs and individuals realize that their expectations were inflated and that their jobs, their place in the organization, and the organization itself are very different than anticipated. For some individuals, this results in a loss of idealism, rejection of the organization, and increasing cynicism.[55] Individual personality differences reflected in the needs, goals, and values of the individual determine how reality shock is handled and the extent to which he or she is willing to buy into the organization. The importance of job, career, and upward mobility varies for individuals, and for some they remain secondary concerns that must compete for commitment with other roles and activities of equal or greater importance. For some individuals, roles as parent, spouse, or friend will always be given priority over their role in the organization. For others, leisure activities may be viewed as more important and satisfying than work. For still others, the satisfaction of nonconformity, of holding onto their own preorganization values and behaviors and being free to express themselves, outweighs the satisfactions or rewards of conformity. All of these factors determine how receptive to organizational socialization individuals are and how they will accommodate themselves to the demands and expectations of the organization.

Robert Presthus identified three major patterns of accommodation that individuals adopt in response to the demands of organizations: upward mobility, indifference, and ambivalence. Upward mobiles are the most susceptible to socialization. They accept the organization and are committed to maximizing accumulation of the rewards that it can provide: status, authority, power, and money. To achieve those rewards, they are willing to conform to the organization's expectations. For them, acceptance into the Men's Hut is a powerful motivating force, and they are willing to pay the price demanded for membership. The price is frequently high: in addition to constant conformity to the expectations of those with greater authority and status, sacrificing one's personal life and always putting the organization first is often required. Working overtime, dressing right, living right, even selecting the right type of spouse are necessary.

Indifferents view the organization very differently and consequently are much less receptive to its socialization process. Although some individuals may begin their work careers indifferent to the status system, values, and goals of the organization, the majority of indifferents are those who are unable to recover from the disenchantment experienced during the entry phase of socialization. Their response is to withdraw mentally and emotionally from the work arena and to transfer their interests to activities outside the job.

Ambivalents constitute a relatively small minority, but they are the least well adjusted and the most neurotic of Presthus's categories. Ambivalents can neither completely reject the organization and its reward system nor completely accept its demands or fulfill its expectations. Professionals and highly trained specialists are most likely to become ambivalents. Their preorganization socialization process has usually convinced them of their superiority and their right to autonomy, and the status and authority systems of the organization (which frequently make them subordinate to persons from outside their profession) appear illegitimate and unfair. They thus resist the organization's socialization process. Their desire for status and power and their unwillingness to accommodate themselves and conform to the extent necessary to succeed within the organization makes their situation the most unpleasant of those faced by the three patterns of accommodation.[56]

Van Maanen presents a different typology of individual responses to the socialization process. His classification is based on the extent to which an individual conforms to the values of both the immediate work group and the larger organization. An individual who conforms to the demands of both is a team player. Although this type of adjustment is the most comfortable for the individual and the organization, it is possible only if the norms of the work group are compatible with those of the overall organization. When those norms diverge, the individual must make a choice. The isolate opts for the organization's norms and pays the price of being ostracized by the group. The ratebuster, the dedicated upwardly mobile person (frequently referred to in quite different terms by colleagues), resists group pressure in favor of the rewards and benefits of organizational approval. The warrior chooses the opposite route of work group approval and acceptance, overtly or covertly battling "the system," criticizing or ignoring the rules and policies, violating the norms, and challenging the authority system. Warriors are frequently regarded as heroes by their work group and are supported and protected by it. Outsiders conform to neither the group's nor the organization's norms, and the anxiety associated with that role is so severe that few individuals maintain it for very long. They either leave the organization or convert to one of the other roles.[57]

The varying effectiveness of organizational socialization poses problems for both the organization and its members. While total commitment is dysfunctional for both because it may lead to excessive conformity and stagnation as well as the complete loss of individuality, total rejection is even more undesirable. For the organization, rebellion leads to excessive conflict and inability to accomplish substantive goals. For the individual it leads to alienation or complete lack of belongingness. The determinants of effective socialization remain unclear. Even those organizations with the most intense socialization processes are far from uniformly effective in socializing new members. For example, both Harris and Van Maanen found that the most prominent effect of police socialization was not so much the instilling of organizational commitment as it was the instilling of commitment to fellow officers and to maintaining a low profile.[58]

A useful analogy may be the decreasing effectiveness of the political socialization process in the United States. Although children and adolescents are subjected to a prolonged socialization effort in their homes and schools to indoctrinate them into the desired role of citizen and into internalizing the right beliefs about the political system, overt measures of its effectiveness, particularly voting participation and levels of approval of the behavior of public officials, indicate disappointing results. The creation of excessively high expectations and unrealistic illusions that cannot withstand the reality shock of actual experience may be at fault in both socialization processes.

The Psychological Contract Renegotiated

One of the major consequences of the disillusionment of reality shock is the realization on the part of the individual that the psychological contract as originally negotiated is not going to be fulfilled. Both individuals and organizations have developed responses for managing the broken contract. For the individual, the most common response is to renegotiate the contract, accepting the reality of the job and organizational situation, accepting that the job will not be quite as exciting or meaningful as anticipated and that the organization is not quite as rational and fair as anticipated. If the shock of entry is too overwhelming and the disparity between reality and expectations too great, the individual may either terminate the relationship or, if this is impossible because of lack of alternatives, economic pressures, or inertia, may remain but become alienated from the job and the organization.[59]

The longer the individual remains with the organization, the more difficult it becomes to terminate the relationship. The "golden padlock" that binds the individual to the organization becomes increasingly tight, chaining the individual psychologically, emotionally, and economically to the job and the organization. As seniority accumulates, its benefits become more appealing and the idea of starting all over decreasingly so. Some organizations purposely manipulate the cost of leaving for some individuals by giving them rapid promotions and salary increases. Further, as time in the job increases, one's expertise becomes more specific to the current organization, limiting employability in other organizations. Similarly, the longer one works for an organization in a specific occupation, the more one comes to identify with both and to believe in the value of what one does and of the organization itself. Such beliefs increase the individual's sense of self-worth and self-esteem and are for many people essential to sanity. Admitting that one's work is meaningless and the organization is senseless or worse is admitting that one's life, or a major part of it, is similarly meaningless and purposeless. Consequently, people prefer to believe in the value of what they do and the organization for which they work.[60] All of which makes it more difficult to change jobs or organizations. Albert Hirschmann offers a similar categorization of individual reactions to disappointment and dissatisfaction with the organization. The choices available to the individual are three: exit, voice, or loyalty.[61] Hirschmann's approach is economic and underestimates the psychological and emotional factors that pressure individuals to remain silently loyal to the organization and also underestimates the penalties associated with voice (openly trying to change the organization).

Despite this increase in identification and renegotiation of the psychological contract, many individuals are doomed to further disillusionment and disappointment with jobs and organizations. As previously indicated, organizational recruiters always promise more than the organization can deliver. Particularly for the professional and the upwardly mobile person, promises made are frequently promises broken. Upward mobility is limited by the pyramidal structure of the hierarchy: there is never enough room at the top for all those who would like to be there, and for professionals the opportunities are even more limited. But both professionals and upwardly mobile employees are essential to the organization, and even though it cannot fulfill all their expectations, it must retain them if proper functioning is to continue. Consequently, organizations have provided ways for "cooling out the mark."[62] In con games generally, after the sting, the mark is motivated to seek revenge, which requires the organization to provide a "cool out," a way for the mark to define the situation in a way that makes it easy for him to accept what has happened. For professionals and management personnel with great expectations about advancement, the sting is frequently a critical event that signals the end of upward mobility or possibly the removal from a critical position.[63] For the mark the crucial loss is of self-respect and self-esteem. So the organization provides a cooler, a new definition of the situation or some way to release frustration and anger. A second chance may be provided; the mark may be allowed to blow up and express otherwise unacceptable feelings. Substitute rewards may be provided or, in the case of professionals, a separate status system may be created. If successful, the cool out placates the mark, restores his or her self-respect, and maintains his or her commitment to the organization, at least until the next sting.

One of the best examples of cooling out the mark happened to a colleague, a political scientist who had grown increasingly restive at seeing university administrators reap the bulk of the rewards in the university system: higher salaries, larger raises, better offices, and more perquisites, power, and status than faculty. Although an outstanding academic, the colleague had had little success in moving into the administrative hierarchy. Finally, the position of assistant dean of the graduate school opened and he applied for it. He did not get it, and his frustration and disappointment were increased by the realization that the individual who did had considerably less impressive credentials than he. Then came the cool out. Walking across campus one day he encountered the dean of the graduate school, who greeted him warmly, put his arm around his shoulder and explained, "Be thankful you didn't get that assistant deanship. Why, for a man of your qualifications, it would just have been a waste. It's just a go-for position."

Over time, individuals constantly renegotiate their psychological contracts with their organizations, just as organizations do with individuals. Combined with the impact of continuous socialization, this renegotiation enables individuals to come to terms with and accept the reality of their positions and prospects. If they are not as enthusiastic or as committed or as ambitious or diligent as when they first entered the organization, they still, for the most part, contribute what they consider a reasonable share to the organization. Given the extremely low rate of dismissal for cause in both the public and private sectors, organizations evidently revise their expectations of members as well. Once again, satisficing emerges as the dominant organizational and individual response to a critical problem.

CONCLUSION

Culture, whether of a society or an organization, is deeply rooted in the historical experience of the entity under consideration. It forms gradually, changing imperceptibly over time. Attempts to change it quickly or radically rarely succeed and may well result in initial social upheaval followed by rebellion. Organizational culture has long been ignored or underestimated as a determinant of organizational behavior and performance. Faults or problems that previously have been attributed to structure, such as bureaucratic inertia or bureaucratic arrogance, may well be more a result of the culture of a specific bureaucratic agency than of bureaucracy in general. Because of the relative newness of organizational culture as a theoretical approach, much remains to be explained about how organizational culture relates to other organizational variables. It seems likely that initial choices of structure, goals, and technology will become embedded in the organization's culture and over time become unconscious assumptions about the proper structure, goals, and technology of that organization. What we do and the way we do it become deeply embedded values for organization members, and attempted changes directly threaten those values. For individuals, few things are more distressing or frightening than having their basic values challenged and declared inadequate. Resistance may be as unconscious as the values themselves, which further explains why organizational change is difficult to implement successfully. The extent and rules of organizational politics are also part of an organization's culture, just as they are of a society's culture. The relationships among these variables are also likely to be reciprocal, further complicating an already complex relationship.

Organizational culture is shaped by the organization's environment. Cultural values of the society in which an organization is located are incorporated and reflected in the cultures of organizations, and members' attitudes and values are shaped initially in society and they bring those values and attitudes into the organization. For many public organizations, such as educational organizations, social values concerning their functions and the nature of their clientele determine basic organizational culture. Similarly, social attitudes toward poverty and crime are reflected in the value structures of organizations created to deal with those problems.

Admirers of Japanese organizations who advocate the incorporation of their management style into American organizations have seldom recognized the difficulties or limitations of this approach. To a large extent, management style is determined by organizational culture, which in turn is determined by the culture of the broader society. Japanese cultural values, which discourage individual competitiveness, stress cooperation over personal advancement, equate the firm with family, and allow only limited social mobility, are radically different from American values, as many Japanese corporations with American facilities have learned. Japan also has the advantage of being socially and culturally unified, another marked contrast to this country. The differences between the cultures of the two countries make it unlikely that their management styles or organizational cultures will be easily or effectively transferrable. Beyond the question whether it is possible to change the cultures of American organizations to match those of their Japanese counterparts is the question whether it is desirable to do so, particularly in the public sector. Public organizations that come the closest to matching the conformity, loyalty, and indoctrination characteristic of Japanese organizations are also those most criticized for excessive intrusion into the private lives and rights of individual members. Finally, one weakness of Japanese management that receives little attention is its limited track record on developing innovative products and technological breakthroughs. Seemingly, even if the public sector were to somehow manage to create organizations with Japanese-style cultures, they would not become more innovative.

Organizational socialization processes attempt to instill the organization's values in its members. Yet as we have seen, even the most rigorous, unrelenting socialization processes are not always successful. The effectiveness of the socialization process is muted by the persistence of subcultures within the organization and by the conflicting roles that members must play both within and outside the organization. The limitations of organizational socialization processes reinforce the difficulty of changing culture. Until organizational management can develop more effective socialization methods, management's ability to control and change culture is limited. Regardless of the difficulties of managing them, culture and socialization are the central, and perhaps the most important, determinants of organizational and individual behavior.

NOTES

1. Charles Perrow, *Complex Organizations*, 3rd ed. (New York: Random House, 1986), p. 158.
2. Ibid., p. 167. See also Philip Selznick, *Leadership and Administration* (New York: Harper & Row, 1957).
3. Thomas Peters and Robert Waterman, *In Search of Excellence* (New York: Harper & Row, 1982); William Ouchi, *Theory Z* (Reading, Mass.: Addison-Wesley, 1981).
4. Richard Pascale and Anthony Athos, *The Art of Japanese Management* (New York: Warner Books, 1981), pp. 73–75.
5. Edgar Schein, *Organizational Culture and Leadership* (San Francisco: Jossey Bass, 1985), p. 7.
6. Ralph Kilmann, Mary Saxton, Ray Supa, et al., *Gaining Control of the Corporate Culture* (San Francisco: Jossey Bass, 1985), p. ix.
7. Burton R. Clark, *The Distinctive College: Antioch, Reed, and Swarthmore* (Chicago: Aldine Publishing, 1970).
8. Jay Shafritz and J. Steven Ott, *Classics of Organization Theory*, 2nd ed. (Chicago: Dorsey Press, 1987), p. 375.
9. Edgar Schein, "How Culture Forms, Develops and Changes," in Kilmann et al., *Gaining Control of the Corporate Culture*, p. 20.
10. Anthony Jay, *Management and Machiavelli: An Inquiry into the Politics of Corporate Life* (New York: Holt, Rinehart and Winston, 1967), p. 96.
11. Richard N. Harris, *The Police Academy: An Inside View* (New York: John Wiley, 1973), p. 99.
12. Peter Blau and Marshall Meyer, *Bureaucracy in Modern Society*, 2nd. ed. (New York: Random House, 1971), p. 53.
13. Gareth Morgan, *Images of Organization* (Beverly Hills, Calif.: Sage Publications Inc., 1986), p. 135.
14. Schein, *Organizational Culture and Leadership*, p. 15.
15. Harris, *The Police Academy: An Inside View*, p. 47.
16. Ibid., p. 100.
17. Kilmann et al., *Gaining Control of the Corporate Culture*, p. 5.

18. R. Ritti and G. Ray Funkhouser, *The Ropes to Skip and the Ropes to Know*, 2nd. ed. (Columbus, Ohio: Grid Publishing Co., 1982), p. 37.

19. Emily Bunnell Gillett, "Higher Education's Caste System: Injustice Is a Daily Experience," *The Chronicle of Higher Education* (February 4, 1987): p. 96.

20. Ian Mitroff and Ralph H. Kilmann, et al., "Corporate Taboos Are the Key to Unlocking Culture," in Kilmann et al., *Gaining Control of the Corporate Culture*, p. 184.

21. Harrison M. Trice and Janice Beyer, "Using Six Organizational Rites to Change Culture," in Kilmann, et al., *Gaining Control of the Corporate Culture*, p. 372.

22. J. A. C. Brown, *The Social Psychology of Industry* (Baltimore: Penguin Books, 1956), p. 147.

23. Ibid., p. 147.

24. Trice and Beyer, "Using Six Organizational Rites to Change Culture," p. 380.

25. Morgan, *Images of Organization*, p. 135.

26. Brown, *The Social Psychology of Industry*, p. 146.

27. Ibid.

28. Ritti and Funkhouser, *The Ropes to Skip and the Ropes to Know*, p. 3.

29. Victor Thompson, *Modern Organization* (New York: Knopf, 1961), p. 70.

30. Peter Frost, Larry Moore, Meryl Reis Louis, Craig C. Lundberg, and Joanne Martin, *Organizational Culture* (Beverly Hills, Calif.: Sage Publications, Inc., 1985), p. 95.

31. John Van Maanen, "Cultural Organization: Fragments of a Theory," in Peter Frost et al., *Organizational Culture*, p. 41.

32. Kilmann et al., *Gaining Control of the Corporate Culture*, p. 12.

33. Caren Siehl, "After the Founder: An Opportunity to Manage Culture," in Frost et al., *Organizational Culture*, p. 127.

34. Ritti and Funkhouser, *The Ropes to Skip and the Ropes to Know*, p. 96.

35. Herbert Kaufman, *The Forest Ranger* (Baltimore: Johns Hopkins University Press, 1967).

36. John Van Maanen, "Breaking In: Socialization to Work," in Robert Dubin, *Handbook of Work, Organization and Society* (Chicago: Rand McNally, 1976), p. 75.

37. Roosevelt Thomas, "Managing the Psychological Contract," in Paul Laurence, Louis Barnes, and Jay Lorsch, *Organizational Behavior and Administration*, 3rd. ed. (Homewood, Ill.: Richard D. Irwin, 1976), p. 466.

38. Edgar Schein, *Organizational Psychology* (Englewood Cliffs, N.J.: Prentice Hall, 1970), p. 211.

39. See Erving Goffman, "On Cooling the Mark Out: Some Aspects of Adaptation to Failure," *Psychiatry* (1952): pp. 451–463, for a general discussion of how society generally creates expectations that cannot be fulfilled and then provides methods for allowing the disenchanted and disappointed to work out their frustrations.

40. Thomas, "Managing the Psychological Contract," p. 467.

41. Meryl Reis Louis, "Surprise and Sensemaking: What Newcomers Experience in Entering Unfamiliar Organizational Settings," *Administrative Science Quarterly* (1980): p. 230.

42. Kilmann, et al., *Gaining Control of the Corporate Culture*. p. 24.

43. Reis, "Surprise and Sensemaking: What Newcomers Experience in Entering Unfamiliar Organizational Settings," pp. 235–238.

44. Van Maanen, "Breaking In: Socialization to Work," p. 91.

45. Thomas P. Rohlen, *For Harmony and Strength* (Berkeley: University of California Press, 1974), pp. 203–207.

46. Sanford M. Dornbush, "The Military Academy as an Assimilating Institution," *Social Forces* (1955): p. 377.

47. Edgar Schein, "Organizational Socialization and the Profession of Management," *Industrial Management Review* (1965): p. 6.

48. Van Maanen, "Breaking In: Socialization to Work," p. 92.

49. John Van Maanen, "Police Socialization: A Longitudinal Examination of Job Attitudes in an Urban Police Department," *Administrative Science Quarterly* (1975): p. 221.

50. Richard Harris, *The Police Academy: An Inside View*, p. 160.

51. Ibid., p. 163.

52. Van Maanen, "Police Socialization," pp. 225–226.

53. Ibid., p. 226.

54. A. Gouldner, "Cosmopolitans and Locals: Toward An Analysis of Latent Social Roles," *Administrative Quarterly* (1958): pp. 444–480.

55. Van Maanen, "Breaking In: Socialization to Work," p. 109.

56. Robert Presthus, *The Organizational Society*, 2nd. ed. (New York: St. Martin's Press, 1978), pp. 143–251.

57. Van Maanen, "Breaking In: Socialization to Work," pp. 112–113.

58. Harris, *The Police Academy: An Inside View*; Van Maanen, "Police Socialization."

59. Thomas, "Managing the Psychological Contract," p. 467.

60. Barry Stau and Gerald Salancik, *New Directions in Organization Behavior* (Chicago: St. Clair Press, 1977), p. 21.

61. Albert Hirschmann, *Exit, Voice and Loyalty* (Cambridge: Harvard University Press, 1970).

62. Erving Goffmann, "On Cooling the Mark Out: Some Aspects of Adaptation to Failure," *Psychiatry* (1952): p. 456.

63. Ritti and Funkhouser, *The Ropes to Know and the Ropes to Skip*, p. 263.

8

OF INDIVIDUALS, ORGANIZATIONS, AND WORK

Organizations are collections of individuals, and successful organizational control and management ultimately depends on the organization's ability to control and direct the behavior of individuals toward the achievement of organizational purposes. From the organization's perspective, this is somewhat unfortunate, because individual behavior is difficult to understand and even more difficult to control systematically and consistently. The attempts to control that behavior generally, from structural design and formal and informal controls through technology and socialization, have varying degrees of success. Consequently, contemporary organization theory has increasingly utilized psychological approaches to understand and predict individual behavior and to provide a basis for improved management techniques. The first part of this chapter covers some of the psychological theories that have received the most attention in organization theory.

A crucial part of individual work behavior is individual orientations towards work: expectations about work and the role it plays in the individual's life. Those orientations determine the individual's susceptibility to organizational control and manipulation and set limits on the individual's commitment to the work organization. Expectations weighed against reality form the basis of job satisfaction or dissatisfaction, a topic that has received an enormous amount of attention, perhaps undeservedly so, in organization behavior. Extreme dissatisfaction may lead to alienation, a concept that since Karl Marx has also received extensive attention. The second part of the chapter addresses the roles of work, job satisfaction, and alienation in contemporary society.

PERSONALITY: WE ARE ALL THE SAME BUT WE ARE ALL DIFFERENT

No two individuals are exactly the same. They differ in intellectual abilities, motor skills, interests, attitudes, levels of aspiration, energy, needs, education, and training.[1] This is not to say that human beings share no similarities. Every person is in some ways like all other persons, in some ways like some other persons, and in some ways like no other person.[2] Further complicating the attempt to understand individual behavior, individuals change over time: what I am today, I was yesterday, I will be tomorrow and next week and in ten years, but with certain modifications—and those modifications may more strongly affect my actual behavior than do the underlying consistencies in my personality. For effective management, individual differences must be recognized and, when possible, taken into consideration in recruitment, hiring, job design, and employee motivation and evaluation.

Psychology is a social science, so it is not surprising that there is no agreement as to what personality is, what causes it, or how to identify or change it. Similarly, no agreement exists as to what commonalities are shared by individuals. Because there is no single, acceptable theory, to understand individual personality several theories must be studied and since none of the theories is supported by hard empirical evidence, they all should be viewed with a degree of skepticism. There are at least fifty different definitions of personality,[3] but underlying those definitions is agreement that:

1. Everybody has one;
2. Personality consists of a pattern of consistent behaviors, characteristics, attitudes and values;
3. It is dynamic—it develops throughout life;
4. It is partially inborn and partially acquired, shaped by a variety of factors: heredity, biology, early and later life experiences, group membership, role determinants, society, and culture.[4]

For Sigmund Freud, personality was primarily the outcome of the constant struggle between the id and the superego. The id, which seeks pleasure through satisfaction of our unrestrained biological instincts, is constantly at war with the superego, which is our internalization of the values, morals, ideals, and expectations of society: our conscience, in everyday language. The struggle is mediated by the ego, which determines which of the id's demands can be satisfied and the acceptable methods of satisfying them. For Freud, the biological instincts and drives were the key motivating factors of human behavior and the restrictions society imposed on their satisfaction a primary source of frustration and, in many instances, neurosis.[5]

In some respects, Freud's id, ego, and superego are comparable to the child, adult, and parent ego state of transactional analysis (TA), which has been used extensively in organizational development. The child is the pleasure-seeking, uninhibited, emotional aspect of our personality; the parent is the voice of authority, the constant replay in our minds of parental admonishments; the adult is the mature, rational, problem-solving aspect of our personality.[6] All three ego states are present in all of us, but one will be dominant at any given time. Although TA asserts that each of the three ego states may be appropriate bases for behavior in different situations, in organizations the clear preference is for the adult ego state, and the most effective transactions are in adult-adult circumstances. The most frustrating transaction is adult-child—when for example, a professor comes into class prepared to discuss important concepts and is greeted with, "Oh, do we have to have class today, it's so nice outside." If the class persists in its collective child ego state, the adult (professor) is likely to become frustrated and resort to the voice of authority. For both Freud and TA, behavior (personality) is the outcome of the struggle among ego states, and the constant need to suppress our instincts imposes a considerable strain on individuals.

Most psychologists agree that needs are a key concept in explaining and understanding human behavior. "A need is a construct . . . which organizes perception. . . . Each need persists and gives rise to a certain course of overt behavior (or fantasy) which . . . changes the initiating circumstances in such a way as to bring about an end situation which stills the organism."[7] In other words, the quest to gratify an unfulfilled need is the source of human behavior. The attempt to identify human needs has preoccupied many psychologists and organization theorists.

No theory of personality has received more attention in organization behavior than A. H. Maslow's hierarchy of human needs. Although lacking in empirical verification and running counter to a great body of empirical evidence, Maslow's hierarchy has assumed an almost mythical position in contemporary organization theory. Basically, Maslow theorized that human beings share common needs and that these needs are hierarchically arranged. Higher needs do not emerge until lower needs have been satisfied. Needs are goal states that an individual strives to achieve; the search for gratification of an unfulfilled need explains behavior. Unsatisfied needs dominate the individual's thoughts and concerns, but once satisfied, a need is no longer relevant in determining behavior.

According to Maslow, the lowest level needs are physiological: our needs for food, water, sex, and shelter. Next to emerge are safety needs: the need to be secure and protected from danger. After safety comes the need for belongingness: social needs develop. Social needs include the need for friendship, love, affection, acceptance, and association. The fourth-level needs are ego needs: the needs for differentiation, achievement, autonomy, status, recognition, and prestige emerge at this level. Finally, at the apex of the hierarchy, emerging only after all the lower-level needs have been satisfied, is the need for self-actualization.[8]

Self-actualization is a complex psychological state, difficult to define, understand or achieve. Maslow defined it as

> the individual doing what he is fitted for. . . . This need we call self-actualization . . . the desire for self-fulfillment, namely to the tendency for one to become actualized in what one is potentially. This tendency might be phrased as the desire to become more and more what one is, to become everything that one is capable of becoming.[9]

Maslow believed that although very few truly self-actualized people existed, many people, perhaps most of us, have moments of self-actualization, which he termed peak experiences. During such moments one experiences "a special flavor of wonder, of awe, of reverence, of humility and surrender before the experience as before something great. . . . The person at the peak is godlike not only in senses . . . but . . . in the complete, loving, uncondemning, compassionate and perhaps amused acceptance of the world and of the person."[10]

Completely self-actualized persons are characterized by an openness to experience; they are in tune with themselves, spontaneous, autonomous, and independent, dedicated completely to some cause outside themselves to which they devote total effort. They resist conformity, are detached and private, and relate to a few specially loved others on a deep, emotional level.

Since Maslow's theory appears in almost every textbook on business and public administration, frequently as uncontested truth, it deserves close scrutiny, and regrettably, much about the theory does not withstand this scrutiny. The evidence on which the theory was based was at best flimsy, primarily anecdotes drawn from the treatment of neurotic and psychotic individuals.[11] Testing the theory has proven difficult, if not impossible.[12] In general, Maslow demonstrated little concern with the need for empirical verification of his theories, at one point estimating that in American society physiological needs are generally 85 percent satisfied; safety needs, 70 percent satisfied; social needs, 50 percent satisified; ego needs, 40 percent satisifed; and self-actualization needs only 10 percent satisfied, without any empirical evidence to support the generalizations.[13] Solancik and Pfeffer concluded that "the evidence indicates that the need satisfaction model must be seriously re-examined and does not warrant the unquestioning acceptance it has attained in organizational psychology literature."[14]

A certain puritanical bleakness characterizes Maslow's needs. Nowhere in his hierarchy does any need to play, to laugh, to go to a baseball game and drink beer and eat hotdogs appear. And self-actualized people do not seem to have any fun at all. Although in some later versions of his theory Maslow considered the need to know and understand and aesthetic needs (vaguely defined as a craving for beauty), both were regarded as tentative and not characteristic for all people. Perhaps that is why managers like his theory: the only universal needs are those that can be directly satisfied by work, admittedly with considerable effort on the organization's part.

The concept of prepotency, that lower needs must be satisfied before higher needs emerge, is equally troublesome from an empirical perspective. For example, other psychological theories indicate that the need to be loved and accepted emerges almost at birth, clearly long before physiological and safety needs have been satisfied. Anecdotal evidence indicates that some of the greatest works of art and literature were created by individuals who lacked the most basic necessities and were scorned and ignored by colleagues and society, left to satisfy their needs for acceptance and differentiation only after years of deprivation.

The basic concept of self-actualization is similarly troublesome. Maslow says that it is the need of individuals to maximize their potential; but he also gives a rather detailed description of what one must be to be considered self-actualized. What is left unclear is whether individuals can maximize their potential, be all that they can be, without meeting Maslow's prescription and still be considered self-actualized. Surely not all people have identical potential and why maximizing that potential should require that they conform to one ideal is unclear. The alternative is to concede, as Maslow occasionally did, that not all or even most people are capable of self-actualization, in which case it is clearly not a universal need and is instead an elitist concept. One aspect of Maslow's writings that has been given far less attention than his hierarchy of needs, his description of the aggridant (superior) personality, tends to confirm the suspicion that elitism permeates his concept of self-actualization.

> Some people are superior to others in any given skill . . . and there is some evidence to indicate that some people tend to be generally superior. . . . Those people who are selected out because they are physically healthy tend to also be superior in everything else. (A thought here. Could this general superiority be part of the explanation for those who seem to be unlucky all the time . . . ? Or maybe this is the place to talk about the schlemiel personality.)[15]

After discussing the characteristics of the aggridant person (and the individual's I.Q. is a key measure for Maslow), he goes on to discuss the necessity of inferiors (his term, and he subsequently refers to them as "losers") respecting, obeying, and admiring their superiors. That we in American society do not do this causes Maslow considerable discomfort and leads to the following recommendation: "I think the thing to do is to reread Nietzsche on the slave morality or the morality of the weak in contrast to the morality of the strong. It raises questions."[16] Coming from the spiritual founder of organizational humanism, this is somewhat disconcerting.

All of this criticism is not intended to debunk Maslow but rather to put him and his theory in proper perspective. The concept of a hierarchy of needs is interesting; it may even be true for some people. Similarly, positing universal needs shared by all humans satisfies the theoretical quest for simplicity and at least partially identifies some of the needs that motivate some of the people some of the time. The problem arises when a weak and unproven theory is treated as an irrefutable presumption. No one argued this more persuasively than Maslow himself:

> I, of all people, should know just how shaky this foundation is as a final foundation. . . . I am quite willing to concede this because I am a little worried about this stuff which I consider to be tentative being swallowed whole by all sorts of enthusiastic people, who really should be a little more tentative in the way that I am.[17]

Because unsatisfied needs are recognized as the cause of behavior, many other psychologists have also attempted to identify and explain human needs. Alderfer combined Maslow's five categories into three—existence, relatedness, and growth (ERG)—but found no evidence of hierarchial ordering. Rather, he theorized that extreme fear or anxiety about any particular need precluded thoughts and concerns about other needs.[18] Thus, an individual who is extremely concerned about successfully completing a project in order to receive praise, recognition, and promotion may be temporarily oblivious to all other needs, including physiological needs.

David McClelland has theorized that although a variety of needs exist and those needs are mixed in people, for most individuals one need constantly recurs and dominates. Needs are learned and not necessarily inherent, and they do influence behavior. Although many needs exist, the three that McClelland concentrated on and that have considerable relevance in organizational settings are the needs for achievement (nAch), affiliation (nAff), and power (nPow).[19] Individuals dominated by achievement needs are task oriented, usually prefer to work alone, and dislike collaboration and sharing responsibility. Because successful accomplishment of a goal or a task is the overwhelming need for these individuals, they dislike taking risks. They are competitive, driven by a quest for excellence and generally concerned with other people only insofar as they are helpful in performing tasks. Affiliators (those high in nAff) are driven by the need to be liked, to be accepted by others, and to maintain or restore positive affective relationships. Neither people high in nAch nor those high in nAff are likely to be effective managers because their primary need is not directing and coordinating the efforts of others. For McClelland, the most effective managers are people high in nPow, who are motivated mainly by a need to dominate others. They are aggressive and highly argumentative and place considerable value on prestige and status. Their greatest satisfaction comes from controlling and dominating others.

As long as their need for power is directed toward the accomplishment of social purposes, people high in nPow make the best leaders. Organizations attract all three personality types, and all three make different but important contributions to an organization. To function successfully, an organization must have a mixture of all three; an organization composed of only one type could not survive very long.

Basically, McClelland's methodology relied on the Thematic Apperception Test (TAT), which consists of showing individuals a series of simple pictures. The subjects are then asked to write stories describing what was happening in the pictures, what led up to the situation, what the people in the pictures were thinking, what they wanted, and what would be the outcome of the situation. Because McClelland used a verifiable and easily duplicated methodology to identify his personality types, his method can be used by organizations for selection of employees and managers and also for motivation.

Personality Development

Need theory tends to focus on individuals in a somewhat static fashion, yet psychology also teaches us that personality is dynamic and continues to develop throughout life. This further complicates successful management by indicating that people in their twenties are different from people in their forties; they behave differently, have different concerns (needs), and respond differently to organizational incentives. Freud once again was the first to identify discrete stages of personality development, though he believed that these ended at age eighteen with the completion of the genital stage. Later psychological theorists have believed that development continues throughout life. Erik Erikson identified eight major stages in human development: the first five are the oral-sensory stage; the muscular-anal stage; the locomotor-genital stage; latency; and puberty and adolescence (all of which occur before age eighteen). The last three stages are young adulthood (nineteen to twenty-five years); adulthood (twenty-six to forty); and maturity (ages forty-one and beyond).[20] Each stage is characterized by a specific life conflict that must be resolved before the individual can move to the next stage. In young adulthood, the conflict is between intimacy and isolation, between the need to establish a relationship with an "intimate other" and the need for aloneness, supported by a fear of rejection. Adulthood is characterized by the conflict between generativity, which focuses on parenting and mentoring, and stagnation, the reluctance or failure to do this. Maturity is characterized by the conflict between ego integrity, a satisfactory resolution of the puzzle of the meaning of life, and despair, which results from not resolving earlier conflicts the way Erikson believes they should have been resolved. Erikson's theory has a strong normative basis, and he leaves no doubt as to the one best way to resolve life's conflict regardless of individual differences.

Daniel Levinson focused specifically on adult development, identifying the major stages and transitions in adult personality development.[21] Like many other psychological theorists, he concentrated exclusively on men, and consequently the relevance or irrelevance of his theory to the stages of adult female development is unknown. The Early Adult Transition occurs between the ages of seventeen and twenty-two. Like the other transition periods, this is a time of considerable turmoil and confusion. The initial break from parents and home occurs, initial career and job choices are made, new relationships are established, marriage often occurs, and the individual is still struggling to "grow up." Organizations that employ or educate large numbers of individuals in this age group should recognize that the difficulties inherent in this transition period have an impact on the individuals' behavior. On the positive side, these people are likely to be enthusiastic, energetic, and considerably more malleable than they will be in later stages. On the negative side, however, they are still struggling to establish self-discipline and control; they are likely to be less reliable, less predictable and less work oriented than older employees. This is one reason why some organizations prefer not to hire workers under the age of twenty-one. This transition is followed by the Getting Into the Adult World (GIAW) period, from age twenty-two to twenty-eight. In this stage individuals begin to settle down. They make a more definite occupational choice and a choice of work organizations. On the job they explore the nature of their work, seek out a mentor, and learn what the job and the organization demands. They become more independent and predictable, and personal relationships become more stable.

Unfortunately for both individuals and organizations, this relatively peaceful stage of development terminates with the Age-Thirty Transition, actually the age-twenty-eight-to-thirty-two transition. Initial choices are questioned and reevaluated. The result of that reevaluation may be an organization switch or even a career shift. Some individuals decide at that point to return to college to make a complete change in career. On the personal side, many of those who married young, get a first and frequently devastating attack of the "seven year itch" and divorce, with all its consequent emotional, mental, and financial disruptions occurs. An employee who appeared reliable and competent, with good advancement prospects, becomes, inexplicably to the manager who has forgotten his or her own age-thirty transition, unreliable; his or her work deteriorates and he or she may even decide to leave the organization.

Most individuals pass through the Age-Thirty Transition into a period of Settling Down (age thirty-three to forty). New commitments are made or old ones are reaffirmed, and stability, security, and career advancement emerge as dominant concerns. Goals are established, and the individual concentrates on working towards them. Attention gradually turns towards Becoming One's Own Man (BOOM), establishing control and autonomy, achieving goals through personal effort. This constructive, relatively quiescent goal-oriented period terminates in the much-noted midlife crisis or, in Levinson's terminology, the Midlife Transition (ages forty-one to forty-five).

No transition has received more attention or caused more worry for many people than the midlife crisis, perhaps because most of us initially assumed that if we could just survive adolescence, life would flow tranquilly and serenely. It should be noted that not everyone, perhaps not even a majority, actually experiences a traumatic and wrenching crisis at midlife, and even for those who do go through a marked transition, its severity and duration varies considerably. It seems equally likely that the crisis phenomenon is not innate but socially and culturally created and blown out of proportion in literary works and the media. For those who do experience it, the Midlife Transition is the Age-Thirty Transition writ large. The questioning of one's choices, personal and professional, is more intense, critical, and prolonged, and for those who conclude they have made the wrong choices, the realization may be devastating. The reactions may range from divorce through quitting one's job to emotional breakdowns and engaging in a variety of behaviors that are frequently aimed at recapturing the aura of youth. The traumatic and devastating consequences of this type of transition have received the majority of attention, but it is equally possible that one may go through the extreme questioning process and conclude that one did make the right choices.

From the relative turmoil of the Midlife Transition one proceeds to Middle Adulthood, a period characterized for some by a new sense of values, self-awareness and restabilization of life structure. They regain interest and involvement in their jobs and organizations, although this is less intense than it was earlier. Outside interests become more important. For others, the turmoil may continue; the changes they have made in their lives—new jobs, new marriages, new life-styles—may or may not prove satisfactory. Some may experience an Age-Fifty Transition, which involves further questioning and reassessment, before achieving serenity. Late adulthood is a time of reflection and acceptance of what one has done and what one is.

Chris Argyris, one of the most prominent organizational humanists, also believes that human beings go through a distinct developmental process. Argyris did not identify discrete phases of individual development but instead proposed that as we develop from childhood to adulthood we change in several ways:

Child	Adult
Passive	Active
Dependent/submissive	Independent/autonomous
Few ways of behaving	Multiple ways of behaving
Shallow interest	Deep interest
Short time perspectives	Long time perspectives
Lack of awareness of self	Self awareness
Few abilities/skills	Varied abilities/skills
Short attention span	Longer attention span[22]

For Argyris, these developmental trends were nearly universal, at least for individuals in our culture. Development, for the healthy adult, occurred continuously along each of the dimensions. Individuals differed in pace, but the final outcome of the developmental process was the self-actualized individual (unless, of course, something prevented that development).

Psychological Theory, Individuals, and Organizations

Although all of this psychological theory may seem remote from the concerns of organization theory, it directly relates to managing organizations and assessing their impact on individuals and society. All of motivation theory and practice is based on understanding human needs and using that understanding to elicit desired behavior from workers. Motivation theorists have used Maslow's hierarchy of needs to construct their own theories of how to extract maximum performance out of workers. When these theories proved less than uniformly successful, other theorists turned to other need-based approaches.

Theories of personality development also have clear relevance for management. Basically, they tell us that individuals' personalities change predictably over time and that this will be reflected in their work behavior. Particularly when an individual is going through one of the transition stages, pronounced and occasionally disruptive and dysfunctional behavioral changes may occur. Management can either facilitate the passage of the crisis or exacerbate the problems associated with it. The price of ignoring these crisis transitions may be the loss of a valuable employee. Both job and organizational satisfaction appear to be correlated with stages of the life cycle.[23] Young, new employees are likely to be overly idealistic about both work and the organization, and initial reactions to reality are likely to be plummeting organizational and job satisfaction. Dissatisfaction bottoms out during the age-thirty crisis and then satisfaction gradually develops and increases until the midlife crisis. Job and organizational satisfaction decline markedly for those forty-one to fifty years old. With the emergence from the age-fifty crisis, satisfaction again increases until individuals enter preretirement (age fifty-five and up). At that point, individuals apparently begin the process of detaching themselves from their job and organizations. Organizational satisfaction decreases more sharply than job satisfaction, perhaps because individuals perceive, usually accurately, that the organization has little interest in them and no further rewards or punishments to offer other than to ease them out through forced retirement.

Psychological theories also provide the basis for theories on the impact of organizations on individuals and society. For Freud, the basic conflict between the id and the superego was reflected at a higher level in the conflict between the individual's struggle for autonomy and self-expression and society's struggle to maintain order and harmony. We cannot live without society and the security, solidarity, belongingness, and material values it provides us. But living in society requires that we give up some of our freedom and individuality and accept the constraints and restrictions society imposes. We are compelled, in Freudian terms, to repress a large part of our nature as the price for civilization, but we cannot do this easily or without problems. "A good part of the struggles of mankind center round the task of finding an expedient accommodation—one, that is, that will bring happiness—between this claim of the individual [for autonomy] and the cultural claims of the group."[24] Few ever find a truly satisfactory accommodation, and the result is that we are all neurotic to one degree or another.

What is true of civilization and its constraints is equally true of organizations. We create organizations to help fulfill our needs, and organizations are essential to our personality development. Like civilization, however, organizations also constrain our behavior and require that we give up our autonomy and individuality. For Argyris, the essence of the conflict was that organizational goals were either independent of or antagonistic to individual needs, and the more formal the organization, the more it forced individuals to behave as infants. Many individuals were thus never allowed to develop as adults. Those who tried to do so in organizational settings experienced frustration, psychological failure, and conflict.[25] The result might be called "Organizations and Their Discontents."

Organizations do constrain behavior and significantly restrict the freedom of their members but the extent to which this prevents individuals from developing psychologically and causes neurosis is subject to debate. Kohn, for example, found that bureaucratization is associated with "greater intellectual flexibility, higher valuation of self-direction, greater openness to new experience and more personally rewarding moral standards."[26] Clearly a certain degree of restraint and discipline facilitates psychological, moral, and intellectual development. Man in a pure state of nature, unrestrained by any conventions, is likely to be primitive and undeveloped in every sense. Further, by providing human beings with the economic means to satisfy basic human needs, organizations, to use Maslow's terminology, set the stage for the development and satisfaction of higher needs. Organizations also provide for the satisfaction of many of those higher needs: security, society, differentiation, status, prestige, and esteem are all partly fulfilled within the organizational setting. To a certain extent even self-actualization, the development of one's capabilities and potential, is facilitated for many by the organizations for which they work. This is true, however, only if one's capabilities and potentials are useful for the organization's purposes. If they are not, then their development will be stunted and discouraged. For people at the highest level of self-actualization, those Maslow would have considered truly self-actualized, the conflict is likely to be more severe. These were not "ordinary" people (Jefferson, Lincoln, Eleanor Roosevelt, for example), and for them the constraints of the organization far outweighed the benefits.

At least part of the perceived conflict between organizations and individual self-fulfillment stems from the role that many theorists have assigned to work in the individual's life. For many organization theorists, individuals seem to have no life at all other than their work lives, and so work and the work organization must satisfy all needs and provide the only outlet for fulfilling activity. To the extent that organizations fail to do that, by inference, they restrict human potential and stunt psychological development. Consequently, assessing the impact that the work organization has on the human psyche requires an understanding of the role of work in the lives of individuals.

INDIVIDUALS AND WORK

Work, the engaging in a physical or mental activity to provide the physical necessities of life, has always been part of life. Whether hunting, fishing, gathering, or tilling, mankind has always worked to survive. The view that work is the central interest of individuals and that it must satisfy all their social, mental, psychological, and intellectual needs is of relatively recent origin. The ancient Greeks viewed work as brutalizing to the mind, rendering man unfit for considering truth or practicing virtue. The Old Testament regarded work as a curse imposed on man as a punishment for his sins, a necessity that the sensible man engaged in solely to support himself and to allow him to do the things he really liked. It is only since the Reformation and the rise of the Protestant work ethic that work has begun to assume a higher, nearly sanctified position in life. Work then became a predestined calling that man must engage in because it is the will of God, and the best way to serve God was to do most conscientiously one's work.[27]

Karl Marx elevated work to an even more central position in life: people were defined by the work they did; work was the essence of their being, basic to establishing their identity.

Ironically, the organizational humanists share with the Marxists the basic concept of work inherent in the Protestant work ethic—that work is and should be the central life interest of individuals—and, one occasionally suspects, its Calvinist abhorrence of idleness, leisure, and pleasure. This may explain why almost all humanist motivation theories seem to be based on the assumption that workers do not work hard enough, that they do not give their total effort to their jobs and that ways, humanistic ways unquestionably, must be found to correct this problem. All other aspects of life—family, friends, hobbies, recreational activities, community involvement—are relegated to a position of insignificance: work is and must be everything. If your work does not totally fulfill you, you are unfulfilled. From an organizational perspective, this is a convenient view because under the guise of providing fulfillment, the organization can seek maximum commitment from workers at the expense of their personal lives. After all, it appears to work well for the Japanese.

That this view of work may be not only erroneous but also detrimental to individuals, organizations, and society receives little attention. Dubin reviewed a variety of survey research studies conducted from 1956 to 1972 on work as the central life interest. The major conclusion from these studies was that workers vary considerably in the extent to which they locate their central life interests in work: the results ranged from 12 to 82 percent who considered work their primary life interest.[28] Compounding the complexity of these results was the diversity of aspects of their jobs to which people were attached. These included work groups, the organization, the union, the profession, technology, routine, autonomy, personal space, pay, benefits, power, authority, status, and career.[29] In reality, work means different things to different people, and people vary considerably as far as what they most value in a job situation. The expectation that any job will satisfy all of an individual's needs lays the groundwork for the reality shock that most new workers experience. This expectation perpetuated throughout life may be one of the major contributing factors to the midlife crisis. By trying to fulfill this expectation, many of us pin all of our hopes for fulfillment on our jobs; work and its demands and rewards overshadow all other aspects of life. As Carl Jung pointed out,

> We wholly overlook the essential fact that the achievements which society rewards are won at the cost of a diminution of the personality. Many—far too many—aspects of life which should have been experienced lie in the lumber room among dusty memories. Sometimes, even, they are glowing coals under grey ashes.[30]

Similarly, when many individuals reach retirement age, their inability to conceptualize life without work makes retirement seem like a death sentence.

Unrealistic perspectives about the centrality of work may also be dysfunctional for organizations and their management. First it creates unrealistic expectations about how workers should behave, basically reinforcing the attitude that workers are not nearly as productive or motivated as they should be. This in turn leads to the endless and frequently expensive quest to determine why they are not and how they can be made so. Further, it engenders in many organizations (and probably particularly in public organizations) guilt that jobs are not as totally fulfilling as they should be. Finally, it results in organizations attempting to make work—the job—into what it should be, further encroaching on the individuality and lives of workers.

Society also pays a price for this unrealistic overemphasis on work. With everything other than jobs and careers relegated to secondary importance, other social institutions and activities are neglected. Family ties and devotion of time and attention to the family are denigrated in a work-oriented society: energy, time, and commitment devoted to family are seen as energy, time, and commitment taken from the job. Thus, it becomes acceptable and even necessary to turn traditional family responsibilities over to other organizations: from sex education to teaching moral values to caring for the aged, the family has gradually abrogated responsibility. The truly work-oriented individual has little time for volunteer community activities and in all likelihood little interest in or information on politics and political participation. If adults are basically uninformed, unread, and unconcerned about their own mental and intellectual development (as is frequently lamented), perhaps it is because we have communicated to them that these activities are unproductive and, worse yet, unfulfilling.

What role does and should work play in the individual's life? Work serves many different purposes for people. For most people, work is a source of economic security: it provides us with the money to secure the necessities and frivolities of life. Work is also a primary source of social interaction, and it provides fellowship and social life. It provides us with a source of recognition, power, and status; beyond that it is a source of ego satisfaction, of self-esteem. It is, after all, how most of us spend eight hours a day, five days a week for most of our adult lives. But even at that, the major portion of our lives is lived outside the work place, and what happens outside may well be far more crucial for overall life satisfaction than what occurs on the job. We might all be healthier and more content if we accepted the advice, based on Taoist philosophy, offered by Ralph Siu:

> The individual should therefore conduct himself at work almost in self protection, as it were, against the natural propensities of organizations in his attempt to preserve the primacy of his own mental health. . . . A person is born alone and dies alone. He lives alone through many days of childhood

and old age. Not quite alone—but alone in the world of nature. . . . It is from this totality that he came . . . and it is into this totality to which he must return. . . . If he is able to retain the joy of living alone . . . with nature . . . then he would be able to realize the harmony of himself. . . . The most important meaning of work, then, is a negative one. . . . Certainly work by all means. And do a good job while you're at it. Enjoy the rewards. But do not be attached to them. . . . Work should have no special commitment. It is just one of the many activities of man.[31]

ALIENATION, JOB SATISFACTION, AND DISSATISFACTION

Although the concept of alienation had long been a central concept in theology, Karl Marx's formulation of work alienation has been the basis for contemporary sociological and psychological studies of the phenomenon. Marx considered work to be central to human life, "an existential activity of man, his free conscious activity—not as a means for maintaining life but for developing his universal nature."[32] The capitalist system resulted in a separation, an estrangement of the worker from his labor:

> What then constitutes alienation of labor? First that work is external to the worker, that it is not part of his nature; and that, consequently, he does not fulfill himself in his work, but denies himself, has a feeling of misery rather than well-being, does not develop freely his mental and physical energies but is physically exhausted and mentally debased. The worker, therefore, feels himself at home only during his leisure time; whereas at work he is homeless.[33]

Work was no longer an expression of our own creativity and personality: our work was taken from us and turned into an object. Thus, we were alienated from our work and ourselves, our basic nature, and from one another, our interactions devoid of human qualities.

Contemporary sociologists generally define work alienation "as a form of dissatisfaction or a feeling of disappointment with jobs, occupations, or work in general, which do not provide intrinsic need satisfaction or opportunities for self-direction and self-expression."[34] Industrial psychologists define alienation similarly and measure its extent by the degree of job involvement, job satisfaction, intrinsic motivation, occupational and work role involvement, and central life interests expressed by workers.[35] The actual measurement of alienation has always been considered difficult because the consensus of research opinion from Marx to the present has been that a truly alienated worker would be unlikely to recognize his or her own alienation. Thus, measurement has generally taken one of two approaches. The first approach has been for the researcher to analyze the nature of jobs and, based on the characteristics of the job, to determine whether alienation was present. Hackman and Oldham, for example, identified five job characteristics—variety, autonomy, task significance, task identity, and feedback—whose presence or absence were used as a measure of alienation.[36] This completely eliminates the need to solicit workers' opinions and provides an "objective" measure of alienation. The second approach involves the use of questionnaires designed to measure job satisfaction or involvement on the part of workers.

The results of both types of research are controversial and subject to varying interpretations. In 1973, the federal Department of Health, Education, and Welfare (HEW) published a study called *Work in America*. That study concluded that significant numbers of American workers were dissatisfied with their jobs, finding them dull, repetitive, seemingly meaningless, and lacking in challenge or autonomy.[37] A major point of controversy is what constitutes a significant number. Gallup polls taken nationally from 1958 to 1973 showed that job satisfaction rates varied from 81 to 90 percent, increasing steadily throughout the time period. Evaluation of those figures depends on how one chooses to look at them. To paraphrase, is the glass 10 percent empty or 90 percent full? For the HEW study authors and many organizational humanists the glass is clearly empty. For them a 10-to-19-percent dissatisfaction rate in the work force constitutes significant numbers and establishes that alienation was widespread in this country; and for the HEW study authors, this was only the tip of the iceberg. If workers do not know when they are alienated, they do not know when they are satisfied either.

> Does this mean that such high percentages are *really satisfied* with their jobs? Most researchers say no . . . Those workers who report that they are "satisfied" are really saying that they are not "dissatisfied" in Herzbergian terms—i.e., that their pay and security are satisfactory, but this does not necessarily mean that their work is intrinsically rewarding.[38]

The Department of Labor in 1974 concluded quite the opposite: that no evidence of widespread job dissatisfaction existed, nor was there any detectable decline in rates of job satisfaction.[39]

Analysis of job characteristics leads to similarly conflicting conclusions. Once again the organizational humanists conclude that a major portion of jobs in the economy are boring, meaningless, and monotonous, allowing workers little control over their schedules, pace, or procedures. For them, too, alienation is a prevalent de facto characteristic of many workers. Conversely, some researchers urge caution in accepting the validity of these conclusions.

> To impute boredom, alienation, anomie or the seeds of mental illness to another man's work or existence is a hazardous thing. To some blue collar workers, the social scientist's preoccupation with books, dry articles, tables of statistics and obsessive academic discourse must seem boring, more alienating, more fraught with anomie, than his own existence. That worker might provide excellent evidence that the lonely, dissatisfied social scientist has a

much higher rate of surveyed mental illness, psychiatric utilizations and suicides than any UAW population.[40]

The meaningfulness or meaninglessness of a job, as well as its monotony, lies in the eyes of the beholder. Academics, researchers, and members of the middle and upper classes in general are more prone to see their own jobs as more meaningful than the jobs of blue-collar workers and bureaucrats. Questioning just how meaningful lecturing three times a week to an assemblage of moderately bored students who will forget 99 percent of everything they were forced to memorize within a relatively brief time after a class concludes tends to be viewed as heretical. That teaching the same classes semester after semester, year after year could be construed by some as boring is likely to be equally discounted. All of us tend to look at jobs that we would not like to have and underevaluate the importance of the job. But to the worker holding that job, things may appear very differently.

> There is little intrinsically bad about being a janitor or trash collector. What is so bad about them is that in such jobs you cannot earn a living. Where the pay for garbage and trash collectors approaches a living wage, as in New York City, there is intense competition for the work that is elsewhere shunned. . . . So would it be, perhaps, with [other] jobs that are presently considered menial, dead end jobs. If a man could earn a living at these jobs they would not be dead end.[41]

At least part of the conviction of humanists that alienation is widespread relates directly to their concept of work as the central (only) life interest and their beliefs about what work should be. When the reality of work in many jobs fails to meet their preconceived standards, they conclude that alienation exists. "Organizational humanists overstate their argument when they proclaim that people can only achieve inner peace through intrinsically satisfying work; and it is implicit in their ideology that blocked self-actualization in the job not only leads to conflict in the workplace, but adversely affects society."[42] But many workers share neither the ideology nor the perceptions of the humanists. While few workers love their work, most like it and very few hate it. This is reflected in the proportions of workers who indicate they would continue to work even if it were unnecessary to do so and in the attitudes of the unemployed who overwhelmingly prefer working to drawing unemployment checks. Work is for the majority a necessary way to earn a livelihood, but not a way of fulfilling their existence.[43] The workers derive satisfaction off the job, and especially for blue-collar workers, extrinsic job factors are more salient than intrinsic factors.[44]

Excessive job involvement may actually be related to poor mental health. A study conducted by Kanungo found that "greater involvement in one's job is associated with greater worry, anxiety, and apprehension concerning how the job needs to be done. . . . Psychological identification with the job may sensitize individuals to view even minor problems . . . as matters too serious to be taken lightly."[45] This may lead to feelings of frustration and hostility, which in turn may result in drug abuse, alcoholism, and psychosomatic symptoms, reactions typically associated with burnout, which will be discussed in Chapter 10.

The vast majority of American workers clearly do not think of themselves as alienated; they view themselves as satisfied with their jobs. From a societal perspective, it is clearly important that they do so. Large numbers of dissatisfied workers could present a threat to social and political stability. From a moral perspective, it is equally important that people not be forced to labor in jobs that they dislike and that dissatisfy them. Whether it is equally important from an organizational perspective is considerably more difficult to ascertain. Although it might seem that job satisfaction should equate with productivity and organizational commitment (and many theories of motivation have been constructed on that premise), little evidence exists to support that contention. Countless research studies have found that there is at best a weak relationship between satisfaction and productivity. In a review of the literature, Tannenbaum found that correlations between satisfaction and productivity ranged from .14 to −.18.[46]

In 1983 a team of researchers from Indiana University compared job satisfaction rates of American and Japanese workers. The results of the study were somewhat perplexing. Although Japanese workers and the Japanese management style are widely admired in the United States for the high productivity they have achieved, Japanese workers are considerably less satisfied with their jobs than their American counterparts. While 81 percent of American workers expressed satisfaction with their jobs, only 53 percent of the Japanese did. What was even more surprising was that 88 percent of the Americans agreed that the organization and its employees were like one big happy family, compared with 36 percent of the Japanese. Action-oriented commitment, however, was not particularly high for either group of workers: when asked if they would give up earned personal time off to help the organization when things were busy, 23 percent of the Americans said they would, compared with 39 percent of the Japanese.[47]

The Japanese results should not really come as a surprise. Although the Japanese management style has been widely praised and American organizations, public and private, have been urged to emulate it, its proponents have been relatively selective in portraying its total impact on workers. Japanese management sounds good and humanistic, but Japanese working conditions are not all that desirable. The six-day-a-week, 12-hour work day is standard in Japan. Wages, although relatively high, are not high enough to maintain material standards of living equal to those of American workers because necessities, food, housing, and utilities are extremely expensive. Work emerges as the central life interest (at least for males) because that kind of work schedule leaves little time for anything else. The human results of this are becoming increasingly apparent: alcoholism, suicide rates, and divorce rates are increasing.[48] Excessive work involvement is no better for Japanese mental health than it is for American mental health.

If satisfaction is not clearly related to productivity or motivation, it does seem to be related to turnover rates and absenteeism. The greater the level of satisfaction, the lower both turnover rates and absenteeism are likely to be in an organization.[49] Since both turnover and absenteeism are costly from an organizational perspective, some concern with satisfaction rates does appear to be economically justifiable. Similarly, high dissatisfaction rates may make workers more susceptible to unionization and, for those already unionized, more willing to resort to strikes.

The lack of correlation between satisfaction and productivity may not be as puzzling as first appears. High productivity probably does equate with intense job involvement. That in turn equates with putting in long hours on the job, identifying oneself completely with the job, and identifying one's self-worth with success and failure on the job. The price of such involvement is likely to be high levels of stress, little time for family, friends, or off-work interests, and expressed dissatisfaction with the job. The ultimate irony of organizational humanism may be that its insistence that work be the central life interest (which humanists equate with an absence of alienation) may in reality be a major cause of alienation.

CONCLUSION

Individuals are the building blocks of organizations, and cementing a collectivity of diverse individuals into a coherent, cohesive whole is a difficult task. Certainly, the formal structure of the organization is an important part of that task, as is socializing members into the norms and culture of the organization. But no matter how well those two functions are performed, the personalities of the individuals who compose the organization remain distinct and discrete variables that managers must attempt to understand in order to mold continuing commitment to organization purposes. Whether individuals make good workers—ones who are productive from the organization's perspective—depends on a great many factors. Their basic personality structure, their most important needs, their skills, abilities, and training, their perception of the role of work in their lives, and their orientations toward their jobs and even their ages affect the level of performance and output of workers. They affect the variety of attitudes that are collectively grouped under the term "motivation," the subject of the next chapter.

From this chapter it should be apparent that we know very little definite about human personality, and consequently our attempts to control human behavior have had less than universal success. Cherished theories frequently fail to pass the test of reality; sometimes we discard them in favor of new theories, but sometimes, lacking new theories that appear viable, we cling to the old and discredited because they are, if nothing else, familiar. Verifiable or not, the hierarchy of human needs seems likely to be with us for a long time.

Similarly, because it seems logical that satisfied workers should be productive workers, evidence to the contrary seems unlikely to shake our belief in that principle. Consequently, management theory will continue to concentrate on ways of increasing satisfaction to increase productivity. So will surveys that indicate that the vast majority of workers are satisfied be either ignored or discounted.

Organization theory and management are both heavily normative in their approach to work and workers. That work should be the central life interest is a strongly held belief, as is the belief that only meaningful work, by the theorists' definition, can be satisfying. Perhaps part of the lack of success of many theories aimed at increasing productivity is attributable to the reality that many workers share neither of those beliefs. To the extent that this is true, organization theorists may be guilty of E_{III}—solving the wrong problem.

NOTES

1. Wendell French, *The Personal Management Process* (Boston: Houghton-Mifflin, 1978), p. 71.
2. Clyde Kluckholn and Henry A. Murray, *Personality in Nature, Society, and Culture* (New York: Knopf, 1953), p. 53.
3. Dorothy Harlow and Jean Hanke, *Behavior in Organizations* (Boston: Little, Brown, 1975), p. 44.
4. Theodore Herbert, *Dimensions of Organizational Behavior*, 2nd ed. (New York: Macmillan, 1981), p. 187.
5. Calvin S. Hall, *A Primer of Freudian Psychology* (New York: The American Library, 1954), p. 122.
6. See Eric Berne, *Games People Play* (New York: Grove Press, 1964) and Thomas Harris, *I'm OK, You're OK* (New York: Harper and Row, 1969).
7. Henry A. Murray, *Explorations in Personality* (New York: Oxford University Press, 1938), p. 155.
8. A. H. Maslow, "A Theory of Human Motivation," *Psychological Review* (July, 1943): pp. 370–396.
9. Ibid., p. 392.
10. A.H. Maslow, *Toward a Psychology of Being* (New York: Van Nostrand Reinhold, 1968), pp. 87–88.
11. Clifford T. Morgan, Richard A. King, and Nancy Robinson, *Introduction to Psychology*, 6th ed. (New York: McGraw-Hill, 1979), p. 534.
12. Douglas T. Hall and Khalil E. Nougaim, "An Examination of Maslow's Need Hierarchy in an Organizational Setting," *Behavior and Human Performance* (1968): pp. 12–35.
13. W. Clay Hamner, "Motivation Theories and Work Applications," in Steven

Kerr, *Organizational Behavior* (Grid Publishing Co., Columbus, Ohio, 1979), p. 43.

14. Gerald R. Salancik and Jeffrey Pfeffer, "An Examination of Need Satisfaction Models of Job Attitudes," *Administrative Science Quarterly* (September 1977): p. 453.

15. A. H. Maslow, *Eupsychian Management* (Homewood, Ill.: Dorsey Press, 1965), p. 133.

16. Ibid., p. 135.

17. Ibid., p. 55–56.

18. C. P. Alderfer, *Existence, Relatedness, and Growth: Human Needs in an Organizational Setting* (New York: Free Press, 1972).

19. David McClelland, *Studies in Motivation* (New York: Appleton-Century-Crofts, 1955), pp. 226–34.

20. Erik Erikson, *Childhood and Society* (New York: Norton, 1950), pp. 270–271.

21. The following discussion is based on Daniel Levinson, *The Seasons of a Man's Life* (New York, Knopf, 1978).

22. Chris Argyris, *Personality and Organizations: Conflict Between the System and the Individual* (New York: Harper and Row, 1957).

23. Manfred Kets de Vries, Danny Miller, Jean-Marie Toulouse, Peter H. Friesen, Maurice Boisvert, and Roland Theriault, "Using the Life Cycle to Anticipate Satisfaction at Work," *Journal of Forecasting* (1984): pp. 161–172.

24. Sigmund Freud, *Civilization and Its Discontents*, trans. *James Strachey (New York: Norton, 1961), p. 43.*

25. Chris Argyris, "Personality Versus Organization," in Donald White, *Comtemporary Perspectives in Organizational Behavior* (Boston: Allyn & Bacon, 1982), pp. 40–43.

26. Melvin L. Kohn, "Bureaucratic Man: A Portrait and an Interpretation," *American Sociological Review* (June 1972): p. 472.

27. Stanley Parker and Michael Smith, "Work and Leisure," in Robert Dubin, *Handbook of Work, Organization and Society* (Chicago: Rand McNally, 1976), p. 38.

28. Robert Dubin, "Attachment to Work," in Dubin, *Handbook of Work, Organization and Society*, p. 283.

29. Ibid., p. 290.

30. Carl Jung, "Stages of Life," in *Collected Works of C. J. Jung*, vol. 8 (Princeton: Princeton University Press, 1960), p. 396.

31. Ralph Siu, "Work and Serenity," in John Senger, *Individuals, Groups and Organizations* (Cambridge, Mass.: Winthrop Publishers, 1980), p. 106.

32. Karl Marx, in Robert C. Tucker, ed., *The Marx-Engels Reader* (New York: Norton, 1972), p. 62.

33. Ibid., p. 60.

34. Robindra N. Kanungo, *Work Alienation* (New York: Praeger Publishers, 1982), p. 21.

35. S. Rabinowitz and D. T. Hall, "Organizational Research on Job Involvement," *Psychological Bulletin* (1977): pp. 265–88.

36. J. R. Hackman and G. R. Oldham, "Motivation Through the Design of Work: Test of a Theory," *Organization Behavior and Human Performance* (1976): pp. 250–279.

37. Department of Health, Education, and Welfare, *Work in America: Report of the Special Task Force to the Secretary of HEW* (Cambridge, Mass.: MIT Press, 1973).

38. Department of Health, Education, and Welfare, "Work in America" in Dale S. Beach, ed., *Managing People at Work*, 2nd ed. (New York: Macmillan, 1975), p. 55.

39. U.S. Department of Labor, *Job Satisfaction: Is There a Trend?* (Washington, D.C.: Government Printing Office, 1974).

40. I. Siassi, G. Grocetti, and J. R. Spino, "Loneliness and Dissatisfaction in a Blue Collar Population," *Archives of General Psychiatry, American Medical Association* (February 1974): p. 265.

41. E. Liebow, "No Man Can Live With the Terrible Knowledge That He Is Not Needed," *New York Times Magazine* (April 5, 1970).

42. H. Roy Kaplan and Curt Tausky, "Humanism in Organizations: A Critical Appraisal," in Dean L. Yarwood, ed., *Public Administration* (New York: Longman, 1987), p. 149.

43. Mitchell Fein, "Motivation to Work," in Dubin, *Handbook of Work, Organization and Society*, p. 493.

44. Kaplan and Tausky, "Humanism in Organizations," p. 150.

45. Kanungo, *Work Alienation*, p. 151.

46. Arnold Tannenbaum, *Control in Organizations* (New York: McGraw-Hill, 1968). See also Victor Vroom, *Work and Motivation* (New York: John Riley, 1964), and W. W. Ronan, "Individual and Situational Variables Relating to Job Satisfaction," *Journal of Applied Psychology Monograph* (February 1970): pp. 13–31.

47. Stanley J. Modie, "Satisfaction Guarantees Nothing," *Industry Week* (November 28, 1983): p. 7.

48. Leslie Helm and Charles Gaffney, "The High Price the Japanese Pay for Success," *International Business* (April 7, 1986): pp. 52–54.

49. Vroom, *Work and Motivation*, pp. 175–78.

9

MOTIVATION

The quest for organizational productivity underlies the concern of organization theorists and management with motivation. An organization can achieve maximum productivity only if its individual workers are maximally productive, and they in turn will be maximally productive only if they are motivated to be productive. From Frederick Taylor to the present, theorists have believed that neither workers nor organizations are attaining maximum levels of productivity and, by inference, that workers are not properly motivated. What is assumed to be true in the private sector is assumed to be more so in the public sector. One of the most prevalent popular and current political beliefs is that public sector organizations are inefficient and wasteful and that their productivity levels are lower than those of private sector organizations. The public sector is labor intensive, so any increase in its productivity depends heavily on increasing the productivity of workers. Logically this seems to indicate that public sector workers must be less motivated than their private sector counterparts. Consequently, motivation of employees emerges as a central concern for public sector organizations.

Productivity in the private sector is defined as the ratio of outputs to inputs: one hundred widgets per person-hour, for example. Productivity thus measured can be increased by either increasing the number of widgets produced or decreasing the person-hours required to produce the same number of widgets. Productivity may also be measured by cost per unit of production. Either way, it is a measure of efficiency and becomes especially meaningful when one organization's or one nation's productivity is compared with that of another. Defined in this fashion, productivity ignores any other considerations, such as quality of output, treatment of employees, or such externalities as air and water pollution caused by production. Despite the vast differences between the public and private sectors, a measure used for the private sector is also assumed to be valid for the public sector.

Productivity is an inadequate measure of the functioning of the private sector, and its use in the public sector is even more questionable. The problems with measuring public sector productivity begin with attempting to specify the output of public organizations. The lack of goal clarity characteristic of public organizations makes even identification of outputs difficult. Should the output of a police department be number of arrests, number of convictions, number of calls responded to, or family disputes resolved? If the majority of people arrested are innocent, number of arrests would not truly indicate productivity; convictions, however, are not within the control of police department—pressures on prosecutors and courts may result in dropped charges for many valid arrests. Should a school's output be measured by number of students taught or number passed from one grade to the next, even if those students can neither read nor write when they graduate? And what is the output of the Defense Department?

All of the previously discussed differences of public organizations from private sector organizations make measuring public sector productivity very different from and far more complex than measuring private sector productivity. Ambiguity of goals and the problems of determining desired outputs is but one of the difficulties. The intangible nature of many public services compounds the difficulty of productivity measurement: equal opportunity and justice, for example, are difficult to achieve, and their accomplishment difficult to quantify. Productivity measurement in the public sector has always included effectiveness as well as efficiency as a necessary aspect of true productivity, but this further complicates quantification. The quality of education, of mental health services, of medical care for the aged are as important an aspect of productivity as is their quantity, even though little agreement exists on what *quality* means or how it should be measured. When requirements for equity, responsiveness, and constitutionality are added, defining, measuring, and improving productivity becomes even more difficult. Nevertheless, the convictions that efficiency is a primary criterion for evaluating an organization and that the public sector compares poorly with the private sector have made productivity measurement and improvement an unavoidable part of contemporary public administration.[1]

Concern with productivity leads in turn to concern with motivation. If the public sector is plagued with low productivity (although the evidence to support this belief is spotty and inconclusive), it is assumed to be the fault of public employees, whose low productivity is in turn at least partially attributed to a lack of motivation. If motivation is increased, then productivity will improve.

This simplistic assumption should be viewed with some skepticism. First, low motivation, like low productivity, is basically an unproven assumption. Motivation is extremely difficult to measure, and it is not the same as job satisfaction or dissatisfaction, though some theorists assume that it is. Second, employee motivation is only one aspect of performance (productivity). In Victor Vroom's formulation, performance is a function of motivation and ability: $P = F(M \times A)$.[2] Ability includes the education, skills, training, and experience of the employee. Beyond that, however, performance also depends on broader organizational factors, especially technology and resource availability. The basic technological inadequacies of public sector organizations has already been discussed, but it is important to realize that if no one really knows or agrees on how to accomplish the organization's mission, this will inevitably affect the performance and output of individual employees. The lack of adequate resources, money, personnel, and equipment also directly diminish organizational and employee performance. Finally, situational variables—the nature of clientele; political, legal, and constitutional restrictions; public expectations and demand—all play a major role in determining the performance and productivity of public sector organizations.

Despite all these qualifiers, motivation is an important determinant of individual employee performance, and a multitude of theories have been developed to explain what motivates individuals and what organizations should do to ensure that their employees are highly motivated. This chapter analyzes some of the most popular of these theories.

MOTIVATION: INTERNAL DRIVE OR EXTERNAL FORCE?

Although most administration textbooks stress that the primary task of managers is to motivate employees, many psychologists believe that one person cannot motivate another. Motivation is internal, "all those inner striving conditions described as wishes, desires, drives. . . . It is an inner state that activates or moves."[3] Motivation is the "why" of human behavior, the reasons we do things we do. All behavior is motivated; individuals have their own reasons for behaving as they do. When certain individuals work harder and longer than others, presumably it is because they are motivated to do so.

For those motivation theorists who have followed Maslow's lead, the driving force of behavior is unsatisfied needs. "Need" is an ambiguous, value-laden and somewhat misleading term when used to explain human behavior. Its ambiguity lies in the lack of clarity as to whether it applies only to those things that are required for maintaining our physical and mental well-being or whether it also includes our wishes, wants, and desires above and beyond the necessities. Maslow and his followers restrict needs to those things that they have determined are requisite for physical and mental well-being, and therein lies the misleading nature of the term. No one, unless he or she lives on an island or fishes for a living, needs a sailboat. But many people want one and would willingly work overtime if that would result in the ability to purchase the boat. People desire many things that strictly speaking they do not need; they want many things that strictly speaking are detrimental to their physical and mental well-being (e.g., drugs, alcohol, cigarettes). The things people want are just as important in motivating their behavior as the things they need. Ignoring desires as a cause of behavior results in only partial understanding of what causes people to behave as they do, and from an organizational perspective limits the ability to control and channel behavior.

Unsatisfied desires and needs result in a drive to satisfy them; they cause us to behave in such a way that we may fulfill them:

To control someone's behavior, you must first determine what they need or desire, then make satisfaction of their desires contingent on behaving the way you want them to behave. That is motivation in a nutshell, and all motivation theories are built around that basic premise. If organizations want workers to behave differently, more productively, they must determine what type of behavior this involves and whether it falls within the capabilities of employees, next ascertain what employees' needs or desires are, and then ensure that those needs or desires are satisfied as a result of changed behavior and increased productivity. Katz and Kahn identified the minimum general behavioral requirements for effective organization functioning as

1. attracting and retaining sufficient personnel to perform the essential functions of the organization;
2. members must know and conform to role expectations; do a lot of work and do it well;
3. they must engage in innovative spontaneous and cooperative activities to protect, improve and create a favorable climate for the organization.[4]

Linking those general requirements to specific behavioral expectations is, however, a major source of problems.

Unfortunately, in many public organizations, the specific behaviors associated with increased productivity and motivation are not easily identifiable. For an organization to know how it wants its employees to behave, it must first know what it is trying to accomplish and how it can best do that. Once again, the presence of vague and conflicting goals and uncertain technology creates problems for public organizations.

Ascertaining the needs and desires of workers has been the major focus of motivation studies, but no clear, universal, and agreed on set of needs and desires has emerged; nor has one best way to motivate everyone been identified. Although for theorists and managers it would clearly be best if they could operate from the assumption that all individuals are the same, for motivation purposes it seems that individual differences make this impossible. The difficulties of ascertaining the desires of diverse individuals remains one of the most complex problems in motivation, and satisfying those desires through work is equally difficult. Compounding these difficulties is the lack of direct and perceived connection in many organizations between superior performance and rewards. Money, promotions, and job security are desired by many workers, but rewarding them on the basis of seniority rather than job performance nullifies their utility as motivators. In practice, however, many private and public organizations do exactly that. Even worse, many organizations actually penalize workers for increased productivity. If workers increase production, overtime pay is cut back and reductions in force may be undertaken.[5] Consequently, not only individual workers but also employee unions may regard productivity improvement programs with suspicion and resist their implementation.

Motivation is internal; why we do the things that we do is a result of our individual personalites. To that extent, it is true that no one can motivate another. What can be done is to determine what another wants and then make satisfaction of that want an integral part of their job situation. To that extent motivation can be externally manipulated.

CLASSIFYING MOTIVATION THEORIES

One of the most common typologies for classifying motivation theories is the content-process typology.[6] Content theories, also referred to as cognitive theories,[7] attempt to specify the internal needs and drives that energize human behavior and to explain how organization structures and processes can be created and maintained to satisfy those needs. Process or acognitive theories focus on external environmental factors that influence behavior. "The emphasis is on the structural features . . . of ongoing work situations, particularly those characteristics of organizations which can be managed or administered in order to elicit particular behaviors from participants."[8] According to this classification, Maslow's hierarchy of human needs and McClelland's need theory as well as the theories of Herzberg, McGregor, and Argyris are content theories; proponents of behavioral modification, expectancy theory, and equity theory are process theorists. Content theories emphasize universalistic needs and intrinsic rewards—job content, characteristics of the job itself as motivators. Process theories take a more individualistic approach to needs and desires, emphasizing the use of extrinsic as well as intrinsic rewards to control behavior. "Content theories emphasize the adaptation of structures to fit needs, whereas process theories urge the adaptation of organizational inducements in directions which produce valued payoffs for participants *if* they contribute toward organizational goals."[9]

Although the two types of theories are different in some respects, they have underlying similarities. Both have an identical purpose: to obtain maximum productivity from individual workers in the interest of overall organizational productivity. Although some process theories (behavioral modification especially) have been criticized for unethical manipulation of human beings, all motivation theories and practices are manipulative. They are attempts to control and direct human behavior for organizational purposes. In addition, both types of theory require managers to know the needs and desires that motivate worker behavior. Finally, both assume that to ensure maximum productivity, organizations must find and use ways to fulfill those needs.

ORGANIZATIONAL MOTIVATORS

Organizations possess a variety of rewards, punishments, and methods to motivate workers. Katz and Kahn identified three major types of organizational motivators: rules, extrinsic rewards, and intrinsic rewards.[10] Although an organization may emphasize one, most organizations use a combination of all three to achieve their purposes. Formal machine bureaucracies rely heavily on formal rules and detailed job descriptions backed by a system of rewards and punishments to secure the desired behavior of their members. Although this type of motivational system is frowned on by organizational humanists, it is not as ineffective as they have portrayed it; in fact, it satisfies basic needs for many of its members. Clear rules and expectations are important for many people and satisfy basic needs for order, predictability, and security. Punishment of inadequate performance can improve the quality of work because it provides necessary feedback as to what is acceptable behavior.

Extrinsic rewards are benefits and incentives provided by the organization to its participants: pay, fringe benefits—health insurance, pensions, sick leaves, vacations, day care for children, group outings—and bonuses, promotions, praise, and recognition. Extrinsic rewards are of two types: system rewards, which are general rewards provided to everyone in the organization (pay, job security, fringe benefits) and individual rewards, which are based on meritorious performance. System rewards tend to be ignored by many organizational theorists but they play an important role in determining worker orientation to the organization. They are especially important in attracting and retaining people for the system. The public sector is frequently evaluated negatively by potential employees because of the perceived inadequacy of the most important system rewards: pay scales. On the other system rewards—security, and fringe benefits in the past at least—the public sector compared favorably with the private sector. The perceived adequacy of system rewards is important in maintaining a minimum level of productivity; adequate system rewards also help build loyalty and commitment to the organization. This in turn encourages cooperation within the system, reduces turnover and absenteeism, and helps create a favorable opinion of the organization in the external environment.[11] System rewards also help satisfy basic needs for survival, security, and belongingness.

Individual rewards can also be important in maintaining and increasing performance, but only if they are properly administered. They must be awarded directly as a result of outstanding performance. Members of the organization must believe that such rewards are distributed fairly and equitably. If the reward is money, it must be a large enough amount for workers to feel that it is worth the extra effort required to obtain it.[12] A twenty-five dollar merit bonus is unlikely to inspire much additional effort; depending on the pay of the individual, a $5,000 bonus is much more likely to do so. Promotions, awarding of status symbols, praise, and recognition satisfy our desire for differentiation, enhance our self-esteem, and gratify our ego needs.

Intrinsic motivators relate to the nature of the job itself: the degree of challenge, responsibility, and power it affords, the opportunity it provides for self-expression and creativity—its perceived meaningfulness. Intrinsic motivation also includes internalization of the values of the organization and the resulting identification with that organization and belief in what it does. The inculcation of a "my organization right or wrong" attitude results in dedication and willingness to do what the organization wants and to derive a sense of satisfaction from doing it.

All organizations possess a wide variety of inducements that motivate their members. Even the formal machine bureaucracy characteristic of many public organizations provides the opportunity for satisfaction of many needs and desires of its members. Beyond the system of formal rules, it can offer valued extrinsic and intrinsic rewards. An organization plagued with low productivity cannot necessarily attribute this to organization structure or to an absence of rewards. More likely, the low productivity is attributable to poor management of the incentive system or provision of the wrong rewards (or punishment) to the wrong persons at the wrong time.

WHAT DO WORKERS REALLY WANT?

Incentives accomplish little or nothing in motivational terms if they are not desired by the workers, and similar problems occur if the incentives desired by the workers are not provided by the organization. Content theorists tend to assume that they know what workers want and need and that these wants and needs are common to all workers. To a certain extent they may be right, but by ignoring individual differences they may end up with theories lacking in practical validity. Individual personality differences determine the strength and importance of various needs, aspiration levels, behavior, orientation to work, and reaction to frustration.[13] What an individual values in work reflects his or her personality. To understand motivation, we need to know both what workers generally want and what the specific worker we are trying to motivate wants at the time we are trying to increase that worker's productivity.

Work in America, the study by the Department of Health, Education, and Welfare (HEW), reported that based on survey research what workers wanted was

1. Interesting work,
2. Enough help and equipment to get the job done,
3. Enough information to do their jobs,
4. Enough authority to do their jobs,
5. Good pay,
6. Opportunity to develop special abilities,
7. Job security,
8. Seeing the results of their work.[14]

The list is interesting, if not conclusive, both for what it includes and what it does not include. It includes several job characteristics directly related to Maslow's higher-level needs, which certainly lends support to some of the contentions of the organizational humanists. It also includes, however, two characteristics that the humanists have given minimal importance: pay and security.

The humanists' decision that money is not a motivator has always been received with considerable approval by management and by those who determine salaries. Certainly in the public sector it is a welcome and comforting idea. Money and security were assumed to have lost relevance in the affluent society. Douglas MacGregor, for example, contended that "the high standard of living created by our modern technological know-how provides adequately for the satisfaction of physiological and safety needs."[15] Satisfied needs, of course, do not motivate behavior; money consequently is no longer a motivator.

There are three basic errors in that contention: it overestimates the extent to which physiological and safety needs are actually satisfied in this society; it ignores human wants and desires that can be satisfied only with money; and it underestimates the role that money plays. With a poverty rate of 14 percent and an unemployment rate of 6 percent, this society has a rather sizeable proportion of its population whose physiological needs are satsified barely or not at all. According to the Bureau of Labor Satistics, the median wage in the United States in 1986 was $18,616; real median household income (base year 1973) was $23,618. That may be sufficient to satisfy physiological needs, but it is surely not sufficient to satisfy the need for security. Even for many of those who are earning sufficient money to satisfy basic needs, the desire for the endless parade of consumer items available remains unsatisfied. Houses, cars, stereos, video recorders, vacation trips are expensive and desired by a great many people, even people whose salaries are not adequate to purchase them. That is why consumer debt is so high in this country.

Beyond that, money (salaries and wages) plays an important symbolic role for most people. We tend to judge our own worth and the worth of others on the basis of what we or they are paid. Money is a major source of status and satisfaction of ego needs. High salaries and big bonuses prove the worth of the receiving individual both to him- or herself and to others. Equally important, money as such a measure is one of the primary sources of feelings of inequity and relative deprivation. Even for the individual earning $150,000 a year, which is surely sufficient to satisfy needs and desires, the knowledge that a colleague of equal or lesser rank or ability is earning $175,000 becomes a source of frustration and anger, fueling beliefs about the unfairness of the organization and life.

Money remains very important to most workers (the humanists notwithstanding), and it is a motivator.[16] It remains the primary reason that most people work, and without money the other motivators are ineffective.[17] This is surely unfortunate for the public sector, which is currently plagued with continuing fiscal scarcity as well as with personnel systems that generally allocate salary increases on the basis of seniority, not job performance.[18] But it should serve as a caution for those who lament low public sector productivity. To the extent that that is true, perhaps we really do get what we pay for and the price of increased productivity may be more than we are willing to pay.

Workers also want job security. "Job security is an essential precondition to enhancing the will to work"[19] Job security guarantees continuity of income and helps build organizational loyalty and identity. It also ensures that workers will not be punished (RIFs) for increased productivity. Despite its importance, few workers have true job security. Once again, the fiscal crunch of the 1980s has undermined what was once one of the most characteristic aspects of public employment: the guarantee that once individuals had survived their probationary period, they had employment security. Now, that security is far more uncertain and dependent on the ability and willingness of government to fund public services.

The desires of workers for interesting work, for opportunities to develop their abilities and see the results of their work, fit nicely with the assumptions of the humanists. The extent to which public organizations allow for satisfaction of these desires varies considerably, as is equally true for private sector organizations. Some public sector jobs are inherently meaningful and interesting at least some of the time; any job held long enough, however, becomes occasionally uninteresting and repetitive whether it is police work, teaching, or medical practice. Other jobs are likely to be viewed as less interesting or meaningful by analysts but, as was pointed out in the last chapter, that assessment may not be shared by the jobholder. Buchanan has contended that the lack of goal clarity in public sector organizations makes it difficult for employees to see the connection between their efforts and organizational success.[20] Despite the ambiguity in expressed public organization goals, as we saw in Chapter 3, this ambiguity may be far more bothersome to theorists than to organization participants.

The desires for sufficient equipment, authority, and information to do the job relate directly to a need that to this point has not been discussed: the need to achieve a sense of competence. Most, perhaps all, human beings need to feel that they have mastered or successfully interacted with their environment.[21] To be unable to perform the tasks assigned to one because of inadequate equipment, authority, or information clearly leaves the need for competence unsatisfied. Such dissatisfaction results in continued frustration and, because it is not within the power of the individual to correct, results in a loss of motivation.

The HEW list, though not comprehensive, provides insight into some of the things that most workers want from their jobs. To reiterate, though different individuals seek different things in their jobs, good social relationships, pleasant location, fair and competent supervisors, status, and respect from society are very important job characteristics for many workers. Linking what workers want to their performance and productivity is the essence of motivation theory. Before examining specific theories, it is necessary to recognize that much about the linkage remains unknown, and many of the assumptions are purely theoretical. Satisfaction does not cause productivity (see Chapter 8); a satisfied worker is not necessarily a highly productive one.

HOW THEN DO WE MOTIVATE WORKERS?

Content Theories

Content theories are universalistic, rely on intrinsic rewards, and emphasize the need to change organizational structures and job design to better satisfy the higher-level needs on Maslow's hierarchy. Their basic assumptions and prescriptions were summarized by Douglas McGregor in *The Human Side of Enterprise*.[22] McGregor contended that there were two basic approaches to management: Theory X, the conventional approach, and Theory Y, the correct (McGregor's) approach. Theory X is based on the assumption that individuals are indolent by nature, lacking in ambition, inherently self-centered, resistant to change, gullible, not very bright, and basically authoritarian, preferring to be led and disliking responsibility. They desire job security and economic rewards above all else. From this rather grim view of human nature, Theory X then advocates, rather logically, that it is the job of management to persuade, reward, punish, control, and direct the worker: authoritarian management for authoritarian workers.

Theory Y, based on the work of A. H. Maslow, is "based on more adequate assumptions about human nature and human motivation."[23] People are not passive by nature but rather seek responsibility. They want to exercise autonomy and creativity; they have a need to find fulfillment at work, to be committed to goals that enable them to self-actualize. Theory Y management accepts the responsibility of arranging organizational conditions so that people can satisfy their needs by directing their efforts toward organizational objectives. According to Theory Y, organizations and jobs must be restructured to allow workers more autonomy, more responsibility. They must provide interesting, meaningful work that allows for the development of the full potential of workers. The adoption of Theory Y "will not only enhance substantially . . . our materialistic achievements, but bring us one step closer to 'the good society'.[24]

Chris Argyris arrived at similar conclusions, based on similar assumptions. For Argyris, the mature personality is active and independent, desires equality and self-control, and has deep interests. Conventional organizations, with their rigid hierarchies and excessive specialization (Theory X), are hostile to the mature personality. They prefer the infantile personality and block individuals from realizing their full potential, from self-actualizing. Argyris's solution was to redesign jobs and organizations to accommodate and require mature personalities. The promised result was not only self-actualized individuals but increased satisfaction, motivation, and productivity.[25]

Frederick Herzberg.   No content theorist has received more academic or practical attention than Frederick Herzberg. "Satisfiers," dissatisfiers," and "hygiene factors" appear and reappear with monotonous consistency in management and administration textbooks and are voiced with reverence by many management professors. His theory is also well received by managers because it relegates material rewards, pay, and fringe benefits to an insignificant role in motivation and productivity.

In Herzberg's original study, he asked 203 accountants and engineers to describe times "when you felt exceptionally good or a time when you felt exceptionally bad about your job."[26] They were then asked a series of questions to determine what factors of the job were associated with these attitudes and what consequences these had on job performance, tenure and interpersonal relationships. From this emerged the list of satisfiers, those aspects of jobs that made workers feel satisfied, and dissatisfiers, those aspects that were associated with feelings of dissatisfaction. Satisfaction and dissatisfaction were *not* two ends of a continuum but rather two separate and discrete concepts. "The opposite of job satisfaction would not be job dissatisfaction but rather *no* job satisfaction; similarly the opposite of job dissatisfaction is not satisfaction but no dissatisfaction."[27]

Dissatisfiers, which were also termed maintenance or hygiene factors, were company policy and administration, supervision and technical aspects, interpersonal relationships, working conditions, and sometimes salary. Satisfiers, which were termed motivators, were achievement, recognition, work itself, responsibility, and advancement. Herzberg was somewhat ambivalent about salary. Although the original study definitely classified money as a hygiene factor, Herzberg subsequently stated, "Because of its ubiqitous nature, salary commonly shows up as a motivator as well as hygiene. Although primarily a hygiene factor, it also often takes on some of the properties of a motivator, with dynamics similar to those of recognition for achievement."[28] As the terms "hygiene factors" and "motivators" indicate, Herzberg has come up with far more than a list of factors that workers like and dislike about their jobs. The dissatisfiers are primarily environmental characteristics of the job. If they are inadequate, workers will complain and be dissatisfied. If they are adequate, workers will not be dissatisfied, but neither will they be satisfied. Improving dissatisfiers will not result in either positive feelings about the job or high performance. Only the satisfiers will do that, and the satisfiers all relate to job content. The only way to motivate individuals to work is through job enrichment: changing the structure of jobs so that the individual has "some measure of control over the way in which the job is done in order to realize a sense of achievement and of personal growth."[29]

Are the satisfiers truly motivators in the sense that they actually lead to high performance and increased productivity? Herzberg's evidence on this point is shaky. The original study relied on the reports of the subjects of the impact of satisfying incidents on performance, which is hardly an objective measure. The assertion is that satisfaction causes performance, but it is equally possible that performance causes satisfaction.[30] If I were to identify a time when I felt particularly satisfied with my teaching, it would be when I delivered a well-prepared lecture that was extremely well received by the students. Although rare, such events do occasionally occur. I performed well; I was satisfied. Conversely, if I gave a lackluster lecture which was received with yawns and all-too-apparent boredom, ego needs being what they are, I would have been likely to attribute my dissatisfaction to the declining intellectual capabilities of the students, my subordinates. What caused what is not all that clear, nor is how it relates to my motivation to work.

Herzberg's methodology has been criticized for the basic reason illustrated in the preceding example. Victor Vroom believes that responses on satisfiers and dissatisfiers are primarily the result of ego-defensive reactions of the respondents. When people are asked to recall something that made them feel good, they are more likely to recall successes that they attribute to their own efforts; when recalling things that made them feel bad they are more likely to identify events or failures attributable to external forces than failures due to their own deficiencies.[31] This may be why researchers using different methodologies have been unable to replicate Herzberg's results.

If the role of satisfiers in work motivation is unclear, so is that of the dissatisfiers. To Herzberg, dissatisfiers are not motivators, but that stretches credulity to the breaking point. Common experience indicates that if two workers have jobs identical in content but one is employed by an organization that pays well, has good fringe benefits, fair and effective policies, good supervision, and pleasant interpersonal relationships and the other works in an organization that has none of the preceding, the first worker is likely to be more motivated and productive than the second. Further, by Herzberg's theory it is possible for a worker to be totally satisfied and totally dissatisfied simultaneously, but the impact of that on motivation should be positive. As Katz and Kahn point out, "the theory is stated in too extreme a form. . . . [T]hat hygienic factors are non-motivating and intrinsic factors non-productive of dissatisfaction is too far fetched a proposition. . . too idealized a logical position to fit the psychological complexities of the real world."[32]

Although Herzberg's theory is based on Maslow, it departs from Maslow's theory on two significant points. As far as Maslow was concerned, *any* need, higher or lower, could be a motivator, but only *unsatisfied* needs could be motivators. Herzberg disagrees on both points: lower-level needs, even if unsatisfied, are never motivators, and higher-level needs are motivators even when satisfied. Similar to Maslow, Herzberg has only weak evidence to support his contentions.

Not only is his evidence weak, but a considerable body of research directly refutes his theory. "In general, the evidence against the theory seems to be greater than the evidence for it."[33] Considerable evidence indicates that maintenance factors are motivators and that workers are more concerned about the fundamental conditions of their work environment than intrinsic elements of the jobs.[34] As far as increasing productivity is concerned, Katzell and Yankelovich contend that "a careful analysis of the findings shows that from a humanist point of view, the most popular, highly publicized and appealing techniques . . . have only a minimal impact. These include . . . job enrichment, management by objectives, autonomous work groups, participative management."[35]

Despite these criticisms, Herzberg remained committed to his theory. In an article entitled "One More Time: How Do You Motivate Employees?" Herzberg reiterated his basic points. You do not motivate by improving working conditions, raising salaries, or even through participative management. Motivation can only be accomplished by "building into people's jobs quite specifically, greater scope for personal achievement and recognition, more challenging and responsible work and more opportunity for individual advancement and growth."[36]

Other content theories, all based on A. H. Maslow's concept of the hierarchy of human needs, share certain similarities with Herzberg's theory. Like Maslow's, they assume that all human beings have identical needs; and in the work place, this means all workers have identical needs. All the content theorists pay little attention to the lower-level needs. They assume either that those needs are satisfied or that they just are not work motivators. From their basic assumptions comes their primary conclusion, that there is indeed "one best way"—actually only one way—to motivate workers: by changing the content of the job to make it meaningful and the structure of the organization to allow the workers control over and responsibility for their jobs.

Content theories are immensely appealing from both a practical and an academic perspective. For humane, ethical, and moral reasons their prescriptions are attractive. They coincide nicely with the theory, if not the practice, of democracy in our society. Arguing against them seems almost un-American, they support so well our normative biases. They are also simple to understand and (on a superficial level) to implement. Their prescriptions are universal, applying to all workers, all jobs, all organizations, private and public sector. From a management perspective, they have additional appeal. They are inexpensive to the organization. Salary increases, merit bonuses, and comprehensive fringe benefit programs cost a great deal of money, which is always scarce in the public sector. Better yet, content theories absolve management from any real responsibility for low motivation and productivity. At worst, management is a dissatisfier, so no real productivity gains can be expected from improving it. If workers are not motivated to perform at maximum levels, the fault lies not with managerial performance but with the way the jobs and organizations are structured.

The weaknesses of content theories, other than their lack of demonstrated effectiveness, are closely related to their appeal. While providing enriched jobs and participatory management may be morally satisfying, ignoring the reality of low pay and job insecurity demonstrates a marked insensitivity to the actual needs of workers and illustrates the elitist bias of the content theorists. They claim to have determined what the workers' needs are, possibly projecting their own needs on to them. Although job enrichment sounds easy to implement, in reality it is not, and neither is it clear what constitutes an enriched job, particularly for many public sector positions. Hackman and Oldham identified five characteristics that determine the level of enrichment of a job: task variety, task significance, task identity, autonomy, and feedback.[37]

The first problem arises when examining some of the more common public sector jobs: police work, teaching, social work. At least superficially all appear to be fairly enriched jobs, especially when autonomy is translated as discretion. Whether much more enrichment could be added without engendering accountability problems is questionable, and whether further enrichment would increase motivation and productivity or increase burnout rates is equally unclear. Certainly teachers have made it clear through their unions that what they want is not job enrichment but monetary enrichment. Many other jobs could be enriched, but every enrichment potentially requires a change in job description, and in the civil service system that means a change in position classification. That in turn might cost money, which is scarce in the public sector.

Process Theories

Process theories view work as inherently neither attractive nor repellant to workers. Rather work's attractiveness or repulsiveness depends on the rewards and penalties associated with it. Process theories concentrate on the process of evoking behavior by providing rewards. Their fundamental premise is that behavior is a function of its consequences. Rewarded behavior will be repeated; behavior that is not rewarded or is punished will be extinguished. Therefore to motivate people to do what you desire, you must reward them for doing it.

Although process theories do not deal explicitly with the concept of needs or desires, they do deal with them implicitly. In order to reward or punish, managers must know what the recipient regards as rewards and punishments: an inappropriate or undesired reward is not a reward at all. Process theories do not claim that all individuals differ in terms of what they recognize as rewards, but the burden is on the one who seeks to control behavior to determine what any particular subject desires to have or wishes to avoid. From an organizational perspective, process theories of motivation advocate that organizational incentive systems must be directed toward rewarding desired performance. To them that is the essence of motivation and the only way to ensure sustained productivity increases.

Expectancy Theory.   Basically, expectancy theory posits that most human behavior is voluntary. Confronted with a specific situation or stimulus, an individual has a choice of responses. The response chosen depends on what the individual expects the outcomes of the chosen response will be and the value the individual attaches to those outcomes.[38] Few things in life, and theories especially, are quite that simple, however, and expectancy theory is no exception. Consider the following example:

A state budget analyst is working at her desk, which is loaded with budget requests, budget estimates, and reports. At 9:30 A.M. her supervisor walks in and states that a legislative committee chairman has requested a special report on a project conducted by one of the agencies assigned to the analyst. He wants the report by 1:00 P.M. that day. The analyst is already overloaded, or feels she is, and has rapidly approaching deadlines on several other reports. However, the supervisor gives her no choice; she must take on the new report. Expectancy theory allows us to predict how much effort the analyst will put into completing the new report.

First, the individual identifies first- and second-level outcomes. In this situation, two first-level outcomes are possible: either she will complete the report or she will not. For each of these outcomes a variety of second-level outcomes are possible:

First-Level Outcome	Second-Level Outcomes
1. Report is completed	1. Supervisor is pleased and praises her work
	2. Analyst feels competent and pride in completing work
	3. Analyst misses lunch
	4. All other work is delayed; analyst must work overtime (without pay) to meet deadlines
	5. Committee chairman is impressed and sends a note of thanks
	6. Other analysts resent both the willingness to work overtime and the praise received
	7. Plans for evening must be cancelled
	8. Family complains about being neglected

2. Report is not completed

1. Supervisor is displeased
2. Analyst feels inadequate and distressed
3. Analyst misses lunch
4. All other work is delayed; analyst must work overtime (without pay) to meet deadlines
5. Committee chairman is critical
6. Other analysts are sympathetic and supportive
7. Plans for evening must be cancelled
8. Family complains about being neglected

The first step involves estimating probabilities for each of the first- and second-level outcomes. Then valences, or value preferences, are assigned to the second level outcomes. Valences may be either positive or negative. The predicted amount of effort can be calculated using the following formula:[39]

$$\underset{\text{(motivation)}}{\text{Effort}} \;=\; \underset{\substack{\text{(probability}\\ \text{that effort}\\ \text{will result}\\ \text{in desired}\\ \text{performance.)}}}{E{\to}P} \;\times\; \underset{\substack{\text{(probability of each second-}\\ \text{level outcome times the}\\ \text{valence attached to that}\\ \text{outcome.)}}}{\Sigma \; (P{\to}o(v))}$$

Thus, if the analyst estimates that there is no probability that the report can be completed, regardless of the desirability or undesirability of the second-level outcomes, she will put little effort into production. If the probability of completion is higher, then the values attached to the second-level outcomes become more important. The strength of the valence assigned is an individual calculation: the analyst might assign a value of $+1$ to supervisor approval and a -10 to peer disapproval or vice versa. Once those valences have been assigned and totaled, she will make the determination of whether increased effort is worth the payoff.

First it should be stressed that probably no one goes through these complicated calculations explicitly in deciding how much effort to devote to a task. Rather, the calculations are performed subjectively, frequently unconsciously. What emerges from the expectancy theory perspective is that motivation is considerably more complex than it appears in content theory. An outcome generally has a variety of consequences, and from the individual's perspective some of these consequences are positive and some negative. Using rewards to elicit specific behavior is far from simple; as Lawler points out:

> Tying a valent reward, such as pay, to a desired behavior, such as good performance, will not be enough to motivate the desired behavior. Pay can be highly valued and can be seen as closely related to performance; but if negative consequences, such as feeling tired, or being rejected by the work group, are also perceived as related to good performance, there may be no motivation to perform. . . . Performing well can have a strong force, but if performing poorly has a stronger force, the person will not be motivated to perform well.[40]

Further, individuals have different needs, desires, and goals, and even when these are similar, the strengths of these needs vary among individuals.

Expectancy theory requires managers who wish to motivate their employees to determine what outcomes each employee values. Management must also know and identify what kind of behavior it desires. Although this is often taken for granted, in reality what constitutes high productivity is not always known—and if it is, it is not clearly communicated to employees. Desired levels of performance should be challenging but realistic. The requirement that individuals believe that through increased effort they are capable of achieving the desired first-level outcome is central to expectancy theory. Without that, there is no motivation. Desired outcomes must be linked to desired performances: Vroom termed this "instrumentality." The individual must also be convinced that achieving the desired first-level outcome will lead to a desired second-level outcome. The situation must be analyzed for conflicting expectancies. If perceived negative outcomes outweigh perceived rewards, once again there will be no motivation to high performance. To increase motivation, changes in outcomes (rewards) must be significant. Trivial changes will not be sufficient to modify behavior. Finally, the system must be equitable, or rather perceived as equitable by the employees. Unfairness in the reward system undermines the basic concept of expectancy: that good performance is rewarded and bad performance is not.[41]

Organizations should be sure that their pay and reward systems are tied to performance, not seniority or loyalty. Similarly, performance evaluation systems should be structured to identify expected behavior, not personality traits. Jobs should be designed for individuals. If workers want enriched jobs, they should be provided with them; but if they do not, as some workers do not, they should be allowed that flexibility. The role and importance of groups should be recognized, and because groups are key determinants of individual behavior, rewards should also be provided for group performance.[42]

Expectancy theory is considerably more demanding of both supervisors and organizations than are content theories. For most organizations, expectancy theory requires a sweeping reorientation of the pay and reward system because most organizations, public and private, do not base either pay or promotions on performance. Good performers, mediocre performers, and even bad performers are all paid the same. Performance evaluations are .frequently poorly designed and ineffectively administered. Promotions and other benefits tend to be based more on seniority than performance. For supervisors, motivation becomes a major, continuous, and demanding part of their jobs, requiring that they know what each individual employee wants and does not want. The burden for maintaining high performance levels rests squarely on supervisors and requires their constant attention.

Expectancy theory in its theoretical formulation is somewhat complex. It clearly presumes that individuals are rational and that the amount of effort they devote to their assigned tasks is the result of a rational thought process in which they determine all the consequences, direct and indirect, of their behavior and weigh the costs and benefits of those consequences before deciding how to behave. It also assumes that humans always seek to maximize their satisfaction. The problem with these assumptions is that there is very little evidence to prove that humans are that rational. Sometimes some of us may be, but most of the time, most of us are not; if that is true then the best we can obtain from applied expectancy theory is that some of the time, for some of the workers, it will deliver the results it promises.

Equity Theory. One of the most disturbing realities that most of us must contend with is the realization that life is unfair. No matter how many times we are told that that is how life is, few of us ever accept that that is how it should be. Similarly, no matter how many times we are victims of perceived unfairness, we are still likely to react with anger, dismay, and disappointment. (Our reactions when we are the beneficiaries of perceived unfairness are somewhat different.) So powerful is this desire for fairness that J. Stacy Adams has contended that the major motivating force in people's lives is a striving for equity.[43]

Perceptions of unfairness or inequity always involve comparisons. In the work situation, individuals regularly compare their situation and treatment with those of others. Individuals assess their input—their education, training, skill, seniority, effort, and performance—and the overall treatment they receive from the organization—pay, promotions, recognition, job situation, punishments, and rewards. The assessment is based on comparison with some other person or persons, a reference person or groups, and includes assessment of the referent's input and treatment. When individuals perceive that their outcome/input ratio is significantly different from that of the reference person or group, feelings of inequity result.

If the perceived inequity is one of underreward, the reacton is likely to be anger, frustration, and resentment of both the reference person or group and the organization, and the longer the perception of inequity persists, the greater grows that rankling feeling of "why should I work hard? Why should I give a damn about this organization when it doesn't care about me?" Some individuals may deal with perceived inequity by mentally distorting their own contribution, convincing themselves that their contributions or input are less than they initially believed, but unstated feelings of inequity almost inevitably result in behavioral responses. One of the most common responses is to demand equity: an increase in the inducements they are receiving. An equally common response is to reduce effort. Some individuals respond by leaving the organization physically, if they have job mobility, or mentally, if they do not; others choose, for various reasons (the golden padlock), not to exercise their mobility. Other options include acting on the reference source or changing the basis of reference.[44] If feelings of inequity are widespread, and all are based on the same reference person or persons, peer pressure will be applied to that person with the intent of either modifying his or her behavior or driving him or her from the organization. The response chosen depends on the individual and the nature, extent, and duration of the inequity. Perceived inequities that are central to individual self-esteem and self-concept will be resisted most strenuously. Changing reference sources is rare, and, leaving the organization seems to be a last resort utilized only when other methods of dealing with the inequity have failed. Frequently, individuals will try a combination of responses in the attempt to reduce the frustration and tension associated with inequity.[45]

Regardless of the response chosen, the results are damaging to the organization. Cohesion diminishes, conflict increases, commitment and morale decline, and performance suffers. The image of the organization presented to the external environment is tarnished, and depending on the type of inequity involved, lawsuits may be filed. Underreward inequity is one of the most potent dissatisfiers, in Herzberg's terms, in organizational life, and one of the most commonly voiced complaints of workers. Its relationship to expectancy theory is clear and strong. If workers perceive that rewards are administered unfairly, that equal inputs are not equally rewarded, the link between performance and rewards is broken. The belief is created that merit and performance are unrelated to the reward system, and so one should not expect good performance to be rewarded. Equally important from the organizational perspective is the set of expectations that inequity creates. To the extent that the process theorists are correct that behavior is a consequence of rewards and punishments, employees will make their own estimates of what type of behavior the organization does reward. If sycophantic kowtowing to those in positions of authority is the major type of behavior rewarded, then one should expect that behavior to increase.

Underreward inequity clearly reduces motivation; and an organization characterized by widespread inequity is likely to experience high rates of absenteeism, turnover, and dissatisfaction. Eliminating or reducing the inequity would be expected to have the results Herzberg associated with removing dissatisfiers: dissatisfaction would decrease, and absenteeism and turnover would do the same. Whether motivation and productivity increase depends on linking performance and rewards.

To this point, only underreward inequity has been considered. The more controversial aspect of equity theory deals with overreward inequity. For many of those times when individuals feel they have been underrewarded, there is another who presumably has been overrewarded: the colleague who got the promotion or the raise, the student who got the "A" and did not "deserve" it. Theoretically, we are supposed to react to being the beneficiaries of inequity, and according to equity theory we react with guilt, which is supposed to make us uncomfortable. Responses to guilt may take several forms. First, individuals may try psychological distortion: revising their estimates of their own abilities and efforts upward and those of their reference persons downward, or devaluing the rewards received. For Adams, however, the most important and likely response to guilt was for individuals to increase their effort—to work harder to justify the inequitably high outcomes. Adams tested this aspect of his theory in five different studies; each of the studies supported the hypothesis that overreward inequity will lead to increased effort, though sometimes the outcome was increased quality rather than increased quantity of work.[46] Thus, if you wish to motivate people to work harder, overpay them.

Such a recommendation should be viewed with considerable skepticism. Despite Adams's findings, it seems likely that people are much less likely to perceive themselves as overrewarded than underrewarded. Self-esteem and ego-defensive needs are likely to convince individuals that they deserve all the rewards they are receiving, and to switch reference sources if necessary to prove it to themselves. Some people feel physicians are overrewarded; physicians rarely agree, pointing to the salaries of top business executives, professional athletes, movie stars. Some people feel members of Congress are overcompensated, a perception not shared by the members, who stress the importance of the duties they perform, the expenses they incur in their jobs, and the salaries of business executives, athletes, movie stars, and doctors. The business executives, athletes and movie stars also tend to feel that they are worth what they earn, and that because their careers are so short or insecure or they are so talented they should be justly rewarded. Thus not only are people less likely to perceive overreward inequity, if they perceive it they are also more likely to rationalize it as being just. If overreward inequity is perceived and reacted to as Adams predicts, a clear conflict with expectancy theory exists. Again, the linkage between effort and rewards is broken, the relationship between high performance and high payoff eliminated. Expectancy theory gives little clue as to how individuals would behave in this situation, other than to experience confusion; equity theory says they will work harder. Somehow, this seems unlikely.

Equity theory's greatest importance in motivation theory has been its clarification of the impact of adverse inequitable treatment on employee behavior. Although that impact may appear to be really a self evident truth, it is constantly ignored or overlooked in many organizations and frequently those same organizations are afflicted with productivity problems. One of the first assessments that management (political or administrative) of an organization concerned about productivity and motivation should make is how equitably they treat employees and how employees perceive their treatment. If inequity, either perceived or actual, exists, identification of reference sources is essential. Those reference sources may be either external or internal and for public organizations a multitude of references sources are possible: the private sector, other levels of government, or other jurisdictions, and/or other professions/occupations viewed as comparable. Although pay comparability has received considerable attention, what is comparable is usually determined by management or the personnel commission. That may be legal and constitutional, but that is not really what equity theory advocates. Equity is in the eyes of the worker, not the employer. If public employees do feel they are treated inequitably, then one of the primary sources of alleged low productivity has been identified. Whether we have the resources to eliminate it is, of course, another problem.

Organizational Behavior Modification

The intellectual founder of organizational behavior modification was B. F. Skinner, although Skinner, like Maslow, was not initially or primarily concerned with organizational behavior and management; he expressed interest in them only after others had attempted to apply his theory in the organizational setting. Skinner's primary focus was on behavior and learning, and he became convinced that both were environmentally determined. Although his initial work was with animals, he eventually applied the same principles and techniques that he used to teach pigeons to play ping-pong to controlling the behavior of human beings.

Behavior is the response of the organism to some stimulus from the environment. Such responses fall into two categories; respondent behavior, which is the result of involuntary, reflex actions such as salivating at the sight of food, and operant or learned behavior.[47] Skinner and organizational behavior modification theorists are primarily concerned with operant behavior and how that behavior can be controlled through operant conditioning. The underlying principle of operant conditioning is the law of effect first formulated by Edward Thorndike in 1913: "Of several responses made to the same situation, those which are accompanied or closely followed by satisfaction . . . will be more likely to recur; those which are accompanied or closely followed by discomfort . . . will be less likely to recur."[48]

Behavior is thus seen as a function of its consequences. When behavior in response to a stimulus has been rewarded, it will be repeated. The more often it is rewarded, the more often it will be repeated.[49] Learning involves a relatively permanent change of behavior, and such a change is the result of an initial behavior being rewarded and then reinforced. In housebreaking a puppy, you must first make clear to the puppy what behavior is desired—go outdoors—and then arrange the circumstances so that that behavior is possible. Every time the puppy does go outdoors, you reward the behavior. Puppies are easy; their favorite rewards are lavish affection, praise, and food. The keys to successful operant conditioning are patience, consistency, and rewards, so at least with puppies and pigeons, operant conditioning works well. Human beings are animals, so the same principles are assumed to be applicable.

If you want an individual to behave in a certain way, you must first specify what behavior is desired; and when that behavior is displayed, you must reward it. Rewards in behavioral modification are termed positive reinforcers. Behavior modification proponents contend that there is no reason to be concerned with internal states, needs, or goals that influence individual behavior, but on this point they are guilty of either misrepresenting or misinterpreting their theory. People are not puppies; one person's reward may be another's punishment, and to select the appropriate reward, it is necessary to know what the subject regards as a desirable consequence. Most people probably do like to be praised, but for some praise causes discomfort and is regarded as something to be avoided. People may be similar as far as the general principles of what evokes behavior, but they are decidedly different in terms of what they value. Anyone— teacher, manager, parent—seeking to use behavioral modification successfully must recognize those differences and structure the reward to fit not only the behavior but also the individual.

Skinner and most organizational behavior modification proponents stress positive reinforcement and frown on the use of punishment, even to eliminate undesired behavior. Their arguments against punishment as a form of behavior control are impressive but unlikely to persuade a great many people. They contend that punishment (the use of aversive stimuli such as physical pain or disapproval) is not only ineffective but also frequently counterproductive. When someone is punished for engaging in a specific type of behavior, there is a good probability that they will avoid that behavior in the future only when the possibility of punishment is perceived to exist ("what he doesn't know won't hurt him"). Punishment serves only to reduce the probability of the specific behavior punished; it does not necessarily produce the desired response and may result in the substitution of an equally undesirable alternative behavior. If workers are reprimanded for talking too long around the coffee machine, they may cease conversation there but transfer their conversations to someone's office or to the lounges. Punishment in any form causes discomfort for the subjects— emotional tension, stress, resentment, and anger are common reactions. Not only are these dysfunctional for the person being punished, but very frequently they are transferred to the punisher and can have lasting and negative effects on the relationship. Puppies forgive easily; people do not necessarily do so. They frequently end up disliking the punisher and resisting and resenting any further attempts to control their behavior. In some individuals, punishment may generate counteraggression.[50]

Despite these limitations and disadvantages, punishment remains the most widely used method of behavior control in our society: in our homes, our schools, our work organizations, our social institutions, and our interpersonal relationships we are a punishment-oriented society. The reason lies in the role of punishment as a reinforcer for the punisher. When someone or something engages in behavior that we disapprove of or dislike, it frustrates us. Punishing them allows us to release this frustration, and thus it makes us feel better. Futher, it does have the immediate effect of stopping the undesired response, and it is easier and faster than reward, so we will no doubt continue to rely on it.

Organizational behavior modification is aimed at maximizing overall performance of both individuals and the organization. It requires that desired performance be identified and defined strictly in behavioral terms. This performance audit should establish a baseline for measuring future performance. Next, measurable performance goals should be established for each worker. Then employees must maintain continuing records of their work. At this stage a schedule of reinforcement must be established.

Behavioral modification identifies five different reinforcement schedules: continuous, fixed interval, variable interval, fixed ratio and variable ratio. Continuous reinforcement provides a reward every time the desired behavior is manifested. Although it produces the most rapid learning rate, it also tends to have the most rapid extinction rate—that is, if the behavior is not rewarded each time, it disappears. Fixed interval reinforcement occurs at a set period of time—every two weeks or months, for example; variable intervals may also be used. Fixed ratio reinforcement is provided after a determined number of responses has occurred; variable ratio reinforcement is believed to produce the most stable performance levels. The final stage is evaluation and feedback:

> The supervisor looks at the self-feedback report of the employee and/or other indicators of performance . . . and then praises the positive aspects of the employee's performance. . . . Since the worker already knows the areas of his

or her deficiencies, there is no reason for the supervisor to criticize. . . . Use of positive reinforcement leads to a greater feeling of self-control, while the avoidance of negative reinforcements keeps the individual from feeling controlled or coerced.[51]

Behavior modification can also be used in specific situations to replace undesirable or unwanted behavior with appropriate behavior. Again, it requires identifying, measuring, and analyzing the performance-related behavior problem. This involves determining the frequency of the behavior and identifying the stimulus that triggers the behavior. The analysis should form the basis for the development of an appropriate strategy, whether it be removing the stimulus or suggesting a more suitable behavior, determining appropriate rewards, and administering them according to a determined schedule. The final step, as always, is measurement and evaluation.[52]

A number of organizations, both private and public, have used behavior modification on a large-scale basis, the most reported of which has been Emery Air Freight. In a metropolitan school program instituted to reduce teacher absenteeism by fixed interval monetary rewards, initial results were positive, but by the end of five years absentee rates were again increasing.[53] The Emery Air Freight program was much more extensive and involved a concerted attempt to increase performance organization-wide by targeting specific areas of low performance. Supervisors were given detailed training and a workbook identifying 150 different kinds of positive reinforcers, primarily different kinds of praise and recognition; they also emphasized continuous feedback.[54] Although the results of the program were impressive ($3 million in savings over a three-year period), as the program continued it began to experience the same difficulties as the school program. The president of Emery reported, "Inasmuch as praise is the most readily available no-cost reinforcer, it tends to be the reinforcer used most frequently. However, the results have been to dull its effect as a reinforcer through its sheer repetition, even to risk making praise an irritant to the receiver."[55]

As is true with the other process theories, behavior modification is easier said than done, and when implemented on a large scale it involves several difficult and expensive problems. It requires a clear understanding and specification of desired behavior. If this involves only having employees show up on time and not take unnecessary sick leave it is easy, but when it involves specifying how teachers, police officers, or caseworkers are to behave it becomes considerably more difficult. Similarly, figuring out appropriate positive reinforcers is more complex than the theory seems to suggest. As the Emery Air Frieght program illustrates, praise, although inexpensive and easy, loses its reinforcement value if overutilized, and even praise is not universally effective. To develop individualized reinforcers and reinforcement schedules would be extremely time consuming and difficult and could result in equity problems. Positive reinforcement may require not only differe   reinforcers but different amounts of the same reinforcer to be effective, and successful implementation also requires extensive training for supervisors. As Skinner pointed out, "It [behavior modification] is not something that can be taken over by the nonprofessional to use as a rule of thumb."[56] Even with training, successful behavior modification requires a great deal of time, effort, patience, and commitment on the part of supervisors. And even with that its success depends on whether or not people, normal adults, are as malleable as the theory suggests. By ignoring internal forces, needs, values, attitudes, and beliefs and their impact in determining individual behavior, behavior modification remains an excessively oversimplified explanation of human behavior.[57]

The strongest criticisms of behavior modification are those charging that it is unethical and immoral. To humanist critics, behavior modification is manipulative, consisting of little more than bribery and dehumanizing both its subjects and its practitioners. It is portrayed as dictatorial, or at best authoritarian, threatening personal autonomy and stunting human growth and development.[58] To a certain extent behavior modification is all of those, but then so are all other motivation theories, even the most benevolent and humanistic. The bottom line in all motivation theories is modifying (manipulating) employee behavior to maximize productivity, and even though content theories take the "we're only here to help you help yourself" approach, they determine, quite authoritatively, what the worker wants and needs and how that can best be provided. If giving people what they want in exchange for doing what the provider desires is bribery, all work and all organizations constitute legalized bribery.

ONE MORE TIME . . .

Ensuring that all employees perform at the highest levels and produce maximum outputs is one of the most widely sought objectives in organziation theory and practice. To achieve that objective, organizations must create and maintain conditions that recognize and reward effective performance in ways that are desired by and meaningful to individual employees. On that point, at least, all motivation theorists are in agreement. They disagree on the issues of whether all individuals have the same needs and desires and even on what constitute desired rewards in the work place. Content theorists assume that individuals are all the same and have identical needs, which in terms of work are for self-actualization (defined as the need for meaningful work, autonomy, responsibility, and challenge and variety). Consequently, the one best way to motivate all employees is through the job content. Jobs must be structured, enriched, to satisfy the employees' need for self-actualization. Beyond that, content theory provides no further rewards. Work is supposedly its own reward. Given meaningful work and the freedom to do it the way the employee deems best, content theorists believe that all workers will be identically motivated to achieve maximum productivity.

Process theory is a type of contingency theory. It starts with the assumption that individuals are alike only in that their behavior is determined on the basis of whether it results in rewards or punishments. As to what constitutes rewards, individuals vary: different strokes for different folks. To motivate employees managers must clearly specify what type of performance is desired and determine what each individual wants or needs. Rewards must be tailored to the individual, and thus they must be as varied as the desires of individuals. Money, fringe benefits, merchandise, praise, recognition, enriched jobs, promotions, time off, vacation trips—all are possible rewards to be provided if the employees perform in the desired manner. The provision of rewards must always be linked to performance, and employees must know and understand that. Rewards must be provided continuously, because if good performance ceases to be rewarded, good performance ceases.

Combined, the two types of theories provide a profile of the maximally motivating organziation. Such an organization would provide adequate system rewards to satisfy the lower-level needs of all employees. It would pay good wages, provide job security and ample fringe benefits, and maintain safe, comfortable, and attractive physical working conditions. It would know exactly what it wants in performance terms for each employee and would clearly communicate that to employees. It would recognize the differences among individuals and ensure that individuals fit their jobs. It would establish and maintain a reward system that rewards only good performance, but does so with rewards tailored to the desires and needs of individuals, and does so continuously. It would always treat all employees fairly and equitably. In return, the organization would achieve the highest possible level of productivity.

No public organization does this, and probably no private organization does either—nor does it seem likely that such an organization will emerge in the near future. To achieve that ideal state would require more money, a change in union philosophies, a change in civil service regulations, and a reorientation of management style, none of which seem likely to occur. In motivation and productivity, as in everything else in administration, maximizing is too demanding. Satisficing, piecemeal approaches with limited results, will remain the dominant approach.

NOTES

1. Donald Klinger and John Nalbandian, *Public Personnel Management*, 2nd ed. (Englewood Cliffs, N.J.: Prentice Hall, 1985), p. 190.
2. Victor Vroom, *Work and Motivation* (New York: John Wiley, 1964), p. 203.
3. Bernard Berelson and Gary Steiner, *Human Behavior: An Inventory of Scientific Findings* (New York: Harcourt Brace, 1969), p. 239.

4. Daniel Katz and Robert L. Kahn, *The Social Psychology of Organizations*, 2nd ed. (New York: John Wiley, 1978), p. 403.
5. Mitchell Fein, "Motivation for Work," in Robert Dubin, ed., *Handbook of Work, Organization and Society* (Chicago: Rand McNally, 1976), p. 490.
6. Curt Tausky and E. Laucke Parke, "Job Enrichment, Need Theory and Reinforcement Theory," in Dubin, *Handbook of Work, Organization and Society*, p. 543.
7. Debra W. Stewart and G. David Garson, *Organizational Behavior and Public Management* (New York: Marcel Dekker, 1983), p. 10.
8. Tausky and Parke, "Job Enrichment, Need Theory and Reinforcement Theory," p. 534.
9. Ibid., p. 535.
10. Katz and Kahn, *The Social Psychology of Organizations*, pp. 406–407.
11. Ibid., p. 414.
12. Ibid., p. 410.
13. James Donnelly, James Gibson, and John Ivancevich, *Fundamentals of Management*, 3rd ed. (Dallas: Business Publishers, 1978), p. 187.
14. Department of Health, Education and Welfare, *Work in America: Report of a Special Task Force to the Secretary of HEW* (Cambridge, Mass.: M.I.T. Press, 1973), p. 13.
15. Douglas MacGregor, *The Human Side of Enterprise* (New York: McGraw Hill, 1960), p. 41.
16. E. E. Lawler III, *Pay and Organizational Effectiveness* (New York: McGraw Hill, 1971).
17. Fein, "Motivation for Work," p. 486.
18. Jay Shafritz, Albert Hyde and David Rosenbloom, *Personnel Management in Government*, 2nd ed. (New York: Marcel Dekker, 1981), p. 334..
19. Fein, "Motivation for Work," p. 582.
20. B. Buchanan, "Government Managers, Business Executives and Organizational Commitment," *Public Administration Review* (1974): pp. 339–347.
21. Robert White, "Motivation Reconsidered: The Concept of Competence," *Psychological Review* (1959): pp. 227–233.
22. McGregor, *The Human Side of Enterprise*.
23. Ibid., p. 88.
24. Ibid., p. 92.
25. Chris Argyris, "Personality and Organization Theory," *Administrative Science Quarterly* (1978): pp. 141–167.
26. Frederick Herzberg, Bernard Mausner, and Barbara Snyderman, *The Motivation to Work* (New York: John Wiley, 1959), p. 141.
27. Frederick Herzberg, *Work and the Nature of Man* (New York: World Publishing Co., 1966), p. 75.
28. Frederick Herzberg, *The Managerial Choice: To Be Efficient and to Be Human (Homewood, Ill.: Dow-Jones-Irwin, 1976), p. 71.*
29. Herzberg, Mausner, and Snydermen, *The Motivation to Work, p. 132.*
30. Charles N. Greene, "The Satisfaction-Performance Controversy," in John M. Ivancevich, Andrew D. Szilagyi and Marc Wallace, *Readings In Organizational Behavior and Performance*, (Santa Monica, Goodyear Publ. Co., 1977), p. 93.
31. Vroom, *Work and Motivation*, pp. 128–129.
32. Katz and Kahn, *The Social Psychology of Organizations*, p. 40.
33. William Scott and Terence Mitchell, *Organization Theory* (Homewood, Ill.: Richard D. Irwin, 1976), p. 119.
34. Arthur Whitehill, "Maintenance Factors: The Neglected Side of Worker Motivation," in Donald White, *Contemporary Perspectives in Organizational Behavior* (Boston: Allyn & Bacon, 1982), p. 122.

35. Raymond Katzell, Daniel Yankelovich, Mitchell Fein, Oscar Ornati, Abraham Nash, and assisted by Jeffrey A. Berman, "Improving Productivity and Job Satisfaction," *Organizational Dynamics* (1975): p. 71.

36. Federick Herzberg, "One More Time: How Do You Motivate Employees?" *Harvard Business Review* (January/February 1968): p. 53.

37. J. R. Hackman and G. R. Oldham, "Motivation Through the Design of Work: Test of a Theory," *Organization Behavior and Human Performance* (1976): pp. 250–279.

38. Vroom, *Work and Motivation*.

39. E. E. Lawler III, *Motivation in Work Organizations* (Monterey, Calif.: Brooks/ Cole, 1975), p. 51.

40. Ibid., p. 46.

41. David Nadler and E. E. Lawler III, "Motivation: A Diagnostic Approach," in White, *Contemporary Perspectives in Organizational Behavior*, pp. 115-117.

42. Ibid., pp. 117–119.

43. J. Stacy Adams, "Toward an Understanding of Inequity," *Journal of Abnormal and Social Psychology* (1963): pp. 422–436.

44. Joseph A. Litterer, *The Analysis of Organizations*, 2nd ed. (New York: John Wiley, 1973), p. 490.

45. J. Stacy Adams, "A Framework For the Study of Modes of Resolving Inconsistency," in Robert P. Abelson, ed., *Theories of Cognitive Inconsistency: A Sourcebook* (Chicago: Rand McNally, 1968), pp. 655–660.

46. John B. Miner, *Theories of Organizational Behavior* (Hinsdale, Ill.: Dryden Press, 1980) pp. 113–117.

47. B. F. Skinner, *Contingencies of Reinforcement* (New York: Appleton-Century-Crofts, 1961).

48. Edward L. Thorndike, *Educational Psychology*, vol. 2 (New York: Columbia University Teachers College, 1913).

49. George Homans, *Social Behavior: Its Elementary Forms* (New York: Harcourt Brace, 1961).

50. Walter R. Nord, "Beyond The Teaching Machine: The Neglected Area of Operant Conditioning in the Theory and Practice of Mangement," in Robert T. Golembiewski, Frank Gibson, and Gerald Miller, *Managerial Behavior and Organization Demands*, 2nd ed. (Itasca, Ill.: Peacock Publishers, 1978), p. 133.

51. W. Clay Hamner, "Worker Motivation Programs: The Importance of Climate, Structure and Performance Consequences," in Hamner and Frank L. Schmidt, eds., *Contemporary Problems in Personnel* (Chicago: St. Clair, 1977), p. 261.

52. Fred Luthans and Robert Kreitner, *Organizational Behavior Modification* (Glenview, Ill.: Scott, Foresman, 1975), p. 150–173.

53. Walter Nord, "Improving Attendance Through Rewards", *Personnel Administration* (1970), pp. 37–41.

54. Amacom, "At Emery Air Freight: Positive Reinforcement Boosts Performance," in Dale Beach, *Managing People At Work*, 2nd ed. (New York: MacMillan Publishing, 1975), pp. 265–274.

55. W. Clay Hamner and Ellen P. Hamner, "Behavior Modification and the Bottom Line," *Organizational Dynamics* (1976): p. 15.

56. B. F. Skinner and William Cowling, "Conversation with B. F. Skinner," *Organizational Dynamics* (1973): p. 40.

57. White, *Contemporary Perspectives in Organizational Behavior*, p. 65.

58. Ibid.

10

STRESS AND BURNOUT

Stress and burnout have emerged in the 1980s as major concerns of organization theorists, management, and the media. Magazine articles, books, and television programs lament the dire consequences of stress for individuals and offer varied prescriptions for avoiding stress or, when that is impossible (as it usually is), coping effectively with it. Organizations, private and public, alarmed by the economic and perhaps human costs of stress have responded by creating stress management and wellness programs to help their employees deal with stress, which, often as not, has been caused by working conditions within the organization. Burnout has entered the language and is used commonly by countless people every time they are bored or tired or frustrated. The two concepts have become the fad of this decade, and that is unfortunate. Fads tend to give way rather quickly to new fads, and both stress and burnout are enduring problems that when understood help explain much about human behavior in organizations and the human consequences of the organizational society. They also help clarify links between organizations and their environments and illustrate how environmental change can directly and indirectly affect individuals within organizations.

Quantifying the costs of stress and burnout is difficult, if not impossible. Excess stress and inadequate coping abilities make people sick, and that is where the direct tangible costs associated with stress begin. The economic costs of peptic ulcers and cardiovascular disease, both recognized as stress-related illnesses, are estimated at approximately $45 billion annually.[1] Health care and health benefit payments, absenteeism, turnover, and decreased productivity associated with stress were estimated in 1978 to cost between $17 and $25 billion; the costs of drug and alcohol abuse, also frequently stress-related conditions, were estimated at $42 billion annually.[2] To these must be added the costs of worker's compensation claims and settlements in liability cases. From 1980 to 1982, 11 percent of all occupational disease claims in thirteen states were for mental disorders related to stress. The claims fell into three categories: physical-mental, mental-physical, and mental-mental. Physical-mental claims arise from a job related physical injury that subsequently results in a mental disorder; mental-physical claims occur when mental (psychological) stress causes a physical disorder, such as a heart attack. Mental-mental claims are the result of psychological stress that results in an emotional or mental illness. Forty-one states recognize such claims as valid, and in 1983, 11,600 claims were filed and accepted at a total cost of $30 million. Examples of such claims include a library clerk in Arizona who suffered a nervous breakdown after his supervisor criticized his work and transferred him to a new department without clearly specifying his responsibilities and a deputy sheriff in Oregon who developed emotional problems as a result of constant harassment by his boss. Although some states will allow only claims based on allegations of unusual stress as in the preceding incidents, seven states allow stress-based claims for any reason, such as frustration with the job or inability to perform assigned duties.[3] Stress management programs are an additional cost.

Even more difficult to estimate are the intangible costs associated with stress and burnout: the psychological and emotional costs to individuals and the costs to clients who frequently bear the brunt of negative behavioral and attitudinal changes of stressed or burned out employees.[4] Perhaps even more costly is the loss of the most sensitive and dedicated human service professionals who finally decide that the only way to cope with burnout is to leave their professions.

Everyone has to endure stress; it is a universal problem (and, from the organizational perspective, an expensive one). Consequently, understanding stress is important for all of us both personally and professionally. As has been true with other aspects of organization behavior, there are many different theories about what causes stress, how it affects individuals, and how it should be managed. This is the focus of the first part of the chapter, and the second part of the chapter deals with burnout. Burnout, the result of excessive psychological stress, is of particular concern to public sector organizations. As the term was used initially, and as it will be used in this chapter, burnout is associated primarily with occupations that work directly and constantly with people: social workers, child protection workers, teachers at all levels of education, police officers, parole and probation officers, prison personnel, managers, and mental and physical health care workers—occupations that account for a sizeable proportion of public sector workers.

STRESS

Consequences and Causes

Stress is "the nonspecific response of the body to any demand made on it."[5] A demand may be any event, circumstance, situation, or experience that the individual perceives, consciously or subconsciously, as creating tension: it may be as catacylsmic as the death of a spouse or as minor as misplacing the car keys. Further, what is regarded as stressful is a matter of individual perception: an event regarded by one individual as highly stressful, such as giving a report at a staff meeting, may be a matter of unstressful routine to another. Both pleasant and unpleasant events cause stress: receiving a long-desired promotion or losing a job can both result in stress. The stress resulting from pleasant events is called eustress; unpleasant events cause distress. Although specific responses to stress vary considerably, the basic pattern of response, which Hans Selye termed the General Adaptation Syndrome is similar for all: alarm, resistance, and exhaustion.

The initial shock causes alarm and sets in motion various physiological and psychological responses. The hypothalmus gland triggers the physiological reaction, followed by the pituitary gland, which secretes ACTH, which in turn acts on the adrenal cortex. If the demand is severe enough, the result will be the secretion of adrenaline, preparing the body for "fight or flight," the classic responses to unmitigated stress.[6] The body continues to resist as long as the stress is unabated, until exhaustion occurs.

Psychological and emotional reactions follow a similar pattern. Initial response to stress ranges from laughing, crying, cursing, boasting, overactivity, and daydreaming to compulsive eating or loss of appetite. If the stress continues, the individual will experience increasing nervousness, worry, tension, confusion, and emotionalism. The next level of response is one of growing discomfort, feelings of uselessness or guilt accompanied by expressions of socialized aggression. Some individuals at this level will resort to increased use of alcohol, tobacco, or drugs to alleviate the tension. This is frequently followed by overt aggression or violence and mild paranoia, leading finally to severe blowups and temper tantrums.[7]

Unabated stress affects every major system in the body, especially the immune system, making people more susceptible to illness, especially colds and influenza. The muscular system responds to stress by tensing, and chronically tense muscles are associated with a variety of psychosomatic disorders: migraine headaches, backaches, sleep disorders, spasms of the esophagus and colon, posture problems, eye problems, asthma, and muscle tears and pulls. Responses of the gastrointestinal system include nausea, increased stomach acidity, and increased salivation. These responses lead to a variety of physiological problems, including digestive upsets, ulcers, and gum problems. The cardiovascular system's responses include heart palpitations, arrhythmia, increased heart rate, hypertension, and athe-rosclerosis.[8]

These physiological and psychological responses are the immediate sources of the organizational and human costs of stress. They are inevitably reflected in job performance and personal behavior. They result in lowered intellectual functioning and decreased ability to communicate. In terms of job performance, they frequently result in erratic work habits; absenteeism; flying off the handle at colleagues, superiors, and clients, decreased productivity; increased error rates; job dissatisfaction, accidents, serious errors in judgment; slower reaction time; and withdrawal of interest and involvement in work. The individual's personal life is likely to deteriorate similarly; hostility and anger may be displaced to spouses, children, and friends. The individual may become accident prone. Family quarrels erupt, and marriages may be terminated and friends lost; social isolation may result. Excess stress is a vicious cycle: it results in behavioral changes that in turn cause events and circumstances that increase the stress experienced by the individual.[9]

Stressors

The sources of stress can be divided into two categories: those associated with work and those occurring outside work. These in turn can be subdivided into major life events and hassles. Although the situation varies from person to person and time to time, the National Institute of Mental Health estimates that the major sources of stress are equally divided between work and nonwork.[10] Any experience that creates a psychological or physiological imbalance in a person is a stressor, and although concern with stress is relatively recent, stress is not. Every era has been an "age of anxiety,"[11] but ours may be characterized by a proliferation in the number and severity of stressors affecting everyone. Change, whether negative or positive, has always been a source of stress, and the rate of societal and technological change has accelerated in the past few decades. This led Alvin Toffler to warn of the limits of human adaptability: "We are not infinitely resilient. Each orientation response, each adaptive reaction exacts a price, wearing down the body's machinery bit by minute bit, until tissue damage results. Man remains . . . a biosystem with a limited capacity for change. When this capacity is overwhelmed, the consequence is future shock."[12]

Initially, stress researchers emphasized major life events as the primary sources of stress. Table 10–1 lists the major life changes that were

TABLE 10–1. Major Life Event Stressors

1. Death of a spouse	(100) _____
2. Divorce	(73) _____
3. Marital separation	(65) _____
4. Jail term	(63) _____
5. Death of a close family member	(63) _____
6. Personal injury or illness	(53) _____
7. Marriage	(50) _____
8. Job firing	(47) _____
9. Marital reconciliation	(45) _____
10. Retirement	(45) _____
11. Change in health of family member	(44) _____
12. Pregnancy	(40) _____
13. Sexual difficulties	(39) _____
14. Gain of a new family member	(39) _____
15. Business readjustment	(39) _____
16. Change in financial state	(38) _____
17. Death of a close friend	(37) _____
18. Change to different line of work	(36) _____
19. Change in number of arguments with spouse	(35) _____
20. Mortgage of more than $10,000	(31) _____
21. Foreclosure of mortgage or loan	(30) _____
22. Change in responsibilities at work	(29) _____
23. Departure of son/daughter from home	(29) _____
24. Trouble with in-laws	(29) _____
25. Outstanding personal achievement	(28) _____
26. Wife's beginning or stopping work	(26) _____
27. Beginning or end of school	(26) _____
28. Change in living conditions	(25) _____
29. Change of personal habits	(24) _____
30. Trouble with boss	(22) _____
31. Change in work hours or conditions	(20) _____
32. Change in residence	(20) _____
33. Change in schools	(19) _____
34. Change in recreation	(19) _____
35. Change in church activities	(18) _____
36. Change in social activities	(17) _____
37. Mortgage or loan less than $10,000	(16) _____
38. Change in sleeping habits	(16) _____
39. Change in number of family gatherings	(15) _____
40. Change in eating habits	(15) _____
41. Vacation	(13) _____
42. Christmas	(12) _____
43. Minor violations of the law	(11) _____

Source: From Thomas Holmes and R. H. Rahe, "The Social Readjustment Rating Scale," *Journal of Psychosomatic Research* (1967): p. 215. Reprinted by permission.

identified as causing individuals the most stress. To assess your stress level, check each event that you have experienced within the last two years; if an event has occurred more than once, make an appropriate number of checks. Multiply checks by the point value assigned to the event (the numbers in parenthesis) and then total the points. A point total below 150 is relatively low and within the range of adaptability for most individuals. Point totals between 150 and 300 indicate major stress and an increased probability of a stress-induced mental or physical illness within the next year. Point totals exceeding 300 are clearly in the danger zone and are accompanied by a 90 percent probability of physical illness within a year.

As serious and as debilitating as major life changes are, from a stress perspective they constitute only the tip of the iceberg. Far more difficult to identify and assign quantitative values are the hassles of everyday life—the "irritating, frustrating, distressing demands and troubled relationships that affect individuals day in and day out."[13] Any experience that creates a physiological or psychological imbalance for the individual is a source of stress, and most of our lives are filled with such stressors. Some may be fleeting: a flat tire, an unpleasant encounter with a client or a coworker, a minor automobile accident. Others may be chronic: an incompetent, arrogant supervisor who makes work life uncomfortable for everybody, an unpleasant neighbor, constant worry about one's weight. Everybody's list of hassles will be different and will vary from day to day, but hassles, as minor as they may seem ("You'll look back on this and laugh"), add up to a considerable drain on our resources to cope and may in fact be more predictive of psychological problems and somatic disorders than major life changes.[14]

Certain personal habits also contribute to stress level. Diet is particularly important because the ingestion of certain substances chemically triggers the discharge of the stress response or makes a person more anxious or irritable. The worst offenders are sugar, salt, and stimulants, specifically caffeine and nicotine.[15] Unfortunately, many people who are already under stress will compound the problem by increasing their intake of coffee, soda pop, tobacco, and alcohol. Candy bars and potato chips are viewed as either comfort or convenience food by many people experiencing stress and time pressure, and they unwittingly increase their stress level and add to their problems in a futile attempt to alleviate their anxiety.

Stress results from any situation in which environmental demands exceed the resources of the individual. Ironically, stress also results from any situation in which resources greatly exceed demands. Such a condition, referred to as hypostress, is the major reason that boring, unchallenging jobs result in considerable stress with the same psychological and physical results as hyperstress for some individuals. For each of us an optimal stress level exists: below that level we are bored and anxious and our job performance and personal life suffer; above that level we are overloaded, tense, and anxious and our job performance and personal life suffer. What constitutes a stressful situation depends on the individual's perception of the situation.

Given the multiple and diverse sources of stress that we encounter, calculating our exact stress level is difficult. Beehr contends that the amount of stress that any one event causes is a "multiplicative function of uncertainty, importance and duration."[16] Total stress level is determined by the following formula:[17]

$$\text{Stress} = \left[\sum_{i=1}^{n} = (Uc_i \times I_i \times D_i) \atop \text{work domain} \right] + \left[\sum_{j=1}^{n} = (Uc_j \times I_j \times D_j) \atop \text{nonwork domain} \right]$$

Stressful events that require long-term and repeated coping are the most debilitating and may eventually result in "learned helplessness," a conviction that one is powerless to control the event, and eventually to an inability to even try.

Organizations and jobs are a primary and constant source of stress, for they place what at times appear to be limitless demands on the individual. Many of the major organizational processes and characteristics covered throughout this book represent major stressors. Organization structure is for many members a source of stress. In a bureaucracy, the hierarchy, the seemingly endless and trivial rules, may create stressful, anxiety-provoking conditions for some. Conversely, the absence of rules or vague, ambiguous rules can cause stress for those who dislike uncertainty. Role ambiguity, a lack of clarity about what one is supposed to do or how to behave or perform properly, is characteristic of many public sector occupations and is directly related to the vague and conflicting goals of those organizations. The continuing uncertainty of public and organizational expectations as to what constitutes good teaching or policing or regulation is a chronic source of stress. Similarly, matrix organizations, with their ambiguity of authority and potential for conflict, are equally likely to cause stress for some members. Physical work conditions, Herzberg's dissatisfiers, may also be the source of considerable stress: excessive heat or cold, noise, overcrowding, lighting, or even uncomfortable furnishings may pose severe physiological and psychological demands on workers. Time pressure is always stressful.

Conflict is stressful for almost everybody, whether with supervisors, coworkers, or clients. As is true with other stressful events, the duration, intensity, and importance of these conflicts determines the total amount of stress felt by the individual. Organizational politics and power struggles inevitably involve conflict and just as inevitably cause stress for participants and nonparticipants as well.

Role conflict—conflict internal to the individual—is caused by conflicting demands imposed from external sources. Some occupational roles are characterized by explicitly conflicting requirements: social workers must ensure that clients receive all the assistance to which they are entitled but also must ensure that fraud or abuse does not occur; teachers are expected to maintain discipline (an increasingly difficult task in some schools), to be understanding, and to teach; police officers are expected to be polite, courteous, and respectful of constitutional rights while making arrests and fighting crime. Intrasender role conflict occurs when one person asks another to accomplish conflicting objectives: when a supervisor orders a subordinate to do a report quickly but to be sure it is thorough, accurate, and well written. Intersender conflict arises when two or more people give a third conflicting orders: for example, when the president orders an agency head to relax environmental regulations and a congressional committee urges that regulations be stringently enforced. Stress may also result when an individual's values conflict with those of the organization—for example, when a university professor who believes that undergraduate teaching should be the primary goal of the university is informed that teaching is regarded as secondary to research. Finally, as most of us play several roles—professional, friend, parent, spouse—we frequently find that the expectations of these various roles conflict with each other.

Certain characteristics of work are also major sources of stress. Work overload, whether quantitative (too much work) or qualitative (work that requires more skills or ability than the individual possesses) places demands on individuals that overtax their resources. Complex jobs that require large amounts of information and diverse methods and skills may become stressful for some individuals. Conversely, boring jobs or those that are overspecialized and underutilize the worker's abilities are equally likely to cause stress. Shift work, hazardous work, and job insecurity are also potential stressors. Status anxiety, which arises from uncertain professional status, is a common stressor in the public sector. Although public servants provide important and essential services and many are highly educated, highly skilled individuals, they are rarely accorded commensurate status by the public, the media, or their political superiors. Professionals who work in bureaucratic organizations are also likely to suffer from status anxiety.

Although proponents of democratic management and humanism advocate greater participation and greater responsibility for workers, both concepts are stressful for many people.[18] Participation frequently involves conflict, delay, and ambiguity, which in turn cause discomfort and anxiety. Decision making, because it almost always involves uncertainty, is stressful. The amount of stress involved varies depending on the importance and complexity of the decision, the adequacy of the information on which the decision must be based, and the amount of time allowed for decision making.[19] Similarly, responsibility, particularly responsibility for other people, can be very stressful. Thus, a study of NASA managers found that the greater their responsibility, the higher their stress levels, which was reflected in increased smoking and increased blood pressure.[20] Occupations characterized by constant responsibility for people (e.g., air traffic control and the human services professions) are almost invariably high-stress occupations, and their stressfulness is compounded when that responsibility is combined with insufficient authority and inadequate resources to perform tasks.

Change of any type causes stress. Within the organizational work setting, some of the most stressful changes that individuals must cope with are starting a new job, technological change, reorganization, job relocation, changing jobs, promotion, demotion, dismissal, and retirement. Entering a new organization to begin a new career is for many people a frustrating experience and is frequently made more so by the socialization process of the organization. For those with unrealistic expectations, it is a time of anxiety, reality shock, and disillusionment.[21] Turnover rates are high for new workers, who frequently take one of the most effective routes for alleviating stress: get out of the situation that is causing the stress. Technological change that demands new skills or results in a more boring, routinized job is similarly stressful. Personal changes, life transitions, and midcareer crises, which may occur simultaneously with organizational and work changes, are extremely stressful because they touch so many aspects of the individual's life.

Special Stressors for Special People

Although many job-related stressors are common to private and public sector organizations, public employees are confronted with special and specific circumstances that magnify the stress with which they must contend. Some of these have already been mentioned: ambiguous and conflicting organizational goals that are reflected in role ambiguity for individual employees; status anxiety resulting from a lack of public respect and constant criticism from the press, the public, and politicians; and, more recently, budget cuts and increasingly scarce resources to carry out assigned programs and responsibilities. Because demands for public services have not decreased correspondingly, the classic stress situation has been created: demands clearly exceed the resources and capabilities of the organizations and individuals on which they are placed. When an uncertain fiscal situation and the uncertainty associated with it are extended, the stress level of public sector organizations and their members escalates.

Budget cuts create multiple sources of stress for employees. Employees are confronted with uncertainty and instability in their work lives as they deal with constant change and decline. They must contend with the fear of job loss and the burden of doing more with less, which brings with them the fear that job performance will be adversely affected. Constant pressure to cut costs has resulted in an increase in paperwork to document all spending and activity and in many organizations has created conflict between administrators and staff over the mission and direction of the agency.[22] The consequences of this increased stress have varied, but at the federal level one of the consequences appears to be an increase in use of federal employees health systems. In the Department of Health and

Human Services, for example, the number of employees treated for stress-related symptoms, such as nausea, hypertension, dizziness, and diarrhea, tripled in 1981.[23] Employees of a large California city that was required to implement reductions in force, pay cuts, and reorganizations reacted initially with feelings of extreme anxiety, followed by feelings of powerlessness and submission. Job satisfaction and intrinsic motivation significantly decreased, and intentions of leaving the job increased.[24]

Managers are subject to special stressors, caught in the middle of the frequently conflicting demands and expectations of their subordinates and those of their superiors. Role conflict is frequently combined with role ambiguity, a lack of clarity about what they are supposed to do and how they are supposed to behave. They must accept the responsibility for the performance of other people as well as responsibility for organizational decisions affecting their subordinates, and they are at the cutting edge of organizational changes. They may also be subject to quantitative work overload: too many meetings, too much paperwork, too much responsibility, and too little authority. Unlike their subordinates, they may also lack close peer contact and support.[25]

Street-level bureaucrats—police officers, teachers, social workers, public lawyers (legal aid, public defenders, prosecutors), judges, and health care workers—face stressors of tremendous intensity and duration and thus are prime candidates for burnout. Their work situation was described accurately but unsympathetically by Michael Lipsky whose sympathies definitely were reserved for the clients.[26] Nearly every aspect of their job is a potential stressor, starting with goals that are ambiguous, vague or conflicting, which makes performance measurement difficult and subjective. Their resources are chronically inadequate, even in the best of times, for the problems that they must handle. The result is constant work overload: too many clients, students, or crimes, and too little time, with no control over the pace of their work or their work loads.

On one hand, they do have considerable discretion, though this translates into role ambiguity for the workers. They must make decisions with serious consequences for other individuals with guidelines from their agencies that are either unclear or nonexistent. If those decisions are wrong, the workers must accept the criticisms or sanctions imposed. On the other hand, despite the tremendous amount of discretion these street-level bureaucrats possess, in reality they have little or no control over the ultimate outcome of their work. The police depend on prosecutors and public defenders, who in turn depend on the courts, which in turn depend on the capabilities of the judicial and correctional system. Teachers seldom really know whether they have educated or not and whether they have depends more on the students and their overall environment than the skills of educators. Social workers and mental health workers have neither the resources nor, at this point, the technology to solve the problems of their clients. Some must work under conditions of physical danger (the police and, increasingly, teachers); others must work under conditions of undesirable physical environment, such as run down, shabby, overcrowded offices. Without exception, they must devote considerable time to extensive paperwork, which many view as taking time from what they perceive their real job to be. Finally, their agencies are frequently the focus of political controversy, caught between conflicting demands of the public, politicans, and clients.

Police work involves additional stress, although not necessarily from sources that were traditionally identifed as their major stressors: physical danger and the need to make split-second life-and-death decisions. High on the list of stressors associated with police work are court scheduling and leniency, lack of support by police administration, faulty equipment, and community apathy.[27] Other stressful elements of police work include boredom, low pay, arbitrary rules, rotating shifts, limited opportunities for advancement and career development, and the ineffectiveness of the criminal justice system in preventing, solving, and punishing crime. The impact of all this stress is partially indicated by a study by the National Institute of Occupational Safety and Health (NIOSH) of police officers in twenty-nine departments. The NIOSH study found that 37 percent of the officers had serious marital difficulties; 36 percent had health problems; 23 percent had problems with alcohol abuse; and 10 percent had drug problems.[28]

Working women are subject to a variety of special stresses starting with overt and covert discrimination and sexual harassment. Affirmative action notwithstanding, many jobs in the public sector are still not completely open to women: police work, firefighting, and high-level management remain largely male preserves, and the women who persist in breaking into their ranks must be prepared for resentment, ridicule, and condescension from colleagues, superiors, subordinates, and clientele. Conversely, some of the highest-stress jobs—nursing, teaching, and social work, for example—are predominantly female occupations. Sex-role stereotyping compounds their problems: women are pressured to be feminine (warm, supportive, unassertive, compliant), but if they succumb to that pressure, they are deemed to be unsuited for "male work." If they behave assertively (aggressively), they are viewed by their male colleagues as threatening. "Women teachers are expected to act like 'ladies,' not women. A woman who is assertive or who works for change politically gets a negative response. Catcalls and sexual games are used to undermine the efficacy of women."[29] Further, working women with families frequently find themselves in the position of holding the equivalent of two full-time jobs: homemaker and their paying job. This almost inevitably results in work overload and role conflict. And for those women with the superwoman complex— the need to do it all and do it perfectly, it results in not only exhaustion but also feelings of failure and guilt for not being the perfect mother, wife, and career woman.

Almost everything that has been said of women applies equally to minorities. In addition to the stresses of everyday life, they too must cope with the stresses imposed by racism and discrimination. They too must struggle against stereotyping in applying for jobs and competing for promotions. They must contend with harassment once on the job and the verbalized or unverbalized belief that the only reason they got the job was because they are minority members. They must also cope with pervasive job insecurity—last hired, as they usually are, first fired when reductions in force occur. They too must frequently be superhumans, tougher, smarter, and harder working, just to prove the stereotypes false and stay even with their white male counterparts. Blacks, as a group, have an extremely high incidence of high blood pressure. Perhaps some physiological explanation for that exists, but perhaps their stress level is at least partially the cause.

Determinants of Stress Reactions

If it seems that almost everything causes stress, this is only because almost everything does. What must be remembered, however, is that different people react differently to the same events and circumstances and that individuals also differ considerably in tolerance of stress. The Person-Environment Fit Model of stress contends that stress resides neither in the situation nor in the person but rather in the transaction between the two. Stress arises from how the person perceives an event. Only if the person construes a situation as presenting a threat or a challenge will stress occur. If that challenge is perceived as clearly exceeding the resources of the person to handle it, stress will continue and increase until the challenge is removed.[30]

According to the Person-Environment Fit Model, job stress results from a mismatch of the individual to the job or the organization. Two types of fit are necessary to minimize stress. The first type of fit is whether the job provides rewards and activities that satisfy the individual's needs and desires. If a misfit exists—if the individual's needs, whatever they may be, are not satisfied—stress results. The second type of fit is the extent to which the skills, training and abilities of the individual satisfy the demands and requirements of the job. A misfit in this area results in stress for the individual and strain for the organization.[31] Consequently, a stressful job for one individual may not be so for another. Nevertheless, some jobs may be so unsatisfying or demanding that they will cause stress for anyone who holds them.

The individual's specific response to stress depends on the nature of the stressor, the individual's vulnerability, and the context in which the stressful situation occurs; the duration, intensity, and magnitude of the stressor as perceived by the individual also affects the response. Individual vulnerability to stress depends on genetic factors, personality, general physical and mental condition, preparedness, and coping skills.[32] Much also depends on the amount of stress the individual is already experiencing when the new stressor is introduced. We all have stress thresholds, which determine the amount of stress that we can accomodate without undue negative responses. Once we have reached that threshold, even minor incidents can trigger major stress reactions.

One of the most common typologies used to differentiate individual responses to stress is the Type A–Type B personality dichotomy, originally developed by Friedman and Rosenman to determine personality characteristics of individuals most susceptible to coronary disease.[33] The Type A personality is more likely not only to suffer heart disease but also to cope with stress more inadequately and more self-destructively. Type A people have four major personality characteristics: an intense sense of time urgency; a tendency toward inappropriate aggression and competitiveness; a tendency toward polyphasic behavior; and a propensity for rushing into tasks without planning or even knowing how to accomplish the desired goal.[34] Type A people are always in a hurry; they eat fast, talk fast, drive fast, and move fast. They are as impatient with slowness in others as in themselves. Their chronic sense of time urgency leads to polyphasic behavior: constantly attempting to do several things at once to squeeze as many activities as possible into limited time. Although they are intensely competitive about almost everything and are frequently aggressive, nothing brings out a Type A person's competitive and aggressive tendencies as much as another Type A person. Type A people can seldom relax, and they almost never have any fun.[35] In fact, they sound almost like the ideal personality that some motivation theorists would like workers to emulate. Ironically, not only are Type A workers more susceptible to a wide variety of stress-induced illnesses, they also are frequently less effective in their work, particularly in management positions, than the more laid back Type B personalities.[36] Type A people not only suffer from stress, they also cause stress for those around them.

Other personality characteristics are also associated with individual reactions to stress. Locus of control refers to whether a person believes that he or she is primarily responsible for what happens to him or her or that what happens is controlled by fate, luck, destiny, or the system. Those with an internal locus of control are better able to cope with stress in the long run, although initially they may react with greater anxiety. Sooner or later, however, a person with an internal locus will take action to either remove the stressor or to reduce its consequences. A person with an external locus is more likely to suffer passively and lapse into learned helplessness.[37] Similarly, individuals with high self-esteem seem to cope better with stress and be less susceptible to heart disease than those with low self-esteem.[38] Optimists handle stress better than pessimists. Finally, those who rank high on need achievement (nAch) are also highly susceptible to stress. Those high in nAch tend to be superachievers (as well as, one suspects, Type A personalities), and much of their stress is likely to be self-induced. They set extremely demanding and frequently unachievable goals for themselves and then relentlessly drive themselves towards goal accomplishment.[39]

Coping with Stress

The sources of stress are primarily external to individuals, many of them a result of their work situation. But reactions to stress are internal to individuals, and the consequences of excess stress are both individual and organizational. Successful coping with stress is thus a concern of both individuals and organizations and the most successful stress management strategies require the involvement and commitment of both. Coping includes all "efforts, both action oriented and intrapsychic to manage (i.e., to master, tolerate, reduce and minimize) environmental and internal demands and conflict among them which tax or exceed a person's resources."[40] Successful coping means developing methods for handling stress that minimize its adverse psychological and emotional effects.

Without exception, the experts agree that efforts to cope with stress must begin with the individual. The first step is self-analysis, determining your stress level and identifying how you react to stress.[41] This requires identifying the stressors in your life, both in your work life and personal life, and recognizing the signs of distress, any or all of those physical, emotional or behavioral responses previously mentioned. Clearly the best time to prepare for coping with stress is before it exceeds your capacity to cope, and the best way to do this is through good health habits. A proper diet, emphasizing fresh fruits and vegetables, fish, poultry, lean meat, and moderate salt and refined sugar intake, and regular sleeping habits help build physical resistance to stress. Regular, noncompetitive aerobic exercise at least three or four times a week is an essential part of any stress management program. Exercise makes people feel better emotionally, socially, intellectually, and spiritually and acts as a natural antidepressant. Over time it results in improved self-esteem and increased mental energy, concentration, and will power.[42] For those experiencing increased stress, vigorous physical exercise aids in venting frustrations and pent-up emotions.

To mitigate the impact of excess stress, attitudinal change may be necessary. Selye recommends that people practice altruistic egoism, which requires that you love yourself and use your resources for your own benefit as well as for others.[43] This requires learning to say no to excessive work demands. It also means learning to compartmentalize work and nonwork life. Leave the problems and stresses of the job when you leave the job; bringing them home only exacerbates the stressful situation. Similarly, leave the problems and stresses of home life at home. Getting away from stressful situations even temporarily is beneficial; constantly rehashing and fretting about them only increases anxiety and emotional stress. Altruistic egoism means learning to indulge yourself occasionally and using leisure time for fun. If overload is contributing to your stress level, examine your life work and nonwork, and cut out the deadwood.[44] Eliminate all the stressors that you can.

Learning to relax is also essential in effectively coping with stress, and many organizational stress management programs include training in either transcendental meditation (TM) or other techniques of relaxation. New York Telephone, IBM, and Arthur Little Co., encourage their executives to learn and practice TM.[45] Transcendental meditation results in a state of deep rest and relaxation combined with a mental state of restful alertness. Individuals who regularly practice TM are likely to be less tense and anxious and more energetic than those who do not. At least one study has found that TM increases productivity and job satisfaction of executives.[46] A simpler but equally effective method is the Relaxation Response developed by cardiologist Dr. Herbert Benson.[47] This method requires finding a quiet place and sitting in a comfortable position with eyes closed. Muscles are relaxed in sequence and slow diaphragmatic breathing is combined with silent repetition of the word "one" with each breath. Ideally this should be practiced at least once a day for twenty minutes to achieve maximum antistress effects.

One of the most commonly recommended work-related antistress measures is talking through job related stresses with peers. Letting off steam with colleagues who may be sharing the same stresses is a cathartic experience that reduces emotional tension. It also fosters a sense of belongingness and reduces feelings of isolation. Talking it through may also provide practical advice and technical information on how to deal with problems.[48] The negative aspect of rehashing one's grievances with peers is that if overdone, it can actually increase frustration and anxiety and spread dissatisfaction and stress to workers who may previously have been unaffected.[49]

Other work-related strategies include knowing and understanding your organization, acquiring necessary skills and training, keeping current with developments in your field, pursuing further education, and setting realistic goals.[50] Many, perhaps most, people who work in public bureaucracies have little knowledge or understanding of how large organizations operate, of bureaucratic procedures or organizational politics, and that lack of understanding is the basis for many of their frustrations. Paperwork, which emerges as one of the major stressors for so many public service employees, from police officers to social workers and teachers, might not be quite so frustrating if employees understood and accepted that it is just as much a part of their job as dealing with people and that beyond that it helps keep the institution accountable. Having multiple interests and constantly expanding abilities and knowledge makes work more comprehensible and interesting and minimizes the time available for dwelling on grievances and frustrations.

Obviously, one of the best ways of dealing with stress is to avoid it. But just as obviously, avoiding all stress is neither possible nor desirable. Nevertheless, if a situation becomes so stressful that it threatens a person's mental or physical health and other stress management techniques prove ineffective, the individual ought to get out of the situation. If a job has become intolerable and the thought of going to work is sufficient to cause a headache, it may be time to change jobs. A change of this magnitude is itself a potent stressor, so before undertaking it, the individual must determine whether it is the job or perhaps just the specific organization that is the primary stressor. Although organizations with similar functions tend to be alike in many respects, they may differ in significant ways related to individual stress. For example, police departments in large cities differ from those in small towns, management styles differ and work loads differ. Consequently a change in organizations may help alleviate stress, but sometimes more may be required. A severe misfit between the individual and the demands and rewards of the chosen profession can only be corrected by selecting a new, more appropriate career.

A multitude of methods for coping with job stress exists. Of all the available methods the five best appear to be:

1. Build resistance by regular sleep and good health habits;
2. Compartmentalized work and nonwork life;
3. Engage in physical exercise;
4. Talk problems through with peers on the job; and
5. Withdraw physically from the situation.[51]

Coping with stress is extremely difficult, and while many of the most effective methods are basically simple and reflect what mothers and grandmothers have been telling their children for generations, they are difficult to put into practice. For many individuals those methods require a nearly total reorientation of their life-styles and attitudes, which does not come easily to most people. That is why organizations most concerned with helping employees manage stress have created mandatory stress management programs. Organizations do not do this out of pure altruism (though it would be nice, for a change, if they did). They do it because they recognize that the costs and consequences of stress have serious negative effects on organization performance and productivity. Mandatory programs, whether they are called wellness programs, stress management programs, or employee assistance programs, are not without problems. From any perspective, they constitute another intrusion of the organization into the private lives of individuals. "Don't smoke; don't drink; eat properly; exercise regularly," is clearly well-meaning advice, but if it was irritating when your parents said to do it, it is even more so when the boss orders you to do it. From a civil liberties perspective it is troublesome and it would clearly be preferable if, instead of placing the burden on individuals (victims of a sort) to change their life-styles organizations would change their behavior to eliminate or minimize the stressors they create. This is unlikely to happen, so perhaps we must settle for the lesser of two evils—stress management programs.

As indicated previously, many large private organizations have developed extensive employee wellness programs: for example, Johnson, IBM, AT&T, PepsiCo., Coca Cola, General Foods, New York Telephone. Increasingly, public organizations are doing the same. Several large urban police departments, such as those in Boston, Detroit, and New York and the Los Angeles County Sheriff's Department, have developed comprehensive programs to help employees and spouses deal with job-related stress. Many agencies offer drug and alcohol rehabilitation programs and provide psychological counselling. Mandatory and voluntary physical fitness programs are increasingly appearing in agencies at all levels of government. One of the most extensive stress management programs is provided by the United States Secret Service, and it includes agency policies to minimize stressful working conditions as well as individually oriented training. Job rotation from stressful assignments, the worst of which are protective assignments to public officials, is mandatory. No agent may serve more than three years on such an assignment. Overtime is strictly limited. Regular stress management seminars are offered and required. The Secret Service Employee Assistance Program provides drug, alcohol, and marital counseling for employees and their families under guarantees of strict confidentiality.[52] The effectiveness of all these programs remains unclear. What remains clear is that stress is a serious and continuing problem for both organizations and individuals.

BURNOUT

The term *burnout* was first applied to human beings in 1974, by Herbert Freudenberger, although the condition itself clearly existed before that time.[53] Since then its original meaning—"to fail, to wear out or become exhausted by making excessive demands on energy, strength, or resources," as defined in Webster's dictionary—has been so expanded as to render the term almost meaningless; now every time people have a bad day, they are likely to report that they are burned out. But burnout in the original sense and as it will be used here is more than a temporary fatigue and discouragement. Burnout is a pervasive and enduring condition that strips the affected individual of energy, caring and strength: "a general malaise, emotional, physical and physiological fatigue . . . of hopelessness, helplessness and a lack of enthusiasm about work and even life in general . . . a general erosion of the spirit."[54] A person in the final stages of burnout feels physically, emotionally, and mentally exhausted. Physically, burnout victims suffer from the same reactions as those who experience severe and prolonged stress: psychosomatic illnesses, sleep disorders, and pervasive weariness. Emotionally, they become so depressed and apathetic that they stop caring about anything or anybody, feeling entrapped by events and circumstances beyond their control. In this sense, burnout is primarily an affliction of human service workers who work constantly with other people: social workers, child protective workers, police officers, teachers, lawyers, doctors, nurses, dentists, day care workers, and mental health professionals.

Burnout does not occur overnight. It unfolds in distinct phases. In some jobs, such as child protection services, burnout may occur within a year. In other jobs, such as teaching, the process may take as long as four or five years.[55] The first phase is the honeymoon phase, the initial period on the job, marked by high enthusiasm, idealism, and a conviction that one can solve the problems of society and other people.[56] Potential burnout victims are strongly committed to their jobs and to helping others and usually put in long hours on the job. Even when they leave work, they take the job home with them mentally and emotionally, thinking about cases that they have been assigned, talking about them, living their jobs twenty-four hours a day. They live in what Edelwich terms "the small world," a world where all their basic satisfactions in life come from one source.[57]

At some point the demands of the job begin to overwhelm. There are too many cases and too little time or resources to deal with them effectively, and the problems of clients are seldom solved. The ideal goals of the agency, whether fighting crime, educating students, eliminating poverty, or curing the mentally ill, seem remote and unrelated to the tasks the employees actually perform. Reality shock, with all of its disillusionments, hits hard. Things in employees' nonwork lives are probably not going too well either. Job demands and commitments have minimized the time available for family, friends, and leisure activities.

In phase two, fuel shortage, the strain begins to show, and anxiety and tension develop and increase. Fatigue and sleepness nights lead to physical exhaustion. Early symptoms of inefficiency at work appear, and stagnation sets in.[58] The job begins to lose its appeal, and job dissatisfaction develops. Frequently, the burnout victim begins to drink more, as a way to relax, to unwind, and escape from the pressures of the job.

Initial problems of fuel shortage evolve into chronic symptoms. Exhaustion becomes a wearing constant of life, frustration with the job grows, and depression develops and deepens. Anger with clients, family, friends, and life is quickly triggered but slowly dissipated. Attitude toward clients changes from empathy to apathy. An "I've heard it all before" attitude hardens into one of cynicism and suspicion. The victim increasingly feels powerless to solve the problems of clients or even to cope with the demands of work and life.

In the crisis phase, symptoms mount and become an obsession. The victim feels overwhelmed by the demands of life and unable to cope; frustration, anger and despair mount.

The final phase of burnout has been termed "hitting the wall,"[59] and total professional deterioration is likely to occur. Apathy replaces enthusiasm; detachment replaces committment. "Turning off" and "tuning out" become chronic states of mind and behavior. One of the most marked job-related behaviors is physical, emotional, and mental withdrawal from clients.[60] Avoiding physical contact with clients may take the form of rearranging one's office so that maximum physical distance is maintained, finding excuses for not being in the office, not returning phone calls, not keeping office hours, and purposely failing to notice clients whenever or wherever encountered. As one burned out college professor described her case of "undergraduatitis," "I find myself crossing the street whenever I see someone in their twenties approaching. I do not think I like teaching anymore."[61] Emotional withdrawal is reflected in a loss of caring about clients, as well as coldness, nastiness and resentment openly demonstrated to them. "Sometimes I feel like telling my clients, 'Who cares?' You think you're the only one that has problems?" was how a burned out social worker expressed her attitude.[62] Depersonalization and dehumanization of clients is a key component of burnout.[63] A police officer referring to suspects as "animals" (or worse), or a social worker referring to clients as "people like that," or mental health workers referring to patients as "loonies," are all reducing individuals to a subhuman state so that they can be treated correspondingly. Stereotyping further alleviates the need to respond to clients as individuals; and put downs, humorous or otherwise, help complete the emotional withdrawal. Mental withdrawal frequently takes the form of excessive reliance on the rules, going by the book to avoid having to think about or exert oneself on behalf of clients. It also means no longer listening to or concentrating on what clients are saying.

Burnout victims withdraw not only from clients; they withdraw from colleagues, family, and friends. As a physician suffering from burnout explained, "Everything my colleagues do gets on my nerves: their vocabulary, the way they talk, they way they walk, and the way they think. They all seem so stupid to me now, and to think I once thought they were an exciting, stimulating bunch is quite inconceivable."[64] Withdrawal and isolation continue off the job; few marriages are able to tolerate the strain, and divorce is likely. Everything seems purposeless; getting out of bed in the morning becomes ever more difficult, a sense of failure permeates the victims' thoughts, and with it comes the guilt for feeling the way they do, for having failed, for having let everyone down. And with it too comes the increased probability of all the psychological and physiological problems associated with extreme stress.[65]

Burnout makes Marx's or anyone else's concept of alienation seem like a case of minor job dissatisfaction, and although some researchers identify burnout with alienation, it is considerably different both in symptoms and causes. Burnout is not an affliction of assembly-line workers but rather of professionals with jobs that involve considerable responsibility and discretion, too much of both sometimes, and their jobs are meaningful, if impossible to perform successfully. Burnout is a slow process and not necessarily a linear one. It may occur in varying degrees, the process may be halted or reversed, and the duration varies. Burnout may be experienced more than once, and the victims may or may not be aware that they have burned out.[66] The physiological consequences of burnout were unknown to Marx and are seldom considered by contemporary writers on alienation. The psychological consequences are similar, although those associated with terminal burnout appear to be more extreme and extensive. Nonetheless burnout victims are unquestionably alienated from their work, their fellow workers and themselves.

Causes of Burnout

The causes, or at any rate the sources, of burnout reside in the organizations where burnout occurs, the individuals who develop it, and the broader social, economic, and political environment in which they must operate. Burnout primarily affects those who work with other people, and it is the result of the constant or repeated emotional pressure associated with intense involvement with those people.[67] Almost invariably, the people with whom they deal are in a dependent, subordinate postion, emotionally charged, and frequently behaving at their worst. In many instances, the clients are nonvoluntary and resent the position in which they find themselves. They are frequently worried, anxious, frightened, resentful, belligerent, hostile, angry, or apathetic. The professionals become emotional dumping grounds for other people's problems and the targets for their anger, fear, and resentment. Day after day the professionals must absorb the emotional outpourings of others. Even in the best of circumstances this is emotionally taxing, and human service professionals in the public sector rarely work in the best of circumstances.

To a certain extent, these workers are ill prepared for the reality of the work situation, regardless of how much education and training they have had. Some professionals have been socialized to believe that they are there to help people, and when those people not only resent and resist being helped but turn the helping relationship into an adversarial one, the professionals are likely to feel resentment, which they are not allowed to express. Professional norms and public expectations require that they, whether they are police officers, social workers, or teachers, be unemotional, courteous, and professional.[68] Teachers must cope with students who do not want to learn or even be in a classroom. As both classroom vandalism and violence have escalated, teachers increasingly find that instead of teaching, their major task is maintaining discipline. Police officers, social workers, and child protective service workers must constantly deal with the seamy side of life: with people at the bottom of society who live in conditions that on the one hand are heartbreaking but on the other hand are appalling, and the people are not very nice. As one police officer said in a workshop, "About the third time some drunk pukes all over your uniform which you have just had cleaned, you begin to develop a bad attitude." Even college professors, who do not have to work under such taxing circumstances, find they are increasingly confronted by underprepared, apathetic students who expect and even demand higher grades.[69]

Equally frustrating is the lack of appreciation and gratitude from clients, supervisors, and the public for services provided or assistance rendered.[70] The lack of positive feedback, particularly when negative feedback is common, is demoralizing and discouraging and contributes to feelings of frustration and powerlessness: "Why am I doing this? Nobody gives a damn anyway." The lack of objective criteria for measuring accomplishment (results are both intangible and slow in developing) limits the availability of psychological rewards inherent in the work. No one knows for certain when a mental patient is cured or a student educated. Little control over outcomes exists, and service delivery is fragmented; thus, task identity is lacking. Similarly, both responsibility and credit are fragmented. As a child protective officer explained,

> Protecting children from abuse is an impossible job. When you interview they don't tell you that you won't have the power to carry out the life and death decisions you are responsible for making. You don't get sufficient time, resources or access to information. . . . The police won't get involved unless you have specific evidence and you can't get it because people don't want to go to court.[71]

Powerlessness and lack of autonomy and control are pervasive. Role ambiguity is characteristic. Players lack information about how to perform their jobs, about what constitutes adequate performance, about what the scope and responsibilities of the job are, and about how they will be evaluated.[72]

Role overload, both quantitative and qualitative, is endemic. In large cities, welfare caseloads average between 180 and 200 cases per social worker.[73] Chronic overload has been exacerbated by funding cutbacks. Although resources have diminished and personnel has been reduced, demands for the services of the police, the educational system, legal services, and the welfare system have actually increased, and only rarely is triage viewed as a legally or morally acceptable method of allocating resources. Qualitative overload and role conflict are particularly apparent in police work and teaching. Police officers are expected to enforce the laws, arrest offenders, and be psychiatrists, marriage counselors, social workers, and masters of bureaucratic paper pushing. Teachers are expected to be educators, disciplinarians, family counselors, purveyors of appropriate morals and values, sex educators, guidance counselors, and psychological counselors. Without exception, human service workers are expected to be agents of social control and rehabilitation and assistance. Professional and bureaucratic norms also conflict; bureaucrats are supposed to be impersonal, treating everyone equally, but professionals are supposed to be involved, recognizing that everyone is different and tailoring their approaches individually.

From a career perspective, many of these jobs are clearly frustrating. Sexism is pervasive. The jobs are low paying at all levels, and upward mobility is limited, usually only possible by moving into administrative positions far from the actual work for which the professional was trained. Promotion means less or no work with clients, more paperwork, and alienation from peers. Physical work conditions are frequently crowded, uncomfortable, unclean, and unchanging.

Other organizational characteristics add to the stress of the jobs. Supervisors are frequently untrained in administration and, worse, may themselves be burnout victims who have moved into their positions to escape from the hassles of front-line duty. Consequently their supervisory styles are characterized by either autocratic behavior or disinterest in the problems their subordinates are experiencing; they provide little assistance, support, information, or feedback.[74] While they may be aware of the burnout process, their attitude is frequently, "Let them burn out and quit; there are three people out there eagerly waiting for each position opening up who will be willing to promise to remain forever both cheerful and grateful."[75] Although burnout affects individuals, it rarely occurs to just one individual in an organization. Rather "like a staph infection, it gets around."[76] It taints all it touches, and relationships with coworkers as well as clients deteriorate. Burnout causes some to redirect their attention to office politics, and the work situation becomes even more intolerable as status and power games proliferate. And when those games are played by the essentially powerless, they tend to be particularly vindictive and cruel, serving to reinforce the burnout process. Yet many organizations lack either the interest, the ability, or the will to become involved in helping prevent or treat burnout.

Individual Determinants of Burnout

Even though the basic sources of burnout are inherent in the jobs and organizations characterized by high burnout rates, burnout is an individual phenomenon, and some individuals are more susceptible to it than others. Although there is no known personality trait or configuration that by itself will cause someone to burn out, it is clear that it is the best and the brightest, the most idealistic, dedicated, and committed of human service workers who are most susceptible to burnout.[77] "You can't burn out if you've never been on fire."[78] In addition, the motivation and needs of people who enter human services work make them as a group particularly likely to burn out.

While people who enter human services work do so in order to make a living, they are obviously not primarily motivated by greed or the desire to make a great deal of money. Cherniss contends that the need for competence, for mastery and efficacy, is particularly pronounced in human service professionals.[79] Other motivations that predominate are the need to help people and the need for control or power.[80] Their personal needs and beliefs and their training reinforce their expectations that they will make a difference and that they will be able to solve problems quickly. They expect to be appreciated by clients and the public and, if not to be paid well, to at least have status and prestige in the community.[81] These needs and beliefs are even more pronounced in the most idealistic and enthusiastic new professionals. Given what has already been established about the actual nature of their jobs in the real world, these individuals are doomed to disillusionment and severe need deprivation. Motivation theories tell us that the unavoidable result of that disillusionment will be severe job dissatisfaction, declining productivity, and a loss of motivation. As the need deprivation continues and workers recognize that their work expectations will never be fulfilled, motivation and morale continue to decline. What motivation theory does not predict is the full consequences of burnout, perhaps because most motivation theorists could not and cannot believe that a job situation so intolerable can exist.

Beyond the characteristics shared by human service professionals, certain individual personality characteristics also seem to be associated with burnout. Predictably, Type A personalities are more likely to burn out than Type B people, as are those high in nAch and nPow, neither of whom will have their dominant needs satisfied in their work situation. Neurotic anxiety, a related set of personality traits including low self-esteem, strong, punitive superego, emotional instability, and excessive concern with the opinions of others, similarly makes the individual less resistant to stress and more susceptible to burnout.[82] Individuals with an internal locus of control are less likely to develop burnout than those with an external locus, who are prone to learned helplessness when confronted with stressful situations.[83]

As was true with those who coped most effectively with any type of job-related stress, workers who have vital interests outside of work, who have expanded "the small world" to include diverse interests, activities, and relationships not associated with their work, are less likely to burn out.[84] Similarly, a limited commitment to the job and the ability to leave the problems of work at work also are associated with resistance to burnout. Whatever the advantages of work as the central or only life interest may be, the individual who is overcommitted to the job is likely to pay a high price in psychological and social terms if the job is as emotionally demanding as many human service jobs are.

Environmental Sources of Burnout

Although burnout existed well before its initial recognition by social scientists in 1974, most researchers agree that it has increased substantially in the late 1970s and 1980s. Neither the basic nature of the jobs involved or the type of individuals seeking them have changed substantially, so major responsibility for the increase in burnout resides in changes that have occurred in the political, social, and economic environment. According to Cherniss, one of the major changes can be clearly explained by organization theory. The 1960s marked the popularization of the belief that work must be self-actualizing, as well as the belief that bureaucratic organizations crushed the spirit and blocked self-actualization. Before and, even more emphatically, immediately after the great depression, a job that paid well, was secure, offered some opportunity for advancement, and provided safe and comfortable working conditions was almost universally regarded as a very good job, in many respects the epitome of the American dream. But then came organizational humanism and the popularization of Maslow, and what had been a very good job was reevaluated and found wanting. Such a job at best eliminated dissatisfaction, but a good job—to which all were entitled—had to provide more than that; it had to allow and encourage people to self-actualize.[85] Particularly for the college educated, attitudes toward work changed. Work had to be meaningful, to allow for autonomy and creativity and that vague maximization of human potential. With those changed attitudes came changed and unrealistic expectations about what work should be like and what workers could accomplish. And in those unrealistic expectations lay the foundation for reality shock, frustration, and burnout.

At the same time, the professional mystique flourished and was popularized by television, movies, and books. Police shows glamorized police work and established that justice always prevailed and that no crime was so complicated that it could not be solved in sixty minutes or less. In mental health work, the mystique was communicated through books and movies like *David and Lisa* and *I Never Promised You a Rose Garden*, in which a dedicated professional was able to restore attractive but very ill patients to normal functioning. Elementary and secondary teaching was similarly fictionalized and dramatized. This once again created expectations in the minds of both the public and those entering the professions that that was how it really was. It never was, it is not now, and it never will be, but again, in disillusionment lie the roots of burnout.

In the political arena, the 1960s were also a time of great expectations. At long last racial and then sexual equality were going to be achieved. The War on Poverty was going to eradicate proverty and urban blight. Crime would be attacked and eliminated; equal educational opportunity would be provided to all, and presumably all were breathlessly awaiting its arrival. Mental illness would be eradicated, and those shameful public mental hospitals would be changed into model treatment centers. In the cold reality of the Reagan Era it may seem impossible that people ever really believed those things and even more impossible that government was the chosen instrument for achieving them. But they did, and the political system responded by creating policies and organizations to accomplish those goals. When created, those organizations were filled with enthusiasm and zeal and attracted employees, young and old, who believed that all things were possible and that they were going to do them.

We know now, or at least we think we know, how naive those people were. They really did not understand the problems; they knew nothing about their complexity, and they had no proven or feasible methods for accomplishing their goals. They burned out when faced with the cruel realities of the people they were to help and the problems they were to solve. We, at least, will not burn out; we have never been on fire: we no longer believe government can solve our problems and the private sector has not demonstrated much interest in solving them either, so maybe they were not really important problems after all. But for those who did believe, burnout remains a painful reality, and the change in political attitudes only makes their situation worse. And when the massive budget cuts that have accompanied the subsequent shift in public and political attitudes were added, the stresses and frustrations of the jobs were compounded.

The nature of the policymaking process and the policies that emerge from it also contribute to the causes of burnout. Even in the height of the idealism of the sixties, policies tended to be more symbolic than substantive, and from a political perspective, the symbolism was far more important than actually solving the problems. Adequate funding was never provided for social programs. Both federalism and pluralism ensured that programs and service delivery systems would be fragmented and uncoordinated, making an effective attack on problems impossible and guaranteeing frustration for those who tried. The needs and demands of the political branches for visible and quick results added to the problem. True results were likely to be neither quick nor visible, so to provide what was demanded, goal displacement occurred. Quantity became more important, and pressure to increase numbers added to job stress and detracted from qualitative results. In some programs the pressure for results lead to "creaming"—selecting those least in need of service and consequently the easiest to help—and ignoring those most in need. For the committed professional, such goal displacement is extremely distressing.[86]

The Social and Organizational Costs of Burnout

For the individual affected the costs of burnout are enormous, but the individual costs are only part of the total costs of burnout. Organizational costs include "high turnover, low morale, we-they polarization, increased concern with bureaucratic turf, conflict over authority, scapegoating of organizational leaders, increased absenteeism and replacement of informal communication by rigid, role defined channels."[87] Interpersonal conflicts of all types increase: between staff and clients, between staff and the public, between coworkers, and between subordinates and superiors. On-the-job accident rates also increase.

Burnout victims have two choices: they can either leave the organization or job or remain in the situation and either choice is costly from an organizational and social perspective. Burnout affects the most dedicated and committed, whose departure deprives the organization and society of its most talented and valuable workers; and if all burnout victims depart, the organization is left with only indifferent employees, those who don't care much about it or their job. Quality of work and concern for clients deteriorates commensurately. If burned out employees completely leave the profession, the societal costs associated with their training and education are also lost. Turnover is expensive: not only are the costs of recruitment and training lost, but it also means a temporary decline in productivity and a break in continuity of performance. Yet if the burnout victims remain on the job the costs are equally high. Their continued presence will spread burnout to other staff members and clients. As they progress throughout the burnout process, their job performance will steadily deteriorate, and the quality of care and treatment they provide to clients will similarly decline. The emotionalism and irritability associated with burnout result in increased conflict with colleagues and clients. Motivation gradually declines and job dissatisfaction increases. In the final stage of burnout, if the victims remain on the job, they become deadwood, "trapped in a gilded cage," staying for the sole reason that they need the job to survive economically.[88]

If they move or are pushed into administrative positions, the organizational consequences are equally unfortunate. That an organization would willingly and knowingly put a burnout victim in an administrative position might seem peculiar, but sometimes the organization may have little choice. When supervisors perceive that job performance has deteriorated to the point that clients, students, the public, or (in the case of police officers) suspects and the courts are beginning to complain, they may be reluctant to dismiss the individual for several reasons. They may not wish to go through the tedious, time-consuming, and always uncertain process required by civil service regulations. They may not wish to antagonize the union, which would be certain to intervene. Or simply for humane reasons, they may be reluctant to penalize an individual who at one time was a dedicated and valuable employee. If no treatment programs are provided—and frequently there are none—the remaining alternative is to move the individual into administration, with usually dire results. The individual may prove incompetent, and the apathy and indifference associated with burnout will be turned toward the new job responsibilities and new subordinates and peers. Other employees will resent what they perceive as inequitable treatment, seemingly indicating that the only way to get a promotion is to perform poorly, and morale will plummet, fostering accelerated burnout for other employees.

The organization and the public have a clear interest in preventing burnout and providing care and assistance for its victims. Even though prevention and treatment programs and strategies inevitably involve costs, those costs are likely to be considerably less than the costs of ignoring burnout. Convincing organizations and their political supervisors of this may be difficult because so many of the costs of burnout are indirect and intangible, while the costs of treatment programs are likely to be a direct and tangible drain on already scarce resources. A comprehensive and empathic understanding of burnout may provide the basis for persuading political and organizational decisionmakers to commit resources for dealing with the problem.

Prevention and Treatment

As was true with stress management, effective strategies for coping with burnout fall into two categories: individual and organizational. Both must be based on the realization that burnout will happen, perhaps repeatedly, and must be dealt with on an ongoing basis.[89] Blaming the victim is neither fair nor productive in dealing with the problem, and actually serves to worsen it. For both individuals and organizations, the first step in coping with burnout is awareness: awareness of what it is, what its symptoms are, and why it occurs. The second step is reality therapy—learning to accept reality and develop realistic expectations:

> Expect to be doing a difficult job without sufficient resources or rewards. Expect to have to get along with some disagreeable people and to have to show tolerance for outrageous viewpoints. Expect to be unable to do any of these things all the time. Expect to be far from perfect, and expect clients and colleagues to be far from perfect.[90]

Developing and maintaining a realistic approach to the job means recognizing one's own limitations and realizing that one is not responsible for the clients or the organization. It requires setting realistic goals for oneself and knowing what can and cannot be changed.[91] The ultimate goal of reality theory is not cynicism or lack of involvement but the development of detached concern.[92]

Whether such realism can be conveyed in educational and preservice training programs remains debatable. Although educational programs encourage and reinforce unrealistic attitudes towards occupations with high burnout rates, they are not the only or perhaps even the most important sources of such perceptions. Presenting a more balanced view of the demands of the job and the limited abilities of individuals and organizations to solve problems would be helpful. Beyond that, it may not be possible to prepare individuals to cope with the stresses of experiences with which they are basically unfamiliar.[93] Simply providing knowledge of what will likely happen will not have a long-term effect unless it is followed with continued on-the-job assistance.

For individuals, developing awareness of burnout means consciously and constantly monitoring themselves for symptoms. The recommendations provided for effective stress management are equally appropriate and especially important for those in jobs with high burnout potential. Establishing and maintaining a complete compartmentalization of work and nonwork is particularly important, as is expanding "the small world," developing off-the-job interests, and making time to engage in them.[94] Seeking further education, expanding skills and knowledge, and improving competence is also highly recommended. Ultimately, however, exercising the option for getting out, changing either jobs or occupations, may be necessary. If the other methods for preventing or dealing with burnout have been tried and have failed and the overwhelming negative attitudes towards the job and life persist, calling it quits is preferable to continuing in a situation that will continue to deteriorate along with one's mental and physical health.

Organizations can play a major role in preventing and treating staff burnout. Many of the job conditions associated with high burnout rates are organizationally created and can be eliminated only by the organization. Client loads can be reduced and jobs structured so that the amount of time spent on the most stressful activities is limited and systematically alternated with work on less stressful activities. Similarly, the organization can ensure the availability of "times out" as a matter of policy, for all workers when needed. Physical work conditions can also be improved.

Specific policies should be developed for staff support and development. Organizationally developed social support systems can provide technical and emotional support and assistance for all workers. Problem-solving groups, the equivalent of quality control circles, counseling, and an understanding and concerned administrative climate can be invaluable in preventing burnout. Staff development programs that provide training, teach coping strategies, and encourage education should be combined with specific career development programs for workers. Staff should be continuously monitored for signs of burnout, and focused assistance should be provided at the earliest stages for those who display symptoms. Clearly accepting that the organization has as much responsibility for preventing burnout as the individual alleviates much of the guilt and self-recrimination of affected workers as well as providing the best basis for systematic and positive action to deal with burnout.

CONCLUSION

Although stress and burnout may be the fads of the eighties, their fashionableness should not be allowed to obscure their enduring importance for understanding individual behavior in organizations. Understanding stress, its causes, and human reactions to it helps individuals better understand many aspects of organizational behavior. It gives a clearer perspective on why individuals oppose change and the consequences of too rapid or too much change. Similarly, reactions to conflict and the aversion of many people to conflict appear to be as much physiologically as socially determined, and this raises doubts about the wisdom of recommendations to stimulate conflict. The positive and negative impacts of bureaucracy are also clarified by an understanding of stress. On the positive side, bureaucracy minimizes many of the conditions that cause stress: uncertainty, ambiguity, and change. On the negative side, in practice it frequently contributes to role conflict, overload, and boredom.

Understanding stress and burnout also helps in understanding job satisfaction, motivation, and alienation. Many of the suggested correlates of job dissatisfaction are in reality also stressors for many individuals, with the result that attempting to remove job satisfiers may decrease stress and improve job performance. Like job satisfaction, stress is individually determined. Motivation and stress are also linked. Both arise from unfulfilled needs, which initially serve as a stimulus to behavior. If the needs remain unfulfilled, motivation declines and stress increases, often causing physical and psychological disorders. Conversely, however, the goal of motivation theory—to get employees to identify with their job and organizations so that they will work harder—not only increases their stress levels but also contributes to burnout.

Understanding burnout helps explain the causes of some of the most criticized aspects of the behavior of street-level bureaucrats. Too often, they have been labeled villains of the public service by critics who have little concern for the circumstances that cause that behavior. A knowledge of burnout teaches us that they are as much victims of the system as their clientele. Burnout emerges as the ultimate form of alienation, though its causes differ in many aspects. If research on burnout is accurate, it teaches us the ultimate folly of overemphasizing the importance of work in life, for that results not only in a unidimensional life but also in a deep disillusionment with both work and life.

The role of the political system in the increased rates of stress-related illness and burnout is clear. From basic characteristics that have resulted in unclear and conflicting goals and the creation of unrealistic expectations to current attitudes and behaviors that have resulted in negative public attitudes and inadequate resources, the political system has been the source of many of the contributing factors to stress and burnout. Budget cuts and constant criticism exacerbate the problems, and the future seems to promise little relief. Demographic trends, particularly the aging of the population and geographic population shifts, indicate that the demands on many human service agencies will continue to increase. There is little indication that resources for the agencies that will be called on to respond to those demands will increase commensurately.

Dealing with stress and burnout should be an organizational priority, for the sources of stress and burnout can be dealt with only at that level. Unfortunately, the probability of this occurring is low. The dominant approaches to stress and burnout at this point are individualistic and frequently punitive. The emphasis of most stress management programs is not on eliminating causes but on improving individual capacity for coping. Implicit in this approach is blaming the victim; if individuals led better lives, they would not suffer ill effects from stressful conditions. Drug and alcohol abuse programs tend to be even more punitive, always carrying with them the real possibility that the victims will be subject to disciplinary or legal action. The philosophy of individualism prevails: responsibility resides with the individual, not the organization or society.

NOTES

1. Terry Beehr and Rabi S. Bhagat, eds., *Human Stress and Cognition in Organizations* (New York: John Wiley, 1985), p. 6.
2. Thomas McGaffey, "New Horizons in Organization Stress Prevention Programs," *Personnel Administrator* (1978): pp. 26–32.
3. "Insurance Covering Some Job Related Stress Problems," *Spokane Spokesman Review* (February 24, 1984): p. C1.
4. Robert F. Minnehan and Whiton S. Paine, "The Bottom Line," in Whiton S. Paine, ed., *Job Stress and Burnout* (Beverly Hills, Calif.: Sage Publications, 1982), p. 100.
5. Hans Selye, *The Stress of Life* (New York: McGraw Hill, 1956), p. 311.
6. Ibid.
7. John Stratton, *Police Passages* (Manhattan Beach, Calif.: Glennon Publishing Co., 1984), p. 289.
8. George Stotelmyer and David Girdano, *The Stress Mess Solution* (Bourie, Md.: Robert J. Brady, 1980), pp. 11–15.
9. L. Territo and J. J. Vetter, "Stress and Police Personnel," *Journal of Police Science and Administration* (June 1981): p. 197.
10. Keith Davis and John Newstrom, *Human Behavior at Work* (New York: McGraw-Hill, 1985), p. 479.
11. Selye, *The Stress of Life*, p. 311.

12. Alvin Toffler, *Future Shock* (Bantam Books, 1971), p. 342.
13. A. Delongis, J. Coyne, G. Dakoff, S. Folkman and R. S. Laqzarus, "Relationships of Daily Hassles, Uplifts and Major Life Events to Health Status," *Health Psychology* (1982): p. 122.
14. Ibid., p. 130.
15. Stotelmyer and Girdano, *The Stress of Life*, p. 61.
16. Beehr and Bhagat, *Human Stress and Cognition in Organizations*, p. 7.
17. Ibid., p. 14.
18. Manfred Kets de Vries, "Organizational Stress: A Call for Management Action," in Donald White, *Contemporary Perspectives in Organizational Behavior* (Boston: Allyn and Bacon, 1982), p. 319.
19. Stotelmyre, *The Stress Mess Solution*, p. 35.
20. Kets de Vries, "Organizational Stress, A Call for Management Action," p. 319.
21. Ralph Katz, "Organization Stress and Early Socialization Experience," in Beehr, and Bhagat, *Human Stress and Cognition*, in Organizations, p. 117.
22. Todd J. Dick, "As the Axe Falls: Budget Cuts and the Experience of Stress in Organizations," in Beehr and Bhagat, *Human Stress and Cognition in Organizations*, p. 84.
23. Ibid.
24. Ibid., p. 103.
25. Annette Gaul, "Burnout," *Management* (Spring 1982): p. 3.
26. Michael Lipsky, *Street and Police Personnel*, p. 196.
28. John Blackmore, "Police Stress," in Clinton Terry III, *Policing Society* (New York: John Wiley, 1985), p. 394.
29. Jerry Edelwich with Archie Brodsky, *Burnout* (New York: Human Sciences Press, 1980), p. 146.
30. Richard Lazarus, quoted in Daniel Galeman, "Positive Denial: The Case for Not Facing Reality," *Psychology Today* (November 1979): p. 52.
31. R. Van Harrison, "The Person-Environment Fit Model and the Study of Job Stress," in Beehr and Bhagat, *Human Stress and Cognition in Organizations*, p. 24.
32. Donald White and H. William Vroman, *Action in Organizations*, 2nd ed. (Boston: Allyn and Bacon, 1982), p. 317.
33. Meyer Friedman and Roy H. Rosenman, *Type A Behavior and Your Heart* (New York: Fawcett Crest, 1975), pp. 101–103.
34. Stotelmyer, *The Stress Mess Solution*, p. 56.
35. Andrew Dubrin, *Fundamentals of Organizational Behavior*, 2nd ed. (New York: Pergammon Press, 1978), pp. 141–142.
36. John Senger, *Individuals, Groups, Organizations* (Cambridge, Mass.: Winthrop, 1980), p. 184.
37. C. R. Anderson, "Locus of Control, Coping Behaviors, and Performance in a Stress Setting," *Journal of Applied Psychology* (1977): pp. 446–451.
38. J. M. Ivancevich and M. T. Matteson, *Stress and Work: A Managerial Perspective* (Glenview, Ill.: Scott, Foreman, 1980).
39. Gaul, "Burnout," p. 3.
40. R. S. Lazarus and R. Launeir, "Stress-Related Transactions Between Person and Environment," in L. A. Pervin and M. Lewis, eds., *Perspectives in Industrial Psychology* (New York: Plenum, 1978), p. 287.
41. Hans Selye, *Selye's Guide To Stress*, vol. 1 (New York: Van Nostrand, Reinhold, 1980) p. 341.
42. Stratton, *Police Passages*, p. 304.
43. Selye, *Selye's Guide to Stress*, p. 341.
44. Gaul, "Burnout," p. 5.
45. Dubrin, *Fundamentals of Organizational Behavior*, p. 142.

46. David R. Frew, "Transcendental Meditation and Productivity," *Academy of Management Journal* (June 1974): p. 368.
47. Herbert Benson, *The Relaxction Response* (New York: Morrow, 1975).
48. Cary Cherniss, *Staff Burnout: Job Stress in Human Services* (Beverly HIlls, Calif.: Sage Publications, 1980), p. 120.
49. Terry Beehr, "The Role of Social Support in Coping With Organizational Stress," in Beehr and Bhagat, *Human Stress and Cognition in Organizations*, p. 392.
50. Ayala Pines and Elliot Aronson with Ditsa Kafra, *Burnout: From Tedium to Personal Growth*, (New York: Free Press, 1980), p. 86.
51. John H. Howard, Peter A. Rechnitzer, and D. A. Cunningham, "Coping with Job Tension: Effective and Ineffective Mechanisms," in Donald White, *Contemporary Perspectives in Organizational Behavior*, p. 333.
52. Robert Snow, "How the Secret Service Handles Stress," *Management* (Spring 1982): p. 68.
53. Herbert Freudenberger, "Staff Burnout," *Journal of Social Issues* (1974), pp. 159–65.
54. Pines et al., *Burnout: From Tedium to Personal Growth*, p. 3.
55. Ibid., p. 2.
56. Robert Vening and James Bradley, *The Work Stress Connection: How to Cope with Job Burnout* (New York: Ballantine Books, 1981), p. 38.
57. Edelwich, *Burnout*, p. 82.
58. Ibid., p. 28.
59. Vening and Bradley, *The Work Stress Connection*, p. 78.
60. Christina Maslach, "Burned Out," *Human Behavior* (1976): p. 18.
61. Quoted in Pines et al., *Burnout*, p. 20.
62. Ibid., p. 18.
63. Christina Maslach, *Burnout: The Cost of Caring* (Englewood Cliffs, N.J.: Prentice Hall, 1983), p. 8.
64. Pines et al., *Burnout*, p. 21.
65. Cherniss, *Staff Burnout*, p. 17.
66. Jerome F. X. Carrol and William White, "Theory Building: Integrating Individual and Environmental Factors Within an Ecological Framework," Paine, *Job Stress and Burnout*, pp. 45–46.
67. Pines et al., *Burnout*, p. 3.
68. James I. Reese, "Life In the High Speed Lane: Managing Police Burnout," *The Police Chief* (June 1982): p. 49.
69. Winifred Melandez and Rafael de Guzman, *Burnout: The New Academic Disease*, ASHE-ERIC Report No. 9 (Washington D.C.: Association for the Study of Higher Education, 1983), p. 15.
70. Edelwich, *Burnout*, pp. 133–135.
71. Ibid., pp. 188–189.
72. Cherniss, *Staff Burnout*, pp. 89–90.
73. Pines et al., *Burnout*, p. 65.
74. Cherniss, *Staff Burnout*, p. 98.
75. Ayala M. Pines, "Changing Organizations: Is Work Environment Without Burnout an Impossible Goal?" in Paine, *Job Stress and Burnout*, p. 181.
76. Edelwich, *Burnout*, p. 25.
77. Carroll and White, "Theory Building: Integrating Individual and Environmental Factors Within an Ecological Framework," p. 48.
78. Pines et al., *Burnout*, p. 4.
79. Cherniss, *Staff Burnout*, p. 49.
80. Edelwich, *Burnout*, p. 47.

81. Ibid., pp. 52–55.
82. Cherniss, *Staff Burnout*, pp. 127–136.
83. Eli Gogow, "Burnout and Locus of Control," *Public Personnel Management* (Spring 1986): p. 81.
84. Ibid.
85. Cherniss, *Staff Burnout*, p. 151.
86. Cary Cherniss, "Cultural Trends: Political, Economic and Historical Roots of the Problem," in Paine, *Job Stress and Burnout*, pp. 83–85.
87. William White, *Managing Personal and Organizational Stress in Institutions of Higher Education* (Rockville, Md.: N. C. S. Inc., 1980), p. 4.
88. Edelwich, *Burnout*, p. 182.
89. Ibid., p. 14.
90. Ibid., p. 212.
91. Pines et al., *Burnout*, p. 12.
92. Ibid., p. 109.
93. Jack L. Wilder and Robert Plutchik, "Preparing the Professional," in Paine, *Job Stress and Burnout*, p. 115.
94. Edelwich, *Burnout*, pp. 243–44.

11

THE GOOD ORGANIZATION: MEASURING ORGANIZATIONAL EFFECTIVENESS

Organizational effectiveness has been and remains the central theme of organizational theory and behavior. From Max Weber to the most recent culture, power, and motivation approaches, organizational effectiveness has emerged as the unifying concept underlying the disparate and conflicting approaches to the study of organizations. The unity shatters, however, over definitions of effectiveness and its determinants. No single, operational definition of organizational effectiveness exists; there are as many definitions as definers. Although dictionaries define *effective* as producing the intended or expected result, there is no agreement on what the intended result of organizations is or should be.

Some theorists argue that the goals are the intended results, but as has been demonstrated repeatedly, goals are usually neither clear nor easily ascertainable. Open systems theorists believe that the intended result is system maintenance or growth; human relations theorists believe that it should be satisfaction of the needs of the members of the organization. Public organization theorists add that responsiveness, accountability, and adherence to democratic values must be considered primary criteria for effectiveness. Depending on the theorist or theoretical approach, the effectiveness of an organization has been attributed to its structure, its technology, its relationship with its environment, its use of strategic planning, its adaptability to change, its ability to manage conflict, its culture or power structure, or the way it treats individual employees. Frequently the definition and determinants of effectiveness are synonymous; just as frequently no explicit definition of effectiveness is provided.

In the midst of all this diversity, some consensus has emerged—an agreement to disagree. All theorists recognize that whether an organization is effective is a value judgment and that there are no universal criteria that should be applied to all organizations. The world of organizations, private, public, and nonprofit, is too rich and diverse for any universal criteria to be appropriate. Even within each of the three sectors, the diversity of organizations inhibits the use of universal criteria.[1] The result has been that for private sector organizations, multiple criteria have been developed and are regularly utilized. Campbell has identified thirty separate criteria that have been used as measures of organizational effectiveness.[2] These are summarized and grouped by approach in Table 11–1. When criteria for public organizations are added, the total reaches thirty-five. Criteria are derived from social values, and as social values do, many of the criteria conflict.

TABLE 11–1. Organizational Effectiveness Criteria

GOAL APPROACHES	HUMAN RESOURCE APPROACHES
Achievement emphasis	Job satisfaction
Productivity	Motivation
Efficiency	Morale
Profit	Value of human resources
Quality of services/products	Training and development
Planning and goal setting	Absenteeism
Goal consensus	Turnover
Internalization of organizational goals	Accident rates
Readiness	Role and norm congruence

INTERNAL PROCESS APPROACHES	SYSTEMS APPROACHES
Control	Stability/maintenance
Conflict/cohesion	Growth
Managerial interpersonal relations skills	Flexibility/adaptation
Managerial task skills	Utilization of environment
Information management and control	Evaluations by external actors (strategic
Participation and shared influence	constituencies)

POLITICAL APPROACHES	OVERALL EFFECTIVENESS
Responsiveness	
Accountability	
Representativeness	
Constitutionality	
Adherence to democratic values	

Source: Adapted from John P. Campbell, "On the Nature of Organizational Effectiveness," in Goodman and Pennings, *New Perspectives on Organizational Effectiveness* (San Francisco: Jossey-Bass, 1977), pp. 36–39.

And, as is also true with social values, there is no means of resolving the conflict. Effectiveness is a multidimensional concept, and the criteria do not necessarily correlate.[3] Consequently, no organization can be effective on all criteria.

The assessment of effectiveness is further complicated by two additional factors: time dimension and the necessity for comparison. Although most studies of effectiveness examine organizations at one particular time, organizations are dynamic, and their effectiveness as measured by any specific criterion will vary considerably over time, reflecting both environmental and internal changes. Thus the time frame chosen for the assessment is a critical factor.[4] Similarly, the age of the organization, its stage in the life cycle, should play a major role in determining the selection of appropriate criteria. Just as we evaluate the behavior of children differently from that of adults, so should we differentiate between organizations in their youth and those in maturity.[5] Effectiveness criteria tend to be relative rather than absolute: effective compared to what or whom? Even the simplest private sector criterion—profit—is meaningful only in a comparative sense: if a business is making a profit of 9 percent it is effective, but not as effective as one that is making a 15 percent profit. In the public sector where simple, numerical criteria are nearly nonexistent, comparison becomes even more essential (and more difficult). The effectiveness of one community's schools, fire departments, or police services tend to be determined by comparing them with the services of another community. Thus, effectiveness is assessed through a process of social comparison.[6] The selection of comparable organizations further complicates the task of assessment and makes its results more open to argument.

Although in contemporary political rhetoric efficiency has been identified with effectiveness, or occasionally emphasized to the exclusion of effectiveness, efficiency and effectiveness are totally different concepts. Efficiency measures the amount of resources used to produce a unit of output.[7] Efficiency is also always a comparative judgment, and it is always possible to be effective without being efficient and vice versa. The cost of producing a well-trained, employable individual from a job program for hard-core unemployables has been estimated to be higher than that of producing a college graduate from a private university. Assuming that the goal of the jobs program is to train and place in private employment the hard-core unemployed, the program, by one measure of effectiveness at least, is effective but inefficient. If the jobs program surreptitiously replaced the hard-core unemployed with college graduates in computer science, it could easily become efficient without being effective. Efficiency is important, because all organizations, and public organizations particularly, have limited resources. Whether it is as important as effectiveness is, of course, a value judgment. What is clear is that these are two different approaches to organizational assessment that are frequently contradictory.

As Table 11–1 indicates, there are four major conventional

approaches to assessing organizational effectiveness: the goal approach, the human resource or human relations approach, the internal process approach, and the systems approach. This chapter will first examine the assumptions, strengths, and weaknesses of goal-based, open systems, and strategic constituencies approaches. The competing values approach to organizational assessment, which is not actually a separate approach but rather a comparison of the underlying premises of the other major approaches, will be used to compare and contrast the human relations approach, the internal process approach, the goal approach, and the systems approach. Finally, the special values relevant to public organizations will be presented—in the consideration of organizational effectiveness, their criteria are special. Although all of the approaches used for private organization have relevance for their public counterparts, they are not in themselves sufficient. Once again, contingency theory makes a necessary point: "What constitutes a good organization depends on what the organization is attempting to do and on the conditions under which it is attempting to do it."[8] What organizations attempt to do in the public sector is very different from what organizations try to do in the private sector, as are the conditions under which they attempt to do it.

THE GOAL-BASED APPROACH

Technically, all effectiveness approaches are goal based; they differ only in their definitions of goals. Open systems approaches perceive goals as systems goals; human relations approaches define goals in terms of appropriate treatment of employees; strategic constituencies theorists believe organization goals are the satisfaction of key clientele; and for the internal process approach, the goal of organizations is establishment and maintenance of appropriate management methods and processes. The goal-based approach, however, is by definition concerned with measuring and evaluating the extent to which organizations have achieved their intended purposes. The goal-based approach is rooted in the concept of the rational organization, that organizations are rational entities created to maximize attainment of specified purposes.

Several assumptions underlie this approach, starting with the belief that organizations have clearly identified specific goals that are agreed upon and understood by all members of the organization, and that the organization is in the hands of a set of rational decision makers who are committed to achievement of those goals. It further presumes that goals are few in number, progress towards them must be measurable, and that the organization knows how to achieve its goals and possesses the necessary resources to do so.[9] The goal-based approach was the earliest approach to organizational effectiveness, dating back at least to Chester Barnard:

"When a specific desired end is attained, we shall say that the action is effective."[10] Despite its problems and inadequacies, it remains the most widely used approach for measuring organizational effectiveness.

By now, those problems and inadequacies, particularly for public organizations, should be familiar to most readers. Organization goals are not clear—they are frequently vague and ambiguous, established more for symbolic political reasons than as clear-cut guides to action. Etzioni contends that goals are not even meant to be achieved; they are ideal states established at a certain point, and there will always be a difference between an ideal state and actual performance.[11] Organizations are quite likely to have multiple and conflicting goals, making simultaneous achievement impossible. Outputs and outcomes are likely to be as ambiguous as the goals themselves, resulting in the development and use of subjective and arbitrary indicators of achievement. Members' goals are likely to conflict with organizational goals; clientele's goals are equally likely to conflict with organizational goals; and the goals of individual units conflict with each other. Short-term goals may conflict with long-term goals. Technology to achieve goals may be unknown or inadequate.

Even when goals are clear, few in number, and agreed on by all participants and when their achievement is subject to quantitative measurement, their accomplishment or nonaccomplishment may have little to do with the organization's efforts or performance. Performance may be attributable to factors beyond the control of the organization. Variations in inputs, particularly clients, may more strongly determine variations in outputs than anything the organization does.[12] A high school in an upper–middle class suburb clearly has a different clientele than one in a central city low income neighborhood. Neither has control over its clientele, but the clientele are largely determinative of the quality of output. Similarly, environmental conditions beyond the control of the organization can either encourage or impede the accomplishment of goals, so two organizations identical in every respect can still have very different performance ratings. But if organizational efforts have no relationship to performance, why should one organization be considered more effective than the other?

Simon established that organizations and individuals do not attempt to maximize attainment of goals; they satisfice. Which leads to one of the underlying themes of this book: organizations are not rational; individuals are not rational; society is not rational; and most assuredly, politics is not rational. The goal-based approach to organizational effectiveness is clearly grounded in rationalism, and despite its inadequacies as a descriptive theory, it remains one of the dominant myths of this society. That is why goal-based approaches remain the dominant approaches to assessing organizations.

Their dominance is particularly pronounced in the public sector, where they have the least validity. Anyone even vaguely familiar with program evaluation will recognize the pervasiveness of goal-based approaches. One of the ironies of program evaluation is that its staunchest proponents and practitioners are clearly aware of its largest problem: the problem of goals. Goals must be identified before the evaluation can proceed, and because goals are elusive, a variety of techniques, all scientifically objectionable, are recommended for deriving (making up) goals: the legislative history of the program may be checked; official statements of politicians and agency officials may provide goals; the understanding of the policy by affected interest groups may be used; goals may be "translated" from vague policy language by the evaluator; goals most consistent with the evaluators' research requirements; or a preferred methodology may be used.[13] What is true for goals is equally true for objective performance indicators: when in doubt, make them up. The image of rationalism is more important than the reality.

Despite all this, under certain limited circumstances, the goal-based approach may be a valid method of assessing organizational effectiveness. Thompson suggested that the nature of goals and technology should determine the methodology and criteria used to measure organizational effectiveness. In Thompson's typology, goals and output measures were classified as either clear or ambiguous. Technology, or what he termed cause-effect relationships (the degree of knowledge concerning the relationship between organization actions and outcomes), were classified as either complete or incomplete. Figure 11–1 summarizes the resulting typology and evaluation criteria.

FIGURE 11–1.   Contingency Framework for Measuring Effectiveness

CAUSE-EFFECT RELATIONSHIPS

		Complete	Incomplete
CLARITY OF GOAL/OUTPUT STANDARDS	*Clear*	Goal achievement: efficiency criteria Examples: Fire departments (for fire suppression), the postal service, city water departments	Goal achievement: output criteria Examples: baseball teams, National Institutes of Health, fire departments (for prevention)
	Ambiguous	Internal process criteria: satisfaction of organizational climate Examples: research and development organizations; Rand Institute	Social criteria: satisfaction of external constituencies Examples: schools, human service agencies, Department of Defense

Source: Adapted from James A. Thompson, *Organizations in Action* (New York: McGraw Hill, 1967) p. 86.

For those organizations or activities in which goals are clear and the organization members know exactly what must be done to accomplish the goals, not only is goal achievement an appropriate measure of effectiveness but efficiency is also an appropriate criterion. The fire suppression activities of a fire department fit into this category: the fire department knows exactly what it is supposed to do, and better yet, it knows exactly how to do it. Unfortunately, fire departments also have another major goal. And though it is clear and does not conflict with fire suppression, fire prevention cannot be achieved with the same certainty that fire suppression can. Fires are caused by many factors, including human behavior, and the knowledge of how to prevent fires is incomplete and in many circumstances beyond the jurisdiction of the fire department. Even so, the fire department engages in many activities aimed at fire prevention, and the effectiveness of those activities can be measured by the number of fires per population. Thompson might not agree with placing the National Institutes of Health in this category because they are research organizations and it seems a little unfair to measure their effectiveness by the sole criterion of output, but nevertheless they do know what they are trying to accomplish: to find successful methods of preventing, treating, and curing diseases. They just do not quite know how to do that, so cancer, AIDS, arthritis, and other diseases remain serious health problems.

Pure research organizations, such as the Rand Institute, have only the most general of goals, although their research methodologies are likely to be precise, quantitative, and technical. It is not at all clear what they are supposed to produce, so goal output measures are inappropriate. Thompson suggests instead that they be evaluated according to internal process criteria, perhaps because those measures associated with job satisfaction and organizational climate are presumed to be strongly correlated with creative activity. The fourth quadrant is for those organizations that do not know exactly what they are supposed to be achieving and, even if they did, would not know how to do it—in other words, schools, human service agencies, the Department of Defense, and a wide variety of other public agencies. For this type of organization, goal-based measures are, if not absurd, at least misleading. Thompson suggests that the appropriate criteria for these organizations are social criteria that measure how satisfied external constituencies are with the organization, which ironically will turn out to be a different sort of goal-based measure. Each constituency will have its own perception of organization goals, and its level of satisfaction will be determined by the extent to which the organization has achieved those goals.

Even if one concedes that organizations are irrational, it is still difficult, intellectually and practically, to ignore goal accomplishment when considering whether an organization is effective. This is partly because the concept of goals is inherent in the definition of an organization; without goals there would be no organization, and without organizations there would be no organization theory.[14] Consequently, perhaps goals should be handled in organizational effectiveness studies just as they are in organizations: made operational, prioritized, viewed as variable constraints over time, recognized and accepted in their multiplicity and diversity, and used as one of many criteria for determining effectiveness.

THE SYSTEMS APPROACH

The focus of systems theory generally is on the relationship of the organization and its environment. As an open system, the organization depends on the environment for the resources for organizational functioning and for accepting the organization's output. The overriding goal of the organization in systems theory is survival, which has little connection with the organization's ability to accomplish substantive goals. Organizations that fail to accomplish goals do not necessarily fail, and those that achieve their goals do not necessarily survive. This is clearly true in the public sector, where many organizations have been assigned unachieveable goals, and if by some quirk those goals were achieved, the organization would have no reason to continue to exist. If poverty were eliminated, we would not have organizations to alleviate the problems associated with it. Such organizations would either have to acquire new goals, as did the March of Dimes when polio was effectively eliminated, or face extinction. Nonetheless, this is not to contend that substantive goals are completely irrelevant to organizational survival. Substantive goals serve important symbolic functions and are necessary for establishing legitimacy and attracting resources from the environment.[15]

If survival is the ultimate measure of organizational effectiveness, the intermediate criteria of effectiveness are the organization's ability to control and manipulate its environment, acquire inputs, process those inputs, and maintain stability. Effectiveness is "the ability of the organization, in either relative or absolute terms, to exploit its environment in the acquisition of scarce and valuable resources. It is most effective when it maximizes its bargaining position and optimizes its resource procurements."[16] This depends on the organization's ability to establish and maintain a successful bargaining position with the environment, which requires at a minimum the ability to perceive and correctly interpret the real properties of the environment and to respond to changes in the environment.[17]

Successful maintenance of organization-environment relationships requires continual surveillance of the environment so that reactions to organizational outputs are monitored and, if necessary, adjustments in those outputs made. With a complex and dynamic environment, such as many public organizations have, this can be particularly difficult. Outputs desired and demanded by one set of environmental actors, the presidency for example, may be received with hostility by another set of environmental actors, Congress for example. The effective organization successfully negotiates with these conflicting actors to avoid negative consequences.[18]

The key measure of effectiveness—the ability to maintain an optimum balance in the organizational-environmental transaction—poses two major problems. First, no one has ever defined what optimum is, and this probably cannot be defined. So both evaluators and the organization itself find it almost impossible to determine the organization's actual level of effectiveness. For the organization, this poses an additional problem. In the pursuit of resources, organizations are tempted to extract not the optimal level (whatever that is) but the maximum level of resources. The danger in that course of action is that in its greed the organization may deplete its resource base and also stimulate countervailing forces in the environment.[19] Thus an organization constantly increasing its resources may give the appearance of being effective, but it may in reality be undermining its future potential for effectiveness.

To a certain extent this is what governments at all levels in the United States did in the 1960s and 1970s. They grew in both resources and responsibility at an impressive rate, but this growth was accompanied by a growing perception on the part of taxpayers and politicians that they were overutilizing their resource base. These perceptions formed the basis for countervailing pressures, which eventually resulted in Proposition 13 and the Reagan administration. What systems criteria leaves unanswered is whether government was effective during those years of growth or whether it exceeded the optimal balance and consequently should be considered ineffective. A similar situation existed in the Department of Defense during the early years of the Reagan administration. From the short-term perspective, it was effective. It succeeded, when other federal agencies were failing, in increasing its resource base; but in the process of doing that, it antagonized significant groups in its environment. From the long-term perspective, the result may well be diminished capability to demand more resources. Again, it remains unclear whether it should be considered effective.

Other measures of effectiveness in systems theory only partially clarify the ambiguity of the base measure. The other measures direct attention to the organization's internal processes and use of resources, and are primarily efficiency measures. "To assess an organization's effectiveness, one should try to find out whether an organization is internally consistent, whether its resources are being judiciously distributed over a wide variety of coping mechanisms, whether it is using up resources faster than it should and so forth."[20] In addition, one should try to determine whether the organization is efficiently using resources to produce a specified output. These internal processes can be measured by comparing inputs to outputs.[21] For this to be possible, outputs must be clearly and quantitatively specified (which again for public organizations is not always simple or, for that matter, desirable). For some it works well: tax collection agencies, for example, can measure the amount of taxes collected. For schools, mental health clinics, or environmental protection agencies, the output measures are more problematic and run into the same difficulties as goal measures. Internal processes are more difficult to measure, and again no absolute standards exist. Effectiveness is always relative, but little guidance is provided for selecting suitable comparisons.

Using systems criteria provides a valid measure of the relative power of an organization and can help us understand how the organization is utilizing its resources. What should not be overlooked are the values implicit in open systems theory: growth, efficiency, quantity (but not necessarily quality), means (processes) rather than ends (results). Although they may be acceptable values to apply to business enterprises, they are not the values normally applied to the political system. Using them as standards of effectiveness is in effect saying that these are the values the organizations should internalize and that the good organization will pursue them to the exclusion of other values.

The Strategic Constituencies Approach

The strategic constituencies approach may be classified as both an open systems approach and a political approach to measuring organizational effectiveness. It shares with the open-systems approach an emphasis on the environment as the primary determinant of organizational effectiveness. Open systems uses the amount of resources extracted from the environment as the primary measure of effectiveness; strategic constituencies looks instead to the key actors in the organization's environment as the judges of its effectiveness. Open systems theory is compatible with a rational concept of organizations, at least to the extent that it views organizations as purposive entities pursuing an overriding, albeit nonsubstantive, goal, but the strategic constituencies approach starts from the premise that organizations are not necessarily rational. They are instead viewed basically as bargaining arenas where individuals and groups compete to secure outputs that they desire.[22] Those individuals and groups have their own perceptions and definitions of the organization's goals, and they evaluate its effectiveness on the basis of how well it satisfies their desires and needs. Strategic constituencies is the pluralist approach to evaluating organizational effectiveness.

As is true with pluralism, the strategic constituencies approach recognizes that not all groups or individuals are equal, at least in the sense that not all their opinions and evaluations are to be weighted equally. A constituency is any group that has a stake in the organization's performance.[23] Thus alcoholics and drug addicts are constituencies for a drug and alcohol rehabilitation agency; prisoners are a constituency for a prison.

Theoretically, they are even strategic constituencies: a strategic constituency is any group from whom the organization requires support for its continued existence.[24] If the addicts and alcoholics absolutely refuse to participate in the agency's programs or if the prisoners, as they did at Attica, break into open, prolonged, and violent resistance, the organization's existence would be endangered. But as strategic constituencies go, both groups are likely to be viewed as relatively unimportant and powerless.

Use of the strategic constituencies approach requires first that the organization's strategic constituencies be identified. Most organizations are likely to be very aware of who those constituencies are because they are critical to the organization's survival. For the outside evaluator, it may not be quite so obvious; strategic constituencies satisfied with the organization's performance may be quiescent and appear uninterested in the organization, somewhat similar to latent or potential groups in pluralist theory. Because their silence and inactivity may be interpreted as approval, this is likely to indicate that they feel the organization is effective.

Once strategic constituencies are identified, their expectations and demands relating to organizational performance must be determined. Again, although the theory makes this seem relatively simple, in reality it is not likely to be simple at all. Expectations are not always clearly articulated; like goals, they are likely to be vague and ambiguous, and even a single constituency may have conflicting expectations. Congress is a strategic constituency for the Department of Health and Human Services (DHHS), but Congress is a diverse institution. Trying to ascertain its collective expectations for that department is in reality the same as trying to determine what the department's substantive goals are: exceedingly difficult. The presidency, though less diverse, presents no easier determination and raises the question of which demands—yesterday's, today's, or tomorrow's—should be used as guides to performance expectations. At least with single-issue interest groups, ascertaining their expectations is relatively simple: the expectations of right-to-life groups from DHHS are clearly articulated and well understood even if they conflict with the expectations of other single-issue groups. The resulting list of the expectations of strategic constituencies is in fact a list of the perceived goals of the organization and criteria of effectiveness.

If to this point operationalizing this approach has been difficult, it now becomes even more complex. The resulting list of goals and criteria for many public organizations will be the same conflicting mishmash encountered in the goals approach. The president has different criteria than Congress; within Congress, the appropriations committee has different criteria than the substantive, authorizing committees; the right-to-life groups have different criteria than the pro-choice groups. At this point the evaluator must assign relative power weights to each of the constituencies, which is at best an imprecise exercise and at worst an impossible one.

Does the president have more power than Congress over an agency? Or, in strategic constituencies terminology, who has the most control over the agency's continued existence? Theoretically, Congress would seem to because only it may abolish agencies and only it may pass appropriations. But practically, the president has a vast array of powers that can be used to reduce the agency's existence to meaninglessness. If power is determined to be equal and if expectations are conflicting, the strategic constituencies approach gives us no conclusion as to the effectiveness of the agency.

The proponents of the strategic constituencies approach make determination of effectiveness seem deceptively easy:

> Effectiveness in organizations is not a thing, or a goal, or a characteristic of organizational outputs or behavior, but rather a state of relations within and among relevant constituencies of the organization. An effective organization is one that is able to fashion accounts of itself and its activities in ways which constituencies find acceptable.[25]

From a practical perspective, the approach appears to be feasible with only a limited number of organizations: those with homogeneous, simple, and stable environments. For those organizations, the approach is relatively easy to operationalize, and using it will give a clear-cut assessment of the organization's perceived effectiveness. For organizations whose environments are complex, dynamic, and populated with diverse and conflicting constituencies, the approach is difficult to operationalize and will give no clear measure of effectiveness. Strategic constituencies cannot be identified easily or with certainty; their power standings are not clear; and conflicting perspectives cannot be reconciled. For organizations in this situation, pleasing some of the constituencies some of the time is the best to be expected, but whether that equates with effectiveness is debatable.

From a normative perspective, for public organizations the strategic constituencies approach has both desirable and undesirable aspects. Its strength lies in its presumption that effectiveness must be evaluated in terms of organizational responsiveness. The effective organization is one that is responsive to demands from its environment, and this is an important political value in our system. Its weakness lies in its response to the question of to whom the organization should be responsive. To contend that the effective organization should be responsive to the most powerful actors in its environment may be realistic, but it is contrary to democratic values and lends itself to the classic flaw of interest group liberalism: those that have get more, and the public interest is lost in the process.

THE COMPETING VALUES APPROACH

Concepts of the good organization are clearly value judgments derived from the beliefs, interests, and perspectives of the evaluator. The evaluator determines what the most important aspects of organization processes and behavior are or should be and what its ultimate goals should be. That determination made, the evaluator proceeds to ascertain how close the organization in question is to what it is supposed to be. The values that underlie assessments of organizational effectiveness are diverse and conflicting. The competing values approach identifies three dimensions of organizations that are the sources of value conflicts among evaluators: organizational focus, organization structure, and closeness of organizational outcomes, means, or ends, that should be the primary concern of evaluators.[26] From these three sets of competing values, four models of what organizations should be are derived: the human relations model, the internal process model, the open systems model, and the rational goal model. Each model is complete with its own criteria for evaluating organizational effectiveness.

The organizational focus dimension centers on whether the primary concern of the organization and evaluators should be internal or external. Those who support an internal focus believe organizations should be viewed as sociotechnical systems whose primary concern should be the development of their own resources and processes. Those who favor an external focus view organizations as rational enterprises that should be primarily concerned with ultimate goal achievement or the maintenance of a supportive environment. Based on this focus only, Kilmann and Herdon developed a model for evaluating organizations on both effectiveness and efficiency.[27] The resulting matrix (Figure 11–2) is very similar to that resulting from the overall competing values approach, raising the possibility that the major conflicts in values are over internal versus external focus and effectiveness versus efficiency as the primary evaluation criteria.

FIGURE 11–2. Domain Framework for Organizational Evaluation

ORGANIZATIONAL FOCUS

		Internal	*External*
EVALUATION CRITERIA	*Efficiency*	Focus of Evaluation: Outputs to inputs Measure: Cost per unit of output	Focus: Bargaining position with environment Measure: Amount of resources, change in resources
	Effectiveness	Focus: Employee satisfaction Measures: Turnover, absenteeism, organization climate, employee commitment, interpersonal relations	Focus: Constituent and societal satisfaction Measures: Community satisfaction surveys

Published with permission from: Ralph H. Kilmann and Richard P. Herdon, "Towards a Systematic Methodology For Evaluating the Impact of Interventions on Organizational Effectiveness," *Academy of Management Review* (1976): p. 89–90.

The structural variables that are identified as the major source of conflict are control and flexibility. Those who favor bureaucratic structure tend to do so because they believe it maximizes the overall capability of the organizational hierarchy to maintain control over the organization and its members. This control ensures better ability to accomplish organization goals and ensure conformity in members. Proponents of control as a necessary aspect of organization functioning also tend to favor stability as an important requisite to proper functioning. At the opposite end of the spectrum are those theorists who believe that flexibility is the most essential aspect of an effective organization structure (e.g., the organic structure of Burns and Stalker, the temporary organization of Bennis). Flexibility allows the organization to adapt quickly to environmental changes, to treat individuals as individuals, and it encourages innovation and creativity.

The conflict over organizational outcomes has two aspects: ends versus means and, more basic, what ends and means are best. Some organization theorists concentrate on the ultimate ends or substantive goals of organizations as the primary focus for effectiveness, and they usually agree on the appropriate means for accomplishing those ends, but the means are always less important than the ends. Other theorists focus on processes, means, as the most important aspect of organizational effectiveness, either implicitly or explicitly asserting that the most effective means guarantee the most effective accomplishment of goals. For them, however, means are more of a concern than goal accomplishment, and their concept of the appropriate ends of the organization is phrased in terms other than goal accomplishment. Figure 11–3 summarizes the four approaches that result from the competing values approach.

The rational goal model of organization is the basis of goal approaches discussed previously. It is also the rational bureaucratic model of Max Weber. Its methods of control, in addition to goal setting, planning, monitoring, and evaluation, should by now be familiar: emphasis on regulations, rules, and informal behavioral expectations. Its faith in rationality is exemplified by its belief in the necessity and possibility of strategic planning, policy analysis, and rational decision making.

The open systems model also emphasizes an external focus, but rather than being on the outputs of the organization, the emphasis is on the environment and the crucial role it plays in determining organizational effectiveness. Only if the environment, or key actors in the environment, views the organization as effective will the resources and supports necessary for organizational functioning and survival be forthcoming. Consequently, the organization must constantly monitor the environment and be attuned to any changes occurring within it. Whether those changes are threatening or supportive, the organization must be able to respond to them quickly. Thus, the means emphasized are flexibility, adaptability, and the willingness and ability to bargain and negotiate with key actors. Sub-

FIGURE 11–3. **Competing Values Model of Organizational Effectiveness**

STRUCTURAL VARIABLES

		Flexibility	Control
ORGANIZATIONAL FOCUS	*Internal*	*Human Relations Model* **Means:*** Development of employee morale, satisfaction, cohesion Ends: Human resource development	*Internal Process Model* **Means:*** Management information systems; internal communication systems; internal transformation of inputs (T/I) Ends: Control, stability
	External	*Open Systems Model* Means: Flexibility, adaptability, bargaining **Ends:*** Growth, resource acquisition	*Rational Goal Model* Means: Planning, goal setting, evaluation **Ends:*** Goal achievement, productivity, efficiency

*Boldface print indicates model emphasis.
Source: Adapted from John Rohrbaugh, "The Competing Values Approach: Innovation and Effectiveness in the Job Service," in Richard H. Hall and Robert E. Quinn, *Organizational Theory and Public Policy* (Beverly Hills, Calif.: Sage Publications, Inc., 1983), p. 267.

stantive goals are as much subject to flexibility and bargaining as any other aspect of the organization. The observers judge organizational effectiveness—success—by organizational ability to acquire resources and grow.

The Internal Process Approach

The internal process model shifts focus to the internal functions of the organization. It shares Herbert Simon's emphasis on the importance of internal communications and providing adequate information at the right time and to the right people. The primary means emphasized are management information systems, which ensure the proper flow of information and facilitate management control. Control is one of the desired ends of the organization; the other is stability. The good organization is one whose internal operations are characterized by smoothness, minimal conflict, orderliness, continuity, and predictability. Internal process approaches are also likely to stress efficiency as a criterion for organizational effectiveness. The smoothly running organization of their model transforms inputs into outputs with a minimal waste of resources.[28] In many respects, the internal process model is very similar to the concept of organization implicit in the scientific management of Frederick Taylor as well as to Simon's newer management science: the organization as a smoothly running machine.

The Human Relations Approach

The human relations model's focus is on the people in the organization, and the satisfaction of their needs is the most important end of the organization. The means for achieving this have been described throughout this book: job enrichment, democratic management, and creating an organization climate that maximizes job satisfaction and encourages the self actualization of individuals. To do this, the organization must be flexible not in response to the environment but to the needs and demands of individuals. The desired end of the organization is the fullest development of the capabilities of its human resources.

Although the models present sharply contrasting formulations of organizational effectiveness, the underlying similarity is that when all the differences are eliminated, the models are all goal based, and beyond that they are substantive goal-based models. It is not by whim, caprice, or error that the concept of goals is inherent in every definition of organizations. Organizations are created to pursue, if not necessarily to achieve, substantive goals. They are not created to achieve stability or control; they are not created to grow; they are not created to pursue efficiency; they are not created to satisfy the needs of employees. They are created because their creators have some purpose in mind that they wish to see accomplished. Most assuredly, the goals of the creators may not be the ones that the organization ends up trying to accomplish. That has been clearly established. But if not these goals, then operational goals created by the organization become the raison d'etre for its operations and continued existence. Without some kind of substantive, operational goals, the organization will cease to exist; in reality what differentiates the models is disagreement over the best ways to accomplish those goals. Open systems theories believe the best way is by being responsive to the environment; internal process theories believe the right internal control sytems guarantee success; rational goal theories believe rational planning and control is best; and human relations theorists believe that satisfying employees will result in maximal effectiveness. As to which theory is right, we simply do not know. There is no overwhelming empirical evidence to support any contention that has been made in organization theory. Contingency theory offers not the answer, but at least the approach: it all depends. Unfortunately at this point, we do not even know on what it all depends.

NONE OF THE ABOVE

One of the most peculiar descriptions of the effective organization has been offered by Karl Weick. Weick suggests that the effective organization is "(1) garrulous, (2) clumsy, (3) superstitious, (4) hypocritical, (5) monstrous, (6) octopoid, (7) wandering, and (8) grouchy."[29] These are not qualities likely to meet with the approval of theorists of the other approaches, but Weick's explanation is, if not completely persuasive, at least interesting. Effectiveness begins with garrulousness: the effective organization talks a lot. It talks to itself and to its environment continuously, about what it has done, what it should have done, what it might have done, and what it might or will do in the future.

The organization is clumsy, stumbling around and not adapting smoothly or quickly to changed circumstances. Although adaptability is frequently highly touted as an organizational virtue, it has its disadvantages. "Whenever people adapt to a particular situation, they lose some of the resources that would enable them to adapt to different situations in the future."[30] By being slightly backward, an organization can profit from the mistakes of more advanced organizations that constantly plan and quickly adapt, not necessarily successfully, to changed circumstances. Similarly, decisions are not made rationally, hence effective organizations are "superstitious." Rationality frequently results in predictability, not just for the organization practicing it but also for its adversaries. One of the advantages of being nonrational or irrational is that the resulting behavior is unpredictable; another is that it avoids overreliance on past experience and the knowledge derived from it, which is not necessarily valid in changed circumstances.

The hypocritical organization is ambivalent, and its words and its deeds frequently contradict. Although we seldom think of it as such, hypocrisy is one of the most common methods of adaptation for human beings. Hypocrites, and at one time or another we are all hypocrites, enjoy the advantage of being able to cling to past beliefs while adapting their behavior to current reality, and when reality changes, as it frequently does, to reassert their beliefs. As it is with individuals, so it is with organizations. This may be especially important for public organizations, for change in political control or political climate requires a change in behavior without abandonment of traditional beliefs and orientations.

Evolution proceeds through mutation, but mutants are frequently regarded as freaks and, in human society, destroyed before they reach maturity. Organizational mutations are equally likely to be regarded as deviations from the acceptable; they will be eliminated, and evolution will be halted. That is why the effective organization does not automatically destroy its "monsters" but allows them to continue to exist. Over time, of course, the organization itself may become a bit monstrous to conventional eyes, but its survival and effectiveness may be directly attributable to that monstrousness.

The octopus is an ungainly creature with a small brain and several tentacles that are neurally poorly connected that has managed to survive as a species for a very long time. Many organizations, and especially many public organizations, are like octopuses: the garbage can organizations described by Cohen and March. Again, to conventional eyes they appear to be monsters, but in reality they may be very effective organizations, effective in the only way possible given their environments, multiplicity of goals, technology, social expectations, and employees. Octopuses wander; they do not seem to have any specific destination in mind as they amble around the ocean. For Weick, that too may be a characteristic of an effective organization; if so, that too is good news for public organizations, for public organizations do wander a lot. Certainly the State Department and Department of Defense do; schools and universities do; welfare agencies do. In the process of their wandering, they employ a lot of people, engage in interesting activities, help people who need it, and keep children off the street. To Weick that is effective.

Finally, Weick believes that effective organizations and their members are grouchy; they complain constantly, and they are never satisfied. While this is the organizational humanist's epitome of the bad organization, for Weick dissatisfaction and complaints may be signs of healthy organizations and individuals. The absence of dissatisfaction or complaints may indicate complacency, or worse, despair. The self-satisfied person or organization does not complain but does not change much either, and complacency is dangerous in a dynamic environment. Those who have lost hope and resigned themselves to circumstances rarely complain either. Only those who want change and believe that it is possible complain. Only those who know there is something better or more are dissatisfied. Only unsatisfied needs motivate; only expressed complaints receive response. As complaints are voiced and sources of dissatisfaction removed, new complaints and dissatisfaction, of a higher level, will emerge. That is how organizations progress.

Effectiveness is in the eyes of the beholder, and the effective organization in Weick's eyes is unlike that of most other theorists. His view is particularly appropriate for public organizations because of the circumstances under which they have traditionally operated and because of new circumstances, particularly those of fiscal scarcity, under which they must operate for the foreseeable future. All of the other approaches are based on assumptions about the circumstances under which organizations operate that do not hold true for many contemporary public organizations. They assume that goals are clear, or that resources are plentiful and easily available, or that the environment is predictable, or that constituency expectations are clearly identifiable and the relative power of constituencies determinable, or that organizations have the ability to satisfy all the needs of their employees. To the extent that these assumptions are not valid, the measures of effectiveness derived from them are equally invalid, and the assumptions do not hold true for most public organizations.

THE EFFECTIVE PUBLIC ORGANIZATION

General organization theory offers a variety of methods to measure organizational effectiveness even if it provides no definitive, universally agreed on criteria. All of the approaches have been and may be applied to public organizations, but even with the multiplicity of approaches, some of the most important aspects of evaluating public organizations remain untouched. To reiterate, judgments about organizational effectiveness are value judgments, and the ascendant values in organization theory are organizational values. Public organizations are more than organizations; they are political entities whose performance and behavior determine the overall nature and quality of the political system. Any overall assessment of their performance must include political values in addition to organizational values, which compounds the difficulty of assessing their effectiveness.

Even the application of general organizational effectiveness criteria is more complex with public than with private organizations. The problems in measuring goal attainment have been covered previously, but they should not be ignored or underestimated. Ironically, despite the recognized problems of the goal approach, it is one of the most frequent approaches used to evaluate at least specific programs of organizations, if not entire organizations. Technical evaluators, whose underlying values emphasize rationality, have not been and will not be discouraged by the problems of vague, multiple, conflicting, or nonexistent goals. When all else fails, they choose what they believe the goals should be and proceed to evaluate attainment of those goals.

Efficiency is equally difficult to determine for many public agencies. Organizations that produce collective goods, such as the Department of Defense, the State Department, and public safety organizations pose nearly insuperable difficulties to measuring their efficiency. Efficiency is the ratio of inputs to outputs, but when outputs cannot be identified or attributed to a specific organization, the measurement of efficiency becomes extremely subjective. Nakamura and Smallwood offer the example of the Strategic Air Command (SAC).[31] Its goal is to prevent war through the development of nuclear deterrence. Its output might be viewed as no nuclear war. Determination of its efficiency by the standard method is meaningless: you can't divide cost by the avoidance of nuclear war. Consequently, indirect measures of efficiency are used: cost trends and individual expenditures are used as surrogate measures. Of course, what we do not know is whether the output, no nuclear war, is attributable to SAC's activities. Any organization that produces intangible outputs presents the same problem in measuring efficiency, and the problems are overcome by similar methodologies. Schools' efficiency is frequently measured by cost per student, but students are not really their outputs—they are in fact one of the inputs. This does not seem to matter; efficiency must be measured if that is what the evaluator's values require.

Certainly, some public organizations are much more suited to goal attainment and efficiency measures than the examples in the preceding paragraphs. Fire departments, sanitation departments, tax collection agencies, water departments, and highway departments produce tangible, measureable outputs that are directly associated with their assigned goals. But even with agencies of this nature, such outputs are only partial measures of goal accomplishment. What is true of efficiency is equally true of productivity, as was discussed in Chapter 9. It can be measured, but the possibility that the wrong thing or not enough of the outputs are being measured always remains.

Growth and resource acquisition, the primary systems criteria, also seem irrelevant as measures of effectiveness in the current environment of massive federal deficits and decreased resource availability. Survival may be a more appropriate measure, and protection of core organizational programs from emasculation even more so. If the criterion is switched to responsiveness to environmental changes and adaptability, which are also systems criteria, then, ironically, the effective organization may be one that seeks or accepts diminished resources and adjusts to the decrease. Fiscal scarcity also clearly affects organizational ability to satisfy the demands of the human relations model. In Chapter 9, a description of the maximally motivating organization was provided. Presumably, if an organization could satisfy the requirement of that description, it would rank high on human relations criteria (and possibly even on goal attainment). Unfortunately, organizations suffering from decreased resource availability are not going to be able to avoid serious employee morale and satisfaction problems. Reality and fairness indicate that a new set of criteria for measuring treatment of employees be derived for organizations experiencing decline.

Adding political values to the measure of effectiveness is a necessary complication for an already tangled process. While we may be able to agree on the dominant political values, the agreement will shatter when operational definitions and measurable criteria have to be developed. That the dominant political values conflict further complicates the task of effectiveness. The dominant political values applicable to public organizations are responsiveness, accountability, representativeness, constitutionality, and democracy. By those values, we judge our political system; by those values we must also judge our public organizations.

Responsiveness requires that organizations be aware of and receptive to and accede to the needs and desires of whoever the definer thinks they should respond to. Responsiveness to the public is certainly one possibility, but determining what the public desires is seldom easy. Public opinion is volatile, unclear, and frequently based on little knowledge concerning the issue at hand. The general public is likely to be unaware of or unconcerned with many specific public organizations. Some organizations do use citizen satisfaction surveys as a measure, and somewhat surprisingly, most of the time, for most organizations, most of the people are relatively satisfied.[32] The argument has been made that the public rarely knows what it needs and that responsiveness really requires an organization to ascertain their true needs and then respond to those rather than to expressed needs. For organizations with low public visibility, this may be an appropriate concept of responsiveness. Others argue that agencies should be responsive to their clientele: welfare agencies should be responsive to the needs and desires of the poor, which unfortunately may cause conflict with public desires. The strategic constituencies approach believes that organizations should be responsive to the most powerful of their constituent groups, which infuriates critics of interest group liberalism such as Theodore Lowi. It is certainly possible that public organizations should be primarily responsive to their political superiors, who in turn may be assumed to be responsive to the public or to interest groups. Of course, under a system of separation of powers, the political superiors may be in disagreement, and no clear-cut solution to responsiveness in that situation exists. Federalism adds the further complication of determining which publics, groups, and political superiors at which level of government should be the focus of responsiveness.

Accountability runs into the same definitional problems. Public organizations must be accountable if they are to be accorded legitimacy, but the same set of contenders exists as to whom they should be accountable: the people, the legislature, the executive, their clientele, different levels of government, and two new contenders: the laws and the courts. The courts frequently see things from a different perspective than elected officials, both executive and legislative. Whose interpretation of the laws does the accountable organization follow?

Representation has been defined and measured in various ways. Two concepts of representation overlap with responsiveness: to represent can be defined as either acting in the best interests of the constituency or as acting on the expressed wishes of the constituency. Representation encounters the same problems of how to ascertain best interests or expressed wishes and how to define constituency as responsiveness did. At least with elected representatives, an agreed on measure of effectiveness exists: the outcome of the representatives' next election. With organizations staffed with nonelected personnel, no clear-cut measure exists. The third concept of representation, virtual representation, establishes a different set of requirements. Virtual representation requires that the aggregate composition of the representative institution resemble as closely as possible the demographic composition of the aggregate constituencies. If women constitute 51 percent of the population, 51 percent of the representative institution should be women; and minorities and whatever other socioeconomic groups are deemed relevant for representational purposes should also receive proportional representation. Affirmative action and equal employment opportunity are aimed at satisfying this concept of representation.

No public organization can be considered to be truly effective if it violates the Constitution. The Constitution resembles many of our laws: it is vague, general, and subject to conflicting interpretations. As many public organizations have discovered, the due process clauses of the Fifth and Fourteenth Amendments must be complied with or the organization and its members may be sued and their actions nullified. Due process, however, is a complex and evolving concept, and what was acceptable last year may not be acceptable this year. Due process can also be slow and inefficient and can interfere with goal achievement. All of the freedoms in the Bill of Rights should be respected and protected by public agencies, but again, conflicting interpretations of their meaning make this difficult, and sometimes the organization cannot comply unless it violates some other law or provision of the Constitution. The Eighth Amendment prohibits cruel and unusual punishment; the courts have said that crowded, unsanitary prison conditions are cruel and unusual punishment. Legislatures, however, have looked with increasing favor on mandatory prison sentences and with little favor on providing sufficient funds to alleviate prison conditions. The equal protection clause of the Fourteenth Amendment requires that no group be singled out and treated in a discriminatory manner. Opponents of affirmative action contend that it does exactly that for white males, but experience teaches that without it women and minorities will not be treated equally. Freedom of the press may conflict with the defendant's right to a fair trial before an impartial jury, and the Fourth Amendment can impede agency efficiency.

Other conflicts exist in basic democratic values. Individualism and individual freedom conflict with equality; property rights conflict with human rights. Many argue that democracy applies to the internal processes of public organization just as it does to their treatment of citizens. Yet maximization of internal democracy may result in decisions and actions contrary to the wishes of the political institutions and in conflict with both responsiveness and accountability. Justice may conflict with both equal protection and due process because true justice is individualized. Procedural justice and substantive justice are two discrete and very different concepts.

No resolution of these conflicts is likely, and consequently no agreement on the performance of the public sector is possible. Despite the difficulties, public organizations are evaluated all the time. The public, the media, the politicians, the courts, political scientists, public administrators, public employees, and other organizations regularly judge the performance of public organizations. All the judgments are based on the values of the judges, and the result is a lack of consistency and clarity in the overall assessment of any specific organization or the public sector generally. Admittedly, this proliferation of vague and conflicting evaluative criteria makes life difficult for those who manage public organizations. As Denhardt noted, it puts

> administrators in a sort of "double-bind," a damned if you do, damned if you don't situation. On the one hand, administrators have been told to be proactive; on the other hand, they have been told to show restraint. On the one hand, they have been attacked for being unresponsive, on the other hand for being overly responsive. They have been encouraged to be efficient, yet criticized for the coldness and impersonality that constrained efficiency produces.[33]

From a broader perspective, this lack of consensus on the effectiveness of public sector organizations is not necessarily bad, and in fact it does produce positive results for the overall political system and perhaps for the organizations themselves. First, business organizations have not proven any easier to evaluate than public organizations; and those who believe that they are believe so out of ignorance. A knowledge of the complexities of assessing organizational effectiveness generally should help alleviate some of the negative consequences of the bias that "business does it better." Maybe, but that depends on what "it" is; for some "its," not even the best businesses do it any better than public organizations. Searching for excellence is always admirable, but the excellence found may not be excellence for everyone or in all situations. Second, our society is characterized by conflicting values, and so is our political system. Consequently, those conflicting values should be reflected in assessment of our public organizations, for without conflict the diversity of opinion in our society is not reflected. Further, the conflicting assessments help ensure both accountability and responsiveness. The knowledge that they will be subjected to scrutiny and judged by conflicting standards helps ensure that organizations will not be able in the long run to ignore any of their evaluators. They will learn to adjust to shifting expectations and demands from various sources and in the process will be reminded that they are accountable to a variety of institutions and groups, and this facilitates responsiveness as well. Even for the organization, the multiple and conflicting criteria of effectiveness have advantages. They translate into the reality that there are many ways to demonstrate effectiveness and that if they fall short on one criterion, they may excel on others. At a minimum, the multiple criteria provide a "yes, but" defense for weak performance: "Yes, we did not do so well on eliminating crime, but that is because we tried to respect all persons' constitutional rights."

In Chapter 6, it was pointed out that conflict is good; it is not something to be suppressed, ignored, or avoided. Out of conflict come progress, innovation, and creativity. The conflict over measures of effectiveness of organizations offers the same advantages. In the absence of conflict, complacency and stagnation may result. Admittedly this makes theory untidy and incomplete, but so is reality.

CONCLUSION

Gareth Morgan, explaining the contrasting images of organizations that emerge from the diverse theoretical approaches, likened organizational theory to the fable of the six blind men describing the elephant:

> The first feels a tusk, claiming the animal to be like a spear. The second, feeling the elephant's side, proclaims that it is more like a wall. Feeling a leg, the third describes it as a tree; and a fourth, feeling the elephant's trunk, is inclined to think it like a snake. The fifth, who has seized the elephant's ear, thinks it remarkably like a fan; and the sixth, grabbing the tail, says it is much more like a rope. . . . If the elephant were set in motion . . . (that) would probably destroy all their previous understandings and further complicate the task of arriving at a consensus.[34]

What is true of organization theory generally is especially true for approaches to measuring organizational effectiveness.

When confronted with the necessity of describing the qualities of an effective organization, we are blinded by our values. So some grab the organization's goals, others narrow in on its systems attributes, others identify the way it treats employees, and still others concentrate on its internal processes. With public organizations, the elephant becomes more like an amoeba, as the blind men find more attributes to describe and disagreement over the essential nature of the beast increases. Naturally, each of the blind men believes that he has best captured the true essence of effectiveness in his description. It would be miraculous if some person with full sight (and insight) could look upon the creature and proclaim, "You are all wrong. This is actually what it looks like and is." Unfortunately, the clear-sighted person is more likely to proclaim, "I see it, but it is so monstrous, I have no idea of what it is or how to describe it." Perhaps it is best understood by dealing with its separate parts, always realizing that the whole is something different than the sum of the individual parts.

That is the ultimate conclusion to be drawn from the various definitions and theories of organizational effectiveness. It is a multidimensional concept, and any specific organization will vary considerably in terms of its performance as measured by the different concepts. It may be extremely effective by some measures, moderately effective by others, and ineffective by still others. That is especially likely to be true for public organizations, which are subject to evaluation by so many different individuals and groups with so many conflicting values and criteria. From that perspective, public organizations fare very well in comparison to private organizations. The best of them are very effective indeed; and if we used some of the political criteria for evaluating private organizations, many of them would be totally ineffective. As in everything else in organization theory, the answer to the question of what is an effective organization is, "It all depends."

NOTES

1. K. Cameron, "Measuring Organizational Effectiveness in Institutions of Higher Education," *Administrative Science Quarterly* (1978): p. 665.
2. John P. Campbell, "On the Nature of Organizational Effectiveness," in Paul F. Goodman, Johannes M. Pennings, and associates, *New Perspectives on Organizational Effectiveness* (San Francisco: Jossey-Bass, 1977), pp. 36–39.
3. Daniel Robey, *Designing Organizations: A Macro Perspective* (Homewood, Ill.: Richard D. Irwin, 1982), p. 225.
4. Arthur Bedeian, *Organizations: Theory and Analysis* (Hinsdale, Ill.: Dryden Press, 1980), p. 118.
5. Stephen Robbins, *Organization Theory* (Englewood Cliffs, N.J.: Prentice Hall, 1983), p. 37.
6. Jeffrey Pfeffer, "The Usefulness of the Concept," in Goodman and Pennings, *New Perspectives on Organizational Effectiveness*, p. 133.
7. Amitai Etzioni, *Modern Organizations* (Englewood Cliffs, N.J.: Prentice Hall, 1964), p. 8.
8. Richard Scott, "Effectiveness of Organizational Effectiveness Studies," in Goodman and Pennings, *New Perspectives on Organizational Effectiveness*, p. 90.
9. Robbins, *Organization Theory*, p. 24.
10. Chester Barnard, *The Functions of the Executive* (Cambridge, Mass.: Harvard University Press, 1938), p. 19.
11. Amitai Etzioni, "Two Approaches to Organizational Analysis: A Critique and a Suggestion," *Administrative Science Quarterly* (1960): pp. 237–277.
12. John Campbell, "On the Nature of Organizational Effectiveness," p. 76.
13. Robert Nakamura and Frank Smallwood, *The Politics of Policy Implementation* (New York: Saint Martin's Press, 1980), p. 74.
14. Michael T. Hannan and John Freeman, "Obstacles to Comparative Studies," in Goodman and Pennings, *New Perspectives on Organizational Effectiveness*, p. 111.
15. Ibid., p. 128.
16. Stanley Seashore and Ephraim Yuchtman, "A System Resource Approach to Organizational Effectiveness," *American Sociological Review* (December 1967): p. 898.
17. J. Barton Cummings, "A Systems Resource Approach for Evaluating Organizational Effectiveness," *Human Relations* (1978): pp. 631–656.
18. Donald Klinger and John Nalbandian, *Public Personnel Management*, 2nd ed. (Englewood Cliffs, N.J.: Prentice Hall, 1985), p. 193.
19. Johannes M. Pennings and Paul S. Goodman, "Toward a Workable Framework," in Goodman and Pennings, *New Perspectives on Organizational Effectiveness*, p. 146.

20. Campbell, "On the Nature of Organizational Effectiveness," p. 18.
21. William M. Evan, "Organization Theory and Effectiveness: An Exploratory Analysis," in S. Lee Spray, ed., *Organizational Effectiveness: Theory, Research, Utilization* (Kent, Ohio: Kent State University Press, 1976), pp. 22–23.
22. Charles Perrow, "Three Types of Effectiveness Studies," in Goodman and Pennings, *New Perspectives on Organizational Effectiveness*, p. 101.
23. Terry Connally, Edward J. Conlon, and Stuart Jay Deutsch, "Organizational Effectiveness: A Multiple Constituency Approach," *Academy of Management Review* (1980): pp. 211–217.
24. Jeffrey Pfeffer and Gerald Salancik, *The External Control of Organizations* (New York: Harper and Row, 1978), p. 11.
25. Gregory H. Gaertner and S. Ramayaran, "Organizational Effectiveness: An Alternative Perspective," *Academy of Management Review* (1983): p. 97.
26. John Rohrbaugh, "The Competing Values Approach: Innovation and Effectiveness in the Job Service," in Richard H. Hall and Robert E. Quinn, *Organization Theory and Public Policy* (Beverly Hills, Calif.: Sage Publications, Inc., 1983), p. 268.
27. Ralph H. Kilmann and Richard P. Herdon, "Towards a Systematic Methodology for Evaluating the Impact of Interventions on Organizational Effectiveness," *Academy of Management Review* (1976): pp. 87–99.
28. William M. Evan, "Organization Theory and Organization Effectiveness: An Exploratory Analysis," *Organization and Administrative Sciences* (1976): pp. 15–28.
29. Karl Weick, "Repunctuating the Problem," in Goodman and Pennings, *New Perspectives on Organizational Efficiency*, pp. 193–194.
30. Ibid., p. 199.
31. Nakamura and Smallwood, *The Politics of Policy Implementation*, p. 148.
32. Charles Goodsell, *The Case For Bureaucracy*, 2nd ed. (Chatham, N.J.: Chatham House Publishers, 1985).
33. Robert B. Denhardt, Center for Public Affairs and Policy Management, University of South Florida, "Excellence in the Public Service," *Public Affairs Reporter* (Winter 1987): p. 3.
34. Gareth Morgan, *Images of Organization* (Beverly Hills, Calif.: Sage Publications, Inc., 1986), p. 340.

AUTHOR INDEX

SUBJECT INDEX

Accountability, 99, 128, 343
Adhocracy, 45, 46, 129, 135–136
Age Lump phenomenon, 68, 170
Agency theory, 94
Agricultural Stabilization and
    Conservation Service, 138
Air Force, 23, 25
Alienation, 253–257, 309, 318
Army, 78, 79
Army Corps of Engineers, 138
Authority, 30–32, 42, 193, 201
Automation, 29–30, 66, 119, 125, 153,
    167

Behavior modification. *See* Motivation
Bureaucracy, 4, 31, 45, 60, 70, 75, 134,
    137, 249–250, 266–267
  and change, 155, 157
  and goal displacement, 104–105
  machine, 39–42, 99, 110, 121, 128, 155
  and politics, 201, 205
  professional, 42, 128, 135
  street-level, 194, 205, 299–300
Burnout
  causes of, 309

costs of, 315–316
definition of, 306
determinants of, 311–315
phases of, 307–309
prevention of, 316–318

Centralization, 30-34
Change
  process of 156–158
  resistance to, 153–156
  strategies for implementing, 158–166
Civil Aeronautics Board, 76, 91, 101
Classical organization theory, 4, 18, 31,
    35, 38, 188
Complexity, 34–35
Computerization, 144, 167
Computers, 29
Conflict
  attitudes toward, 184–185
  management of, 190–192
  process of, 184
  reactions to, 184
  sources of, 186–189
Conglomerates, 49–50, 112
Consumer Product Safety Commission, 48